EUSEBIUS OF CAESAREA AGAINST PAGANISM

JEWISH AND CHRISTIAN PERSPECTIVES SERIES

VOLUME III

EUSEBIUS OF CAESAREA
AGAINST PAGANISM

BY

ARYEH KOFSKY

BRILL
LEIDEN · BOSTON · KÖLN
2000

This book is printed on acid-free paper.

Library of Congress Cataloging-in-Publication Data

Eusebius of Caesarea against paganism / by Aryeh Kofsky.
       p.   cm. — (Jewish and Christian perspectives series, ISSN
1388-2074 ; v. 3)
     Includes bibliographical references and indexes.
     ISBN 9004116427 (cloth)
     1. Eusebius, of Caesarea, Bishop of Caesarea, ca. 260-ca. 340.
2. Apologetics—History—Early church, ca. 30-600.
     I. Title.   II. Series.
     BR65.E76 K64   2000
     239.3—dc21
                                                                00-23048
                                                                CIP

Die Deutsche Bibliothek - CIP-Einheitsaufnahme

Kofsky, Aryeh:
Eusebius of Caesarea against paganism / by Aryeh Kofsky. –
Leiden ; Boston; Köln : Brill, 2000
(Jewish and Christian perspectives series ; Vol. 3)
ISBN 90–04–11642–7

ISSN 1388-2074
ISBN 90 04 11642 7

In memory of my mother

CONTENTS

PREFACE

This study has been completed with the help of many people and I am grateful to all concerned. I began my work on Eusebius of Caesarea as a doctoral thesis (in Hebrew) submitted to the Hebrew University of Jerusalem in 1990. The entire dissertation has been extensively revised and updated and additions have been introduced throughout.

It is a great pleasure for me to acknowledge the aid I have received from friends and colleagues. I wish to express my heartfelt gratitude to my supervisor, Prof. Guy G. Stroumsa, for his continuous assistance and encouragement over the years and for making the writing of this study a pleasurable experience. The *Jewish and Christian Perspectives Series* seems a natural place for a study of Eusebius, who had contacts with Jews in Caesarea and was preoccupied with the complex relations between Christianity and Judaism. I would like to acknowledge the generous assistance of Dr. Marcel Poorthuis and Prof. Joshua Schwartz, coeditors of the *Jewish and Christian Perspectives Series*, who carefully read the present version, and made insightful suggestions. Thanks are also due to Dr. Meir M. Bar-Asher, Dr. Bruria Bitton-Ashkelony, Prof. David Flusser, Prof. Ora Limor, Prof. Lorenzo Perrone, and Prof. Zeev Rubin, for reading the whole or sections of this study, and for their sound and illuminating comments. I should also like to thank Mrs. Rivkah Fishman-Duker for her help in translating this work from the Hebrew and Mrs. Jennie Feldman for her rigorous editing of the English style. What goes without saying should in this case be stated: the responsibility for any errors or shortcomings is mine alone.

It is a special pleasure to thank the staff at Brill Publishers, particularly Freek van der Steen, *Ph.D.*, for their professional work, as well as for their patience and good grace. I would also like to thank Yad Avi Hayishuv—The Rothschild Fund—(Jerusalem), for the support of my study.

Last but not least, special thanks are due to my wife, Bettina, for her patience and encouragement throughout the years.

ABBREVIATIONS

ANRW	*Aufstieg und Niedergang der römischen Welt*
CC	Origen, *Against Celsus* (*Contra Ceslum*)
CH	Eusebius, *Against Hierocles* (*Contra Hieroclem*)
DCB	Dictionary of Christian Biography
DE	Eusebius, *Demonstratio Evangelica*
GCS	*Die griechischen christlichen Schriftsteller der ersten drei Jahrhunderte*
HE	Eusebius, *Historia Ecclesiastica*
LC	Eusebius, *In Praise of Constantine* (*Oratio de Laudibus Constantini*)
LCL	*Loeb Classical Library*
MP	Eusebius, *The Martyrs of Palestine* (*De Martyribus Palaestinae*)
PE	Eusebius, *Praeparatio Evangelica*
PG	*Patrologia Graeca*
PRE	*Paulys Real-Encyclopädie der klassischen Altertumswissenschaft*
OCD	*The Oxford Classical Dictionary*
RAC	*Reallexikon für Antike und Christentum*
SC	*Sources Chrétiennes*
TU	*Texte und Untersuchungen zur Geschichte der altchristlichen Literatur*
VC	Eusebius, *The Life of Constantine* (*Vita Constantini*)

INTRODUCTION

By the end of his life Eusebius had amassed an abundant literary corpus. It is estimated that no more than a half of this body of work has come down to us, but even this is remarkable in its range and breadth, embracing as it does Scripture and its exegesis, history, biography, polemics, apologetics, and theology. The works of Eusebius have stimulated numerous studies. Many have regarded him as a formidably erudite scholar lacking, however, in inspiration and originality, and unable or unwilling to undertake any profound philosophical speculation. This approach assumes that any novel idea or original thematic development in his work has to be attributed to earlier authors, even in the absence of any evidence for such an assumption. However, this view is by no means unanimous and even its advocates disagree as to how far it can be taken. Nonetheless, it would seem to explain why, despite the wealth of research on the works of Eusebius, his apologetic and theological writings have received relatively little scholarly attention.

The apologetic-polemical works of Eusebius, to which he devoted much of his adult life, into old age, constitute the central pillar of his writings. In sheer volume it surpasses every other subject and even, perhaps the rest of his works combined. It may well be that the principal motivation for some of his non-apologetic works was also fundamentally apologetic. The *Praeparatio Evangelica* (*PE*) and the *Demonstratio Evangelica* (*DE*) are two parts of a single treatise that was apparently the most comprehensive apologetic-polemical work to be written in the early Christian era. The *PE* provoked wide interest, not on account of its polemical content, but because it is a gold mine of citations from lost authors. In fairness, one cannot criticize scholars for preferring to deal with those aspects of Eusebius' work which seemed promising and stimulating. Their judgement often appears to have been sound. Yet a close study of the apologetic-polemical writings might alter the picture and modify the verdict; it might reveal Eusebius as worthy of some credit for contending with the pagan offensive against Christianity that was launched in a new guise and under different circumstances during his lifetime. Moreover, the study of these works may clarify somewhat their key importance for Eusebius and his contemporaries.

The volume of the material and the limited scholarly interest in it explain the absence so far of any comprehensive study on the subject of polemics and apologetics in Eusebius. However the subject was not entirely neglected, appearing in the framework of studies of early Christian apologetics, general monographs on Eusebius, studies on specific issues in his work, and commentaries on other aspects of his thought, or in introductions to various editions of his works. My study makes no claim to exhaust the subject but rather aims to fill some of the existing gaps.

Over a hundred years ago M. Faulhaber devoted the first part of his projected study of fourth-and fifth-century Christian apologetics to Eusebius. This part includes a brief general introduction to apologetics in that period and focuses on Eusebius' attack on philosophy and pagan religion in the *PE*. In addition Faulhaber touched upon the differences between Christianity and Judaism reflected in the *PE* and the *DE*, and dwelt on the polemics contrasting Jesus with the pagan hero Apollonius of Tyana in Eusebius' short work *Against Hierocles*. Thus Faulhaber's study focuses primarily on the *PE* and the negative aspect of Eusebius' polemic—the refutation of pagan beliefs— rather than on its positive dimension, consolidating the truths of Christianity and proving their superiority over pagan polemical arguments.[1] Some sixty years later J.R. Laurin published his study on the principal trends in Christian apologetic writing in the years 270– 361. In the framework of his study Laurin surveyed most of Eusebius' polemical works. His short descriptions and analyses go beyond the scope of all previous monographs on Eusebius and create a broad-based picture of Eusebius' apologetic-polemical works.[2] The most recent general discussion of polemics and apologetics in Eusebius appears as a chapter of T.D. Barnes' comprehensive book on Constantine and Eusebius. Barnes, like Laurin, offers a general survey of the structure and content of Eusebius' apologetic works.[3] Within the framework of such studies Laurin and Barnes could offer little more than an overview of key issues. In his extensive study Barnes determined a certain chronological order for Eusebius' works

---

[1] M. Faulhaber, *Die griechischen Apologeten der klassischen Väterzeit. I. Buch. Eusebius von Cäsarea* (Würzburg, 1895).

[2] J.R. Laurin, *Orientations maîtresses des Apologistes chrétiens de 270 à 361* (Rome, 1954 = *Analecta Gregoriana* 61).

[3] T.D. Barnes, *Constantine and Eusebius* (Cambridge, Mass., 1981).

and on this basis developed a thesis regarding the development of
Eusebius' literary career. The question of chronological order is especially complicated in light of Eusebius' habit of reediting his texts.
The sequence that Barnes proposes differs in important details from
the views of previous scholars and seems at times problematic. Barnes
also goes against the general consensus by giving a much later date
for Porphyry's book against the Christians. The date of its composition is a key to understanding Eusebius' early writings and sheds
light on his apologetic enterprise as a response to Porphyry's assault.

In her *SC* edition, M. Forrat devotes a monograph to Eusebius'
polemical treatise *Against Hierocles*, the only monograph on this work.
Eusebius' final apologetic work, the *Theophany*, was written in his old
age. In many ways it is a digest of themes in the *PE* and the *DE*
and may reflect some developments in Eusebius' thinking on certain
issues. In his monograph on the *Theophany* H. Gressmann edited the
Greek fragments and translated the entire work into German from
the Syriac, the only extant version of the original. The monograph
discusses the content of the text and, primarily, the linguistic and
textual queries it raises.[4] We should note, too, the panoramic study
of Eusebius' historical concepts by J. Sirinelli, who also considers
explicit apologetic aspects of apologetic works such as the *PE* and
the *DE*. Although his real interest lay in reconstructing the historical concepts reflected in these works, the breadth of his discussion
contributes greatly to our appreciation of their apologetic-polemical
aspect.[5] Other studies relating to apologetic themes in the works of
Eusebius will be mentioned throughout this study. In summary we
may say that until now studies on the apologetic-polemical works of
Eusebius have been either general or partial; with the exception of
one or two none has offered a comprehensive analysis. This holds
true not least for key passages in the *PE* and the *DE* which constitute Eusebius' major apologetic work.

The important studies of J. Geffcken and P. de Labriolle painted
a graphic picture of the long drawn out struggle by pagans defending their ancient culture against ascendant Christianity. This picture has considerably modified earlier impressions that the pagan

---

[4] H. Gressmann, *Studien zu Eusebs Theophanie, TU* 23,3 (1903).

[5] J. Sirinelli, *Les vues historiques d'Eusèbe de Césarée durant la période prénicéenne* (Paris,
1961).

religions simply succumbed and collapsed in the face of Christian pressure. Their vigorous struggle is a key factor in understanding the Christian polemic and apologetic literature of the time and the development of other branches of ecclesiastical literature such as theology, biblical exegesis, chronology and ecclesiastical history.[6]

---

[6] J. Geffcken, *The Last Days of Greco-Roman Paganism* (Amsterdam-New York-London, 1978), an English translation of the second German edition of 1929; P. de Labriolle, *La Réaction païenne* (Paris, 1934); and see also P. Chuvin, *Chronique des derniers païens* (Paris, 1990), and F.R. Trombley, *Hellenic Religion and Christianization c. 370–529* (Leiden, 1993).

CHAPTER ONE

BACKGROUND

Apologetics and Polemics before Eusebius

The Christian apologetic and polemical tradition dates back nearly
two centuries before Eusebius. In fact, despite its somewhat arbitrary
classification, we may speak of a literary genre whose works shared
salient characteristics and reflected a common struggle. The main
stimulus for its growth was the anti-Christian rumor, slander, and
bias prevalent in the Greco-Roman world. Pagan intellectuals became
increasingly convinced that Christianity posed a threat to the social,
religious, and political order of the Empire. Prominent among these
adversaries of Christianity in the second century CE were Lucian of
Samosata, the philosopher Fronto, tutor of Marcus Aurelius, and,
especially, Celsus, noted for his formidable attack on Christianity.[1]
Until Celsus in the late second century, however, most of the pagan
arguments against Christianity have to be gleaned from Christian
apologetics and not from pagan authors, who apparently had not
yet felt the mounting danger. It seems that such arguments were
common and were thrust at Christians at various times and places.

Several arguments were drawn from the ancient reservoir of pagan
anti-Semitic literature well known from Josephus' *Against Apion*; many
others were specially created to target the new religion. There was
a historic hostility to Christians who were perceived as an exclusive
group that did not fully participate in religious, social, and political
life. Christians, it was claimed, were enemies of humanity; they did
not take part in the worship of the gods, and were therefore atheists[2] who even went as far as shunning religious and cultural events.

---

[1] The most thorough and comprehensive treatment of pagan views of Christianity
and of arguments against it by pagan authors is P. de Labriolle, *La Réaction païenne*.
Authors prior to Celsus appear on pp. 1–108. A similar summary of pagan authors
of the first two centuries CE has more recently been published by S. Benko, "Pagan
Criticism of Christianity During the First Two Centuries AD", *ANRW* 23, I, pp.
1055–1117.

[2] Justin, *First Apology* 5.

Thus they were enemies of the gods, the Emperor, and the laws
and customs of society; in short, they were traitors who had abandoned their ancestral tradition.[3] Moreover Christians were ignorant,
uncultured, and rude. They were incapable of engaging in divine
matters and were unproductive members of society.[4] In fact, Christians were the cause of every catastrophe:

> If the Tiber rises as high as the city walls, if the Nile does not send
> its water up over the fields, if the heavens give no rain, if there is an
> earthquake, if there is famine or pestilence, straight away one hears:
> "Away with the Christians, to the lions! (*Christianos ad leonem*)".[5]

Criticism also focused on the alleged licentiousness of Christian rit-
uals and morals.[6] Detractors claimed that Christians indulged in for-
nication, ritual murder, and cannibalism at secret feasts and orgies.[7]
Their young women behaved immorally and wife-swapping was a
common practice.[8]

A third line of argument confronted the Christian faith, maintaining that it could not be proved and made no sense.[9] Belief in
resurrection was empty and foolish, for how could corporeal matter
be gathered after it had been dispersed.[10] The idea of the existence
of father and son in the divinity was ludicrous and the Incarnation
a fairy tale.[11] Christians were insane to place a crucified person second to the eternal God,[12] and worship this human being as a divine.[13]
Several claimed that Christians worshiped the sun, a wooden cross,
or even a donkey's head.[14] Jesus, they said, used magic and sorcery
to give the impression of being the son of God.[15] Others argued that

---

[3] Tertullian, *Apology* 6,7; 2,16.

[4] Tertullian, *Apology* 42,1.

[5] Ibid. 40,1–2.

[6] Theophilus, *To Autolycus* 3,15.

[7] Tatian, *Address to the Greeks* 32. On Tatian and his apologetic work see A.F.
Hawthorne, "Tatian and His Discourse to the Greeks", *Harvard Theological Review*
57 (1964), pp. 161–188.

[8] Tatian, *Address to the Greeks* 32; Theophilus, *To Autolycus* 3,4.

[9] Theophilus, *To Autolycus* 3,4.

[10] Athenagoras, *A Plea for the Christians* 36. On Athenagoras see L.W. Barnard,
Athenagorsas, a Study in Second Century Apologetics, Paris 1972 (*Théologie historique* 18);
Tatian, *Address to the Greeks* 6; Tertullian, *Apology* 48,5.

[11] Athenagoras, *A Plea for the Christians* 10; Tatian, *Apology* 21.

[12] Justin, *First Apology* 13.

[13] Tertullian, *Apology* 21,3.

[14] Ibid. 16,1–9.

[15] Justin, *First Apology* 13.

if Jesus had only recently been born, i.e., during the governorship of Quirinius, how could those who lived before him be saved and why had he not appeared earlier.[16] Tertullian gives several examples of pagan ridicule in the form of questions concerning Jesus: "Who is this Christ with his fables? Is he an ordinary man? Is he a sorcerer? Was his body stolen from the tomb by his disciples? Is he now in the netherworld or in heaven whence he will return and shake the foundations of the world?"[17] Others argued that Christian Scripture was a new collection of mere tales,[18] and that punishment of sinners by eternal fire was a pompous threat designed to spread terror and to frighten humanity into behaving properly.[19] Heaven, on the other hand, was just a pale imitation of the Elysian fields.[20]

Christian apologists waged a struggle against these and similar arguments in an attempt to protect their coreligionists. In particular, they had to fight against the claim that Christianity was a danger to the state, a crime against the official cult and religion, and even against the Emperor himself. They fought for their legal and moral right to exist. Emphasizing the superiority of Christian morality and decency over the corrupt and degenerate social mores of the pagans, Christian apologists leveled against them the very same accusations which the pagans had used against Christianity. These apologists sought to cultivate public opinion, to weaken anti-Christian bias and to underline the superiority of Christianity over other religions and cults. This endeavor explains the frequently repeated claim that the Christian faith played a major role in maintaining world order, the status of the Emperor and the integrity of state, society, and humanity. Spurred on by anti-Christian invective, the apologist changed his defensive stance for an affirmative presentation of the faith that found expression on two levels: the refutation of pagan cult, mythology, and philosophy, and a vindication of the Christian faith. According to the apologists, a rational vindication of the faith was necessary in order to establish the right of the community of believers to exist. Along with their effort to expose the absurdity and corruption of pagan religion, mythology, and society, the apologists

---

[16] Ibid. 46; *Letter to Diognetus* 1.
[17] Tertullian, *Apology* 23,12.
[18] Theophilus, op. cit. 3,1; 3,16.
[19] Justin, *Second Apology* 9.
[20] Tertullian, *Apology* 47,12.

offered proof that only a Christian possessed a true understanding
of God and of the universe. As a consequence, they defended the
Christian dogmas of monotheism, divine unity, the divinity of Christ,
the Incarnation, and the resurrection of the body.

Thus through a critique of Greek philosophy, Christianity laid
claim to be the true philosophy. Not content with this, the authors
also argued that since Greek philosophy was based upon human
intelligence alone, it could only arrive at a truth that was incomplete and misjudged. In contrast, Christianity held the absolute truth
because the *Logos* descended to earth via Christ. Therefore Christianity was far superior to Greek philosophy; it was divine philosophy. However from the struggle to disprove accusations that the
Christian faith was empty, naive, and irrational, there emerged the
assertion that Christianity did in fact meet the demands of the human
spirit and was in harmony with human intelligence. Armed with
some knowledge of philosophy, many Christian writers went on to
acknowledge the relative value of philosophy and to admit that it
possessed some elements of truth.

Often the antiquity of the Christian religion was cited as further
proof of its authenticity. Christianity, claimed the apologists, was heir
to the Holy Scriptures and the ancient traditions of Judaism. The
New Testament was tightly bound to the Old by prophecies regarding the Redeemer. Since Moses lived long before the earliest Greek
philosophers, Christianity was the most ancient and honorable of all
religions and philosophies.

Therefore the major thrust of apologists was a polemic against
anti-Christian invective, together with a presentation of Christian
doctrine. This was true of the apologetic-polemical works of Aristides, Tatian, Athenagoras, and Theophilus, and of the anonymous
Oratio ad Graecos, *Cohortatio ad Graecos*, and *Epistle to Diognetus*. These
can all be classified as "apologies", as can the apologetic works of
Justin and Tertullian. The ratio of polemic to doctrine varies widely
between texts, lending diversity to an otherwise uniform literary genre.

Not all polemical arguments are original. Many are based on the
critique of Greek religion, mythology, and philosophy by different
schools of Greek philosophers and authors.[21] With regard to the neg-

---

[21] A broad survey of this critique may be found in H.W. Attridge, "The Philosophical Critique of Religion under the Early Empire", *ANRW* 16,1 (1978), pp.
45–78.

ative aspect of apologies, i.e., the critique and refutation of pagan
culture that made use of the pagans' own arguments and vilifica-
tions, apologists were virtually dependent on their Christian predecessors. Hence the frequent repetition of similar claims in different
works. Only rarely did they attempt to adapt to their own times a
polemic better suited to ancient literature. Indeed Christian authors
sometimes appear to be debating with the contemporaries of Socrates,
rather than with those of Marcus Aurelius.[22]

An additional source for Christian apologists is the apologetic literature which flourished in Hellenistic-Jewish circles. Josephus, Philo,
Eupolemus, and Artapanus argued for the superiority of monotheism on the basis of reason and revelation. The antiquity of Jewish
history and tradition, including Moses, together with comparative
chronological calculations, served as proof that the people and Torah
of Israel were the major source of Greek culture. It was from the
Hellenistic-Jewish authors that Christians learned how to use examples from Greek literature. This explains the apologists' zeal in searching Greek literature for anything that matched and corroborated
biblical concepts or even historical events related in the Bible.

Second century apologetic-polemical works are not methodical and
have no logical or consistent structure. Untutored in philosophy or
literature, the authors seem to base their polemics on collections and
anthologies and do not refer directly to, or show real knowledge of,
pagan literary sources.[23] Their polemics are presented haphazardly
to counter a variety of arguments and are followed by critiques of
paganism and assertions justifying the Christian path, the two themes
running parallel and following the sequence of issues in the text. For
most of the second century, however, one cannot speak of a comprehensive program of apology which treats subjects and problems
in a systematic way and which provides a framework for answers to
pagan criticism.

The first systematic attack on Christianity was written c. 177–180
CE by Celsus in his book *Word of Truth* ('Αλητὴς Λόγος). Although the
work has been lost, substantial parts were preserved in Origen's *Contra*

---

[22] A. Puech, *Les apologistes grecs du IIe siècle de notre ère* (Paris, 1912), p. 7. For the
Christian apologists of the second century, see also H.B. Timothy, *The Early Chris-
tian Apologists and Greek Philosophy* (Assen, 1973); R.M. Grant, *Greek Apologists of the
Second Century* (Philadelphia, 1988).

[23] J. Geffcken, *Zwei griechische Apologeten* (Leipzeg-Berlin, 1907), p. 113.

Celsum (*CC*) and from these we can reconstruct the broad lines of Celsus' book.[24] Celsus repeats only few of the claims based on rumor, slander, or unfounded arguments.[25] Instead he relies upon personal observation and a study of Jewish and Christian literature. As a result, his work is generally free of gross errors, even though riddled with prejudice. Together with his critique of Christianity, Celsus makes a real effort to defend the traditional values of pagan culture and even to restore Christians to paganism. With his apparent Platonic leanings, Celsus was a talented rival who pounced on every possible argument to counter the Christians and their faith. At first he attacked Christianity from the vantage point of a Jew arguing against Jesus. Then he veered round to a full-fledged onslaught on both Jewish and Christian beliefs. Presenting Jesus as a wizard and imposter, Celsus derided the messianic idea. As a Platonic philosopher, he claimed that Greek religion and philosophy were superior. He severely criticized the Gospels, especially with regard to the Resurrection of Jesus, an absurd belief invented by the apostles and their disciples. However, Celsus did not totally reject everything taught by Christianity. For example, he affirmed Christian ethics and the theological concept of the *Logos*.[26] In addition, he was prepared to acknowledge the existence of Christianity on condition that Christians left their religious and social isolation and came under the aegis of Roman religion. Celsus was afraid that divisiveness would weaken the Empire. He concluded his work by calling upon Christians to support the emperor, to cooperate with him in preserving justice, to fight alongside him in battle, and to participate in the affairs of state.[27]

---

[24] It is possible that Celsus knew the Apology of Aristides to which he might be responding in his work. See J.R. Harris, *The Apology of Aristides on Behalf of the Christians* from a Syriac ms. preserved on Mount Sinai. Edited with an introduction and translation, and an appendix containing the main portion of the original Greek text by A. Robinson, 2nd ed. (Cambridge, 1893), pp. 19–23. H. Chadwick also argues that it is highly likely that Celsus read some Christian apologetic works. According to Chadwick, Celsus was inspired to write his polemic after reading Justin. He also claims direct evidence that Celsus must have been acquainted with some of the arguments raised in the debate between Marcion and the Church, particularly in his attack on the Old Testament. See H. Chadwick, *Early Christian Thought and the Classical Tradition* (Oxford, 1966), pp. 22, 26.

[25] Origen himself attests that in his time there were fewer libels against Christians, but they did exist (*CC* 6,27).

[26] On Celsus' ambivalent attitude towards the paganism which he defends, see M. Simon, "Christianisme antique et pensée païenne: rencontres et conflits", *Bulletin de la Faculté des Lettres de Strasbourg* 38 (1960), pp. 309–323.

[27] Celsus' polemic against Christianity is the subject of numerous scholarly studies.

Celsus' Christian contemporaries do not refer to *Word of Truth* and its impact on them, confusing or otherwise, is hard to gauge.[28] Only some seventy years later did Ambrose ask his friend Origen to write a response to counteract the potential damage of Celsus' work. Origen was unenthusiastic at first, seeing no particular urgency or importance in the matter.[29] However he gave in to Ambrose's pleas in the hope of thus helping those not yet acquainted with the Christian faith, and supporting those whose conviction was weak.[30] When he began *Against Celsus*, Origen conceived the work as a general, comprehensive response to the arguments of Celsus. However he soon changed his mind and went over to formulating individual responses to the issues presented in Celsus' tract, following the same order. Origen attests to this in his introduction.[31] Origen's profound knowledge of Greek literature and philosophy and his analytical expertise are evident in the context and complexity of his assertions. *Against Celsus* thus raised Christian-pagan polemics to a new level, giving the impression of a debate between two leading intellectuals of the respective camps even though Origen was disputing a work written seventy years earlier.

Eusebius was quite well acquainted with earlier apologetic literature written in Greek, including the Greek translation of Tertullian's apology.[32] He notes authors by name and cites passages from their works. Scholars differ in their assessment of Eusebius' knowledge of Latin. Many hold that it was not sufficient to enable him to read

---

Attempts at reconstructing the text were undertaken by O. Glockner and R. Bader, see O. Glockner, *Celsi Alethes Logos* (Bonn, 1924); R. Bader, *Der Alethes Logos des Kelsos* (Stuttgart-Berlin, 1940). For an analysis of the fragments see Labriolle, *La Réaction païenne*, pp. 111–169, and in the English edition, see H. Chadwick, *Origen: Contra Celsum* (Cambridge, 1953), and K. Andresen, *Logos und Nomos, Die Polemik des Kelsos wider das Christentum* (Berlin, 1955).

[28] For example, Tertullian or Clement of Alexandria. Clement is not an apologist in the conventional sense and his works do not come under the category of "apology". His writings, however, include much apologetic-polemical material. The many issues raised in apologies are discussed in his works with a breadth and profundity that reflect his extensive knowledge of Greek philosophy and his remarkable erudition. Clement explicitly states that his works are intended for pagans as well (*Stromateis* 7,1). He does not mention Celsus and perhaps did not read or even hear of his work. However, several points indicate that he may have had Celsus or another critic in mind as he wrote (H. Chadwick, *Early Christian Thought*, p. 49).

[29] *CC* Introduction, 1.

[30] *CC* Introduction, 6.

[31] Ibid.

[32] Eusebius attests to his use of the Greek translation of Tertullian's *Apologeticus* (*HE* 2,2, 4–6). On the translation, see A. Harnack, "Die Griechiesche Übersetzung des 'Apologeticus' Tertulians", *TU* 8.4 (1892) pp. 1–36.

Latin works, despite Eusebius' claim that he himself translated Latin documents.[33] He does not use or refer to Latin authors in any of his numerous works. When he began to write his masterpiece of apologetics, Eusebius was well aware of his predecessors and of himself as a link in a long and well-established tradition. He refers respectfully to previous authors who responded to anti-Christian arguments in texts devoted to refutation, commentaries on Scripture, or homilies on particular subjects, and who thereby attested to the truths of Christianity and its unique concepts. However, Eusebius also announces that his approach and methods were new and different.[34]

The Caesarean Background

Eusebius lived in Caesarea. He was a disciple of Pamphilus, the teacher whom he revered and whose admiration of Origen he inherited. Pamphilus established a large library housing Origen's original manuscripts,[35] and a school similar in character to the one founded by Origen.[36] Gregory Thaumaturgus, a disciple of Origen, described the curriculum. It began with preparatory studies of Socratic dialogues in order to practice philosophical dialectic thinking. Studies included the three philosophical subjects: physics, logic, and, subsequently, ethics, both as a system of thought and as a way of life. Gregory learned to identify and control irrational feelings and to develop moral virtues. Origen emphasized that the source of all virtues and their ultimate goal is religious piety, and that philosophy should be understood as preparation for theology. The students read Greek philosophical works together with an elucidation of what was true and beneficial in them. The program of study was crowned

---

[33] *HE* 4,8,8. For a similar view, see J.B. Lightfoot, "Eusebius", *DCB* 2, 324. According to J. Stevenson, Eusebius found Latin an insurmountable obstacle. See J. Stevenson, *Studies in Eusebius* (Cambridge, 1929), p. 39. E. Fisher holds the opposite opinion in her study of translations from Latin to Greek in the fourth century CE. She accepts at face value Eusebius' statements that he translated official documents and concludes from an analysis of language and style that he was a talented translator and could read and translate Latin well. See E.A. Fisher, "Greek Translations of Latin Literature in the Fourth Century AD", *Yale Classical Studies* 27 (1982), p. 203.

[34] *PE* 1,3.

[35] *HE* 6,32,3–4. Jerome relates that Pamphilus collected books from all over the world and was a sort of Demetrius of Phaleron of religious studies (*Letter* 34).

[36] *HE* 7,32,25.

by the reading of Holy Scripture which Origen viewed as an inexhaustible reservoir of wisdom and truth.[37]

Origen was guided by a sense of mission: to direct his pupils towards proper lives, to give them a true understanding of the world, and to distance them from the errors of the philosophers. Despite these efforts, however, Gregory's description of the school shows that it was run along the lines of the philosophical academies of his time. Origen used the vocabulary and terminology of contemporary religious and ethical debate, and although the program of study was generally Christian in character, it lacked specific Christian components. This fact may shed some light on Origen's Middle-Platonic and Stoic way of thought. He addressed himself not only to Christian pupils but also, and perhaps even more, to pagans who loved philosophy and were searching for truth. Origen hoped that a general education would, indirectly, bring them closer to Christianity. His school was neither an institution for catechumens nor a theological institute, nor was it an official arm of the Church.[38]

Both Pamphilus and Eusebius continued Origen's well-known project of editing and commenting on the biblical text. Christian communities would send them their copies for revision and proofreading. Pamphilus focused on the text of the New Testament to a greater degree than Origen. They used Origen's *Hexapla* and *Tetrapla*, and in colophons of biblical manuscripts, the names of both Pamphilus and Eusebius are given to validate the copied version.

Eusebius' preoccupation with the text of the Holy Scriptures is prominent in many of his writings, especially his biblical interpretations in which he makes skillful use of his knowledge of the different translations. He also was greatly absorbed by the text of the New Testament and compiled comparative tables of the Gospels, explaining their use in his epistle to Carpianus.[39] According to E. Schwartz, Caesarea served as a center for research on the different versions of

---

[37] Gregory's *Dedication to Origen* was written upon Gregory's departure from Caesarea after five years of study under Origen, *SC* 148 (1969).

[38] On Origen's school see A. Knauber, "Das Anliegen der Schule des Origenes zu Caesarea", *Münchener Theologische Zeitschrift* 19 (1968), pp. 182–203, especially pp. 195–196; H. Crouzel, "L'Ecole d'Origène a Césarée", *Bulletin de littérature ecclésiastique* 71 (1970), pp. 15–27; L.I. Levine, *Caesarea under Roman Rule* (Leiden, 1975), pp. 119–124.

[39] See H.H. Oliver, "The Epistle of Eusebius to Carpianus: Textual Tradition and Translation", *Novum Testamentum* 3 (1959), pp. 138–145. It seems that Eusebius also wrote a commentary to I Corinthians, see Jerome, *Letter* 49.

Scripture, like the *Mouseion* in Alexandria where scholars engaged in textual criticism of Homeric texts.[40] In addition to textual studies, the scholars of Caesarea seem also to have been involved in translating the biblical text. Eusebius mentions his friend, the martyr Procopius, who worked on the translation from Greek to Aramaic. This is plausible as Caesarea was a major crossroads between the Greek and Syriac languages.[41] Given this context, Barnes considered Eusebius first and foremost a scholar and commentator on Scripture, who because of the turbulent times had to deal with other matters later on in life.[42]

Pamphilus and Eusebius also expressed their deep regard for Origen in an apologetic tract which refuted the growing view that Origen had heretical tendencies. It was composed while Pamphilus was in prison during the dark days of anti-Christian persecution.[43] After Pamphilus' martyrdom, Eusebius dedicated a biography (which has been lost) to his beloved teacher,[44] and may have assumed his name (Eusebius Pamphili) as a sign of loyalty. Eusebius' entire spiritual world undoubtedly bore the mark of Origen's influence. However scholarly opinion is divided as to whether Eusebius' ideas and statements came directly from Origen, or, via the interpretation of his teachers, who made their own revisions and changes.[45]

---

[40] E. Schwartz, "Eusebios", *PRE* 11, 1372–1373. On the textual works of Pamphilus and Eusebius and their names in manuscript traditions, see Lightfoot, "Eusebius", p. 310.

[41] *The Martyrs of Palestine* (*MP*) 4 (W. Cureton's edition).

[42] Barnes, *Constantine and Eusebius*, p. 164.

[43] Only the first of the six books of this work is extant, in a Latin translation by Rufinus, *PG* 17, 541–616.

[44] *MP* 11; *HE* 7,32; 6,32; 8,13. This is the first known Greek Christian biography.

[45] For a forthright exposition of the first view see Robert Grant's studies of Eusebius, such as R.M. Grant, "Eusebius, Josephus and the Fate of the Jews", *Society of Biblical Literature 1979 Seminar Papers*, V. 2, Missoula, Montana, pp. 69–86. A less forceful position is taken by G. Bardy, "La Théologie d'Eusèbe de Césarée d'après l'Histoire ecclésiastique*", *Revue d'histoire ecclésiastique* 50 (1955), p. 13. Stevenson (*Studies*, p. 26) gives the opposing view. He claims that Eusebius learned of Origen's ideas through the interpretations of his students Pamphilus, Dionysius, and Pierius, and that any divergence by Eusebius from Origen's thought was traceable to the Alexandrians Dionysius and Theognostus (ibid., p. 85). Pierius was, in fact, Pamphilus' teacher in Alexandria and the head of the school (Photius, *Bibliotheca* 119) and Theognostus was apparently a student of Origen in Alexandria (Photius, ibid., 106). Pamphilus would alter Origen's statements where he thought that Origen had strayed from the more orthodox views found elsewhere in his writings. See H. De Lubac, *Origen, On First Principles* (Gloucester, Mass., 1973), Introduction, p. XXXVIII. For a general view of Eusebius' Origenism see C. Kannengiesser, "Eusebius of Cae-

Origen wrote that in his day wild accusations against Christianity were few; Eusebius states that such libels no longer existed in his times, for the truth had been made public throughout the world.[46] Moreover, Eusebius claims that Origen's comprehensive and forceful *Against Celsus* had answered all the prevalent anti-Christian arguments. Origen, he said, had closely examined all that had been or would be said about the subject, and had answered and anticipated every one of his own responses. Eusebius emphasized that Origen's statements reflected his own views.[47] Here we must ask why Eusebius turned to writing a long series of distinguished apologetic and polemical works despite his claim that there was no need for them. Eusebius gives no explicit answer to this question, but it seems that his motive in writing had become self-evident.

The Persecutions

During Eusebius' lifetime, pagan society launched one of its final major attacks on Christianity. Both the cultural and political powers of the Empire, independent of each other, sought to close ranks against the perceived threat to the venerable splendour of a centuries-old edifice that united religion, culture, law, and politics in a harmonious whole. Some time before the outbreak of the great persecutions by Diocletian, Porphyry had published his anti-Christian tract. It was the most complete and sophisticated attack yet launched against the Christians. His great erudition and his philological training enabled him to focus his assault on the Scriptures and on Christian tradition. Within a short time Porphyry had become the chief enemy of Christianity. Four books were written in direct response to his attack; one of them was by Eusebius.[48]

In their persecution of Christians, the Roman authorities were not satisfied with administrative measures alone. In some areas, the persecution was accompanied by a literary onslaught. Of these tendentious works the best known was *The Lover of Truth* (Φιλαλήθης), written by the government official Hierocles. Even if not originally intended

---

sarea, Origenist", in H.W. Attridge and G. Hata (eds.), *Eusebius, Christianity and Judaism* (Detroit, 1992), 435–466.

[46] *HE* 4,7,12.

[47] Eusebius, *Against Hierocles* 1.

[48] The replies to Porphyry's attack will be dealt with briefly later on.

as part of the propaganda machine for persecution, the book was certainly used for this purpose. Eusebius devoted a minor work to refuting the attack by Hierocles. As persecution increased in the eastern part of the Empire under Maximin, newly forged apocryphal writings such as the *Acts of Jesus* and the *Acts of Pilate*[49] were widely disseminated. According to Eusebius, the initiative came from the court of Maximin or even from the emperor himself.[50] Eusebius witnessed the persecutions, the attempts at a religious revival by Maximin (similar measures were later taken by Julian), and the deaths of his friends as martyrs. Caesarea was one of the centers of persecution and religious coercion instigated by Maximin. According to Barnes, Maximin may even have lived in Caesarea for a time.[51]

Maximin's acts are recorded in Eusebius' account, *The Martyrs of Palestine*.[52] At the end of March 306 Maximin gave instructions to the magistrates in every city to hold a general sacrifice. In November he visited Caesarea for celebrations and spectacles in honor of his birthday.[53] In 309, Maximin ordered a final general sacrifice.[54] Delapidated temples were renovated and children were required to sacrifice and eat the meat of their offerings. Items for sale in the marketplace had to be sanctified by sacrificial libations, and guards were posted at the doors of bathhouses to pour libations upon the bathers. After the death of Galerius, Maximin embarked on a reorganization of religious life, appointing a large number of priests and high priests. It was what might be called the restoration of an organized cult, but not an imitation of the ecclesiastical organization.[55] Maximin's religious zeal was evident in his enthusiasm for building and renovating temples, and revitalising a reordered pagan clergy.[56] Behind this religious fervor lay the same concern for paganism felt

---

[49] This pagan forgery should not be confused with the extant Christian apocryphal *Acts of Pilate*.

[50] *HE* 1,9,3; 1,11,9; 9,5,1. On the escalating propaganda war between Christians and pagans preceding the persecution, see W.H.C. Frend, "Prelude to the Great Persecution: The Propaganda War", *Journal of Ecclesiastical History* 38 (1987), pp. 1–18.

[51] T.D. Barnes, *The New Empire of Diocletian and Constantine* (Cambridge, Mass., 1982), p. 65. Barnes refers to years 306–308 CE.

[52] *MP* 4,8.

[53] *MP* 6,1.

[54] *MP* 9,2.

[55] According to Stevenson, Maximin wished to establish a pagan church against Christianity, but did not succeed (*Studies*, p. 57).

[56] *HE* 8,14,9; *MP* 9,2.

by Diocletian, Galerius, and Maxentius. Maximin seems to have taken seriously the title "Iovius", which he inherited from Diocletian and Galerius. He was influenced by the oracle of Zeus in Antioch,[57] and his letter to the people of Tyre included a short homily on the greatness of Zeus. Before the battle against Licinius, Maximin vowed to Jupiter that should he emerge victorious, he would wipe out the name of the Christians.[58]

Porphyry's Polemic against the Christians

In the wake of the challenge of the great pagan onslaught and the attempted revival of the Greco-Roman cult, apologetic and polemical activity was renewed with evident urgency. However most scholars of Eusebius view his apologetic and polemical writing primarily as a response to the publication of Porphyry's book against the Christians. Such conclusions appear to be based on general impressions and are often offered without proof.[59] Some scholars even contend that virtually all Eusebius' works were prompted by an apologetic-polemical impulse,[60] and have to be understood in light of the polemic against Porphyry.[61] Although no specific evidence has been adduced to prove that Porphyry's tract was the main catalyst for Eusebius' apologetic-polemical writings, it seems that scholarly opinion has been decisively influenced by the presumed date of composition and publication of *Against the Christians*. In fact, some even state that Eusebius was greatly influenced by Porphyry's other works, and by his literary style, and philosophical and religious outlook.[62]

---

[57] *HE* 9,3.

[58] This, according to Lactantius, *On the Death of Persecutors* 46, 2. On the religious tendencies of Maximin, see R.M. Grant, "The Religion of Maximin Daia", *Christianity Judaism and other Greco-Roman Cults, Studies for Morton Smith at Sixty*, ed. J. Neusner (Leiden, 1975), pp. 143–166.

[59] Lightfoot, "Eusebius", p. 329; A. Harnack, *Die Chronologie der altchristlichen Literatur bis Eusebius* II, Leipzig 1904, p. 119. See also E.H. Gifford, *Eusebius' Preparation for the Gospel*, Oxford 1903, Inroduction, p. XV; Stevenston, *Studies,* p. 37; Sirinelli, op. cit. p. 28; Barnes, *Constantine and Eusebius*, p. 175.

[60] Lightfoot, "Eusebius", p. 346; Stevenson, *Studies,* p. 35.

[61] Sirinelli, op. cit. pp. 56–57, 166.

[62] R.M. Grant, "Porphyry among the Early Christians", *Romanitas and Christianitas* (Amsterdam-London, 1973), pp. 181–187. Sirinelli, *Les vues historiques d'Eusèbe*, p. 166. The library at Caesarea was well stocked with works of the later Platonists, including Porphyry. See K. Mras, *Eusebius Werke VIII Die Praeparatio Evangelica*, I (Berlin, 1954), liv–lviii.

Furthermore, Eusebius' polemic against Porphyry may not have been entirely without personal motives. Porphyry was a native of Tyre and studied in Caesarea as a young man. According to the historian Socrates, Porphyry had even been a Christian at one time. However, after being attacked by certain Christians, he left the faith out of anger and frustration.[63] Porphyry states that during his youth he knew Origen, and he seems to have been Origen's student. But disappointment with his teacher led him to attack Origen in his writing, deliberately distorting and ridiculing the man and his ideas. Porphyry could not comprehend Origen's detached attitude to philosophy when the latter's knowledge of the subject was so thorough. Origen, he claimed, was a charlatan who used the tools of the Greeks in order to rationalize the barbarous and primitive superstition which he had adopted after leaving his native faith and culture.[64] In Eusebius' eyes, Porphyry had wronged the great master of the faith, for after the privilege of studying under Origen, Porphyry had become his enemy and detractor.

Given this background, Eusebius may have been spurred by personal motives, or even local patriotism to refute Porphyry's arguments and defend Origen against a major pagan detractor, as he had defended him against Christian critics.[65]

What was it in Porphyry's book that so angered and alarmed Christians? The fact that four major works were written to refute his arguments attests to the threat felt by Christians.[66] Indeed Constantine had scarcely established his rule when Porphyry's book was consigned to the flames.[67] Jerome could not find a copy of *Against the Christians* in the library at Caesarea,[68] and John Chrysostom states that such libelous anti-Christian works were only to be found in their

---

[63] Socrates, *HE* 3:23. This is probably a Christian device. See R. Wilken, *The Christians as the Romans Saw Them* (New Haven & London, 1984), p. 130. According to Stevenson, the source of Socrates' testimony is Eusebius' lost work *Against Porphyry* (*Studies*, p. 36).

[64] *Against the Christians*, in Eusebius, *HE* 6,19.

[65] Regarding Eusebius' motive of local patriotism, see Lightfoot, "Eusebius", p. 329; Harnack, *Chronology* II, p. 119.

[66] This refers to the responses of Methodius of Olympus, Eusebius, Apollinarius and Philostorgius.

[67] After the Council of Nicea in 325. Socrates, *HE* 1,9,30; *Codex Theodosianus* 15,5,66. According to Socrates, Constantine compared Arius to Porphyry and wished to call the Arians "Porphyrians".

[68] *Commentary on the Epistle to the Galatians* 1,2.

complete form among the Christians themselves.[69] However, it seems
that the imperial decrees were not universally obeyed, for in the
mid-fifth century, under Theodosius II and Valentinian III, the prohibition against Porphyry's book had to be reissued.[70] The fact that
Jerome and Augustine also referred to Porphyry's arguments suggests an ongoing influence. The repeated attempts to obliterate his
work indicate that it continued to inspire, directly or indirectly, later
anti-Christian invective.[71] Eventually the campaign against Porphyry's
book succeeded; apart from a few dozens of fragments, the book
was eradicated. Also lost were the four direct refutations,[72] in which
echoes of Porphyry's attack reverberated, as if thereby to erase all
trace of his work.[73]

Several attempts were made to assemble the fragments of Porphyry's tract scattered in Christian works, and to reconstruct the text
of *Against the Christians*. A. Harnack finally prepared the definitive edition of all fragments pertaining directly or indirectly to the book.[74]
To the dozens of relevant fragments, Harnack added nearly fifty others from the apologetic work of Macarius of Magnesia.[75] The literary

---

[69] *Homily on St. Babilas* 1,2. He does not refer specifically to Porphyry's work.

[70] *Codex Theodosianus* 1,6,66; *Codex Justinianus* 1,1,3; Socrates, *HE* 1,9,30.

[71] P. Courcelle thinks that Porphyry's work was the source of many anti-Christian arguments presented by Christian authors, notably Hierocles and Julian. See
P. Courcelle, "Propos anti-chrétiens rapportés par Saint Augustin", *Recherches augustiniennes* 1 (1958), pp. 149–186; Idem., "Critiques exégétiques et arguments anti-
chrétiens rapportés par Ambrosiaster", *Vigiliae Christianae*, 13 (1959) pp. 133–169.

[72] Only a few fragments are extant. Methodius in G.N. Bontwetsch, *GCS*, 27
(Leipzig, 1917); Apollinarius in H. Liezmann, "Apolinaris und seine Schule", *TU*
1 (1904) p. 265; Philostorgius in J. Bidez, *GCS* 21 (Leipzig, 1913). Jerome refers to
the works of Methodius, Eusebius and Apollinarius in the introduction to his commentary on Daniel and in the commentary itself, 4, 12, 13; *Epistles* 48:3; 84:2; *De
Viris Illustribus* 81:3; *Commentary on Matthew* 4,7. Philostorgius notes them briefly (*HE*
8,14) and states that he wished to add his own refutation (*HE* 10,10).

[73] It is possible that the replies to Porphyry did not satisfy Christian sages. See
Lightfoot, "Eusebius", p. 329; Stevenson, *Studies*, p. 37; M.V. Anastos, "Porphyry's
Attack on the Bible", *The Classical Tradition: Literary and Historical Studies in Honor of
Harry Caplan* (Ithaca, N.Y., 1966), p. 424.

[74] On attempts prior to Harnack see T.W. Crafer, "The Work of Porphyry against
the Christians and Its Reconstruction", *Journal of Theological Studies* 15 (1914), pp.
360–395, 481–51. For a survey of attempts prior to Crafer, see ibid., p. 482, and,
Labriolle, *Réaction*, p. 245. Harnack gave the background for the collection of fragments in his exhaustive study "Kritik des Neuen Testament von einem griechischen
Philosophen des 3 Jahrhunderts", *TU* 37, 4 (1911), and in his introduction to the
edition of the Fragments, see idem., *Porphyrius "Gegen die Christen", 15 Bücher: Zeugnisse, Fragmente und Referate* (Berlin, 1916).

[75] This work has been partially preserved in a single manuscript which disappeared

framework of this composition was the five-day debate between Macarius and a pagan opponent. The fragments are gleaned from the arguments of Macarius' anonymous pagan antagonist. Owing to their similarity to Porphyry's arguments, Harnack initially thought that Macarius had taken them from Porphyry and placed them in the mouth of the pagan. However, certain inexplicable differences convinced Harnack that Macarius had become aquainted with Porphyry's views through an anonymous abridged version of *Against the Christians*, without knowing its source. By identifying that source, Harnack effectively doubled the number of fragments known from Porphyry's lost work and enabled us to obtain a clearer picture of its content. Scholars accepted Harnack's position as a basis for reconstructing and analyzing Porphyry's book.[76]

However some scholars disagreed with Harnack's views on the relationship between the arguments of Macarius' pagan and those of Porphyry. T.W. Crafer held that although the fragments were taken from Porphyry, they reached Macarius via Hierocles' work, *Lover of Truth*, which presented Porphyry's arguments without actually citing his words.[77] J. Geffcken thought that although Macarius was dependent on Porphyry, especially with regard to biblical criticism, he also gleaned from other sources.[78] Following both Crafer and Geffcken, S. Pezzella proposed that some fragments came from Porphyry, others, from Hierocles' *Lover of Truth* and other pagan authors.[79] Barnes renewed reservations about identifying the fragments

---

shortly after C. Blondel copied and prepared it for publication. Blondel died before he could have the work published and P. Foucart completed the edition under the title, "The Only Child, or an Answer to the Greeks" (Μονογενὴς ἢ Ἀποκριτικὸς πρὸς Ἕλληνας); *Macarii Magnetis quae supersunt*, ex inedito codice edidit C. Blondel (Paris, 1876). For an English translation of the fragments from Macarius attributed to Porphyry by Harnack, see R.J. Hoffmann, *Porphyry's Against the Christians, the Literary Remains* (Amherst, N.Y., 1994).

[76] Labriolle's description of Porphyry's attack is based on all the fragments which Harnack collected, though he expresses some reservations concerning two of them. He fully agrees with Harnack's conclusions about the fragments from Macarius (*Réaction*, p. 247). See also Anastos, "Porphyry", p. 424. In her study of the Christian vocabulary of Porphyry, J.M. DeMarolle treats the fragments of Macarius as if they derived from Porphyry. See J.M. DeMarolle, "Un aspect de la polémique païenne à la fin du IIIe siècle: le vocabulaire chrétien de Porphyre", *Vigiliae Christianae* 26 (1972), pp. 87–104.

[77] Crafer, "Porphyry", pp. 361–388.

[78] Geffcken, *Zwei Apologeten*, pp. 301–304; see also his book, *Last Days*, p. 62.

[79] S. Pezella, "Il problema del *Kata Christianon* di Porphyrio", *EOS* 52 (1972), pp. 87–104.

as originating from Porphyry, although he did not totally reject the possibility that their source may have been Porphyry, albeit indirectly.[80] A. Meredith and A. Benoît followed Barnes, whose opinion has been accepted by many scholars.[81]

However R. Goulet was to produce a comprehensive study of Macarius' work,[82] which superseded all previous conclusions. He proved that the words and linguistic style of the fragments have much in common with the rest of Macarius' work. Basing his claims on this affinity, Goulet concluded that Macarius molded Porphyry's arguments to his own style and sometimes, perhaps, made changes to the content of the argument as well. Goulet fully accepted the identification of Porphyry as the source for the anti-Christian arguments for the same reasons that Harnack had proposed. However, Goulet did not see any need to predicate these reasons on the existence of an anonymous abridged text serving as intermediary between Porphyry and Macarius; this removed the difficulties which Harnack faced. Goulet concluded that Macarius was acquainted with Porphyry's attack on Christianity, albeit indirectly, through one of the tracts against Porphyry which included his statements. Macarius' goal, however, was not to write yet another work against Porphyry, but rather to demonstrate, in his disputation, how to answer pagan queries concerning Holy Scripture and matters of Christian faith. Therefore he did not want Porphyry to be seen as a literary source for the anti-Christian arguments, and even tried to disguise the fact by referring to another work by Porphyry, *Philosophy from the Oracles*. According to Goulet, Macarius' desire to camouflage his source also explains the striking similarity between the content of Porphyry's other fragments and Macarius' arguments, despite the infrequency of any linguistic parallels. Finally, Goulet proposed that Macarius gleaned Porphyry's arguments directly from Apollinarius' book against Porphyry. Even if we do not accept all of Goulet's views, he seems to have reinstated

---

[80] T.D. Barnes, "Porphyry against the Christians: Date and Attribution of the Fragments", *Journal of Theological Studies*, N.S. 24 (1973), pp. 424–442.

[81] A. Benoît, "La 'Contra Christianos' de Porphyre: où en est la collection des fragments", *Paganisme, Judaisme, Christianisme, Mélanges offerts à Marcel Simon* (Paris, 1978), pp. 263–270; A. Meredith, "Porphyry and Julian Against the Christians", *ANRW* 23.I 2 (1980), pp. 1126–1128.

[82] R. Goulet, *Makarios Magnes, Monogenes*. Introduction générale, Traduction et Commentaire, Thèse inédite (Paris, 1974). Goulet has published his main conclusions in "Porphyre et Macaire de Magnésie", *Studia Patristica* 15 = *TU* 128 (1984), pp. 448–452.

the view that Porphyry served as the source for Macarius, and has explained convincingly how Macarius adapted Porophyry's statements to a new literary framework.

On occasion scholars expressed reservations about the identification of one or another fragment from among those that did not come from Macarius. Generally speaking, however, these fragments were accepted as reflecting the content of Porphyry's statements, if not the actual words. After Harnack's compilation of fragments, several additional passages were identified, by Harnack and by other scholars.[83] These additional fragments did not add much to Harnack's collection. But the fact of their discovery suggests that the corpus of fragments from *Against the Christians* is not yet complete and that additional items will certainly come to light.[84] Porphyry's work served as an arsenal for subsequent anti-Christian polemics; it was also, perhaps, a source for many questions raised by Christian authors.

Eusebius is the only author who gives any indication of the date of composition of *Against the Christians*. He states that Porphyry wrote his book during his stay in Sicily,[85] i.e., from 268 CE, before his return to Rome after the death of Plotinus in 270 CE.[86] Accepting

---

[83] Using a table, Benoît (n. 81) tried to reclassify the known fragments according to their different sources, noting their general characteristics and their possible relation to Porphyry's original text. The fragments added to Harnack's collection are: A. Harnack, "Neue Fragmente des Werkes des Porphyrius gegen die Christen", *Sitzungsberichte der preußischen Akademie der Wissenschaften* (1921), pp. 266–284; 834–835; P. Nautin, "Trois autres fragments du livre de Porphyre 'Contre les Chrétiens'", *Revue biblique* 57 (1950), pp. 409–416; F. Altheim & R. Stiehl, "Neue Bruckstücke aus Porphyrios *Kata Christianon*", *Gedenkschrift G. Rohde, Aparchai, Untersuchungen zur klassischen Philologie und Geschichte des Altertums* 4 (1961), pp. 23–38; C. Shaeublin, "Diodor von Tarsos gegen Porphyrios?" *Museum Helveticum* 27 (1970), pp. 58–63; D. Hagedorn & R. Merkelbach, "Ein neues Fragment aus Porphyrios 'Gegen die Christen'", *Vigiliae Christianae* 20 (1966), pp. 86–90; G. Binder, "Eine Polemik des Porphyrios gegen die allegorische Auslegung des Alten Testaments durch die Christen", *Zeitschrift für Papyrologie und Epigraphik* 3 (1968), pp. 81–95; M. Gronewald, "Porphyrios Kritik an den Gleichnissen des Evangeliums", *ZPE* 3 (1968) p. 96.

[84] Harnack has suggested that various passages of *PE*, *DE*, and the *Theophany* contain sentences or longer fragments from *Against the Christians*, which include a hidden polemic against Porphyry (Harnack, *Against the Christians*, p. 91). His statements, however, were expressed as a general and plausible assumption without actual proof.

[85] *HE* 6,19,2. For a different understanding of this passage and a possibility that Porphyry wrote his book later in Rome, see T.D. Barnes, "Scholarship or Propaganda? Porphyry *Against the Christians* and its Historical Setting", *Bulletin of the Institute of Classical Studies* 39 (1994), pp. 60–62.

[86] Porphyry, *Life of Plotinus* 6,1.

the testimony of both Porphyry and Eusebius, J. Bidez gives their
statements a liberal interpretation and proposes 268–275 (the reigns
of Claudius II and Aurelian) as a plausible date of composition.[87]
Following Bidez's argument, Harnack thought that Porphyry wrote
the book just before or just after the death of Plotinus, in 270 CE.[88]
Scholars accepted without question the conclusions of Harnack and
Bidez regarding the date of composition.[89] Later, A. Cameron proposed a more exact date. Citing Porphyry's dependence on the lost
work of Callinicus, on Alexandria during the brief reign of Zeno-
bia, Cameron proved that the *terminus post quem* should be late 270–271,
or even a little after.[90] When it seemed that the question had been
settled, Barnes adduced a new set of rather speculative arguments,
which led to the assumption that Porphyry had written his work
towards the end of his life, in the early fourth century.[91] In his later
book on Constantine and Eusebius, Barnes relates to this view as a
fact needing no additional proof,[92] and it was subsequently accepted
by other scholars as well.[93] B. Croke, however, who was inclined at
first to accept Barnes' opinion, undertook a thorough and systematic clarification of the matter, which completely changed his view.
In his analytical and critical article on Barnes' position, Croke convincingly rejects his arguments, returning to the earlier dating of
Against the Christians.[94]

The extant writings of Porphyry do not reveal his motives for
writing his anti-Christian work. The view generally accepted by scholars is that Porphyry wrote *Against the Christians* at the request of Plotinus.[95] The latter had embarked on a campaign against the gnostics
and attacked them in a special tract.[96] In the framework of this anti-
gnostic campaign, Amelius, a disciple of Plotinus, wrote a major work

---

[87] J. Bidez, *Vie de Porphyre* (Ghent, 1913), p. 65.
[88] Harnack, *Against the Christians*, p. 1.
[89] See Labriolle, *Réaction*, p. 242.
[90] A. Cameron, "The Date of Porphyry's *Kata Christianon*", *Classical Quarterly* N.S.
17 (1967), pp. 382–384.
[91] Barnes, "Porphyry *Against the Christians*, Date and Attribution", pp. 433–442.
[92] Barnes, *Constantine and Eusebius*, pp. 174–175.
[93] Meredith, "Porphyry and Julian", p. 1126; B. Croke, "Porphyry's Anti-Christian Polemic", *Journal of Theological Studies* N.S. 34 (1983), p. 184.
[94] B. Croke, "The Era of Porphyry's Anti-Christian Polemic", *Journal of Religious
History* 13 (1984/5), pp. 1–14. Barnes, however, still prefers a later date for the
composition, see "Scholarship or Propaganda?" p. 60.
[95] Harnack, *Against the Christians*, p. 1.
[96] Plotinus, *Enneads* 2,9.

against the gnostic apocalypse of Zostrianus. In fact, it was Porphyry
who proved that the *Book of Zoroaster*, a text sacred to gnostics, was
a forgery.[97] Given this background, it is easy to understand Porphyry's anti-Christian zeal, especially in his attacks on Scripture. His
polemic against the gnostics had been similarly fervent.[98] Perhaps
Christians were included in the general category of "gnostics" targeted by Plotinus.[99] The existence of a large Christian community
in Rome, where Plotinus and his disciples lived, may have further
impelled his intellectual struggle against Christianity.[100] Porphyry
claims that once worshiping Jesus had become part of life in the
city,[101] veneration of the gods had declined.[102] Such statements must
remain hypothetical as there is no evidence that Plotinus was hostile
to Christianity. Had he wanted to, Porphyry could have commented
explicitly on these matters in his biography of Plotinus. Harnack suggested that Porphyry may have served as a spokesman and propa-
gandist for the Emperor Claudius.[103] However there is no clear
indication that Claudius intended to persecute the Christians. Furthermore, Claudius died at the beginning of 270, whereas the book
was apparently not written before the end of the year,[104] during the
reign of Aurelian, who did not persecute the Christians. However it
is likely that Aurelian was about to take repressive measures prior
to his assassination in 275. According to Eusebius, Aurelian's change
of heart regarding the Christians was the result of his advisors' counsel.[105] Perhaps his policy towards the Christians is further indication
that Aurelian established a cult of sun worship in 274. Harnack's
suggestion regarding Porphyry and Claudius could also be extended
to Aurelian: Porphyry may have cooperated with Aurelian in matters concerning the Christians.[106]

---

[97] On the anti-gnostic works of Amelius and Porphyry, see Porphyry, *Life of Plotinus* 16.

[98] See Geffcken, *Last Days*, p. 62.

[99] Idem, *Zwei Apologeten*, p. 296; Labriolle, *Réaction*, p. 231. Apparently Porphyry
tended to view the gnostic opponents of Plotinus and his disciples as a Christian
group (*Life of Plotinus* 16).

[100] Labriolle, *Réaction*, p. 240.

[101] Although Rome is not mentioned here, it is clear that it is intended.

[102] Harnack, Fragment (F) 38.

[103] Harnack, *Against the Christians*, p. 1, n. 4.

[104] See Cameron, "The Date of Porphyry's *Kata Christianon*", p. 384.

[105] *HE* 7,30,20–21. See W.H.C. Frend, *Martyrdom and Persecution in the Early Church*
(Oxford, 1965), p. 443.

[106] Cameron, "The Date of Porphyry's *Kata Christianon*", p. 384.

Porphyry knew of earlier polemical traditions. He expanded, changed, developed, and consolidated previous arguments and added new ones. The question remains, however to what extent he drew on specific polemical works by pagan authors, notably Celsus. Despite the fact that some of their arguments are similar, and that there are various parallels and points of convergence, it is not clear whether Porphyry borrowed directly, if at all, from Celsus.[107]

Efforts had been made previously to reconstruct the original fifteen books of *Against the Christians*.[108] The problem was that of nearly a hundred fragments, only seven could be linked to a specific section of the work; even then, determining the content of an entire section on the basis of a single fragment is mere conjecture. Harnack had reservations about such attempts and was content to arrange the fragments according to subjects, regardless of their original sequence. The first fragment served as an introduction, followed by five main categories:

1. A critique of the nature and authenticity of the evangelists and of the apostles (F. 2–37).
2. A critique of Scripture (F. 38–47)
3. A critique of the acts and sayings of Jesus (F. 48–72).
4. A critique of Christian doctrines (Dogmatics, F. 73–94).
5. A critique of the contemporary Church (F. 95–97).

The Contents of the Fragments[109]

The evangelists had made up the stories about Jesus. Historians had not written about him (F. 15). The evangelists had perpetrated a fraud. This was the basic position that Porphyry wished to present by exposing the contradictions within the New Testament. He compared the two genealogical lists in Matthew and in Luke, pointing

---

[107] Harnack, *Against the Christians*, p. 11; Geffcken, *Zwei Apologeten*, p. 297; idem, *Last Days*, p. 63.

[108] On the various attempts to define the structure of the book, see A.B. Hulen, *Porphyry's Work against the Christians: An Interpretation* (New Haven, 1933), pp. 46–47.

[109] A description of the contents of the work, based on the fragments, has been presented on several occasions either partially or in a more complete form. In addition to the books mentioned above, see also R.L. Wilken, *The Christians as the Romans Saw Them*, pp. 126–163. For other descriptions of a more general nature, see J. Moffat, "Great Attacks on Christianity, II: Porphyry, 'Against the Christians', *Expository Times* 43, 1 (1931), pp. 72–78. For a study of more limited scope, see

out the discrepancies between them (Matt. 1; Luke 3; F. 11). Matthew
was guilty of ignorance because he attributed a verse in Psalms to
Isaiah (F. 10).

Likewise, Porphyry condemns Mark for attributing a quotation
only to Isaiah while part of it actually comes from Malachi (F. 9).
There were contradictory versions of the circumstances of Judas Iscariot's death in the Acts of the Apostles and in Matthew (F. 17). Only
John related that a Roman soldier stabbed Jesus on the cross and
that water and blood issued from his wound (F. 16: John 19:34). In
the account of the drowning of the pigs, Mark added details which
were not found in Matthew's version (Mark 5:13; Matt. 8:31). It was
impossible that such a large herd of swine existed among the Jews
and that so many drowned in such a small lake (F. 49). Mark had
deliberately exaggerated and given a ridiculous story. For in such a
small lake there could not be waves and storms such as the stormy
wind which Jesus rebuked (Mark 4:37–39). In fact Mark dramatizes
the incident in order to show how Jesus stopped the storm and saved
his disciples from drowning. Such childish tales as these demonstrated
that the Gospels acted as a "sophists' stage" (ἐκ τοιούτων παιδικῶν
ἱστοριῶν ἐγνώκαμεν σκηνὴν σεσοφισμένην εἶναι τὸ εὐαγγέλιον) (F. 55).

Porphyry finds contradictions in the words and deeds attributed
to Jesus. For example, in John 7:6 Jesus announces that he will not
go to Jerusalem on the Feast of Tabernacles, but does indeed do
(John 7:10; F. 70.). In one passage, he tells his disciples that he will
not always be with them (Matt. 26:36); later he states: "... I am
with you always, to the close of the age" (Matt. 28:20; F. 61). Jesus
threatened sinners with eternal damnation, but also declares that
punishment would be meted out according to the transgression, measure for measure, and within specific time limits (F. 91). The world
continued to exist despite Matthew's message of an imminent end
(24:14; F. 13). Peter died a wretched death in spite of the rewards
promised him (F. 26). John died a natural death despite Jesus' dec-

W. Den Boer, "A Pagan Historian and His Enemies: Porphyry against the Christians", *Classical Philology* 69 (1974), pp. 198–208. On the other hand, little attention
has been given to the echoes of Porphyry's polemic in later Christian apologetic
literature, in part because no Christian polemics against him have survived, but
also because of the difficulty in ascertaining the continuity of arguments not known
from the fragments. Another problem stems from absence of any Christian reference to Porphyry's name after the ban declared against him by the Church and
the authorities.

laration that he would be martyred.[110] New messiahs had not appeared in the past centuries despite Jesus' prophecy that "many will come in my name" (Matthew 24:5; F. 60). Here, Porphyry adds, "unless you mean Apollonius of Tyana, a man who was crowned with all the ornaments of philosophy" (ἄνδρα φιλοσοφίᾳ πάσῃ κεκοσμένον).

Porphyry points out that each Gospel gives a different version of the passion (πάθος) of Jesus. For example, Mark writes that someone offered Jesus a sponge dipped in vinegar (15:36). Matthew states that he was given "wine mingled with gall" (27:34), while John mentions "a sponge full of the vinegar on hyssop" (19:29). Matthew relates that on the cross, Jesus cried out: "*Eli, Eli lama sabachtani? that is to say, My God, my God, why hast thou forsaken me?*" (27:46). Luke, on the other hand, writes that Jesus cried out: "Father, into thy hands I commit my spirit" (23:48). In light of the banal and highly contradictory story, says Porphyry, perhaps several were crucified and not just one man. If the authors of the Gospels could not present a single version of the death of Jesus, then nothing they wrote was worth believing (F. 15).

The apostles were merely simple and poor country folk (*homines rusticani et pauperes*) (F. 4). They followed Jesus because he was the first who knew how to exploit their stupidity (F. 6). They performed several miracles, but that was not such a great thing (*non est autem grande facere signa*). Apollonius and Apuleius also performed quite a number of miracles. The apostles also used acts of magic to obtain money from rich and foolish women (F. 4), and wickedly exploited the inexperience and naivete of their audiences (F. 5).

Porphyry aimed his criticism at the leaders of the apostles. Peter was "the head of a troupe of disciples" (ὁ πρωτοστάτης τοῦ χοροῦ τῶν μαθητῶν) and was in charge of their affairs. Porphyry describes him as a choreographer of a dance troupe or a conductor of a choir (F. 23, 26). The major role given to Peter, however, did not suit his weak character. He denied Jesus three times out of the fear of a humble servant (F. 25–26). Occasionally he acted against the instructions of Jesus. Whereas Jesus commanded infinite forgiveness, Peter severed the ear of the servant of the high priest who had done nothing wrong but simply followed the instructions of his master (F. 24). He behaved mercilessly towards Ananias and Sapphira who had

---

[110] This is the second of the five additional fragments published by Harnack.

rightly kept some of the proceeds from the sale of their property for
their basic needs.[111] When he escaped from prison, Peter in effect
condemned his guards to certain death. It was hard to understand
how such a man held the keys to heaven (F. 26) and why Jesus
trusted him even though he called Peter, Satan. Perhaps Jesus was
inebriated when he called him Satan, or perhaps he was daydreaming
when he handed him the keys to heaven (F. 23). Peter's death was
as unfortunate as his life.

Porphyry deals even more harshly with Paul. According to him,
Paul was contradiction personified. He rejected circumcision, but circumcised Timothy (F. 27). He rejected Jewish Law but continued
to follow it (F. 31). What could his disciples understand from the
confusion of this ignoramus? He stated that he was both Jew and
Roman. The duplicity of his words proved that he was a chronic
liar despite his claims to speak the truth, not lies. He praised virginity but advocated marriage (F. 32). Pauline eschatology seemed
absurd. Paul says, "For the form of the world is passing away" (I
Cor. 7:31), but who should transfer it and for what purpose? If it
were the demiurge, why should it change what had been satisfac-
tory? If to beautify the cosmos, it meant that from the beginning
the world had been created defectively (F. 34). Porphyry lashes out
against Paul's evocation of the Lord descending from heaven and
the resurrected dead and living faithful who ascend to the sky on
clouds to meet him (I Thessalonians 4:15–17). It was totally absurd
that men should fly in the air like birds or ride on top of clouds,
or that heavy living creatures should have the ability of winged beings
to traverse the sky as if it were the sea. It would constitute a mon-
strous aberration from the order of the world. Every creature had
been given its place and its individuality. The divine logos never
changed the order of the world (F. 35).

Porphyry skillfully exploits the controversy between Paul and Peter
over the latter's ambivalent attitude towards Gentile converts and
Judeo-Christians in the Epistle to the Galatians (F. 11–14). This matter bothered Christian commentators long afterwards, to the extent
that some claimed that the man named Caiphas in the epistle was
not really Peter but someone else. Jerome opposed such views (Com-

---

[111] F. 25. Jerome also mentions "the stupid Porphyry" (*stultus Porphyrius*) (*Epistle*
130, 14). Elsewhere, however, he expresses an opinion similar to Porphyry's views
(*Epistle* 109, 3). See Harnack, *Against the Christians*, p. 55.

mentary on Galatians 1,2; F. 21c). According to Porphyry, this controversy demonstrated Paul's envy of Peter for the miracles he performed. This envy prompted Paul's vicious attack on Peter. As for Peter, he grievously erred in his attitude towards Gentile Christians. From Paul's pettiness and Peter's error, and the conflict between them, one could conclude that the doctrines preached by both were made up of fanciful lies which they had invented (F. 21–22).

Porphyry also knew the Old Testament well. From the little that remains of his critique of this part of scripture, a general attitude can nonetheless be discerned. He sharply criticized the tendency to allegorical interpretation popular among Christians. He was well aware that this exegetical approach offered a solution to difficulties presented by the Scriptures, and that it allowed the commentator to elucidate biblical verses according to his own religious or philosophical ideas. By ruling out allegorical interpretation one exposed the difficulties presented by the text. Porphyry argued that allegorical interpretation did not follow the written text but rather expressed the opinions and ideas of the commentators. They claimed that statements made by Moses were riddles (αἰνίγματα) and regarded them as divine prophecies (θεσπίσματα), full of mystery. Thus they suppressed reasonable judgement and promulgated their own interpretations.

Porphyry designates Origen as the father of the Christian allegorical method. He was the inventor of this absurdity (ἀτοπία) among the Christians. Porphyry relates that as a young man he knew Origen, a person of world renown. Origen received a Greek education. He held Greek concepts of the world and the nature of divinity, and into these he integrated foreign myths. He learned the allegorical method of interpretation (τὸν μεταληπτικὸν τρόπον) from the Greeks and applied it to Jewish scriptures (F. 39).

Porphyry presented Christian allegorical commentary as ridiculous to the point of absurdity. He scornfully proposed applying it to the struggle between Achilles and Hector in the *Iliad*, to portray this as the struggle between Christ (Achilles) and Satan (Hector), in the manner of the Christian commentators (Fragment Binder, p. 92).[112]

---

[112] P. Sellew does not agree that Porphyry's allegorical interpretation of passages from the *Iliad* was intended as a *reductio ad absurdum* of Christian exegesis of the Old Testament, suggesting instead that it was a case of "counter-allegorism". See P. Sellew, "Achilles or Christ? Porphyry and Didymus in Debate over Allegorical Interpretation", *Harvard Theological Review* 82 (1989), pp. 79–100; Barnes, "Scholarship or Propaganda?" p. 63.

He rejected the Christians' allegorical interpretation of God's words to the prophet Hosea, and scoffed at the fact that the prophet had intimate relations with a harlot at God's command (Hos. 1:2). He contended that one had to preserve the original "tone" of what was written (*sonare quod legitur*) (F. 45). By Porphyry's time, there was a centuries-old tradition of allegorical interpretation in Greek literature and philosophy, embracing Homer and ancient mythologies.[113] Hellenistic Jewish authors, and subsequently Christian writers, had adopted the allegorical method. As a young man, Porphyry himself was an enthusiastic advocate of allegory and even wrote a fantastic allegory on a brief section of the *Odyssey*, entitled *The Cave of the Nymphs*. In addition, Porphyry made extensive use of allegory in several of his earlier works.[114] His rejection of the Christians' allegorical interpretations may have been a tactical move to attack them at one of their weak points. But it is also possible that in later life, Porphyry grew to dislike allegory in principle.[115]

Porphyry denied the Mosaic authorship of Scripture. He contended that all biblical books had been burned when the Temple was destroyed, and that what had survived under the name of Moses had in fact been written hundreds of years later by Ezra (F. 68). Acquainted with historical and chronographical literature, he dealt with chronographical questions, though it is not clear if he wrote a chronicle.[116] This knowledge enabled him to calculate the date of Moses, and particularly, to examine meticulously the book of Daniel (F. 43).

Porphyry's critique of Daniel is well known. In the twelfth book of *Against the Christians*, he treats the question of the authenticity of the book of Daniel. Jerome's commentary on Daniel preserves many of Porphyry's arguments, and summarizes the latter's basic view that Daniel was not the author of the biblical book. According to Porphyry, it was written during the reign of Antiochus Epiphanes, not

---

[113] See F. Buffière, *Les mythes d'Homère et la pensée grecque* (Paris, 1956); R. Lamberton, *Homer the Theologian. Neoplatonist Allegorical Reading and the Growth of the Epic Tradition* (Berkeley, 1986).

[114] See Porphyry, *Philosophy from the Oracles*, and *Homeric Questions*. See also Buffière, *Les mythes d'Homère et la pensée grecque*, pp. 419–459; Lamberton, *Homer the Theologian*, pp. 108–133.

[115] This subject will be treated in our discussion of Eusebius' views on Christian and pagan allegorical interpretation in the context of polemics.

[116] On the different views regarding this question, see Croke, "Porphyry's Anti-Christian Chronology", pp. 168–185.

Cyrus. The author lived in Judea and was not predicting the future but describing past events. Whatever may have happened before Antiochus corroborated historical fact, but material on events after Antiochus was utter nonsense, since the author could not predict the future. Porphyry attempted to prove his thesis by examining the book of Daniel in light of the power struggle between Antiochus and the Ptolemaic rulers and showed how the upheavals in Antiochus' reign corresponded to Daniel's prophecy.

According to Porphyry, the behavior of Jesus on various occasions seemed incomprehensible and inconsistent with the image of a divine soul or a hero. When he is tempted by the devil at the Temple (Matt. 4:6–7) and told to throw himself down as proof that he is the son of God, Jesus replies: "You shall not tempt the Lord your God." Porphyry rejects this response as unacceptable. Jesus seemed to be avoiding the danger of fall. If he were able to perform miracles and to revive the dead with his words, he should have jumped down immediately and emerged unscathed. He would thus have proved himself capable of saving others from danger, particularly in light of the verse from Psalms mentioning angels: "On their hands they will bear you up, lest you dash your foot against a stone" (91:11–12). Thus Jesus could have proved to everyone at the Temple that he was the son of God and that he had the power to deliver himself and others from all forms of danger (F. 48).

Porphyry was astonished by Jesus' conduct in the land of the Gerasenes (Luke 8 and parallels). Why did he respond to the pleas of the demons (δαίμονες)? Did he not know that they only intended to bring harm to the world? Surely Jesus had come into the world to deliver mankind from them. If the whole story was simply a fabrication, then it taught us about real evil on the part of Jesus (F. 49). Porphyry condemns as illogical Jesus' words, "Now is the judgment of this world, now shall the ruler of this world be cast out" (John 12:31). Who is the ruler and where will he be cast? How will he be cast into a world in which he already is present and which he rules, or perhaps there are two distinct worlds. From whatever vantage point one views these words, they remain enigmatic (F. 72).

Jesus' passivity in the face of insult and injury angers Porphyry. His sorrowful mood at Gethsemane and his prayer, "My Father, if it be possible, let this cup pass from me", showed a foolishness inappropriate for the son of God, especially for a wise man who despised death (F. 62). Afterwards, when he is brought before the high priest and the prefect, why did Jesus not speak in the manner of a wise and divine person? He should have taught them wisdom and helped them become better people. Instead he let them scourge and mock him. Why did he not behave like Apollonius, who before being led to his death spoke harsh words to the Emperor Domitian, and straightaway magically disappeared from the imperial court, to appear several hours later in another Italian city? If Jesus were destined to suffer at God's command, he should have accepted the punishment— but not without a vigorous and harsh reply to Pilate, as befitted a wise man. He should not have put up with insults as if he were some poor wretch emerging from the rabble to speak (F. 63).

Likewise, the resurrection of Jesus takes place under most unfortunate circumstances. Could he not have been resurrected in front of Pilate, Herod, or the high priest, or even better, before the Senate and the Roman people? Then everyone would have known and none would have doubted him. Instead, he revealed himself to Mary Magdalene, a simple woman from a remote village, who at one time had been seized by seven demons (F. 63). Jesus should have ascended to heaven in full view of many Jews and Greeks from all parts of the world, just as in the future he would descend at the time of the Second Coming (F. 65).

Porphyry accused Christians of possessing irrational faith (ἀλόγος πίστις) and of persuading others to share it (F. 1; F. 73). If, as Jesus said, God hid his secrets from wise men and revealed them to children (Matt. 11:25), he should have presented them more clearly and less enigmatically, as befitted children and the simple-minded. Moreover, according to Jesus' words, the major task of the Messiah on earth would be to conceal the light of knowledge from wise men in order to reveal it to children and fools (F. 52). An example of vague and enigmatic discourse was the parable comparing the kingdom of heaven to a mustard seed (Matt. 13:31–32). The parable had no meaning. These were futile fantasies unworthy even of daydreaming matrons. When one is dealing with divine matters, one has to use clear language, especially if the intended audience was children, not wise men (F. 54).

The monarchic concept of the divinity on part of the Christians was simply polytheism in another guise. God could be sovereign only if he ruled over creatures which resemble him in nature, i.e., over other gods (F. 75). In fact, since Christians themselves defined angels as immortal creatures, unchanging and incorruptible, it follows that angels were gods by another name. Porphyry held the view that statues of the gods possessed no inherent divinity but only helped the faithful to remember and honor them. Craftsmen gave the statues human form because man was superior among living creatures. Even Moses spoke of "the finger of God" (Exodus 31:18; F. 76). According to Porphyry, however, even if a Greek were ignorant enough to believe that the gods dwelt inside the statues, this was more acceptable than the belief that the divinity (τὸ θεῖον) descended into the womb of the Virgin Mary and became a fetus to be swaddled in dirty diapers after his birth (F. 77).

Porphyry viewed the Incarnation as unacceptable. Why did Christ appear at so late a date in human history and allow mankind to live so many years without the grace of his advent? Why did he cause so many people to die without salvation? (F. 81–82). How could one believe that the son of God truly suffered on the cross if he possessed an immutable divine nature? (F. 84).

Baptism was a highly immoral practice. How was it possible that mature people who had sinned or committed adultery could, as a snake sheds its skin, simply erase and wash off all their past transgressions in a single act of baptism, uttering the name of Christ? This view simply encouraged sin and evil (F. 88).

The eucharist was an act of cannibalism without parallel even among barbarians.[117] The words of Jesus, "Truly, truly, I say to you, unless you eat the flesh of the Son of man and drink his blood, you have no life in you" (John 6:53) were bestial and absurd, intolerable to the human ear. Even if they had a hidden allegorical meaning, they were harmful to the soul. Even animals without the power of reason did not eat their own kind. Although there were Greeks and barbarians who taught some strange and weird ideas, no philosopher or historian had ever managed to invent such a tragic notion (F. 69). According to Porphyry, Mark, Luke and Matthew felt that these words were bizarre and so removed them from the text.

Porphyry includes earlier arguments against the resurrection of the dead. The life cycle in the cosmos was fixed and eternal, designed

---

[117] It is hard to know whether Porphyry was using this as a time-honored insult, or whether he meant it literally. The fragment derives from Macarius, and perhaps it was he who inserted the idea here (F. 69).

to preserve the existence of the species. There was no reason for God to disturb it. And besides, how could limbs which had been destroyed join the body anew? Consider, for example a seaman who drowns in a storm and is eaten by fish. Fishermen catch the fish in their nets and eat them. When the fishermen die, they become food for dogs whose corpses are preyed upon by vultures. What then has happened to the flesh of the seaman? Christians would answer that God is omnipotent but it was not so. God could not change the fact that Homer was a poet or that Troy fell, or make two and two equal one hundred. God could not become wicked or a sinner, because he was essentially good. Furthermore, how was it possible that God could destroy the heavenly world, the pinnacle of his creation, and yet revive that most miserable creature, man? And even if he could revive the dead, how could the world contain all of mankind born since Creation? (F. 94).

Similarly, Porphyry rejects the Christian view that the resurrection of Jesus or of Lazarus foreshadowed the future resurrection of all humanity. For the body of Lazarus had not yet disintegrated, and Jesus was not born from sperm like other men (*nulla seminis condicione natus est*) (F. 92).

The idea that heaven and earth are not eternal was intolerable as well (Matt. 24:35). It was an insidious idea. How could the words of Jesus be fulfilled after the destruction of heaven and earth? If Christ spoke of such devastation, he was like the cruelest of men who kill their children (F. 92). If pressed, one might believe that the earth could be destroyed, but what of the heavens? How could the embodiment of eternal order come to an end? Have the heavens sinned perchance? Porphyry castigates the Christians for giving moral preference to sinners over those who live holy and innocent lives. Did only sick people or criminals need Jesus? (F. 87). Jesus' statement that "it is easier for a camel to go through the eye of a needle than for a rich man to enter the kingdom of God" (Matt. 19:25) rejected the rich man on principle, even if he may be righteous, and exalted the poor man who was possibly a scoundrel. The poor man had no need to pursue virtue, for his poverty would bring him salvation. Being destitute rather than virtuous would lead one to the kingdom of heaven (F. 58).

Porphyry draws attention to the prophecy: "And this gospel of the kingdom will be preached throughout the whole world, as a testimony to the nations; and then the end will come" (Matt. 24:14). Since the Gospel had indeed spread to the remotest corners of the world, argued Porphyry, surely Jesus' prophecy should have already been fulfilled. But the end, had not come. He ridicules Jesus' promise to those who follow his path: "they will pick up serpents, and if they drink any deadly things, it will not hurt them . . ." (Mark 16:18). This verse should be the test for would-be priests or bishops. They should sip a cup of poison and whoever emerged unharmed should be chosen (F. 33)

Porphyry laughs at the Christian ideal of virginity (ibid.). Women were easy targets. The apostles knew how to extort money from them. Porphyry knew affluent women who were captivated by Christianity, distributed their wealth among the poor and became beggars. Porphyry rejects the idea of choosing to beg, demanding for oneself from the share of others (F. 58). The ideal of martyrdom comes under attack as well. Porphyry castigates Jesus for not sparing his disciples cruel punishment. If he had seen to it that all believed in him, the authorities would not have put Christians to death as heretics (F. 64).

Behind all anti-Christian arguments lies a single dual argument. Christians abandoned the tradition and religion of their fathers for a new and strange way of life. They turned their backs on their ancestral gods in favor of a heretical and atheistic life as the enemies of those very gods who protected them. Thus they betrayed the gods who had long been accepted by kings, legislators, and philosophers throughout the world. Of all the creeds on earth, Christians chose the most heretical and atheistic, thereby becoming fanatical adherents of foreign Jewish mythologies (Ἰουδαϊκῶν μυθολογημάτων) which were universally disparaged. Not only were Christians naive and irrational in adhering to the beliefs of these enemies of all nations, but they did not even worship the God of the Jews according to the latter's traditions and laws.

They strayed from Judaism and forged a new path in the wilderness (καινὴν δέ τινα καὶ ἐρήμην ἀνοδίαν ἑαυτοῖς συντεμεῖν) far from the ways of both Greeks and Jews.[118]

---

[118] F. 1. = *PE* 1,2,2–4. Harnack, following Wilamowitz, assumed that Eusebius took this passage from Porphyry's introduction to *Against the Christians*. See U. von Wilamowitz-Moellendorf, "Ein bruchstück aus der Schrift des Porphyrius gegen die

Christen", *Zeitschrift für die neutestamentliche Wissenschaft* 1 (1900), pp. 101–105; Harnack, *Against the Christians*, p. 45. It seems, however, that this passage is in fact Eusebius' summary of Porphyry's major thesis which may reflect the words of Porphyry. See J. Sirinelli and E. des Places in their edition of *PE* (*SC* 206, Paris, 1974), pp. 224–229; Barnes, "Scholarship or Propaganda", p. 65.

CHAPTER TWO

APOLOGETICS AND POLEMICS IN NON-APOLOGETIC AND EARLY APOLOGETIC-POLEMICAL WORKS

I. *Apologetics in Non-Apologetic Works*

Most of the extant works of Eusebius contain apologetic material, in varying amounts. Some scholars have even considered all his writings as a single multifaceted, apologetic undertaking.[1] Several works were written from the standpoint of internal Christian polemics, such as the apology for Origen, *Against Marcellus* and the *Ecclesiastical Theology*. These do not concern us here. With regard to other works, it cannot be determined whether or not they are apologetic, because their contents are not primarily apologetic or polemical and we are not certain of the motives that inspired them, since Eusebius gives no explicit indication. This is true for the *Onomasticon*, the commentaries on Isaiah and Psalms, and the *Martyrs of Palestine*. More challenging is the apologetic element in the *Chronicle*, the *Ecclesiastical History* (*HE*), the *Life of Constantine* (*VC*), and *In Praise of Constantine*. These works include more apologetic material and may have been written for apologetic purposes. However, they do not possess the combination of features which define them as unequivocally apologetic. Their apologetic-polemical purpose is not defined. They do not constitute a response to an existing work or to specific anti-Christian arguments. They do not contain a systematic attack on pagan religion and culture that combines a rebuttal of anti-Christian arguments with a positive apology on Christianity. Before discussing the unequivocal apologetic works of Eusebius, I shall briefly treat the possible apologetic background of the four above-mentioned pieces and their key apologetic motifs. These descriptions may diverge somewhat from our chronological presentation of the subject, but its scope can be significantly broadened by their inclusion.

---

[1] See Chapter 1, above.

The Chronicle

Prior to Eusebius, Christian apologists made use of chronicles to
prove the antiquity of the Christian tradition as opposed to pagan
arguments.[2] In this they continued an earlier Jewish tradition, but
with the additional motive of refuting pagan polytheism. Through
chronicles, they hoped to show that the gods were mere mortals who
had been deified after death. They rebutted the pagan, two-fold
accusation that Christianity was an innovation and that it rejected
the ancestral gods. The great chronography of Julius Africanus has
been lost, but it seems that he combined the old apologetic motive
with a strong desire to set forth his millenarian concept.[3] Eusebius
rejects his inclination to millenarianism and his preoccupation with
calculating the end of days.[4] Thus he established a different trend
in writing his chronicle from that of Africanus.[5] Eusebius seems to
continue the traditional apologetic task of the chronicle in the manner of his predecessors.[6] He states this explicitly when referring to
the *Chronicle* in a paragraph in the *PE* which illustrates the Christians' interest in comparative chronology.[7] The apologists refuted the
argument that Christianity was a new religion by pointing out that
great Greek legislators and philosophers were much later than Moses
the Lawgiver and the prophets, who had anticipated the coming of
Jesus and taught the religion continued by Christianity.[8]

Perhaps Porphyry's book against the Christians encouraged Eusebius to write the *Chronicle*, for he quotes from it in a central place
in the *Chronicle*. In the introduction to the second, main part of the

---

[2] See Chapter 1. For example: Tatian, *Address to the Greeks*, 36–40; Theophilus,
To Autolycus, 3,16–29; Clement, *Stromateis*, 1.

[3] See A.A. Mosshamer, *The Chronicle of Eusebius and the Greek Chronographic Tradition* (Lewisburg-London, 1979), pp. 146–157. For Eusebius' attitude to the earlier
chronographic tradition, see pp. 128–168.

[4] See *Chronicle*, Introduction.

[5] See Schwartz, "Eusebios", cols. 1378–1379.

[6] According to Sirinelli, Eusebius, unlike earlier apologists, was motivated by a
true "historical spirit" whose originality may be seen in the *Chronicle*. This shows
not only a desire to assemble facts selectively as proof, but a rigorously ordered
approach to history in seeking to clarify the past of cultures and peoples (*Vues historiques*, p. 34).

[7] *PE* 10,9. For Eusebius' *Chronicle* and the Christian chronographic tradition, see
W. Adler, "Eusebius' Chronicle and Its Legacy", in H.W. Attridge and G. Hata
(eds.), *Eusebius, Christianity, and Judaism*, pp. 467–491.

[8] On Eusebius' general apologetic motivation in writing the *Chronicle*, see Geffcken,
Zwei Apologeten, p. 311; Schwartz", Eusebios", col. 1377; Stevenson, *Studies*, pp. 38–39.

Chronicle, namely the tables, Eusebius quotes Book IV of *Against the Christians*. In Book IV, Porphyry dealt with a recurrent question in pagan-Christian polemics, namely, the date for Moses.[9] This question was of foremost importance in the *Chronicle*. It is possible that Eusebius himself discovered a new and more exact date for Moses which encouraged him to write the *Chronicle*.[10] When Eusebius quoted the first edition of the *Chronicle* in his *Prophetic Extracts*, he emphasized the importance of the *Chronicle* in proving the date of Moses and of the other prophets, and its role in supporting the *Extracts*.[11] This impression is strengthened by the passage in the *PE*, recalled above, referring to the *Chronicle*.[12] Here he refers to Porphyry's dating of Moses in Book IV of *Against the Christians*. Moreover, Eusebius states that he is discussing an issue which he had considered earlier, in the introduction to the *Chronicle*, albeit in this case in the polemical context of an apologetic work. This framework enables him to present the views of his predecessors in lengthy quotations rather than fleeting references. Thus Eusebius discusses the matter at greater length in this section of the *PE* than in his introduction to the comparative chronological tables of the *Chronicle*. The "despicable Porphyry" (*impius ille Porphyrius*) plays a major role within this broader framework.[13] The *Chronicle*, one of Eusebius' early works, may contain the first indication of Eusebius' response to the challenge presented by Porphyry, even if this was not the prime motive in writing the *Chronicle*.[14]

Even if the writing of the *Chronicle* was initially motivated by apologetic polemics, its contents did not generally reflect it. Nonetheless, it contained apologetic motifs which Eusebius was later to develop and expand in explicitly apologetic tracts. Since, as we have noted, the *Chronicle* was one of his earlier works, it is worth mentioning

---

[9] Ed. Helm, p. 7.

[10] According to Sirinelli, *Vues historiques*, pp. 54–57.

[11] *Prophetic Extracts*, 1,2, ed. Gaisford = *PG*, 22, 1024.

[12] *PE* 9,10.

[13] *Chronicle*, p. 8, ed. Helm.

[14] Scholars who date the *Chronicle* prior to 303 include: Schwartz, "Eusebios", col. 1376; D.S. Wallace-Hadrill, *Eusebius of Caesarea* (London, 1960), p. 43. Others date it rather earlier. Barnes gives the late 270's (*Constantine and Eusebius*, p. 111), when Eusebius was about twenty. Grant prefers the 280's. See R.M. Grant, *Eusebius as Church Historian* (Oxford, 1980), pp. 7–8. For the view that the *Chronicle* was not written from an apologetic motive, see J.R. Laurin, *Orientations maîtresses des Apologistes chrétiens*, p. 113, and, Barnes, ibid., p. 113.

briefly those motifs which later recur. Eusebius presents Jesus and
Christianity in an apologetic manner. Christ was the fulfillment of
the promise to Abraham,[15] and the prophecies of Moses and Daniel.[16]
When he reaches Jesus' death, Eusebius embarks on a relatively
lengthy discussion, presenting various testimonies to this event. The
prophets had predicted the exact day of Christ's death. Greek sources
also attested to the miracles which took place at the time of his
death, such as a solar eclipse and an earthquake in Bythinia and
Nicea. Such phenomena fully corroborated the account of events
which had occurred during the passion of the Redeemer.[17] Here
Eusebius quotes from *The Olympiades*, the lost work of Phlegon of
Tralles, which documents the natural phenomena mentioned above.
Next, Eusebius cites Josephus on the strange events in Jerusalem on
the eve of the Great Revolt, indicating a chain of calamities that
would plague the Jews, as an external testimony to their punishment.[18] There are three apologetic themes in this passage: the fulfillment of the messianic prophecies through Jesus, the miracles
accompanying his death, and the punishment of the Jewish people.
At the end of the *Chronicle*, Eusebius again points to the chain of
calamities that afflicted the Jews. In the section that opens with the
appearance of Christianity, the religious aspect is more prominent.
A description of Church history is central to this part of the work
which also describes political and military events and pagan rulers.
The misfortunes of the Jews contrast with the portrait of the Church's
stability and its expansion despite harsh persecution. Jesus Christ
stood at the center of history, fulfilling ancient prophecies, strengthening his Gospel through his miracles and his apostles, and founding a new chosen people whose existence was secure, despite heresies
from within and persecutions from without.

The Ecclesiastical History

The *Ecclesiastical History* (*HE*) presents a problem similar to that of
the *Chronicle*. The bulk of the material is historical, but the historical writing is interwoven with apologetic motifs. Eusebius' attempt
to present a quasi-national history of the new Christian nation, in

---

[15] P. 1, ed. Helm.
[16] Genesis 49:10; Daniel 9: 25–27; p. 209, ed. J. Karst.
[17] P. 213, ed. Karst.
[18] *BJ* 6,5,3; *Chronicle*, p. 213, ed. Karst.

the genre of historical accounts of ancient peoples, may suggest a possible apologetic motivation underlying his historical composition. In the introduction to the *HE*, Eusebius does not relate to it as either apologetic or polemical. Immediately afterwards, however, in his description of the timeless beginnings of Christianity through the holy *Logos*, the son of God, Eusebius presents a partially apologetic explanation of his work describing the antiquity of Christianity.

> ... Therefore to make our description of what follows complete we should start the whole narrative concerning him by the most capital and dominant points of the discussion. By this means, moreover, the real antiquity and divine character of Christianity will be equally demonstrated to those who suppose that it is recent and foreign, appearing no earlier than yesterday.[19]

Such statements contributed to the variety of approaches taken by scholars on the question of the main goal and orientation of this work. Many regard *HE* primarily as an historical document containing some apologetic elements which are incidental and secondary to its primary purpose and content.[20] Others regard it as more apologetic than historical—an apologetic undertaking in which the historical data are ingeniously manipulated to support the predominantly apologetic thrust.[21] Even if we incline to the latter approach, the *HE* does not meet the empirical definition of an explicitly definite apologetic work that we have proposed earlier.

---

[19] *HE* 1,2,1. English translation by K. Lake (*LCL*, 1926).

[20] For example, this view is presented by Lightfoot, "Eusebius", pp. 322–327; Laurin, *Orientations*, p. 124; Wallace-Hadrill, *Eusebius*, pp. 165–167; Barnes, *Constantine and Eusebius*, p. 128

[21] See Schwartz, "Eusebios", cols. 1399–1402; F.J. Foakes-Jackson, *Eusebius Pamphili* (Cambridge, 1933), pp. 61–63; M.W. Volker, "Von welchen Tendenzen liess sich Eusebius bei Abfassung seiner Kirchengeschichte leiten?" *Vigiliae Christianae* 4 (1950), pp. 157–180. Volker assembled those fragments which indicate a definite apologetic motif running through the work. According to this approach, one might perhaps discern an apologetic arrangement of historical material not originally conceived as part of an apologetic program. Grant also held that the work was originally apologetic and that its purpose was to show the high esteem in which the Roman state held the Church. According to Grant, *HE* also had an apologetic purpose on a more limited, internal Christian level—to show that the type of Christianity which Origen brought from Alexandria to Caesarea was authentic and orthodox. (R.M. Grant, "Eusebius and his Early Lives of Origen", in *Forma Futuri: Studi in honore del Cardinale Michele Pellegrino* (Turin, 1975), p. 638. For an overview of the apologetic interpretation of *HE*, see A.J. Drogge, "The Apologetic Dimensions of the Ecclesiastical History", in Attridge & Hata (eds.), *Eusebius, Christianity, and Judaism*, pp. 492–509.

As a cursory reading of the work shows, the *HE* has many different and recurring apologetic motifs, most of them discussed in Eusebius' obviously apologetic works. When Eusebius undertook his history of Christianity, some apologetic material evidently crept into the pages. Setting aside for the moment the controversy over the primary motive underpinning the work, we can make the general observation that the numerous apologetic motifs appear only fleetingly, almost as marginal comments within the continuum of the narrative, and not as subjects in their own right. As with the *Chronicle*, I shall present these motifs no more than briefly at this point, and return to them in the course of the discussion of Eusebius' major apologetic works.

The Church had eternal roots in its founder, the Logos, the eternal and primordial Son. From the origins of the history of humanity, the Son-Logos revealed the great truths to the ancient patriarchs. Throughout the course of Israel's history, he inspired the prophets who foretold the coming of the Messiah (Christ) who would repair all flaws and redeem the world.[22] The readiness of the martyrs to die for their faith, the spiritual and charismatic nature of Christianity, and its astonishing expansion throughout the world, served as decisive proof of its truth.[23] The consensus between the testimonies in Scripture and those of Greek authors, the punishment of the Jews, and the tragic deaths of the persecutors of the Church also attested to the truth of the Gospel.[24] Biblical prophecies were fulfilled in the history of Christianity from the advent of Jesus until the time of Eusebius.[25] There was a wonderful correspondence between the revelation of the Christian Gospel and the establishment of peace throughout the Empire.[26]

Certain motifs occasionally appear as specific responses to pagan, anti-Christian arguments, even if Eusebius does not say so explicitly. But as we have noted, the subject appears briefly for the most part

---

[22] *HE* 1,2–4. The historical-theological concept is interpreted at length in *DE*, Book I.

[23] *HE* 8,7,2–3; 5,5,5–6; 9,4,19. According to Stevenson (*Studies*, p. 71), the tendency to exaggerate the description of the Church's prosperity and the victory of Christianity in works written before 324 may be understood in light of the polemical necessity of presenting Christianity as important, powerful and exalted.

[24] *HE* 3,7–8; 8,16,3.

[25] *HE* 10,4,30–33.

[26] *HE* 4,26,7.

and without elaboration. The Christian nation was not formed in a remote corner of the world.[27] The contradictions in the Gospels only seemed to be discordant (διαφωνεῖν).[28] The crude style of the Gospels was an advantage, not a flaw.[29] The power of Jesus to perform miracles was proof of his divinity.[30] Jesus' magical powers acted on subsequent generations, uprooting nations' barbaric customs and cults by waging war against the demons that dominated them and by spreading the Gospel among them.[31]

There is a recurring theme, relatively more elaborated, which integrates an apologetic stance vis-à-vis the authorities with a response to a polemical argument. This is the question of the relationship between the authorities and the Church, which repeatedly surfaces during the historical narrative. The subject is in fact linked to the broader question of Eusebius' theological-political concept, but I intend to discuss only its apologetic-polemical aspect.[32] According to the *HE*, many emperors were initially sympathetic towards Christianity; some, like the Severan house even virtually adopted it. The persecutions by Maximin Thrax were a political reaction to the Severans, who favored the Christians.[33] The Emperor Philip was a Christian and even participated in an Easter service;[34] the persecutions by Decius, according to this apologetic theory, were a reaction to Philip's pro-Christian stance.[35] Moreover, it was because of his sympathy to Christianity that Gallienus was able to strengthen his position.[36] Another apologetic explanation for the unfavorable attitude towards

---

[27] *HE* 1,4,2.

[28] *HE* 1,7,1; 3,24,13.

[29] *HE* 3,24,3.

[30] *HE* 1,13,1–7.

[31] *HE* 7,17,1; 7,18,2–3; 10,4,18.

[32] On the general theological-political concept of Eusebius, see E. Peterson, "Der Monotheismus als politisches Problem", *Theologische Traktate* (Münster, 1951), pp. 86–93; N.H. Baynes, "Eusebius and the Christian Empire", *Mélanges Bidez* (Brussels, 1934), pp. 13–18; J.M. Sansterre, "Eusèbe de Césarée et la naissance de la théorie 'césaropapiste'", *Byzantion* 42 (1972), pp. 131–195 and 532–594; S. Calderone, "Il penserio politico di Eusebio di Cesarea", in G. Bonamente & A. Nestori (eds.), *I Christiani e l'ipero nel IV secolo* (Macerata, 1988), pp. 45–54; M.J. Hollerich, "Religion and Politics in the writings of Eusebius: Reassessing the first "Court Theologian"," *Church History* 59 (1990), pp. 309–325.

[33] *HE* 6,28,1.

[34] *HE* 6,34,1.

[35] *HE* 6,39,1.

[36] *HE* 7,23,4.

Christianity on the part of some emperors, was that their numerous advisors reversed an initially sympathetic attitude, turning the emperors against the Christians. This is how Eusebius explains the stance taken by Valerian and Aurelian towards Christianity.[37]

However the success of the persecution presented a theological problem and lent weight to anti-Christian arguments. So the *HE* presents a brief theological interpretation of the persecutions, justifying them as a divine instrument for the punishment and education of Christians. Only in this manner could the occasional success of the persecutions be understood.[38] Thus the final wave of persecutions under Diocletian was divine punishment for the internal disputes and dissension among the Christians.[39] Although both the persecutions and the emperor were God's instrument in punishing the Christians, the executor of this policy had to suffer divine wrath as well.[40] Peace between the authorities and the Christians was a condition for the prosperity of the Empire.[41] A similar but reverse argument was leveled by Maximin against the Christians. His edict against them blamed them for natural disasters throughout the empire;[42] because of his campaign against them, his reign was free from war, famine and plague, and all was quiet throughout the Empire.[43] (This latter assertion reiterates the old argument but actually contradicts the claim of Christians, including Eusebius, regarding the peace dur-

---

[37] *HE* 7,30,20. On the early Christian tendency to view emperors who did not maltreat the Church as protectors of the Church or covert Christians, see K. Alland, "The Relation between Church and State in Early Times: A Reinterpretation", *Journal of Theological Studies*, 19 (1968), pp. 124–125. This inclination led to a tendentious interpretation of official documents attributed to those emperors, but possibly forged by Christian circles. See A. Linder, "Ecclesia and Synagoga in the Medieval Myth of Constantine the Great", *Revue belge de philologie et d'histoire* 54 (1976), pp. 1029–1030. On Eusebius' presentation of the Roman Emperors, see R.M. Grant, "Eusebius and Imperial Propaganda", in: Attridge & Hata (eds.), *Eusebius, Christianity, and Judaism*, pp. 658–680.

[38] *HE* 7,30,20–21. Eusebius expresses a different opinion on this matter in *PE*, end of Book IV.

[39] *HE* 8,1,87.

[40] *HE* 8,16,3. In *MP* 48, Eusebius relates that God punished with strange forms of death those responsible for the persecutions. The idea that the persecutions were God's punishment of the Church through pagan rulers has parallels in prophetic statements. Assyria and Babylonia acted as instruments in carrying out the wrath of God. Nevertheless they had to perish. See Isaiah 10:5 (Assyria); Jeremiah 25:1–14 (Babylonia).

[41] *HE* 8,13,9.

[42] *HE* 9,7,9.

[43] *HE* 9,8,3.

ing Augustus' rule and the beginnings of Christianity. More on this later.) When Maximin became involved in war, followed by famine and plague, it was almost as if he was refuting his own argument and verifying Eusebius' claim that this was punishment for the persecutions. But the persecutions also served God's purpose in punishing the Christians, and subsequently the perpetrator, who had to pay for his deeds even if he had acted according to divine command.[44] The great victory for Christianity in the final drama was that after his defeat in battle, Maximin gave up his belief in demons, and on his deathbed turned to Christianity and admitted that he had to suffer because of his sin against Christ.[45]

Eusebius regards Constantine as representing a new climax in relations between the authorities and Christianity. He had conceived Constantine as God's messenger designated to save the Christians from Licinius' last plot against them.[46] Actually Constantine himself formulated this Christian apologetic argument in an imperial letter. He stated that the oppression of Christians caused immeasurable harm to the imperial order and to all of humanity, whereas the prosperity of Christianity brought them immeasurable prosperity.[47]

The chapter of persecutions suffered by the Christians was part of the divine plan foretold in biblical prophecies that hinted not only at events in the life of Jesus and the early Christians, but also at occurrences in Eusebius' time, at the persecutions and at God's renewed grace.[48]

The Life of Constantine

The subject of the relationship between the authorities and Christianity in Christian apologetics appears in different parts of the *HE*. The last book of this work hints at the place of Constantine within this framework and his great polemical value for the Christians. This raises the possibility that there was an apologetic purpose behind the later work of Eusebius on the life of Constantine and his laudatory oration celebrating the thirtieth anniversary of the Emperor's reign. As with the *Chronicle* and the *HE*, the literary style and content of

---

[44] *HE* 9,8,15.
[45] *HE* 9,10,6.
[46] *HE* 10,8,19.
[47] *HE* 10,7,1.
[48] *HE* 10,4,30–33.

the *Life of Constantine* (*VC*) do not indicate a distinctively apologetic
work. Scholars attempting to define the work are divided: is it a
biography, a monograph, an encomium, or perhaps a piece of Christian apologetics?[49]

Eusebius' declared purpose was to write a positive biography of
Constantine. But he did not hide his intention of relating only those
details that concerned the Emperor's religious character and Christian devotion, and then, only the most significant.[50] In other words,
the *VC* was to be a highly selective biography designed to present
the Christian Constantine. Eusebius expresses his hope that the
work would be educational, and the figure of Constantine a model
for emulation.[51] The source of his greatness was his absolute faith in
God and his constant devotion to Him. He was an example for
future rulers.

The description of the devoutly Christian Constantine acting as a
messenger of the Christian God is accompanied by apologetic motifs
familiar from the *HE*. When the triumph of Christianity appeared
to be complete, Eusebius' language had become more forceful and
grandiose. By instituting persecution, Diocletian had cast off the
divine providence hitherto protecting the authorities. Through their
persecution, they silenced prayers for their welfare recited by the
Christian faithful.[52] The promotion of Constantius, father of Constantine, to the rank of "Augustus" after the abdication of Diocletian and Maximian, was a divine reward for religious Christian devotion.[53] Constantine was appointed ruler by God as opposed to other
rulers chosen and exalted by their peers.[54] From this point, Constantine's struggle against his political rivals was perceived as a struggle
between the Christian God and demonic forces. In his battle for
Rome against Maxentius, he first required God's help and only subsequently, military force, unlike Maxentius, who needed the intervention of magical arts to guess the wishes of the demons.[55] From

---

[49] For a list of scholars and their differing views, see Laurin, *Orientations*, pp.
394–395.
[50] *VC* 1,11,1–2.
[51] *VC* 1,10.
[52] *VC* 1,15.
[53] *VC* 1,18.
[54] *VC* 1,24. Eusebius presents a letter bearing Constantine's name in which the
emperor asserts that God had chosen him and his services as an instrument to fulfill His will that the world be called to worship Him and to obey His commandments (2,28).
[55] *VC* 1,27. On the cruel divinations of Maxentius, namely the dismemberment

observing the failure of his predecessors who worshiped many gods, Constantine understood that he had to worship the one Supreme God of his father. Jesus revealed himself to Constantine and instructed him henceforth to use the cross as a standard in all his battles.[56] The appearance of a cross in the sky with the words "In this sign, Conquer!"[57] is perhaps one of the most famous episodes in the Christian description of Constantine. The defeat of Maxentius was a heavenly miracle sent to declare the greatness of God to all men. The drowning of Maxentius and some of his men in the Tiber on their retreat into the city over an improvised bridge resembled the drowning of Pharaoh and his riders in the Red Sea.[58] At the end of their lives, both Galerius and Maximin confessed their sins and their error in believing in the cult of the gods, and acknowledged the one true Christian God.[59]

The battle between Constantine and Licinius is described as a campaign between God's troops and the armies of the demons. Surrounded by priests, Constantine prepared for battle by praying. Opposite him, Licinius assembled a group of priests making incantations and consulting oracles, a flight of birds, and the entrails of sacrifices.[60] Eusebius has Licinius deliver a speech which employs the well-worn arguments against Christianity: that Constantine had betrayed the religion of his ancestors and adopted atheistic notions. Licinius said that Constantine was not fighting against him but against the gods which he had forsaken. The campaign would prove who was in error, and would decide between the gods and the one God worshipped by the enemy—the Christians' God—whose origins were unknown.[61] Eusebius knew the results of the battle and placed his *argumentum ex eventu* in the mouth of Licinius. In this campaign, Constantine takes on the image of Moses placing the tabernacle outside the camp.[62] In the tent of prayer, in the midst of battle, Constantine

---

of pregnant women and inspection of the internal organs of babies, see *VC* 1,36. In a letter attributed to Constantine and addressed to the peoples of the provinces concerning the issue of polytheistic error, an oracle of Apollo is cited as blaming "righteous men" for the loss of the prophetic spirit and the cause of great evil to humanity. Those "righteous men" were interpreted as Christians. Thus the oracle became the reason for Diocletian's actions against the Christians (*VC* 2,50–51).

[56] *VC* 1,27; 29.
[57] *VC* 1,28.
[58] *VC* 1,38 = *HE* 9,9.
[59] *VC* 1,57; 59.
[60] *VC* 2,4.
[61] *VC* 2,5.
[62] Exodus 33:7. For the comparison between Constantine and Moses see A. Came-

would receive the necessary inspiration to plan the war and coordi-
nate his campaign.[63] There were even many pagans who acknowledged that the emergence of such a ruler among men was indeed
a wondrous and unprecedented event. Thus they were beneficiaries
of Constantine's rule.[64] At the same time, however, Constantine continued his struggle against demons by destroying centers of pagan
cults.[65] Although the battle tended in his favor, it was not over. Evil
forces at work in the Christian camp, too, plotted to sow discord
and strife, such as the great dispute in the Church of Antioch over
Eustathius, which nearly ended in bloodshed.[66]

In Praise of Constantine

Eusebius' sermons in praise of Constantine and the Holy Sepulchre
(*LC*) are of minimal value for the study of his apologetics. Delivered
during his final years, his speeches include apologetic motifs but contain nothing new. Although the sermon praising Constantine preceded the *VC*, it was more general in nature and included several
apologetic-polemical motifs that Eusebius had developed extensively
in his larger works. Moreover, its essentially Christian presentation
of Constantine does not differ greatly from the *VC* except for being
shorter and without elaboration. Several points regarding the Christian figure of Constantine do not appear in the *VC*. Daniel 7:18 is
interpreted as referring to Constantine and his sons.[67] The destruction of polytheism brought war to an end and created world peace,
thanks to Constantine. Eusebius seem to have drawn a parallel
between the peace of Augustus and that of Constantine. The latter
is viewed as elevating the status of Christian emperor to new heights
by oppressing the demons which had been the cause of wars and
bloodshed in the past.[68] If one takes literally Eusebius' statement that

---

ron, "Eusebius' *Vita Constantini* and the Construction of Constantine", in M. Eduards
& S. Suain (eds.), *Portraits: Biographical Representations in the Greek and Latin Literature of
the Roman Empire* (Oxford, 1997), pp. 158–161.
    [63] Then he would burst forth from the tent and shout the orders (*VC* 2,12).
    [64] *VC* 2,22.
    [65] The Temple of Venus in Jerusalem (*VC* 3,26); the abolition of the pagan cult
in Mamre (*VC* 3,53); the destruction of the temple of Asclepius in Cilicia, and the
temple of Astarte (Venus) in Heliopolis in Phoenicia and its temple prostitution (*VC*
3,56; 66).
    [66] *VC* 3,59.
    [67] *LC* 3,2.
    [68] *LC* 8,9.

Christians spit and trample upon the statues of the gods, this is an interesting indication of the Christians' new sense of security in daily life.[69]

The sermon on the Holy Sepulchre is essentially a compilation of passages from the *Theophany*, which will be discussed later.[70] Perhaps we should note here that in a short section of the sermon, which does not derive from the *Theophany*, Eusebius mentions pagan criticism of Constantine and his Christian projects. It was not proper for a great ruler to deal with tombs and monuments to the dead. It would have been better for Constantine to tend to the traditional cult of gods and heroes, rather than spitting on them and abandoning them on the pretext of a calamity. And if he chose to relate to humans as deities, why did he not consider other men who suffered and died like Jesus to be gods as well? If he had forsaken gods whose origins were human, why not forsake Jesus?[71] Perhaps this passage provided the framework for the sermon which sought to prove greatness and divinity of Jesus and the truth of Christianity, intertwining numerous apologetic motifs derived from the *Theophany*. Several parts of the text seem to indicate a polemical context, as Eusebius addresses an imaginary opponent and lambasts him.[72] At one point,[73] Eusebius admits that his proof of the truth of Christianity and the Gospel, and of the divine power and life of Jesus, are not enough to convince the non-believer, and that additional proof is required. Such

---

[69] *LC* 10,2.

[70] See I.A. Heikel, *GCS*, *Eusebius Werke*, 1, p. 264; H. Gressmann, *GCS*, *Eusebius Werke*, 3, p. 263.

[71] *LC* 11,3–4. On the basis of these and other statements, P. Meyer proposed that *VC* grew out of the campaign to rebut the pagan critique of Constantine and his affinity to Christianity. P. Mayer, "De Vita Constantini", *Eusebiana, Festschrift dem Gymnasium Adolphinum zu Moers* (Bonn, 1882), pp. 23–28. See also H.A. Drake, *In Praise of Constantine: A Historical Study and New Translation of Eusebius' Tricennial Orations* (Berkeley, 1976), 71;152, n.

[72] *LC* 17,7. C. Ehrhardt is inclined to identify Eusebius' rival in the speech as Celsus, stating that Eusebius argued with him and refuted specific points (Ehrhardt does not propose Porphyry as a possible opponent). He admits, however, that he could not prove Eusebius was thinking specifically of Celsus and his work. In fact, there is little more than a suggestion that Eusebius was answering pagan arguments raised in the past and certainly by Celsus. In most cases, his statements come from the *Theophany*, and indirectly, the earlier *PE* and *DE*. Ehrhardt thought that Eusebius read the speech in Constantinople as well, at the thirtieth anniversary celebration. Hence, in his view, its polemical context, since the imperial court still had a large pagan intellectual audience. C.T.H.R. Ehrhardt, "Eusebius and Celsus", *Jahrbuch für Antike und Christentum* 22 (1979), pp. 40–49.

[73] *LC* 16,8,9.

statements seem to arise from a polemical context, and this could
explain the markedly apologetic-polemical character of the sermon
as a whole.

II. *Early Apologetic-Polemical Writings*

The early works of Eusebius include two tracts of a distinctly apologetic-polemical nature. The first, entitled *General Basic Introduction* is
the more general and systematic, while the second, *Against Hierocles*,
is more limited in scope and was written for a specific purpose.[74] Another early polemical work entitled *Against Porphyry* has not survived.

The General Basic Introduction and the Prophetic Extracts

The *General Basic Introduction* (ἡ καθόλου στοιχειώδης εἰσαγωγή) consists
of ten books. Probably only books VI to IX have survived. Considering these four books as a unit, Eusebius gave them the specific
title of *Prophetic Extracts* (προφητικαὶ ἐκλογαί).[75] D.S. Wallace-Hadrill
has pointed out similarities in literary character and content between
the *Extracts* and exegetical material on Luke, written by Eusebius,
which was preserved in a *catena* of patristic commentaries on Luke
edited by Nicetas of Heraclea in the eleventh century.[76] But Wallace-Hadrill rejected the possibility that this exegesis constituted a
commentary on Luke,[77] proposing instead that it formed the lost
tenth book of the *General Basic Introduction*.[78] Both Barnes and, subsequently, F.S. Thielman, accepted this view as a fact which needed
no additional proof.[79] However, despite their similarities in content

---

[74] It was recently suggested, however, that the author of *Against Hierocles* was
another, otherwise unknown Eusebius. See T. Hägg, "Hierocles the Lover of Truth
and Eusebius the Sophist", *Symbolae Osloenses* 67 (1992), pp. 138–150.

[75] The general title of this work is mentioned in *Prophetic Extracts* 3,1; 4,35. The
subtitle, *Prophetic Extracts*, is the title of the extant section of the *General Basic Introduction* and appears in the introduction to the first book of the *Extracts*.

[76] It appeared as Eusebius' *Commentary on Luke* in *PG* 24, 529–605.

[77] Such a commentary is mentioned by neither Jerome nor Photius. See Lightfoot, "Eusebius", p. 338.

[78] D.S. Wallace-Hadrill, "Eusebius of Caesarea's Commentary on Luke: Its Origin and Early History", *Harvard Theological Review* 67 (1974), pp. 55–63. This view
conflicts with that of Schwartz, who claimed that this material is derived from Eusebius' later work, *The Theophany* ("Eusebios", col. 1432). But Wallace-Hadrill analyzed the citations from Luke in the *Theophany* and successfully refuted Schwartz's
claim, although his novel hypothesis is not entirely convincing (ibid., p. 61).

and style, identifying the *Commentary on Luke* with the tenth book of the *Introduction* remains problematic, because while Eusebius had promised that the tenth book would deal with heretical errors,[80] the *Commentary on Luke* does not do this. Perhaps the heresies are those noted briefly in several places in the *Extracts*—the Marcionists, on the one hand, and on the other, the disciples of Artemon and of Paul of Samosata and the Ebionites. In other words, Eusebius may have embarked upon a refutation of their erroneous Christology by using verses from the Prophets, and intending to prove the correct Christology and also, perhaps, to counter non-Orthodox views on the link between the New Testament and the Old.[81]

The first five books of the *Introduction* are lost. It is difficult to reconstruct their contents unless one accepts Stevenson's assumption that they served as the basis for the third book of the *Demonstratio Evangelica*.[82] However, Eusebius refers to their character and contents

---

[79] Barnes, *Constantine and Eusebius*, p. 169; F.S. Thielman, "Another Look at the Eschatology of Eusebius of Caesarea", *Vigiliae Christianae* 41 (1987) pp. 226–237. Regarding attempts at identification, it is perhaps worth mentioning that Schwartz wished to identify two of Eusebius' works, mentioned by Photius but no longer extant, as the *General Basic Introduction*: ἐκκλησιαστικὴ προπαρασκευή = *praeparatio ecclesiastica*, and ἐκκλησιαστικὴ ἀπόδειξις = *demonstratio ecclesiastica* (Photius, *Bibliotheca*, 11.12). According to Schwartz, these two works represent Eusebius' later division of the *General Basic Introduction*. The new names were given after *PE* and *DE*, and the works served as a sort of introduction (Schwartz, "Eusebios", col. 1386). Stevenson saw the *Dem. Eccl.* as belonging to the lost books of the *General Basic Introduction* (*Studies*, p. 65). In contrast, Lightfoot preferred to identify it with a work which assembles Jesus' sayings on the establishment of the Church and compares them to events in the history of Christianity. Apparently, such a collection was written by Eusebius who mentions it in *PE* 1,3,11. Lightfoot states that Eusebius later included this work in the fourth book of the *Theophany* ("Eusebius", p. 331). Schwartz accepted the opinion that this work mentioned by Eusebius was included in the *Theophany*, but rejected its identification with the *Dem. Eccl.* mentioned by Photius ("Eusebios", col. 1387).

[80] *Prophetic Extracts* 4,35.

[81] See *Prophetic Extracts* 3,9; 4,22.

[82] Stevenson went even further and proposed that the lost part of the *General Basic Introduction* was based on Eusebius' *Against Porphyry* (*Studies*, p. 63). His suggestion is worth consideration in light of the fact that while material similar in content to the *Extracts* may be found in the extant books of *DE*, the third book of *DE* contains only one or two parallels. The third book of *DE* does not adduce proof on the basis of prophetic verses and their interpretations, as will be seen later on; rather, it constitutes an anti-pagan polemic. Stevenson's view may be a conjectural notion, but one which could enhance our understanding of the polemical framework of the work. If we take Stevenson's theory further, it might arguably be possible to reconstruct parts of *Against Porphyry* from Book III of *DE* and from the work

in his confused introduction to the first book of the *Extracts*. In the early books of the *Introduction* he went through testimonies on the life and teachings of Jesus and sought to prove their authenticity by adducing direct, convincing evidence, adding further confirmation culled from Jewish Scriptures. The first five books of the general introduction were addressed to "listeners" (ἀκροώμενοι) recently attracted to Christianity and about to study the basic principles of the Gospels.[83] This was not the place to burden initiates with biblical prophecies which they had not yet learned to believe. The *Extracts* were specifically intended for new believers and catechumens, and messianic prophecies in the Old Testament were presented with a brief commentary.

In the *Extracts*, Eusebius notes that the persecution of Christians was still rife and that Christians were forbidden to organize meetings.[84] From this we may infer that the work was written during the persecutions preceding 313 CE, perhaps even earlier, before the Edict of Tolerance issued in 311 CE.[85] Thus it could date from 310 CE.[86] Against the background of ongoing anti-Christian persecution, it is easy to understand both the apologetic motive behind the work and the apocalyptic and eschatological fervor uncharacteristic of Eusebius. Barnes goes as far as to argue that the work was specifically intended to replace the school for catechumens closed during the persecutions.[87] Perhaps the literary structure of the book was influenced by similar introductory works on particular topics which Eusebius knew first hand.[88]

---

as a whole, even from some sections of *PE*. In so doing, additional material would surface, including anti-Christian arguments taken from Porphyry. But such complexities do not concern us.

[83] *Prophetic Extracts* 1,1. See also *HE* 10,4,63; *DE* 7,2,52. For the division of study between beginners and more advanced students, see *HE* 6,15.

[84] *Prophetic Extracts* 1,8.

[85] *HE* 8,17. The work is noted in *HE* 1,2,27.

[86] See Schwartz, "Eusebios", col. 1387. Wallace-Hadrill dates the work after 309, basing his calculation on the mention of Maximin's breaking the statues of Jesus and of the bleeding woman he healed at Paneas (Matthew 9:20), in the *Commentary on Luke*, which he thinks is identical to Book X of the *General Basic Introduction* (*PG* 24,541). The statues are still standing in *HE* 7,18,1–2. Maximin became emperor at the end of 308 (Wallace-Hadrill, *Eusebius*, p. 51).

[87] Barnes, *Constantine and Eusebius*, p. 169.

[88] Barnes has proposed that Anatolius' *Introduction to Arithmetic* and Iamblichus' *Philosophical Introduction*, each containing ten books, may have served as models for Eusebius' work (ibid., p. 168). Anatolius was an Alexandrian Christian philosopher whose teaching incorporated Aristotelian, neo-Platonic, and neo-Pythagorean prin-

In the preface to the *Extracts*, Eusebius explains his presentation of selected prophecies.[89] As a bee gathered nectar from flowers to prepare honey for the health of kings, so he, Eusebius, collected biblical prophecies. But the prophecies were special in a way that surpassed any honey. They required a short, concise explanation by way of introduction. "My commentary will be brief and measured", states Eusebius. "At times it seeks to prove that the holy prophecies of God have been fulfilled by our Redeemer alone, and, on occasion, I will include my opinion on the verses which follow."[90] Eusebius aspired to proving the divine character of the Incarnation and of Jesus' appearance on earth by presenting these as following a series of revelations of the Logos, thereby establishing Jesus as a divine figure already known in the Holy Scripture. This intention, evident in the *Extracts*, relates to its main focus, the prophecies concerning Jesus and Christianity. Indeed, the prophecies heralding the Advent had been handed down directly or indirectly via the patriarchs and the prophets. Thus Eusebius' main purpose in writing the *Extracts* was to prove that the prophecies were fulfilled only by Jesus.

The first book of the *Extracts* deals with prophecies from the Pentateuch, Joshua, Kings, Chronicles, and Ezra. The second is devoted to prophecies from the book of Psalms. The third offers a collection of prophecies from Proverbs, Ecclesiastes, the Song of Solomon, Job,

---

ciples. His work is a neo-Pythagorean treatise on the numerological meaning of numbers one to ten. Later he served for a time as an assistant to Theotecnus, bishop of Caesarea, and subsequently, as bishop of Laodicea (*HE* 7,32,6–21). Perhaps Eusebius had been his pupil. Anatolius was probably the teacher of Iamblichus before the latter began his studies with Porphyry. Iamblichus' treatise on the theology of arithmetic makes use of the above-mentioned work by Anatolius. Anatolius may be the fellow student of Porphyry to whom the latter dedicated his first book of Homeric questions. This would help explain the enigmatic nature of Eusebius' description of Anatolius. If Iamblichus had indeed studied with Anatolius in Laodicea, we may assume that Eusebius had heard of the latter. On this matter and on the similarities in structure and teaching between the Alexandrian and Caesarean Christian schools, and neo-Pythagorean institutions, see R. Grant, "Early Alexandrian Christianity", *Church History* 40 (1971), pp. 140–142; idem, "Porphyry and the Early Christians", p. 185; J. Dillon, "Iamblichus of Chalcis", *ANRW* 2, 36:2 (1987), p. 867. Dillon also believes that Anatolius, bishop of Laodicea, is identical with Anatolius the teacher of Iamblichus, and tends to identify him as the fellow student of Porphyry. According to Dillon, however, Iamblichus did not study under Anatolius in Laodicea, but rather during his stay in Caesarea!

[89] Eusebius is not the first to compile selected verses from Scripture. Melito of Sardis apparently collected verses which could be interpreted as referring to Jesus and the Christian faith (Eusebius, *HE* 4,26,13).

[90] *Prophetic Extracts* 1,2.

Jeremiah, Lamentations, Baruch, Ezekiel, the Twelve Minor Prophets, Daniel, and the Apocalypse of Baruch. The fourth covers Isaiah.[91] For the most part, Eusebius presents the prophecies in a similar manner by quoting the verses and then giving a brief interpretation according to the divine plan (οἰκονομία). In the opening lines of the work, Eusebius declares his intention of showing that the prophecies are fulfilled only by Jesus. He also indicates the divine source of these prophecies. He notes that after describing the antiquity of Moses and the prophets in his *Chronicle*, he naturally proceeded to the next task, namely, writing an anthology of prophecies relating to Christ, intended primarily for newcomers approaching the divine Logos. However, before presenting the subject he had to show that according to the Holy Scriptures the Logos existed not only before the Incarnation but even before Creation. Likewise he had to prove that the prophecies speak of two appearances by Jesus on earth (παρουσία). The first, in humble circumstances, had already taken place, whereas the second, in majesty and splendor, would be accompanied by the heavenly hosts.[92] The Scriptures used the name God to refer to the Logos, as in the verse, "And the Lord came down to see the city and the tower . . ." (Gen. 11:5–6). God descended to earth and spoke. Eusebius argues that since it was not proper for the sovereignty of the deity (αὐθεντία) to act in this manner, it must have been the Logos who went down to earth. God the Father bestowed foreknowledge (πρόνοια) and leadership of the world (οἰκονομία) on the Son, who acted alone through the angels to serve the will of God, for the benefit and salvation of the world.[93]

Eusebius makes a distinction between the revelation of the Logos and that of the angels. The Logos revealed itself to Abraham, whereas it was angels who revealed themselves to Lot and Hagar.[94] He applies this distinction to other passages from the book of Genesis. The Logos was revealed to exalted beings who are as perfect as the patriarchs. To others, such as Lot or Gideon, who had not attained that

---

[91] Eusebius claims that he limits himself to the twenty-two books accepted by the Jews (*Extracts* 3,6). This was a long-standing tenet of Christian polemics which Eusebius repeats. When quoting the Old Testament, one had to limit oneself to the corpus accepted by the Jews to avoid exposing oneself to the Jewish or pagan argument that Christians falsified or revised the text.

[92] *Prophetic Extracts* 1.

[93] Ibid.

[94] *Prophetic Extracts* 1,3.

level of perfection, the Logos was assisted by angels in conveying its message.[95] Regarding Isaac's blessing on Jacob, Eusebius states that the verse, "Let peoples serve you, and nations bow down to you. Be a lord over your brothers . . ." (Gen. 27:29) could not have been intended for Jacob and the Jewish people. From this he deduces that the words of Isaac refer to Christ who is occasionally represented by Jacob in the Holy Scriptures, thus interpreting the text as a prophecy or proclamation of the messiahship of Jesus. Eusebius identifies the angel who struggled with Jacob (Gen. 32:25–30) as the Logos. At this point, he presents his view that, according to Scripture, God did not reveal himself to Adam, Enoch or Noah, and not even to Moses. He appeared only to Abraham, Isaac, and Jacob in the form of the Logos of God.[96] Similarly, Jacob's blessing on Judah could only be interpreted as pertaining to Christ.[97] It was the Logos who spoke with Moses even though it did not reveal itself to him as it did to the patriarchs, who were greater and more perfect than he.[98] And this was true despite the fact that Moses asked to see God face-to-face on the top of Mount Sinai.[99] Joshua was the apostle of God (ἄγγελος) whose mission was given by the Logos; this was the meaning of the phrase ". . . for my name is in him" (Ex. 23:21). Indeed the name "Joshua" was identical to "Jesus". Joshua symbolized Jesus as the true heir of Moses and the Law, who would lead mankind to the Promised Land.[100]

The next three books of the *Extracts* relate to the prophecies heralding the advent of Jesus the Messiah. The apologetic argument is mainly theological and historical. History unfolded according to the age-old plan of the Creator. A proper understanding of Scripture would give us the key to understanding this plan in the past, the present, and even the future. Hence the allegorical interpretation which

---

[95] *Prophetic Extracts* 1,4.
[96] *Prophetic Extracts* 1,7.
[97] *Prophetic Extracts*, 1,8.
[98] *Prophetic Extracts*, 1,12.
[99] Exodus 33–34; *Prophetic Extracts* 1,12. The idea that the Logos-Son was revealed to the patriarchs appears briefly in *HE*, as noted, and is particularly notable in the works of Eusebius. Perhaps it derives from Justin Martyr who sets down such an idea, albeit somewhat primitively (Justin, *Dialogue* 56). This concept seems to have been rejected shortly afterwards. Eusebius may have been returning to the basic concept expounded by Justin. Origen is not Eusebius' source in this case. See Sirinelli, *Vues Historiques*, pp. 268–272.
[100] *Prophetic Extracts* 1,11.

Eusebius constantly invokes. God revealed himself to man through the divine Logos in two periods only: that of the patriarchs, in the ancient past, and more recently, when the Logos became man. However the Law and the prophets paved the way for the most recent divine revelation and foretold it. Moreover, every historical event in the Old Testament anticipated an event in the New Testament. Moses and the prophets actually described in advance every single detail in the life of Jesus. Even historical events after his life were alluded to in Scripture, including the events of Eusebius' own times, such as the culmination of the anti-Christian persecutions, during which he wrote this work.[101] The prophets also spoke precisely about events which the future would reveal. The great drama of the future would be the return of Jesus in all his might to judge the living and the dead. The lovers of God would be separated from the blasphemers and would receive eternal life as a reward for their fidelity.[102]

By presenting the prophecies and their interpretations, Eusebius indirectly confronts heretical groups and Jews, wanting, it seems, both to eliminate the judaizing inclinations of his readers, and also to stress the difference between the correct Christian understanding of Scripture and the simplistic, sometimes foolish understanding on the part of the Jews.[103] This may reflect the readers' awareness of a Jewish interpretation and anti-Christian critique; it may also constitute a response to the pagan critique, such as that of Porphyry, which had attacked Christianity's problematic relationship with Judaism. Eusebius himself states in the *Extracts* that he heard a Jew interpreting Isaiah 7:10–17 not as a messianic prediction but rather as

---

[101] *Prophetic Extracts* 1,15; 3,26; 1,8; 1,19. Barnes hoped to fill in the details of the historical-theological concept of Eusebius in the *Extracts*, taking the *Commentary on Luke* as Book X of the *General Basic Introduction* where it is similar to its final version in *DE*. The patriarchs were actually Gentiles and not Jews. They could be called "Christians." During the period between the patriarchs and Jesus, people were not able to see the Logos directly. Even Moses could not do so. The Jewish people emerged during Moses' time, along with the Law. The Torah and Jewish laws were suited to the historical situation of the Jews who had been corrupted by Egyptian ways and could neither absorb nor live according to great truths. Therefore, the Law of Moses and the Jewish lifestyle were on a lower level than Christianity (*Commentary on Luke*, PG 24, 540,569; Barnes, *Constantine and Eusebius*, p. 171).

[102] *Prophetic Extracts*, 2,15; 2,27–28; 4,3; 4,14; 4,31. Here the eschatology is imminent, but there are no details concerning the catastrophic events of apocalyptic eschatology that can be found in the *Commentary on Luke*. See Thielman, "Another Look at the Eschatology of Eusebius", and Barnes, *Constantine and Eusebius*, pp. 172–173.

[103] *Prophetic Extracts* 3, Introduction.

relating to King Hezekiah.[104] Likewise he recalls that he was a witness to Jewish polemics against the divine person of Jesus.[105] He knew the argument that Jesus was the son of "Panther", or of a man called "Panthera", and rejected it by referring to the verse in Hosea 5:14, where the Hebrew word שחל (lion) is translated as "panther" in the Septuagint. Jesus was the "panther", which in the above verse was a term for the Logos.[106]

Despite the fact that Moses and the prophets predicted every detail in the life of Jesus, the Jews refused to see him as the Messiah mentioned in the prophecies. They blocked their ears to his name and killed him. God punished them by destroying their land and their Temple and he continued to punish them to the present. The Church, on the other hand, had risen as the prosperous heir of truth.[107] The contrast between the fate of the Jews and that of the Church is a recurrent motif throughout the work. In essence, the Jews no longer existed as a nation. They were even forbidden to enter Jerusalem. This constituted divine punishment for their attitude to the Son of God.[108] In contrast, Christianity had spread throughout the world. For three hundred years it had constituted an educating force for humanity. It had taught mankind to control its base inclinations and passions. Many had become Christians even during the persecutions. Even now, all could see the martyrs' steadfastness in face of the atrocities committed by the authorities. Many simple Christians led moral lives according to the ideals of the philosophers—a rare occurrence, even among the philosophers themselves.[109]

---

[104] For Eusebius' commentary on these verses see M.J. Hollerich, "Eusebius as a Polemical Interpreter of Scripture", in Attrrudge and Hata (eds.), *Eusebius, Christiantiy, and Judaism*, pp. 604–605.

[105] *Prophetic Extracts* 4,4; 4,27.

[106] *Prophetic Extracts* 3,10. For this argument, see Origen, *Against Celsus* (*CC*) 1,28; 1,32. Celsus attributes this to a Jew. On the Jewish origin and meaning of *Ben Pantera*, see D. Rokeah, "Ben Stara is Ben Pantera", *Tarbiz* 39 (1970), pp. 9–18 (Hebrew).

[107] *Prophetic Extracts* 1,15.

[108] *Prophetic Extracts* 1,8; 3,36.

[109] *Prophetic Extracts* 1,8; 1,18–19; 2,10; 3,37; 4,8–30. A somewhat unrelated problem to be noted briefly in the course of our discussion of the *Extracts* is Eusebius' theological concept of the divinity of the Son-Logos, and the relationship it bears to God the Father, as evinced in several parts of the work. Barnes previously noted that the *Extracts* retained Eusebius' concept prior to the Arian controversy and the debate on Origen, which may have obliged him to change his ideas. His stance is not vague as it is in other works. The Son-Logos was different or of lower status than God the Father. Despite the fact that the Son was God, he assumed a secondary

Against Hierocles

Against Hierocles is an early apologetic work by Eusebius, written as
a direct response to an anti-Christian polemical treatise. Its exact
date of composition is not clear, but it belongs to Eusebius' early
works. Hierocles was a senior Roman official who established a suc-
cessful career in the service of the Empire in the East and quickly
advanced to senior government positions. He combined literary activity with his political duties and wrote a cogent political tract against
the Christians entitled *Lover of Truth* or *The Word of the Lover of Truth*
(ὁ φιλαλήθης; φιλαλήθης λόγος).

Hierocles served as an official in Syria. He was the governor of
Bythinia when the persecutions began, and later governor in Egypt.
According to Lactantius, Hierocles played a major role in initiating
the persecutions, and as governor was personal advisor to Diocletian.[110] Hierocles wrote his tract against the Christians before the outbreak of the persecutions, but once they had begun he saw to its
publication and distribution. Lactantius relates that a polemical tract
by a pagan sophist was distributed at the same time as Hierocles'.[111]
Hierocles may have written the piece when serving as governor in
Palmyra or elsewhere in the East. He published it again in Nico-
media, the eastern capital of Dicocletian's empire, with the start of
persecutions in 303 CE.[112]

---

position to God the Father and acted on His behalf with the power bestowed by
the Father. The Son was different from and inferior in essence (ὑπόστασις) to the
Father, whose essence was primordial, uncreated and distinct. He belonged to the
realm of creation and was the first created being. The Logos assisted God the
Father in the work of creation, but only in a secondary role. Eusebius interprets
Proverbs 8:22 on the created Logos, in the same way that the Arians subsequently
interpreted it (*Extracts* 3,1; 3,8; 3,31; 4,23; 4,25; 1,2–12; 1,25; 2,5; 2,17–18; Barnes,
Constantine and Eusebius, pp. 173–174). For the further development of Eusebius' sub-
ordinationist Logos theology see H.G. Opitz, "Euseb von Caesarea als Theologe:
Ein Vortrag", *Zeitschrift für die neutestamentliche Wissenschaft* 34 (1935), pp. 17–18;
H. Berkhof, *Die Theologie des Eusebius von Caesarea* (Amsterdam, 1939), p. 30; F. Ricken,
"Die Logoslehre des Eusbiuos von Caesarea und der Mittelplatonismus", *Theologie
und Philosophie* 42 (1967), pp. 341–358; J.R. Lyman, *Christology and Cosmology: Models
of Divine Activity in Origen, Eusebius, and Athanasius* (Oxford, 1993), pp. 106–117.
[110] Lactantius, *On the Death of the Persecutors* 16,4; idem, *The Divine Institutes* 5,2.
[111] *Divine Institutes* 5,2.
[112] According to Harnack, Hierocles wrote this work when he was governor in
Palmyra (*Chronologie* II, p. 118). Thus Harnack accepted the view of S. Duchesne
(ibid.). On the course of Hierocles' political career, see Labriolle, *La Réaction*,
p. 306; T.D. Barnes, "Sossianus Hierocles and the Antecedents of the 'Great Persecution'", *Harvard Studies in Classical Philology* 80 (1976), pp. 239–252. See the monograph on Hierocles and on the work of Eusebius by M. Forrat in the edition of

The original text of *Lover of Truth* has been lost. The little information about its contents may be gleaned from Lactantius and, to a lesser extent, from Eusebius, because he chose to focus his response on only one major aspect of Hierocles' work. Lactantius writes that the tract included an attack on the New Testament as being replete with internal contradictions. The apostles and evangelists were primitive, ignorant and uneducated men who spread lies. Hierocles attacked Peter and Paul in particular. Jesus was a hooligan who surrounded himself with a gang of nine hundred robbers. The Christians were naive and foolish and their faith irrational. Hierocles tries to minimize the importance of miracles which Jesus performed, though he does not deny them. He presents the reader with Apollonius of Tyana and contrasts him with Jesus, claiming that the former performed miracles that were as impressive as those of Jesus, or even greater. But Apollonius maintained an air of modesty, unlike Jesus' boastfulness and claims of divinity. Hierocles was well aware of the contemporary cult of Apollonius and writes about its practice in Ephesus. But he asserts that pagans were wiser than Christians because they did not view Apollonius as a god despite the miracles he performed, whereas Christians believed that Jesus was God because of a number of minor miracles.[113]

Eusebius adds several details to Lactantius' description. Hierocles condemns the Christians for their exaggerated praise of Jesus' miracles, which he compares to those performed by Apollonius of Tyana as described by Philostratus. Hierocles goes on to praise the work of Philostratus and previous biographies of Apollonius, which he views as historical truth. In contrast, the stories about Jesus were written by charlatans like Peter and Paul. Hierocles scoffs at the foolish naivete of Christians who founded their faith on false accounts that paid homage to magic and drew irrational conclusions regarding the divinity of man.[114]

Hierocles' tract included a positive section that drew ironical comment from Lactantius, in which he attempted a compromise between traditional polytheistic religion and philosophical monotheism. In a

---

Against Hierocles, SC (1986). Barnes and Forrat accepted Harnack's opinion, holding that even if Hierocles did not write his book while he was governor in Palmyra, he wrote it while serving elsewhere in the East before he moved to Bythinia (Barnes, ibid.; Forrat, *Against Hierocles*, p. 14).

[113] *Divine Institutes* 5,2.
[114] *Against Hierocles* 2.

list of honorific titles, he emphasizes the unity of the supreme God,
creator and sustainer of all beings. All the traditional gods and spirits of the pantheon were subservient to Him.[115] Such ideas were
prevalent for some time in intellectual circles in the empire, particularly among neo-Platonists. In his introduction, Eusebius argues that
apart from the absurd comparison between Jesus and Apollonius,
there was nothing new in Hierocles' work. All his arguments came
directly from other writings, not only reproducing their content, but
repeating it word for word, syllable for syllable. This was particularly true of Celsus' *True Doctrine.* So instead of writing at length on
the content of *Lover of Truth,* Eusebius instructs his reader to seek
the responses in the comprehensive work by Origen, who gave excellent replies to all of Hierocles' arguments.[116] Eusebius himself chose
to write a tract specifically refuting Hierocles' comparison between
Apollonius and Jesus.[117]

In fact, with the exception of the "nine hundred robbers", the few
arguments in Hierocles' tract are already found in the remaining
fragments of Porphyry's book against the Christians. Even the comparison between Apollonius and Jesus occurs in several of the Porphyry fragments, including a one that was not taken from Macarius
of Magnesia, but from Jerome.[118]

Like Porphyry, both Lactantius and Eusebius note Hierocles' mention of the miraculous disappearance of Apollonius during his trial
before Domitian.[119] It is clear from Lactantius' quotation from *Lover
of Truth* that Hierocles also contrasted the daring disappearance of
Apollonius during his trial with the wretched, helpless death of Jesus
on the cross. In this case, the similarities between Hierocles and Porphyry[120] regarding content and language seem more than coincidental. From this and from Eusebius' comments on Hierocles' use of
sources, it may be concluded that Hierocles derived material directly

---

[115] *Divine Institutes* 5,2.
[116] See Chapter I, above.
[117] *Against Hierocles* 1.
[118] F. 4 (Harnack), drawn from Jerome's *Commentary on Psalms,* states that one
should not exaggerate the importance of miracles. Even the magicians in Egypt
performed miracles, as did Apollonius and Apuleius. Augustine believed that Apuleius
had been transformed into a donkey, and warned the faithful against those who
worshipped him as a miracle-maker whose powers surpassed those of Jesus (*Epistles*
138; 136,1).
[119] Lactantius, *Divine Institutes* 5,3; Eusebius, *Against Hierocles* 38.
[120] F. 63 (Harnack) deriving from Macarius.

from Porphyry as well.[121] If this is the case, it lends weight to Euse-bius' claim regarding the originality of Hierocles' *Lover of Truth*. One may even argue that there is nothing original in it—neither the argu-ments nor the philosophical ideas.[122] At this point, we must ask whether Eusebius was familiar with Porphyry's *Against the Christians* when he wrote *Against Hierocles*, and if so, why he specifically denied this. We shall return to this question shortly.

Hierocles based his comparison between Apollonius and Jesus on the myths and flourishing cults of Apollonius of Tyana, drawing inspiration from Philostratus' legendary biography, *The Life of Apol-lonius*. Philostratus was a member of the intellectual circle of Julia Domna, wife of Emperor Septimius Severus, and wrote the book at her request.[123] Without relating to the historical Apollonius who lived during the first century CE, Philostratus portrayed a figure possessing magical and prophetic powers, a profound philosopher who lived a perfectly ascetic life. The myth of Apollonius had existed before Philostratus, but it reached its apogee in his work. He says that the residents of Tyana dedicated a temple to him which housed statues or pictures (εἰκόνες) of their hero.[124] According to a tradition, Alexander Severus kept statues of Abraham, Orpheus, Jesus, and Apollonius in his private chapel (*lararium*) next to the statues of the deified emper-ors.[125] According to another tradition, when the Emperor Aurelian surrounded Tyana, Apollonius appeared before him and performed miracles in order to lift the siege. Aurelian identified him from the images of Apollonius he had seen in many temples.[126] Perhaps Philo-

---

[121] Labriolle takes this for granted (*Réaction*, p. 310).

[122] See Labriolle, ibid., p. 315. Forrat attempts to support Eusebius' conclusion concerning the originality of the comparison between Jesus and Apollonius, while also assuming that Eusebius knew Porphyry's *Against the Christians* when he wrote his polemic against Hierocles. She proposes that Eusebius meant that Hierocles' innovation was not the comparison itself, but its systematic development, whereas Porphyry regarded it as being of minor importance (Forrat, *Against Hierocles*, p. 50). If Eusebius' statements support such a liberal interpretation, it is difficult to either reject or accept this assumption, on the basis of our knowledge of both works.

[123] *Life of Apollonius* 1,3, ed. F.C. Conybeare (*LCL*, 1912). On the intellectual cir-cle of Julia Domna, see Philostratus, *The Lives of the Sophists* 2,30. For a factual assessment of this circle, see G.W. Bowersock, *Greek Sophists in the Roman Empire* (Oxford, 1969), pp. 101–109.

[124] *Life of Apollonius* 8,29.

[125] *Historia Augusta*, "Alexander Severus", 29,2.

[126] *Historia Augusta*, "Aurelian", 24. On myth and reality regarding Apollonius, see E.L. Bowie, "Apollonius of Tyana, Tradition and Reality", *ANRW* II,16,2 (1978),

stratus' work may be viewed as pagan hagiography that later influenced the development of Christian hagiography.[127]

Apparently Celsus had already thought of diminishing the status of Jesus by presenting him as a sophist and magician, even describing him as inferior to pagan figures such as Asclepius, Dionysus, and Hercules.[128] In the nineteenth century, scholars pointed out numerous similarities between the *Life of Apollonius* and the Gospels. They thought that Philostratus had presented Apollonius as a pagan answer to Jesus, the Gospels, and even to Paul; that the *Life of Apollonius* had been conceived as an anti-Christian polemic offering an alternative to the Gospels in the person of a pagan holy man who represented a superior syncretistic religion common among the upper classes and the imperial court. Even if Philostratus had no intention of creating a pagan rival to Jesus or a Hellenistic Jesus figure, the great similarity between the two shows that the author knew Christian Scriptures and used them.[129]

Philostratus created a fine literary work full of fantastic stories, and succeeded in presenting Apollonius as the personification of an exalted religious idealism based on neo-Pythagorean philosophy, that tended towards monotheism and focused on sun-worship.[130] In his literary description, Philostratus apparently uses form and content derived from Scriptures. He may have been encouraged by a general sympathy towards Christianity that might have existed at the court of Julia Domna. In his work, there is no mention of Chris-

---

pp. 1652–1699. Most of the archeological and literary evidence of the cult of Apollonius has been collected by G.G. Petzke, "Die Traditionen über Apollonius von Tyana und das N.T.", *Studia ad Corpus Hellenisticum Novi Testamenti* 1 (1970), pp. 19–36. For additional material, see also Forrat, *Against Hierocles*, Appendix 1, pp. 215–219.

[127] A.J. Festugière, "Sur une nouvelle édition du 'De Vita pythagorica' de Jamblique", *Revue des études grecques* 50 (1937), pp. 489–494. Festugière showed that the *Life of Apollonius* apparently influenced Athanasius' *Life of Anthony*. Furthermore, the work possibly served as a model for, or at the very least, influenced Eusebius' works on the lives of Origen and Pamphilus. See R. Grant, "Eusebius and His Lives of Origen", pp. 635–648. According to Grant, Eusebius also used Porphyry's *Life of Pythagoras*, particularly as a model for the aspect of the "Divine Man" (θεῖος ἀνήρ) in the life of Origen.

[128] *CC* 7,53; 3,22–24; 1,67.

[129] On the many similarities between the biographical novel by Philostratus and the Gospels, see Faulhaber, *Eusebius*, pp. 108–120, and especially H. Doergens, "Apollonius von Tyana in Parallele zu Christus dem Herren", *Theologie und Glaube* 25 (1933), pp. 292–304.

[130] On the neo-Pythagorean background of the *Life of Apollonius*, see W. Speyer, "Zum Bild des Apollonios von Tyana bei Heiden und Christen", *Jahrbuch für Antike und Christentum* 17 (1974), pp. 47–63.

tianity, and during his lifetime there is no indication that the book was understood as a polemic against Christianity. An environment sympathetic towards Christianity also existed somewhat later, at the court of Julia Domna's niece, Julia Mamaea, mother of Alexander Severus.[131] Even if Philostratus' work had not been originally intended for political purposes, it was later used as such by pagan polemicists such as Porphyry and Hierocles.[132] Perhaps, in the course of the third century, there developed in neo-Platonic circles a systematic presentation of Apollonius, parallel to Jesus. Hierocles made use of this parallel in his work. In the fourth century, the *Life of Apollonius* was translated into Latin in aristocratic circles in Rome dedicated to preserving paganism.[133] Along with the canonization of Apollonius and the growth of such local cults, he had become one of the last heroic figures of pagan religion, and as such, a natural rival to Jesus in the struggle between paganism and Christianity.

The *Lover of Truth* played a role in the intellectual struggle that paved the way for the great persecutions and contributed to their intensification, just as its author was active at the start and during the course of the persecutions. Hierocles included a selection of his predecessors' arguments against Jesus and Christianity, and systematically juxtaposed the legendary image of Apollonius of Tyana with Jesus and the Gospels. Thus he disparaged the image of Jesus and contributed to the religious pride of many pagans. Lactantius dismissed the work derisively and viewed the comparison between Jesus and Apollonius as banal.[134] Eusebius saw it as a grave danger.

It is difficult to know exactly when Eusebius wrote his tract against Hierocles. He does not mention the work in any of his other extant writings. Furthermore, *Against Hierocles* contains no historical information that could resolve this problem. According to Harnack, the book is either a product of his youth or an early work that lacks the great erudition Eusebius displays in his later compositions. Harnack notes that in this book Eusebius does not refer to Hierocles as

---

[131] Eusebius called her "most devout (θεοσεβέστατη)", (*HE* 6,21,3). See the comprehensive treatment by Labriolle, *Réaction*, pp. 181–188, and, subsequently Forrat, *Against Hierocles*, pp. 40–43.

[132] Probably Philostratus' pagan contemporaries had Jesus in mind when they read his book, particularly if there is truth in the story that Alexander Severus (222–235) placed statues of both Apollonius and Jesus in his chapel. See Foakes-Jackson, *Eusebius*, p. 16.

[133] Sidonius Apollinaris, *Epistle* 8,3; Forrat, *Against Hierocles*, p. 35.

[134] Ibid., 5,4.

a persecutor, nor does he mention the persecutions by Diocletian. He concludes that the work was written before the persecutions began in 303 CE.[135] Schwartz, on the other hand, sees in the fourth chapter an allusion to the death of Galerius early in 311. Thus, he dates the work between that year and the death of Maximin in 313.[136] Most scholars follow Schwartz, while Barnes supports Harnack's view.[137] In this chapter, Eusebius writes in general terms about persecutions and the great power of the Redeemer who overcame all his enemies. The persecutors were punished. Here Eusebius' tone is somewhat arrogant, perhaps hinting at the cessation of the persecutions. But the statements are not explicit and could be a general reference to persecutions in the past, before Diocletian. This poses a certain difficulty because it presumes a long interval between the first publication of *Lover of Truth*, before the persecutions, and Eusebius' awareness of the work and his brief reply.

At this point we can raise the question as to whether Eusebius knew Porphyry's *Against the Christians* when he wrote *Against Hierocles*. We have noted that in a chapter of the introduction to his work, Eusebius mentions Celsus, along with other unnamed authors, as Hierocles' main source. He also directs his reader to Origen's *Against Celsus*, which contains answers to all the arguments raised by Hierocles, and even to hypothetical pagan arguments that could be put forward in the future. Eusebius notes that there was nothing new in Hierocles' arguments, with the exception of his comparison between Apollonius and Jesus, and that Hierocles copied his arguments verbatim from his predecessors. The fact that Eusebius does not mention Porphyry does not prove that he had no knowledge of *Against the Christians*. Perhaps he did not want to acknowledge the fact openly or he may have alluded to it among the other sources that Hierocles used. Perhaps at that time he had hoped to write a comprehensive work responding to all the arguments by Porphyry and Hierocles, and directed the reader to Origen only in the interim.[138] But this is also problematic. Porphyry's book contained many new arguments not found in Celsus' work. Eusebius did not hesitate to

---

[135] Harnack, *Chronologie* II, p. 118.
[136] Schwartz, "Eusebios", col. 1394.
[137] Labriolle, *Réaction*, p. 310; Laurin, *Orientations*, p. 130; Wallace-Hadrill, *Eusebius*, p. 18; Forrat, *Against Hierocles*, p. 25; Barnes, "Sossianus Hierocles", p. 240.
[138] See Lightfoot, "Eusebius", p. 328.

mention Porphyry many times in other works. He regarded the comparison between Apollonius and Jesus as original, although it already existed in Porphyry's work.[139] It is difficult, though possible, to solve these problems simply by arguing that Eusebius wanted to avoid mentioning Porphyry and *Against the Christians* at all costs. It is easier to assume that Eusebius did not yet know the work of Porphyry when he wrote *Against Hierocles*. This assumption makes a later dating of *Against Hierocles* more difficult. How can we explain the earlier attention to Porphyry in the *Chronicle* and the *Ecclesiastical History*? This problem may be solved by assuming that the above-mentioned works underwent later editing by Eusebius. Eusebius' practice of revising and editing his earlier works is well known. However, this assumption is also problematic, because those passages seem to be an integral part of the works. Indeed the earlier dating of *Against Hierocles* dispels most of the difficulties. For dating it before 303, when Eusebius wrote his *Chronicle*, enables us to assume that Eusebius had not yet seen a copy of *Against the Christians*. However, these statements probably will remain conjecture for some time.

Eusebius' polemical tract is intended mainly as a comparison between Jesus and Apollonius. Eusebius' aim was to invalidate the comparison. He explicitly states that he could draw up arguments to prove the absolute superiority of Jesus over Apollonius, but that he chose instead to concentrate on the image of Apollonius as it appeared in the *Life of Apollonius*, and thus remove all grounds for comparison. Thus Jesus and Christianity hardly appear in this work. Eusebius defends them without actually dealing with them. The tactical advantage of this method is clear. By shattering the myth of Apollonius, or at least, by lowering his status, Eusebius does not relate to the comparison itself and so prevents the reader from becoming engaged in such a comparison.

In the fourth chapter, Eusebius explains his position and takes the opportunity to include a brief set of arguments which he claims he could have used had he intended to. This well-worn device allowed him to precede the short work with a general apologetic introduction in which he briefly notes a number of well-known topics. Jesus

---

[139] As a result, Harnack concluded that when Eusebius wrote *Against Hierocles* he was not yet aware of *Against the Christians*. See Porphyry, *Against the Christians*, p. 29. Labriolle agreed with Harnack (*Réaction*, p. 310), but accepted Schwartz' later date for *Against Hierocles*.

could not be compared with Apollonius. The advent of Jesus had
been predicted by the prophets and he had many disciples who were
prepared to die for his teachings. His great power overcame all the
persecutions. Jesus was the only teacher considered an enemy by
both the authorities and their subjects, who eventually overcame his
persecutors; they were justly punished. His doctrine continued to
gain adherents everywhere. In his name, demons and evil spirits were
exorcised. Furthermore, his preeminence and unique divinity saved
the entire world. Apollonius was neither a philosopher nor a man
of high moral character, and certainly could not be compared with
Jesus.[140]

Indeed, Eusebius says that he had once thought Apollonius a wise
man, despite his human limitations, and that he could still be considered a philosopher, setting aside the fictitious descriptions by his
biographers.[141] Eusebius sought to show that Apollonius was not the
ideal image of the wise man, philosopher, and man of high moral
character as naive people had thought. A critical examination of the
literary sources of Hierocles, notably Philostratus, proved that he was
not the great paragon of truth he pretended to be. Once it was
proven that Philostratus was not truthful, the entire structure built
around his hero would collapse under the numerous contradictions
and paradoxes in his account. In addition, Hierocles' arguments
would cease to be effective because they would be proved ground-
less.[142] Thus Eusebius' work was designed to undermine the parallels drawn by Hierocles, and hence it constitutes a direct polemic
against him. From a literary point of view, however, the polemic is
indirect since Eusebius focuses his efforts only on the image of Apollonius as seen in Philostratus. Occasionally, after presenting in a
ridiculous manner an event or detail in the life of Apollonius, Eusebius adds a derogatory remark about Hierocles and points to his
naivete in accepting these words as truth. Thus he throws back the
pagan accusations of naivete and foolishness against the Christians.
Moreover, he repeatedly refers to the bombastic name *Lover of Truth*

---

[140] *Against Hierocles* 4. Chapter divisions in the critical editions are not identical
but very similar. For example, Forrat's has 48 chapters, whereas F.C. Conybeare's
has 42 (*LCL*, Appendix to Philostratus, *Life of Apollonius* II, pp. 484–605). I refer to
Against Hierocles, hereafter *CH*, according to the chapter numbers of Forrat's edition.
[141] *CH* 5.
[142] *CH* 4.

assumed by Hierocles.[143] Apart from the above, Eusebius has little to add as far as Hierocles is concerned.

Eusebius wished to present himself as a fair polemicist who did not have to resort to name-calling or counter-claims not based on objective discussion of the historical sources used by Philostratus and Hierocles.[144] He does not oppose the image of Apollonius as a physician and a philosopher of human affairs. He is prepared to admit that Apollonius had a certain wisdom. Thus he is willing to accept as completely truthful details containing an apparent measure of truth, even if the overall description seems exaggerated. For example, Eusebius tends to accept details regarding Apollonius' biography, such as his aristocratic lineage and his extensive education. He admits that Apollonius possessed excellent qualities as a physician and a religious man. Eusebius emphasizes that all these qualities do not constitute anything supernatural. He acknowledges them because they conform with truth and the love of truth.[145] He voices his opposition to Philostratus' image of Apollonius as a miracle worker and divine figure, and to the comparison with Jesus.[146] He does this in a detailed analysis of the *Life of Apollonius*.

Eusebius discusses the unusual miracles of Apollonius in order to point out his grave doubts as to their veracity. He claims that they were probably invented by his biographers.[147] Eusebius' critique strives to diminish the supernatural dimension of the *Life of Apollonius*.[148] He casts doubts on all the miracles performed by Apollonius, explaining many of them as acts of magic whose secrets were acquired in India, thus proving their inferiority.[149] Moreover, Apollonius performed miracles through a spirit (δαίμων).[150] Eusebius passes judgment on each of Apollonius' miracles and attributes them to various δαίμονες. He concludes that all the miracles (παραδοξοποιία) were performed through spirits.[151] Eusebius, therefore, draws the definite conclusion that Apollonius was a magician (γόης) who was assisted

---

[143] *CH* 4; 14; 20; 25.
[144] *CH* 4.
[145] *CH* 12.
[146] Ibid.
[147] *CH* 30; 36.
[148] *CH* 9; 11; 14.
[149] *CH* 26; 29.
[150] *CH* 35.
[151] Ibid.

by demons.[152] Thus Eusebius renews the accusation that had led to
Apollonius' arrest and trial before the Emperor Domitian.[153] He even
accepts as true the story about the miracles performed in jail and
the miracle of his disappearance during the trial though he claims
Apollonius was aided by spirits.[154] Eusebius thus acknowledges Apollonius' ability to perform miracles through demons, but he attacks
the tendency to exalt Apollonius and to attribute to him the divine
status already prevalent in Philostratus' work.[155] Nonetheless, Eusebius maintains that Apollonius' magical and demonic powers were
limited, indirectly admitting a point that he tries to suppress throughout *Against Hierocles*, i.e., that the ability to perform miracles attested
not only to demonic powers, but also to divinity. If we were to
believe all of the miracles related to Apollonius, we would have no
choice but to place him among the gods. Here Eusebius refers to
the story of Apollonius' ascension to heaven accompanied by hymns
and dances.[156] The similarity to the ascension of Jesus is so striking
that Philostratus may have modeled his version on the New Testament. Moreover, Eusebius was definitely aware of the similarity
between the two ascension stories when he wrote his polemic. He
thought it necessary, therefore, to limit the magical powers of Apollonius and to attribute his supernatural acts to demons. For throughout his work, as we shall see, Eusebius states that the unique miracles
performed by Jesus and the apostles constitute an important testimony to the divinity of Jesus and to the truth of Christianity.

Perhaps Eusebius may have been prepared in principle to give
Apollonius some credit. But in the course of writing his polemic, he
painstakingly sifts through the work of Philostratus for contradictions which he endeavors to present in a manner designed to ridicule Apollonius, so that virtually nothing is left of this credit. For
example, if Apollonius claimed to know all the languages—even
though he did not learn a single one[157]—why did he have to learn
the Attic dialect,[158] and why did he frequently use a translator on

---

[152] *CH* 44.
[153] *Life of Apollonius* 8,7.
[154] *CH* 39.
[155] For example, *CH* 32, regarding the description of the Emperor Vespasian as
kneeling in prayer before Apollonius as if he were a god, and the proclamation of
the latter as one who crowns kings.
[156] *CH* 8; 9.
[157] *CH* 8.
[158] *CH* 9.

his travels?[159] He pretended to be omniscient and to know all the sciences, but to his biographer he was ignorant in many fields.[160] Apollonius argued that he understood the language of animals, that he knew the secrets of men's hearts even if they did not speak, and that the mysteries of the future were revealed to him.[161] Still, he found that he was often surprised by things that he did not know.[162] If Apollonius was so intelligent, as was reputed,[163] why were there so many contradictions, absurdities and vexing episodes?[164] Apollonius frequently appeared as a man of the highest moral caliber,[165] but in many cases he was vengeful and arrogant, or eager to please.[166] Although he was considered unusually wise, he appeared to be a normal person.[167] If Apollonius were a god, why did he have to learn from so many teachers?[168] If we accept the criticism of Eusebius, hardly anything is left of Philostratus' idealized portrait of the wise and pious man of Tyana. According to Eusebius, however, Apollonius was not to blame for his biographers' enthusiastic devotion to detail in works that did not distinguish between truth and legend.[169]

In addition to its historical and theological aspects, the critique of the miracles of Apollonius also has a philosophical aspect. In the sixth chapter of *Against Hierocles*, Eusebius invokes the laws of nature to argue that Apollonius could not divest himself of his essentially human nature and intervene in the affairs of the gods. According to this philosophical concept, the laws of nature organize life on earth and limit every creature to the sphere of activity defined by its nature. But Eusebius does not likewise limit the nature of God. He explains that God's essential goodness enabled Him to treat all His creatures well and to intervene on their behalf. Thus Eusebius

---

[159] *CH* 14.

[160] *CH* 37.

[161] *CH* 8; 10.

[162] For example, *CH* 15.

[163] *CH* 12.

[164] *CH* 15; 20; 21.

[165] *CH* 12.

[166] *CH* 33; 38; 43.

[167] *CH* 36; 42.

[168] *CH* 11.

[169] On Apollonius' divine characteristics in Philostratus, and on Hierocles' and Eusebius' differing understanding of these traits, see also A. Mendelson, "Eusebius and the Posthumous Career of Apollonius of Tyana", in Attridge & Hatta (eds.), *Eusebius, Christianity, and Judaism*, pp. 510–522; E. Junod, "Polémique crétienne contre Apollonius de Tyane", *Revue de théologie et de philosophie* 120 (1988), 475–482.

preserves, albeit implicitly, both the principle of divine providence
for individuals and, especially, the dogma of the Incarnation. God
descended from his heavenly abode just as a physician leaned over
his patient and a teacher adjusted his method to the level of his
pupils. However the reverse was not possible.[170]

The end of the work is devoted to a critique of inconsistencies in
Apollonius' astrological determinism.[171] Eusebius finds a contradiction between this concept and the attempts to change the course of
events by magic.[172] The question of determinism was the obverse of
the doctrine of free will. At this point, Eusebius finds a fitting opportunity to present a positive view of free will which explains the intervention of the deity in human affairs,[173] a subject which he is to
develop further in the *PE*.[174] The astrological determinism of the late
pagan world is a major polemical target for Christians.[175] Despite
the concept of predestination expressed by Paul,[176] and later by Augustine,[177] most Christians saw the concept of free will as a precondition for the existence of morality and religion, and of human society
in general.

Eusebius' method was to scrutinize Philostratus' tract for all possible contradictions and inconsistencies. Through this exposé, one
could undermine the credibility of the author, and hence that of
Hierocles. As a result, Philostratus' idealized portrait of Apollonius
is destroyed and the comparison between Apollonius and Jesus, based
on that portrait, is rendered invalid. Eusebius presents his report as

---

[170] It is evident that at this point, Eusebius had not yet developed adequate skills
in grappling with philosophical and theological issues. From the ideas he presents
in *CH*, it is difficult to explain the basic Christian concept of participation of the
faithful in the divine life and nature through Christ, as Paul had taught. It is even
more difficult to explain how resurrection, leading to a life of happiness in the kingdom of God, is possible. In fact, this concept of the laws of nature served as the
basis for one of Porphyry's arguments against belief in resurrection. See F. 34 (Harnack); Laurin, *Orientations*, p. 141. For an analysis of this chapter and its pagan
sources, see M. Kertsch, "Traditionelle Rhetorik und Philosophie in Eusebius' Antirrhetikos gegen Hierokles", *Vigiliae Christianae* 34 (1980), pp. 145–171.
[171] *CH* 43.
[172] In essence, it is only a partial contradiction; one could overcome determinism only through magic. See F. Cumont, *Astrology and Religion among the Greeks and
Romans* (New York, 1912), p. 88.
[173] *CH* 45–48.
[174] In most of the sixth book of *PE*.
[175] See Cumont, *Astrology and Religion*, p. 85.
[176] Romans 8:29–30.
[177] See, for example, *De dono perseverantiae* (On the Gift of Perseverance) 35.

an objective critique, but he is actually rather selective in his treatment of details, and his tone often becomes ironic or sarcastic. Eusebius exploits the contradictions he finds to give a cumulative impression of absurdity in Philostratus' descriptions and in the portrait of Apollonius, thereby creating a caricature.[178]

Eusebius studied Philostratus well, and in *Against Hierocles*, he deals with Philostratus' work according to the order of its books. In this way it resembles Origen's *Against Celsus*, which was written in the form of responses matching the sequence of Celsus' arguments. However, the critical method of examining a work in order to expose its contradictions and then subjecting it to ridicule through the use of irony and sarcasm, is more reminiscent of Porphyry's *Against the Christians* and its critique of Holy Scripture. Since *Against Hierocles* is primarily a detailed criticism of the *Life of Apollonius*, we may assume that it was chiefly intended for readers who knew the biography, for educated pagans, and for Christians with a pagan literary background.[179]

Against Porphyry

Written as a direct response to Porphyry's attack on Christianity, the work entitled *Against Porphyry* (Κατὰ Πορφυρίου) belongs to Eusebius' early polemics. Virtually the entire book has been lost.[180] The fact that two Greek catalogues mention the manuscript in the sixteenth and seventeenth centuries might indicate that one day the work will be recovered.[181] As in the case of *Against Hierocles*, Eusebius does not recall the work in his own extant writings.

A few details about the work were preserved by later Christian writers. According to Harnack, it was written before 300 CE.[182] If so,

---

[178] On the extensive use of irony and sarcasm in *CH*, see Laurin, *Orientations*, p. 144; Forrat, *Against Hierocles*, p. 76. E. Des Places holds that Eusebius tried to imitate, albeit rather awkwardly, the satirical tone of Lucian or Oenomaus. See E. Des Places, *Eusèbe de Césarée commentateur: Platonisme et écriture sainte* (Paris, 1982), p. 139.

[179] Forrat, *Against Hierocles*, p. 70.

[180] There remain a few fragments. See A. Harnack, *Geschichte der altchristlichen Literatur bis Eusebius* (Leipzig 1893) I, p. 594; idem, *Against the Christians*, p. 30.

[181] Harnack, *Chronologie* II, p. 118; Stevenson, *Studies*, p. 36.

[182] Harnack, *Chronologie* II, p. 119.; idem, *Against the Christians*, ibid. The accepted assumption is that the work was written before Maximin and prior to the great apologetical project of *PE* and *DE*, which also were written before Constantine had established himself as the sole ruler in the Empire. See Schwartz, "Eusebios", col. 1395.

perhaps Eusebius' silence regarding *Against Porphyry* followed his practice concerning *Against Hierocles*, which he considered an unsuccess-
ful product of his youth.[183] It is possible that its loss may be similarly
explained. The answers presented in *Against Porphyry* may have been
inadequate, or the force of Porphyry's attack may have reverberated
throughout Eusebius' text.[184] In the previous chapter, we noted that
Against the Christians prompted four substantial replies, which have
been lost. Methodius wrote the first response.[185] Why then did Eusebius have to write an additional work against Porphyry? There may
be several reasons. Jerome states that Methodius' work was relatively
short, consisting of some ten thousands words.[186] It was well-writ-
ten,[187] but its reply to Porphyry's attack on the book of Daniel was
only partial (*ex parte*) and that was perhaps true of the rest of the
work as well.[188] So Eusebius may have considered Methodius' answer
to Porphyry to be inadequate.[189] Furthermore, Eusebius was highly
involved in this matter, particularly in the wake of Porphyry's attack
on Origen, and as a result of his possible Caesarean background.[190]
In addition, Methodius was one of the leading opponents of Origen[191] and his personal rivalry with Eusebius was such that the latter did not mention him in his extant books. Perhaps Eusebius wished
to outdo Methodius in this area as well.

Against Porphyry was long, consisting of twenty-five books.[192] Jerome
states that Eusebius wrote with great talent (*sollertissime*) and responded
to Porphyry's critique of Daniel in books 18–20 of *Against Porphyry*.[193]

---

[183] Likewise, Harnack, *Chronologie* II, p. 119; Stevenson, *Studies*, p. 36.

[184] See Lightfoot, "Eusebius", p. 329; Anastos, "Porphyry's Attack on the Bible",
p. 424.

[185] Jerome, *Epistle* 70 (to Magnus) 3. Methodius was followed by Eusebius, and
subsequently by Apollinarius and Philostorgius.

[186] Jerome, ibid. According to Harnack, the reply apparently included only one
book (*Against the Christians*, p. 30).

[187] Jerome, *De viris illustribus* 83.

[188] Jerome, *Commentary on Daniel*, Introduction.

[189] See also Harnack, *Against the Christians*, p. 29.

[190] From Socrates, who relates the account of Porphyry in Caesarea, we may
infer that it was taken from Eusebius' *Against Porphyry* (Socrates, *HE* 3, 23). See also
Harnack, *Against the Christians*, p. 36, 38.

[191] See H. Crouzel, "Les Critiques adressés par Méthode et ses contemporains à
la doctrine origénienne du corps ressuscité", *Gregorianum* 53 (1972), pp. 679–716;
L. Patterson, "Methodius, Origen, and the Arian Dispute", *Studia Patristica* 17.2
(1982), pp. 912–923.

[192] Jerome, *De viris illustribus* 81; *Epistle* 70,3.

[193] Jerome, *Commentary on Daniel*, Introduction; *Commentary on Matthew*, 24:16; *Against
Rufinus* 2,33.

Porphyry's critique of Daniel appears in books 12 and 13 of his work.[194] From the structure of Eusebius' reply, we may conclude that he followed the order of Porphyry's arguments and answered them one by one.[195] If this is true, then Eusebius wrote *Against Porphyry* along the lines of Origen's *Against Celsus* and his own *Against Hierocles*. Perhaps we may further infer that if Origen's work served as the model for Eusebius here, then his *Against Porphyry* included extensive and complete quotations from Porphyry's book.

Jerome and Socrates regarded Eusebius' reply as adequate.[196] Jerome, however, pointed out that the most powerful work against Porphyry was written by Apollinarius.[197] Sharing this view, Philostorgius stated that the work of Apollinarius was far superior to those of Methodius and Eusebius.[198] Apollinarius had also written a long work comprising some thirty books.[199] It is possible that Eusebius' work was considered an inadequate reply even by contemporaries, hence the additional refutation by Apollinarius. Even Philostorgius, who had praised Apollinarius, found it necessary to write an additional work against Porphyry.[200]

We may assume that much of the material in *Against Porphyry* is to be found in Eusebius' later polemics,[201] though this cannot be proved until sufficient fragments of the work are discovered. Eusebius preferred not to mention his earlier polemics against Hierocles and Porphyry, staunch enemies of Christianity. He would formulate a definitive response to all the enemies of Christianity in the major apologetic project of his life's work.

---

[194] Of the fifteen books of *Against the Christians*. See Jerome, *Commentary on Matthew*, ibid.

[195] See also Lightfoot, "Eusebius", p. 329.

[196] Jerome, *Commentary on Daniel*, Introduction; Socrates, ibid.

[197] *Epistle* 84,2 (to Pammachinus and Oceanus).

[198] Philostorgius, *HE* 8,14.

[199] Jerome, *De viris illustribus* 104; *Epistle* 70,3.

[200] Philostorgius, *HE* 10,10. Barnes holds that perhaps both apologetic works, entitled *Against the Pagans* and *On the Incarnation*, were written by Athanasius when he was a young man as a reaction to Porphyry's *Against the Christians* (*Constantine and Eusebius*, p. 206).

[201] Perhaps mainly in *PE* and *DE*. See Lightfoot, "Eusebius", p. 329; Harnack, *Chronologie* II, pp. 118–119. Stevenson thinks that much material was included in *DE* in particular. He also assumes that the lost first part of the *General Basic Introduction* was based on *Against Porphyry*, and served as the basis for the third book of *DE* (*Studies*, p. 37, 63).

CHAPTER THREE

PRAEPARATIO EVANGELICA AND *DEMONSTRATIO EVANGELICA* – A SINGLE APOLOGETIC-POLEMICAL ENTERPRISE

General Plan, Basic Characteristics and Principal Questions

Before addressing the various issues pertaining to Eusebius' polemics and apologetics in the *Praeparatio Evangelica* (*PE*) and the *Demonstratio Evangelica* (*DE*), I shall present the general structure of both works, several of their basic characteristics, and key points that enable us to view the separate treatment of specific issues as part of the general picture created by these two comprehensive works.

Eusebius regarded the two compositions as forming a single work, which was designed to present the nature of Christianity to those who did not know it. The name "Demonstration of the Gospel" (εὐαγγελικὴ ἀπόδειξις) actually includes both parts, which are united by a single general objective into one apologetic undertaking.[1] Furthermore, the title "Preparation for the Gospel" (εὐαγγελικὴ προπαρασκευή) really means "preparation for the demonstration of the Gospel" (εἰς τὴν τῆς εὐαγγελικῆς ἀποδείξεως προπαρασκευήν), and they should not be seen as two separate apologies.[2] Taken as a whole, the two works comprise a single apologetic treatise whose arguments evolve on two levels. From a literary point of view, the *PE* is an introduction to the *DE*.

This double composition is an exception among the many works by Eusebius, in that nearly all scholars agree upon its date. While some lengthen the time of composition and others shorten it, there is a general consensus that Eusebius worked simultaneously on parts of both the *PE* and the *DE*, beginning no earlier than 312 and finishing by 324.[3] As we have seen, Eusebius is well acquainted with the

---

[1] *PE* 1,1,11–12; 1,3,13; 1,6,6; 15,1,1–9.
[2] *PE* 6,10,49.
[3] The work itself gives no direct evidence of its date of composition, which has to be gleaned from allusions to events. According to Lightfoot, Eusebius began it before the end of the persecutions, apparently in 312 (Lightfoot, "Eusebius",,

apologetic tradition and mentions it early in the work.[4] In the *Ecclesiastical History* (*HE*), he names and describes a list of apologists who wrote before him[5] and even quotes from some of them in the *PE*. However, at the beginning of his work he argues that his method differs from theirs (ἡμῖν γε μὴν ἰδίως ἡ μετὰ χεῖρας ἐκπονεῖται πρόθεσις), without elaborating how.[6]

The first part of this double composition (*PE*) attempts to prove the superiority of Christianity through a critique of pagan religion and philosophy. The second (*DE*) was intended to prove the validity of Christianity and the Gospel as the fulfillment of ancient prophecies, in the New Testament and in Christian history. Such proof, based on prophecies in the holy scriptures, could be presented only after the walls of paganism had been demolished and the superiority of Christianity had been demonstrated according to pagan criteria. The work addresses those Christians and pagans who have a positive attitude towards the ancient Hebrew scriptures and regard them as true prophetic oracles. According to Eusebius, the proof of fulfillment of biblical prophecies constituted the strongest and most definitive proof of the truth of Christianity.[7] The structure of the work may to some extent parallel that of the *General Basic Introduction,* which is made up of two parts. The first apparently dealt with the Christian attitude to Greco-Roman culture; the second focused on Christianity's relationship to Judaism as the fulfillment of biblical prophecies.[8] The first part, the *PE*, consists of fifteen books; the second, the *DE*, comprised twenty, of which only the first ten have survived. This entire corpus is perhaps the longest apologetic work on Christianity written in antiquity.

---

p. 330). Mras accepted this date for the beginning of composition and fixes its completion in 322 (Mras, *PE*, Introduction, p. LV). Sirinelli chose the years 313–324 (Introduction to *PE*, SC 206 (1974) = *PE* 1, p. 13). Barnes shares this opinion (*Constantine and Eusebius*, p. 178; 186). Schwartz limits the period of composition from the end of 314 to 321 ("Eusebios",, col. 1390) and Wallace-Hadrill to the years 312–318 (*Eusebius*, p. 57).

[4] *PE* 1,3,2–5.

[5] *HE* 4–5.

[6] *PE* 1,3,4. Eusebius makes similar remarks about the *HE* (1,1,3), and also about the *Chronicle* (2, Introduction).

[7] However, he acknowledges that one had to devise special arguments to use against pagan enemies of Christianity who did not believe in prophetic Scripture, in order to convince them of the truth of the ancient prophecies (*DE* 3,2). This subject will be discussed later.

[8] See Barnes, *Constantine and Euebius*, p. 178.

Both works are addressed to the same audience—new Christians of Gentile origin, and curious, educated pagans willing to learn about Christianity.[9] The *PE* criticizes the intellectual foundations of the educated pagan. Its encyclopedic character attempts to encompass his traditional world—its religion, mythology, history and philosophy—and to show it in a new and different light.

This dual work has two major interrelated aspects: the first, educational and didactic, and the second, polemical. According to Eusebius, his main goal was to present and prove the doctrine of the Gospel and the dogmas of the Christian faith, i.e., the ἀπόδειξις, a presentation-demonstration of proof.[10] The latter, however, could take place only after the reader of pagan origin had received suitable "preparation" (προπαρασκευή), i.e., the preparation for the presentation-demonstration of the Gospel, or more briefly, preparation of the Gospel.[11] Thus, there is a graduated process of learning at two stages. For those who hardly knew Christianity, it constitutes basic preparatory instruction to enable them to attain a comprehension of the deeper doctrines: "the exact understanding of the essential matters of the mysterious οἰκονομία belonging to our Redeemer." Thus, there are two levels in the formation of the future Christian believer, a two-stage program of instruction. The catechumen moves from the easy to the more difficult, from the superficial to the deep and significant, from the outer to the inner circle, and from the more general to the more particular dogmas of Christianity. The first stage, the *PE*, treats subjects familiar to the educated pagan, such as religion, mythology, philosophy, cosmology, theology, and ethics. Only at the second stage does Eusebius proceed to deal with the particular problems that Christian dogmas present to the educated pagan, such as the Son (the *Logos*), the Incarnation, Virgin Birth, Passion, Crucifixion, and Resurrection. The book opens with a discussion of familiar topics, re-evaluating pagan beliefs and attitudes towards them, and preparing for an acknowledgment of new truths and the superiority of Hebrew scriptures. At this point, the reader reaches the more advanced stage at which he is ready to peruse the *DE*. Here he will discover the true profound meaning of the Holy Scriptures.[12]

---

[9] *PE* 1,1,12; *DE* 2,3.

[10] The word ἀπόδειξις incorporates both meanings, which Eusebius uses for his own purposes interchangeably.

[11] *PE* 1,1,11–13.

[12] On the didactic and pedagogic track, see Sirinelli, *Les vues historiques d'Eusèbe*, pp. 43–44; Laurin, *Orientations*, p. 371.

Beneath the didactic structure lies the main intention of the work, namely, its apologetic-polemical orientation and the desire to demonstrate the truth of Christianity and refute the opponent's arguments. Throughout the work, Eusebius stresses and insists upon the rational character of the faith he is defending, explaining and justifying. He conceives of the work as a single, comprehensive polemic in which he seeks a wiser answer to the criticisms of, and attacks on, the Christians. However, whereas Eusebius' treatise against Porphyry had followed Origen's method of refuting Celsus—namely, a detailed response to each argument in turn—here Eusebius seems to have adopted Origen's original plan for his work. Indeed, Origen had first attempted a general reply to Celsus, subject by subject, but he abandoned this method because of the enormity of the task.[13]

The direct polemical context is immediately apparent in the first book of the *PE*, and later reappears. Accusations against Christianity and the questions posed to Christians served as the primary motive in writing the work.[14] Eusebius notes several major arguments, and replies as follows: Who are the Christians? They are certainly of Greek origin or culture, and have deserted their ancestral religion, to turn to the Holy Scriptures of the Hebrews, without adapting their way of life. The time had come to show how wisely Christians acted when they left the religion and tradition of their ancestors. There was no better way to do this than to present this tradition with all its faults. In this manner, said Eusebius, we shall reveal the divine power of presentation and demonstration of the Gospel, which has come to us to heal all those evils and diseases. Likewise, we must explain why we have rejected the lifestyle of the Jews while adopting their holy scriptures. We must present the essence of Christianity in a positive light as neither Greek nor Jewish, but the new and true divine knowledge.[15] Demonstrating the wisdom of Christianity as a religion not based on blind faith, but capable of rational proof, emerges as a major goal at the beginning of the work. Eusebius had not intended to answer every anti-Christian argument

---

[13] See: *Against Celsus*, Introduction, 1,28.

[14] *PE* 1,2,4. Willamowitz and Harnack identified this passage as taken from the introduction of Porphyry's book against the Christians. See Harnack, *Against the Christians*, F. 1, p. 45 and notes. Perhaps this further strengthens the view that much of the polemical context of the work is aimed at Porphyry. However, this is nowhere stated explicitly by Eusebius. Porphyry is mentioned and cited often in this work. His place in the *PE* and the *DE* will be discussed later.

[15] *PE* 1,5,10–12.

in detail, but wished to present an apology justifying Christianity against the general accusation of unwise abandonment of ancestral traditions for the inferior, barbaric religion of the Hebrews. According to him, the sole purpose of the *PE* was to provide answers to questions directed at Christians concerning their preference for barbaric writings over the noble philosophy of their ancestors, namely, the Greeks.[16] Throughout the entire work, Eusebius repeatedly emphasizes this anti-Christian argument and the importance of responding to it, and finds ample evidence of the Christians' wisdom in leaving their ancestral traditions for the religion and philosophy of the Hebrews.[17]

From a polemical standpoint, the overall structure of the *PE* and the *DE*, taken as a single work, is roughly in the form of a reply to three major arguments against Christianity.[18] The argument that Christians had abandoned the religion of their ancestors serves as the basis for the description and examination of these ancient traditions. The argument that they preferred the barbaric Hebrew religion creates a framework for the investigation of the "Hebrew" beliefs, and a comparison with pagan concepts. The argument that the Christians appropriated Jewish scripture but rejected and deviated from their mode of life and worship, serves as the basis for a positive description of Christianity and for Eusebius' theory of Christian history.

The general discussions also reflect more specific anti-Christian arguments and endeavor to refute them. Some statements seem to constitute reactions or responses to inexplicit arguments. In fact, the detailed polemical framework continues throughout the first three books of the *DE*. Eusebius himself asserts this link in the first chapter of the first book. In the beginning of the third, he also states that the main body of the *DE* begins at this point. Eusebius may have chosen to divide the double work where he did because the first six books of the *PE* tend to deal with one theme,[19] and the next nine books (7–15) with another.[20] That is to say that the *PE* contains a counter-attack against the pagan onslaught on Christianity, although the work also has some positive discussions on Christian-

---

[16] *PE* 1,3; 14,1; 15,1.
[17] For several examples, see *PE* 1,2; 3,13; 7,7–18; 9,1; 10,1–4; 13, Introduction, 21; 14,1–3; 10; 15,1; 62.
[18] See Sirinelli, *PE*, *SC*, p. 46.
[19] *PE* 1,5,10.
[20] *PE* 7,1,2. The division of the books is not always according to subject; a par-

ity. The first two books of the *DE* have a third theme, namely, arguments castigating Christianity for its deviation from Judaism. However, from the refutation of such arguments there emerges a detailed and positive presentation of the development of Christianity from Judaism. The rest of the work (*DE*, 3–10) dwells on the fourth general theme, namely, the presentation of Christian doctrines as the fulfillment of ancient prophecies. The special polemical framework of the third book seems to be part of a general plan presenting Jesus, the apostles, and basic Christian doctrines rooted in the New Testament. This theme may also be considered an adaptation of the *Prophetic Extracts*, in which the prophecies are now arranged according to subject rather than their order of presentation in the Old Testament.

The combination of apologetic-polemical and didactic-educational traits lends the work its unique character as both a polemic and a manual of edification. The urgent need for a comprehensive answer to pagan attacks—one that would offer a strategic offensive against the basic premises and conventions of pagan religion and philosophy—had joined forces with the pressing need for a systematic and thorough instructional text for the educated pagan interested in Christianity or the recent convert, thereby creating an original *magnum opus*. As we have noted, the genre of apologetic literature is characterized by both an apologetic-polemical component and a positive description of the faith to reinforce it. Moreover, it is possible that most of Eusebius' apologetic arguments are not entirely original and may be found in one form or another in earlier works. Even the method he uses to assail religion and philosophy—citing the opponent's statements in order to expose their contradictions—is not new. In fact, it is used by rivals of the various philosophical schools and even occasionally, Christian writers.[21] Perhaps the originality and uniqueness of Eusebius' enterprise derive from the arrangement of arguments around central themes, the innovative use of the apologetic method, the unprecedented systematic organization, and the integration of the two components into one organic complex. Thus polemical and didactic principles become interchangeable.

This dual composition may be regarded as combining, on the one

---

ticular topic may extend from one book into the next. Apparently, the amount of material occasionally determined the internal division into chapters.

[21] For example Tatian, *Address to the Greeks*, 31.

hand, anti-Greek apology and a positive presentation of Christian doctrine, and, on the other, the genre of apology known as *adversus Iudaeos* (against the Jews). I have not dealt with the last and will relate to it later. Each component is limited to a single aspect, e.g., either polemics or edification of the faith. Eusebius' great talent lies in interweaving all three components into a coherent texture. "Against the Greeks" takes up the first part of the *PE*. "Against the Jews" serves as the opening of the *DE* and in the course of the work blends into the refutation of the Jewish interpretation of "messianic" passages of the Old Testament. The positive doctrinal exposition appears mainly in the *DE*, but can also be found in the second part of the *PE*, in a polemical comparison with Hebrew beliefs, which the Christians preferred to Greek concepts.[22]

The structure of this work shows a logical, didactic progression and a consolidated concept of history that is applied from Creation until Eusebius' own time. The first part of the *PE* shatters distorted pagan concepts, making an exception of ideas taken from the ancient Hebrews and not falsified under the rule of evil demons. The author identifies these demons as the gods of the pagan pantheon. The second part of the *PE* compares the truths of the Hebrew faith with pagan concepts, and offers proof of the former's antiquity and superiority. The religion of the Hebrews is depicted as the source of Greek culture and social order. Eusebius wanted to prove that pagan culture borrowed from both the barbarians, and, in particular, from the Hebrews, in order to defend Christianity against the accusation of preferring barbarian philosophy. By proving that the Greeks had turned to "barbarian philosophy" he would undermine the pagans' same charge against the Christians. This motivation differs from that of Hellenistic Jewish apologists who sought to prove both to themselves and to the pagans that Jewish culture and tradition had actually incorporated Greek philosophy. To be sure, this issue was important to Eusebius and other Christian apologists, but it did not have a high priority. In fact, in the *PE*, Eusebius strives to point out the harmony—even the similarity—between Christianity and all that is good in Greco-Roman culture. Finally, the *DE* relates that the Hebrews' beliefs were compromised by prevailing social conditions and

---

[22] On the integration of the genres, see Sirinelli, *PE, SC*, p. 48. For a similar view, see D. Rokeah, *Pagans and Christians in Conflict* (Jerusalem-Leiden, 1982), p. 74.

remained impure under the Law of Moses. In the past, the Law had attempted to struggle against pagan error. It could not succeed, however, because of its historical situation, hence the need for a new covenant and a renewal of the divine revelation.[23] The historical reality of Eusebius' day, which saw Christianity flourish and expand throughout the world was seen to validate this concept and to explain the significance of historical events in the framework of a divine plan of sacred history.

In his book Eusebius criticized Greek philosophy and religion by quoting at length from the writings of Greek authors and philosophers in order to expose their contradictions, thereby demonstrating their confusion and deceit. In the *PE*, this becomes a systematic structural technique, which he applies with unprecedented skill. Schwartz states that along with the *Ecclesiastical History*, the *PE* and the *DE* exemplify Eusebius' talent for adducing large amounts of material to support simple and basic ideas.[24] Other scholars give similar views, albeit less forcefully.[25] Statistically, quotations account for approximately 71 percent of the work,[26] so that only about 29 percent is actually written by Eusebius. We may further subtract the sections in which Eusebius presents or introduces the quotations, as well as his summaries of statements by authors quoted directly or indirectly, and the repetition of facts given earlier. He often states that he could provide many more quotations to support his arguments.

Eusebius rarely voices his thoughts beyond those in the brief passages linking the numerous quotations. He thus creates the impression that a constructive discussion on the value and veracity of Christianity, beyond the evidence found in Scripture, is not crucial to the general plan of his work; indeed, it is fully developed in a few places only. Nevertheless, it underpins this composition. It is not difficult to understand, therefore, why many viewed him as an author of great erudition, however lacking in imagination and speculative thought. Even if one does not fully accept such conclusions, there is no doubt that the most original aspect of this work is its structure, which effectively interweaves the numerous quotations. Eusebius may not have been an outstanding theologian, but he wrote

---

[23] *DE*, Book 1.
[24] Schwartz, "Eusebios", col. 1388.
[25] For example, see Foakes-Jackson, *Eusebius*, p. 126.
[26] Namely in *PE*, see Laurin, *Orientations*, p. 358.

several long works in which he extensively developed different ideas—albeit largely unoriginal—without resorting to many quotations. The encyclopedic character of the *PE* and the *DE* is essential to the strategy of the work. As he states on many occasions, Eusebius wishes to let the quotations speak for themselves. The citations were the best proof because they came from the enemy camp and attacked him on his own turf with his own weapons. He did not wish to elaborate on these quotations, for that could be counterproductive, and his personal intervention might diminish the force of the argument.[27] The citations had to come from a pagan, or, occasionally, a Jewish source. It seems that Eusebius resorts to citations from Christian sources only when he does not have at his disposal a pagan source as proof. Even in this case, the Christian source is occasionally adduced to testify against the pagans[28] or to serve as support, but not as major proof. For one's own testimony regarding oneself was the weakest form of proof, to be used as infrequently as possible.[29]

The sheer volume of his sources is marshaled as evidence of Eusebius' scholarship and of his "scientific" criteria as the spokesman for Christianity. He is careful to identify his sources and notes his inclusion of authoritative writers in the discussion of different subjects.[30] He is consistent in first presenting his opponents' testimonies on a particular issue, then summarizing them and adding brief conclusions that correspond to the general nature of the proof.

Eusebius wants to appear fair and objective vis-à-vis his opponents. As we shall see, this is not necessarily the case. He claims to show impartial judgment throughout the work.[31] He does not distort quotations for apologetic purposes, and usually gives the exact quotation.[32] But as we shall see, Eusebius sometimes made minor changes and omissions that enabled him to interpret quotations as

---

[27] See, for example, *PE* 1,5; 2,5; 3, Introduction; 4,6; 5,5; 6,9; 8,1; 10,1; 11,6; 13,3; 14,1; 15,1.

[28] For example, Clement of Alexandria in *PE* 10,2.

[29] For the minimal value of the New Testament as testimony and proof, see also Rokeah, *Jews, Pagans and Christians*, p. 74.

[30] For example, see *PE* 1,5; 3,1; 5,5, and elsewhere throughout the work.

[31] *PE* 15,1: "διὰ τούτων ἁπάντων τῆς ἡμετέρας γνώμης τὸ κριτήριον ἀδέκαστον ἐπιδεικνὺς τοῖς ἐντυγχάνουσιν."

[32] E. des Places, "Eusèbe de Césarée juge de Platon dans la Préparation Evangélique", *Mélanges de Philosophie Grecque offerts à Mgr Diès* (Paris, 1956), p. 72; J. Coman, "Utilisation des Stromates de Clément d'Alexandrie par Eusèbe de Césarée dans la Preparation Evangélique", *TU* 125 (1981), p. 134.

he wished and to take them out of context. The pagan authors most often quoted are Plato and Porphyry. Eusebius clearly prefers Plato above all the others. Plato was the leading writer; his quoted words, thanks to his superior accomplishments and fame, sufficed to resolving the issues.[33] Eusebius is full of admiration for Plato, even though he enumerates the errors that separated Plato from the Christians. He was the only pagan capable of reaching the gates of truth. Eusebius is apologetic that he has to find fault with Plato.[34] Although Eusebius' attitude to other philosophers is less admiring, he rarely refers to them in sharp or sarcastic language. He explicitly states that his efforts to refute their works do not derive from hostility towards them. On the contrary, he admits that he holds them in high esteem (μέγα θαῦμα ἔχειν ὁμολογῶ) compared to the rest of humanity.[35] Thus the list of pagan philosophers, historians, and authors appearing in his work is a long one. Some actually owe to Eusebius their place in our collective memory.

Latin authors are not quoted by Eusebius, probably because his knowledge of their language was minimal. Otherwise, it is inconceivable that he would not have referred to Cicero's *On the Nature of the Gods*. Roman religion is portrayed in the description of Dionysius of Halicarnassus. We have noted that Eusebius generally prefers contemporary writers to earlier ones. (Aristotle, Zeno, and Epicurus appear in passages from later commentators.) Indeed, with the exception of Plato, classical literature is not a major source for quotations. He also displays his knowledge of middle-Platonic and neo-Platonic works.

---

[33] *PE* 11, Introduction. Here the subject is the affinity between Greek philosophy and the Hebrew "oracles" (λόγια).

[34] *PE* 13, Introduction; 13,14; 13,18. The "Plato" who appears in many of Eusebius' quotations is that of middle-Platonism, dominated by *The Republic*, *The Laws*, and, especially, the *Timaeus*. This version of Plato was more popular and more easily understood. Such a selection gave less prominence to metaphysics, the theory of ideas, and the link between them and the world of phenomena. Its philosophy is mixed with religiosity and lacks doctrinal rigidity. This trend is held in common by Stoicism, neo-Pythagoreans, astrology, the mystery cults, and Christianity. Given this background, one can understand Eusebius' predilection for Platonic texts in which the figure of Socrates emerges positively. Eusebius tends to include selections from Plato which complement the purpose of Christian theology on such topics as the unity and uniqueness of God, the essence of goodness, Creation, the stars, time, and the conditional eternity of the gods. See Des Places, *Eusèbe commentateur*, pp. 35–36.

[35] *PE* 14,1,2.

In the *PE*, Eusebius also uses quotations from the Old and New Testaments to justify the Christians' choice of "the theology of the Hebrews". However, such quotations are relatively few, as Eusebius prefers to use them only to reinforce arguments already proven. He thus recognizes that biblical verses can be a double-edged sword and should be used only with the correct interpretation, namely, that of Origen.[36]

Eusebius' great erudition is perhaps the most convincing aspect of the *PE*. The best way of showing that the Christians had not abandoned the Greeks through an ignorance of their philosophy, was to present a thorough and careful selection of pagan philosophical texts. He demonstrates his vast knowledge of philosophy in order to refute the popular claim that Christians preferred the Hebrew oracles because they were ignorant of Greek culture.[37] Eusebius' polemical method resembles that of Porphyry, namely, meticulously examining the opponent's ideas and beliefs in order to expose his inconsistencies and make him appear ridiculous.

Sometimes, for tactical reasons, Eusebius seems to prefer to contend with the more ancient and primitive pagan religious concepts presented in earlier works. However, other parts of the work show that he is familiar with the development of contemporary pagan thought and religious belief.

In the last seven books of the *DE*, sections from the New Testament are quoted in order to present Christian traditions and doctrines. The emphasis is on the proof itself, which consists of a long and detailed presentation of passages from the Old Testament. For the most part, the various excerpts are accompanied by interpretations, which Eusebius viewed as essential. On occasion, however, quotations appear without a commentary. When interpreting prophecies, Eusebius takes advantage of the different Greek translations in Origen's *Hexapla*, to select the version most suited to his particular purpose, while at the same time emphasizing his desire to maintain "scientific standards".

While the *Prophetic Extracts* was intended to prove the truth of the biblical prophecies and their fulfillment in Jesus, the *DE* was written both to prove that fulfillment, but also, and more especially, to describe the life and works of Jesus Christ and their continuity through

---

[36] *PE* 6,10.
[37] *PE* 14,2.

the Church, by showing that the history of Christianity is the fulfillment of prophecies in the Old and New Testaments. This work
may be regarded as a continuation of Eusebius' concept of the sacred
history of Christianity. Despite the fact that a major part of the *DE*
is constructed on biblical verses and has a considerable element of
exegesis, it is not a commentary and the parallels it draws between
the prophecies and Christ are presented not for their intrinsic interest, but rather as a presentation-demonstration of the truth of Christianity through the prophecies. The historical orientation is seen in
the fact that Jesus is presented not only as the Christ of the prophecies but also as a prophet. The biblical prophecies and those of Jesus
spoke of the expansion of the Church and its contemporary context.
Eusebius conceives of prophecies being fulfilled across the full span
of Christian history. A new understanding of Christian history emerges
which repeatedly indicates a different perspective on prophetic fulfillment.

Internal Division

As I shall discuss issues that relate to the polemical context of the
works—and not necessarily to the subjects as they appear in Eusebius' plan—I shall now present in brief a schematic division of the
books of the *PE* and the *DE* to set the framework of subjects discussed in these works.[38] Eusebius precedes each book with a list of
chapter titles, which are particularly detailed in the *PE*. Eusebius
may have done this for practical reasons. The titles could serve as
a useful aide-mémoire for students and others who needed the book
for polemical purposes. In addition, Eusebius inserted titles in the
different books, according to subject, which occasionally furnished
details that did not appear clearly in the body of the work. Eusebius' internal division of the *PE* differed from the division into chapters
which appears in the printed editions, although the titles are correctly positioned in the critical editions of Mras and *SC*. In both the
first book[39] and the beginning of the last,[40] Eusebius mentions the
definitive program of the *PE*. The first description makes a general

---

[38] For a detailed analysis of individual books of the *PE* see the introductions to
the various volumes of the *SC* edition (1974–1987).
[39] *PE* 1,6,5–7.
[40] *PE* 15,1.

statement concerning the work, while the second is more exact and detailed.

The first six books are devoted to refuting polytheistic paganism. In the first three, Eusebius criticizes traditional mythologies and their different interpretations. In the subsequent books (4–6), he criticizes the oracles, the pagan gods—identified with evil demons—and the fatalism and determinism associated with pagan oracles.[41]

In the next three books (7–9), Eusebius examines the Hebrew "oracles" and their history as the Greeks recorded them. The seventh book is devoted to the concept of the ancient Hebrews.[42] The eighth deals with the Mosaic laws and the ninth conveys Greek testimonies on the Hebrews and the Jews. The tenth book deals with the Jewish heritage adopted by the Greeks, or, in other words, the Greeks' plagiarism of ancient Hebrew culture. In fact, according to the *PE*, the Greeks received all that is valuable and important in their culture from the Jews.[43]

The books which follow (11–13) focus mainly on the common ground between the ideas of important Greek philosophers, especially Plato, and the beliefs and opinions of the Hebrews.[44] The fourteenth

---

[41] The polemical framework of the fourth book is the pagan accusation that Christians showed gross disrespect for the divine powers and their cults (*PE* 3,17). Eusebius proceeds to refute the third kind of polytheistic error, namely, the official, public and state religion; Christians were accused of transgressing against this third form of religion, thereby breaking the law (*PE* 4,1). The polemical framework of the fifth book is the desire to present additional evidence that the gods were simply demons, in order to show more clearly how Jesus extricated mankind from their grasp (*PE* 5,1). The sixth book focuses on the contrast between the oracles and Jesus' doctrine of God, and refutes the belief in fate on the part of both demons and men (*PE* 6, Introduction). For the polemic on the question of fate, astrology, providence and free will in *PE* 6, see D. Amand, *Fatalisme et liberté dans l'antiquité grecque* (Amsterdan, 1973), pp. 355–380; G.F. Chesnut, "Fate, Fortune, Free Will and Nature in Eusebius of Caesarea", *Church History* 42 (1973), pp. 165–182; idem, *The First Christian Histories, Eusebius, Socrates, Sozomen, Theodoret and Evagrius*[2] (Macon, 1986), pp. 33–64.

[42] The polemical framework of the seventh book is a refutation of the accusation that Christians had abandoned ancestral traditions for strange and barbaric religion and customs, and the idealization of the Hebrews in the spirit of Hellenistic Judaism. For an especially detailed analysis of *PE* 7 see G. Schroeder's introduction to his *SC* edition of this book (1975).

[43] On Eusebius' positive presentation of Jewish doctrines and their adaptation by the Greek philosophers, see Schroeder, *PE* 7 (SC), pp. 40–50; D. Rokeah, *Jews, Pagans and Christians*, pp. 185–192. Rokeah also proposes that Josephus' *Against Apion* served as a model for the *PE* and the *DE* (Rokeah, *Jews, Pagans and Christians*, p. 27).

[44] On Plato's debt to Hebrew sources and his affinity to them, see G. Favrelle's

book points to the dissension and contradictions among the philosophers and notes how philosophical systems opposed to the Christian
philosophical faith were condemned by the wisest of the pagan philosophers. The last book proceeds to attack Aristotle and the Stoics.

The general structure of the *DE* is also fairly clear. The original
work contained twenty books,[45] of which only the first ten, and a
few passages of the fifteenth, have remained.[46] From Eusebius' statement at the beginning of the first book, we may ascertain the contents of the entire work. The bulk of the work is a collection of
biblical prophecies relating to Christ, which encompass all aspects
of his divine nature and his life on earth: his nature and origins, the
Incarnation, his activities, his death, Resurrection and Ascension, his
place at the right hand of the Father, and the Second Coming. In
addition, the work included biblical prophecies on the past and present sorrows of the Jewish people after their rejection of Christ, and
on the spread of the Gospel and the worldwide triumph of Christianity up until the time of Eusebius himself. Understood correctly,
these prophecies together constituted a conclusive presentation and
demonstration of the truth of the Christian faith.

The three first books of the *DE* are entirely different in nature
from the rest, as they include lengthy discussions by Eusebius without many quotations. The first book explains why Christians live
according to a new covenant, why they are separate from the Jews,
and what characterizes the Christian way of life and the nature of
this new covenant. Not only that Christians were entitled to the
Scriptures, but only they understood it correctly. They were right in
rejecting the Jewish way of life, because Christ had made a new
covenant with mankind. After the opening of the first book, Eusebius proposes as the central issue of this book a definition of the
essence of Christianity—a return to the religion of the patriarchs

introduction to *PE* 11 (*SC*), pp. 36–41; Rokeah, "The Jewish People and Religion
in Pagan-Christian Polemics in the Roman Empire", *Tarbiz* 40 (1971), pp. 467–468
(Hebrew); Des Places, "Eusèbe de Césarée juge de Platon", pp. 73–76. Apparently
this was one of the topics discussed in Origen's *Stromateis*, of which only a few fragments remain. He wished to express the basic ideas of the New Testament in Platonic language and to show the harmony between Jesus and Plato (Origen, *Commentary
on John*, 13,45; Jerome, *Epistle* 8,4,3). See Chadwick, *Early Christian Thought*, p. 72.
   [45] Photius, *Bibliotheca*, 10; Jerome, *De viris illustribus*, 81.
   [46] In his introduction to the *Commentary on Hosea*, Jerome mentions that Eusebius
argued about a particular issue in the book of Hosea in Book 18 of the *DE* (*quaedam
de Osee propheta disputat*). For the extant fragments of *DE* 15, see Mras, *DE*, pp.
493–496.

and a spiritual emulation of Abraham, because the law of Moses
was not universal nor suitable for everyone. Christianity, however,
also depended on a correct understanding of Scripture, which announced the new lawgiver, the Christ, the word of God. The message of Christ lay in returning to the pristine religion of the patriarchs
and bringing Judaism to its fulfillment. Historical Christianity was a
kind of rebirth of the religion of the patriarchs. To be sure, there
were slight differences between the two, such as the numerous progeny and animal sacrifice. Such differences had to be explained.[47] The
second book recounts the prophecies predicting Christianity's appeal
to the Gentiles, their conversion to Christianity, and the rejection
and punishment of the Jews. According to Eusebius, the main part
of the *DE* begins with the third Book.[48] Here he responds to two
types of pagan opponents: those who refuse to believe the marvelous
things that the apostles told of Jesus, and those who accept the truth
of such stories, but relate to Jesus as if he were a wizard or seducer.
Eusebius refutes such attitudes and deals with the prophetic promises
relating to the life and works of Jesus.[49]

The fourth and fifth books explore the way in which the prophecies shed light on the relationship between the Son-Logos and the
Father, the doctrine of Christ as the Logos incarnate, and the general question of the divinity of Jesus. The subsequent books deal
with prophecies that speak of the coming of Jesus, the Incarnation,
his birth and tribe of origin,[50] the historical era of his appearance
and its signs,[51] and the major events of his life—his works and miracles,[52] his passion, death and descent into the netherworld.[53] The
tenth book ends with brief quotations from Scripture attesting to the
Resurrection of Jesus, his deeds after the Resurrection, and the rise
and spread of the Gentile Church.

The major extant passage from the fifteenth book concerns the
vision of Nebuchadnezzar in chapter two of Daniel, and the Four
Kingdoms that would exist before the coming of the Son of Man.

---

[47] These subjects will be discussed later.
[48] *DE* 3, Introduction.
[49] According to Stevenson, this book is probably the best one written by Eusebius, see Stevenson, *Studies*, p. 37.
[50] Book Seven.
[51] Book Eight.
[52] Book Nine.
[53] Book Ten.

This detailed section on Daniel may have been elaborated in the wake of Porphyry's critique and integrated into the general plan describing the return of Jesus according to the prophecies.

The Jewish Aspect of the Demonstratio Evangelica

As early as the first chapter of the *Praeparatio* Eusebius indicates the polemical context of the twofold work, but he introduces it not only as a response to questions and arguments presented to Christians by pagans. In his words, the work is also a response to claims and questions raised by Jews.[54] He lists their arguments against Christianity: the Christians were foreigners who abused Scripture, which in any case did not belong to them at all; they forced themselves in and made brutal attempts to displace the Jews from their ancient rights. If the prophecies had indeed foretold a Messiah, they meant one who was a Messiah and a king of the Jews, not of all the nations of the world. If Scripture contained certain promises, they were meant for the Jews, and the Christians were mistaken in thinking otherwise. They distorted the prophecies arbitrarily, applying them falsely to themselves and thereby stealing them from the Jews, all the while deluding themselves. Most unreasonably of all, the Christians expropriated for themselves the good reward promised to those who kept the Law, although they themselves did not keep the customs of the Jews according to that Law, breaking it deliberately.[55] Eusebius claims that the Jews regarded this last charge as the most serious of all. The same claim is presented only two paragraphs earlier as a pagan argument, apparently taken from Porphyry, as mentioned above.[56] According to this argument, not only did Christians forsake the ancient customs and traditions of their peoples, unreasonably and uncritically choosing—through blind faith—the teachings of the faithless enemies of all nations, but they also failed to follow the ways of the God whom the Jews worshipped according

---

[54] *PE* 1,1. The discussion of the Jewish aspect of the *DE* is based on A. Kofsky, "Eusebius of Caesarea and the Christian-Jewish Polemic", in O. Limor & G.G. Stroumsa (eds.), *Contra Iudaeos: Ancient and Medieval Polemics between Christians and Jews* (Tübingen, 1996), pp. 61–70. See now J. Ulrich, *Euseb von Caesarea und die Juden* (Berlin-New York, 1999).

[55] *PE* 1,2,5–8.

[56] First fragment of Harnack's collection of fragments from Porphyry's book *Against the Christians*, possibly from his preface.

to their customs, instead carving a new path in the wilderness that
kept neither the ways of the Greeks nor those of the Jews.[57] Porphyry also attacked the Christians for their distorting interpretation
of Scripture.[58] Towards the end of the *Praeparatio*, Eusebius again
explains the polemical motive in writing the two-part work, saying
that the *Praeparatio* intended to respond to the central charge of
deserting the traditions and religion of the ancestors. He goes on to
state that he will answer other pagan accusations at the beginning
of the *Demonstratio*. One of the serious pagan charges against the
Christians, he adds, was that they had rejected the Hebrews' religion and way of life, despite adopting their sacred writings. This
accusation had been a major factor in his decision to write the *Demonstratio*.[59] He ends the *Praeparatio* by repeating that the *Demonstratio* is
the main part of his work, and explains that his main purpose in
writing it is to counter the Jews' accusations against the Christians.
The essence of these charges was twofold: (1) The Christians' use of
holy writings not belonging to them. (2) Their failure to live according to the Law despite their use of Scripture. Here, then, Eusebius
indicates that the *Demonstratio* is primarily a reply to Jewish arguments against Christianity.[60]

In the opening of the *Demonstratio* Eusebius again notes the polemical context of the two-part work, implying that it is meant to arm
Christians for future debates. He claims that the *Demonstratio* is a
work against the Jews (γραφὴ κατὰ Ἰουδαίων), but that this is not its
only role, since it is also written for their own good. Since the work
showed Christianity to be founded on the fulfillment of the ancient
prophecies, it also thereby certified and verified Judaism. The work
was also meant for pagans, however, being designed to convince
them of the truth of Christianity and to silence pagan slanderers by
means of a logical demonstration (λογικωτέρας ἀποδείξεως) of which
the Christians, they claimed, were incapable. In daily disputes, Eusebius says, pagans continued their virulent accusations that Christians
(ὁσημέραι ταῖς καθ᾽ ἡμῶν διαβολαῖς κατὰ κράτος ἐπεντριβόμενοι) were
incapable of providing a rational account of their cause; instead,

---

[57] *PE* 1,2,4.
[58] See, e.g., fragments 39 and 45 in Harnack's collection, and also the fragment
later identified by G. Binder, "Eine Polemik des Porphyrios . . .", 3 (1968), pp.
81–95.
[59] *PE* 15,1,1–9.
[60] *PE* 15,62,17–18.

Christians demanded that neophytes place their trust in faith alone, closing their eyes like unreasoning animals and obeying without question. Here he adds that the *Demonstratio* also rebuts the teachings of Christian heretics against the prophets, by demonstrating the harmony between old and new, i.e., the Old and the New Testaments. The reference here may be to views like those of Marcion, who claimed that the Old Testament was not part of the Christian canon. Soon afterwards, Eusebius again notes the general schematic division of his work into the *PE* and the *DE*: in the first he had responded to the pagan accusation that the Christians had deserted the gods of their ancestors in favor of a barbarian faith; in the second, he would deal with the accusation by the Jews (τὴν αὐτῶν Ἰουδαίων κατηγορίαν) that Christians failed to embrace the Jewish way of life even though they used their sacred writings.[61]

In the Preface to the second book of the *DE*, Eusebius says that, in addition to returning to evidence drawn from Scripture, he will respond more fully to accusations leveled by "the people of the circumcision", who claim that Christians have no share in the promises of Scripture. The Jews asserted that the prophets and the Messiah were destined for them alone, mocking Christians who descended from Gentile peoples, whom the prophets disparaged. The claim that Scripture did not refer to Christians, and that the prophecies and the Messiah were only for the Jews, was a familiar one. It is likely, therefore, that in his description of the Jews' contempt for gentile Christians and his recitation of Jewish charges, Eusebius was echoing the polemical debates or Jewish anti-Christian arguments of his own day; I shall return to this below.

In the first chapter of the *DE*, Eusebius charges that Jews memorized specific prophecies that were beneficial to them, and then made frequent use of them in their arguments with Christians.[62] To counter this, he would present the prophecies relating to the Gentiles and demonstrate that these carried succor and salvation for the Gentiles which could only come through Jesus the Messiah. Later he would prove that the obverse of the redemption of the nations was the destruction of the people of Israel, their religion and their Land.[63] Additionally, in various places in the *DE* Eusebius presents

---

[61] *DE* 1,1,8–11.
[62] *DE* 2,1,44.
[63] Ibid.

a polemic against the Jewish interpretation of verses with a messianic content.[64]

Thus the sum of Eusebius' words conveys a somewhat blurred
and ambivalent picture of his purpose. First he declares that in the
Demonstratio he intends to respond to the arguments of the Jews. Then
he states that, in this work, he seeks to refute the accusations of the
pagans. In yet another place, he notes that the *DE* contains responses
to both pagans and Jews. It is perfectly clear that the first three
books of the *DE*—entirely different in character from the rest—contain explicit answers to specific pagan arguments. How, then, are
we to understand Eusebius' claim that there is at least a dual polemic
in the *Demonstratio*? How serious is his reference to a Jewish-Christian debate? Does the manifestly literary polemic against the Jews
reflect a literary or an oral debate between Christians and Jews in
his time? Or perhaps what we have here is a work in the literary
genre of *Adversus Iudaeos*, which had crystallized within Christian
apologetic literature since the second century?

Scholars differ as to whether *Adversus Iudaeos* literature reflects
polemical reality, or whether it constitutes an internal Christian literary development arising from the need to delineate the problematic character of Christianity's relation to Judaism. An alternative
explanation for the emergence of this genre is that it grew out of
the need to respond to pagan attacks on Christianity that targeted
its relation to Judaism. It is not my aim here to tackle the difficult
questions posed by the *Adversus Iudaeos* literary genre. I shall, however, examine the significance of Eusebius' claim that his work
responds to the arguments of the Jews, and relate to the questions
concerning the existence of a Christian literary polemic against the
Jews, in an endeavor to understand the nature and role of the *Demonstratio Evangelica*.

The question of the existence of Jewish-Christian polemics in the
first centuries CE has been discussed by several scholars.[65] The spe-

---

[64] This tendency continues in Eusebius' later *Commentary on Isaiah*, where he fre-
quently contrasts the historical interpretation of the Jews with the spiritual inter-
pretation of Christians, e.g., in Isa. 35:9–10, 58:12. On this commentary, see
Hollerich, "Eusebius as a Polemical Interpreter of Scripture", pp. 585–615; idem,
Eusebius of Caesarea's Commentary on Isaiah; Christian Exegesis in the Age of Constantine
(Oxford, 1999).

[65] For example, A. Harnack, "Die Altercatio Simonis Judaei et Theophili Christiani, nebst Untersuchungen über die antijüdische Polemik in der alten Kirche",
TU 1,3, 1883; J. Parkes, *The Conflict of the Church and the Synagogue: A Study in the Ori-*

cial social and religious circumstances of Caesarea have also been noted.[66] Both Jewish and Christian sources indicate that in Eusebius' time there existed a certain measure of polemic or spoken debate between Jews and Christians, though there are few references in Talmud and Midrash to conversations and face-to-face disputes between Christians and Jews.[67] In the third and fourth centuries Caesarea was a center of Jewish scholarship. It is known that in Origen's time R. Hosha'ya lived in the city and debated religious issues with Christians.[68] Quasi-academic connections were also maintained between Jewish and Christian scholars. R. Abbahu, Eusebius' older contemporary,[69] enjoyed good relations with the Christians, and the Babylonian Talmud confirms his contacts with Christian scholars.[70] Christians and Jews held public disputes in Caesarea, in which R. Abbahu and others took part.[71] Origen says that he had conversations with Jewish sages,[72] that he consulted them on biblical questions, and that

---

gins of Antisemitism (London, 1934); L.A. Williams, *Adversus Judaeos, A Bird's Eye View of Christian Apologiae until the Renaissance* (Cambridge, 1935); S. Lieberman, "The Martyrs of Caesarea", *Annuaire de l'institut de philologie et d'histoire orientales et slaves* 7 (1939–1944), pp. 395–446; M. Simon, *Verus Israel: A Study of the Relations between Christians and Jews in the Roman Empire (135–425)* (Oxford 1986—an English translation of the second French edition of 1964); E.E. Urbach, *The Sages, their Concepts and Beliefs* (Jerusalem, 1975), pp. 544–558; *idem*, "Homilies of the Rabbis on the Prophets of the Nations and the Balaam Stories", *Tarbiz* 25 (1956) pp. 272–289 (Hebrew); *idem*, "The Homiletical Interpretation of the Sages and the Expositions of Origen on Canticles, and the Jewish-Christian Disputation", *Scripta Hierosolymitana* 22 (1971), p. 247; Rokeah, *Jews, Pagans and Christians*; H. Schreckenberg, *Die christlichen Adversus-Judaeos-Texte und ihr literariches und historiches Umfeld (1–11 Jh.)* (Frankfurt a.m, 1982). N.R.M. de Lange, *Origen and the Jews* (Cambridge, 1976), offers a discussion of Christian-Jewish polemic distinguishing between various possible sources for the polemic: earlier Christian sources, oral communication with Jews and acquaintance with Jewish sources.

[66] See Lieberman, ibid.; L.I. Levine, *Caesarea under Roman Rule* (Leiden, 1975), pp. 80–85.

[67] See Parkes, *The Conflict of the Church and the Synagogue*, p. 113; Urbach, *The Sages*, p. 546.

[68] See W. Bacher, *Die Agada der palästinensischen Amoräer*, Vol. 1–3 (Strassburg, 1892–1899), Vol. I, Part 1, p. 92; Lieberman, "The Martyrs of Caesarea", pp. 397–398.

[69] According to Lieberman (ibid., p. 400), R. Abbahu was in his seventies when the persecutions of 303 began.

[70] *BT, Avodah Zarah*, 4a.

[71] See Levine, *Caesarea*, pp. 83–84. On R. Abbahu, his links with Christians and his polemic against them, see Bacher, *Die Agada*, Vol. II, Part 1, pp. 96–97; S.T. Lachs, "Rabbi Abbahu and the Minim", *Jewish Quarterly Review* n.s. 60 (1969), pp. 197–212; O. Irshai, "R. Abbahu said: 'If a man should say to you "I am God"— he is a liar'", *Zion* 47 (1982), pp. 173–177 (Hebrew).

[72] Origen, *Contra Celsum*, 1, 45; 49.

he had a Jewish teacher.[73] His words also reflect a Jewish-Christian dispute.[74] Jerome names Clement, Origen and Eusebius as Christian scholars who learned from Jews.[75] Indeed, Eusebius makes several references to conversations he had with Jewish teachers and other Jews. In *Prophetic Extracts* he relates that he heard a Jew expounding Isaiah 7:10–17 not as messianic prophecy but as a reference to King Hezekiah.[76] He further states that he witnessed Jewish polemical statements against the divinity of Jesus.[77] He speaks of contemporary Jewish sages who interpreted Scripture as people trained to penetrate to the heart of Scripture.[78] In his late *Commentary on Isaiah*, he at times invokes a Jewish exegesis for certain verses that he claims to have learned from a Jewish rabbi orally.[79] In *Commentary on Isaiah* 39:1, he says: "When I asked and enquired as to the meaning of the verse before us, the rabbi said . . .", and the explanation follows.[80] I have already noted Eusebius' testimony on disputes between Jews and Christians, mostly over interpretations of biblical verses.

From what has been written, it appears that Christian scholars in Caesarea respected the rabbis, who were well-versed in Scripture.[81] According to S. Lieberman, relations between pagans, Christians and Jews in Caesarea at the beginning of the fourth century were generally tolerable.[82] This situation may have been influenced by the special circumstances in Caesarea at the time, where there was no

---

[73] The sources on Origen and the Jews were listed by G. Bardy, "Saint Jérome et ses maîtres hébreux", *Revue Bénédictine* 46 (1934), pp. 145–164. See also De Lange, *Origen and the Jews*, passim.

[74] Origen, ibid., 1,55; see Urbach, *Sages*, pp. 546–547.

[75] Jerome, *Against Rufinus*, 1,13.

[76] King Hezekiah was also considered a messianic figure in Jewish circles. See Urbach, *Sages*, p. 668.

[77] *Prophetic Extracts* 4,4; 27.

[78] *PE* 1,12.

[79] *Commentary on Isaiah* 23:15; 39:3; Hollerich, ibid., pp. 143–153.

[80] For Eusebius' connections with Jewish scholars see also *Chronicle* 50, 9–20 (ed. Karst). On Origen, Eusebius and Jewish scholars, see S. Krauss, "The Jews in the Writings of the Church Fathers", *Jewish Quarterly Review* 6 (1894), p. 84. The question as to whether Eusebius had any knowledge of Hebrew has barely been investigated. An answer to this question may shed more light on his relations with Jews. My survey of his writings indicates that he had at least a moderate lexical knowledge of the language beyond the etymological handbook attributed to Philo (Eusebius, *HE* 2.18.7), now lost. Such knowledge, however, was probably insufficient for an independent study of Hebrew sources. For a similar evaluation, see J. Stevenson, *Studies*, p. 26. For a minimalist view, see Hollerich, "Eusebius as a Polemical Interpreter of Scripture", p. 593. Cf. Ulrich, ibid., pp. 192–201.

[81] See Lieberman, "The Martyrs of Caesarea", p. 398.

[82] Ibid., p. 409.

dominant majority. Lieberman says that the largest religious group in the city was its Samaritan community.[83] Together, Christians, Jews and Samaritans formed an absolute majority in Caesarea. This may also have affected the considerable pagan minority, and might explain their relative indifference to the official pagan religion, a fact which facilitated interaction between pagans and Jews,[84] and possibly between pagans and Christians. The fact that no group was dominant in the city may have contributed to the relatively tolerant atmosphere and encouraged some social mixing. Thus it seems that Jews and Christians in Caesarea did intermingle, and we have reports of conversations and disputes between Jewish and Christian scholars, both in private and in the market place.[85] It also seems that, in general, there was no overt enmity between Jews and Christians.[86] Eusebius does not relate incidents of joy or provocation among Jews who witnessed the execution of Christians during the great persecution.[87] Indeed, one of the martyrs even prays for the Jews.[88] Eusebius also mentions the sympathy and commiseration expressed by the Jews of Lod in reaction to the suffering of the martyrs and their brave endurance.[89]

However, the extent of good relations between the different religious groups should not be overstated. There is no doubt that tension and hatred existed despite the general atmosphere of tolerance. Origen attests to this.[90] Eusebius says that the pagan masses still derided Jesus, sneered at him and condemned him, and that the Jews mocked and spat on him.[91] There may have also been an ongoing rivalry between Jews and Christians in their efforts to proselytize. The extent of contemporaneous Jewish proselytizing activity is a basic factor in fully understanding the Jewish-Christian polemic, but it remains disputed, since the sources give no definite indications in this regard.[92] In addition to the relatively scarce evidence of verbal disputations between Jews and Christians in the third and

---

[83] Ibid., p. 402.
[84] Ibid., p. 415.
[85] On Jewish-Christian relations in Caesarea, see Levine, *Caesarea*, pp. 80–85.
[86] Ibid., p. 81.
[87] *The Martyrs of Palestine* (W. Cureton's edition), p. 30.
[88] Ibid.
[89] Ibid., pp. 27–28.
[90] See Bardy, "Saint Jérome et ses maîtres hébreux", p. 227; De Lange, *Origen and the Jews*, pp. 85–87; Levine, Caesarea, p. 82.
[91] *DE* 10,8.
[92] For differing views on this question, see Simon, *Verus Israel*, pp. 271–305;

fourth centuries, the Jewish sources adduce sayings and homilies of
the sages directed at a Jewish audience but aimed against Christian
arguments. This Jewish response to Christian arguments was perhaps meant not only to reinforce the Jews' inward response to spoken Christian claims, but also to furnish them with appropriate
responses. In other words, this type of evidence may be an indication of direct debate. For E.E. Urbach, it was evidence of Jewish-
Christian polemics and he studied it as such.[93] Rokeah proposed a
distinction between the terms "polemics" and "dispute": a polemic
would be either a comprehensive religious struggle aimed at converting the opponent, or a defense against the opponent's proselytizing onslaught; the purpose of a dispute, on the other hand, would
be to sort out certain problems. Such disputes often accompanied
unfruitful polemical disputations, when both sides were resigned to
the fact that the enemy could not be converted to their camp.[94]
According to Rokeah, the term "polemic" is applicable to the Christian-pagan conflict, whereas the Jewish-Christian antagonism in this
period is only a "dispute".[95] Typically, these disputes were argu-
mentative, "both childish and barren", and instigated mostly by the
Christian side.[96] This view may be more valid with regard to the
direct debates than for the internal apologetic response to Christian
arguments.

The Christian treatises against the Jews, whether in the form of
a dialogue with a Jew, or as a doctrinal tract, pose a problem. Scholars are deeply divided as to whether they reflect a real polemic
against the Jews. This issue does not impinge on the question of the
existence or extent of a Jewish-Christian polemic, since it can be
argued that such a polemic did exist but is not reflected in the treatises against the Jews. According to this view, these treatises do not
reflect a Jewish-Christian polemic and are to be understood as an

---

Urbach, *The Sages*, pp. 550–552; M. Avi-Yonah, *The Jews under Roman and Byzantine
Rule* (Jerusalem, 1984), p. 150; Rokeah, *Jews, Pagans and Christians*, pp. 42–44.
   [93] *The Sages*, pp. 550–558, and in his above-mentioned articles. See also M. Hirshman, *A Rivalry of Genius, Jewish and Christian Biblical Interpretation in Late Antiquity*
(New York, 1996).
   [94] For a similar general appreciation of religious polemics at the time, see G.G.
Stroumsa, "Religious Contacts in Byzantine Palestine", *Numen* 36 (1989), p. 21.
According to Stroumsa, polemics exist less as a dialogue or an attempt at mutual
persuasion, than as an inward endeavor for the sake of edification.
   [95] Rokeah, *Jews, Pagan and Christians*, p. 65.
   [96] Ibid., p. 78.

internal Christian matter, a literary method of dealing with the problematic character of Christianity's relations with Judaism. Another possibility is that these compositions focus on such problems as a consequence of pagan attacks on Christianity because of its problematic links to Judaism, or as a response to difficult questions raised by recent pagan converts to the faith. Of course, different variations, combinations, and modifications of these possibilities have been proposed by different scholars according to complex considerations which cannot be enlarged upon here. Their theories, and the reasoning behind them, have been presented and criticized by M. Simon, and more briefly by Rokeah.[97]

The above digression illustrates the problems inherent in any attempt to understand the genre of the *Adversus Iudaeos* treatises. It is germane to our discussion because in some respects the *Demonstratio* may resemble works of this kind. Indeed, some scholars include the *Demonstratio* in their discussion of *Adversus Iudaeos* literature. Their opinions in this regard determine their respective views on the *Demonstratio*. Thus A.B. Hulen classifies it as part of the second group of *Adversus Iudaeos* writings, in line with his definition of the work as a doctrinal and exegetical composition intended to convert Jews by adducing biblical proof of the truth of Christianity.[98] Simon, too, argued that the *Demonstratio* was a true polemic primarily aimed at the Jews, with the intention of converting them.[99] We have already encountered J. Sirinelli's view, that the *DE* was a treatise in the genre of *Adversus Iudaeos*. However, he also sees the work as Eusebius' polemic against Porphyry. From the point of view of structure, Rokeah regarded the *Demonstratio* as an expanded version of the earlier, smaller apologies against the Greeks. But he regards both the *Praeparatio* and the *Demonstratio* as essentially a polemical response to Porphyry. For despite Eusebius' words in *DE* 1,1,15–16, that he is replying to Jews who reproach Christians for adopting Scripture while adhering to a different way of life, Rokeah claims that this is essentially the same pagan argument voiced by Celsus and Porphyry concerning the deviation of Christians from Judaism. It is well known, of course, that Porphyry attacked Christianity primarily by criticizing

---

[97] Simon, *Verus Israel*, pp. 136–146; Rokeah, *Jews, Pagans and Christians*, pp. 45–48.
[98] A.B. Hulen, "The Dialogues with the Jews as Sources for the Early Jewish Arguments against Christianity", *Journal of Biblical Literature* 51 (1932), pp. 58–70.
[99] Simon, *Verus Israel*, p. 177.

Scripture. Hence, according to Rokeah, the *Demonstratio* is "at the least, a defensive tract to counter pagan charges such as those of Eusebius' adversary Porphyry, rather than a polemic against Jewish accusation".[100]

It may be possible to reconcile Eusebius' contradictory statements concerning the *Demonstratio Evangelica* by viewing the work as containing a twofold response, to both the pagans and the Jews, even though it was intended for sympathetic pagans and Christians of pagan background, rather than for Jews. The contradictions in Eusebius' statements, the various issues in the *Demonstratio* clearly indicating the existence of anti-pagan polemic, possibly in conjunction with a dispute or polemic against the charges leveled by Jews, and the author's own lack of clarity on this subject, are also reflected among scholars who have dealt with this question. Aside from the question as to whether the *Demonstratio* belongs to the *Adversus Iudaeos* genre, there are those who tend to ignore its complexity and take literally Eusebius' statement at the beginning of the *Demonstratio*, that the work responds to the accusations of the Jews.[101] Others disregard this statement and view the *Demonstratio* as part of the polemical response to the pagans, in general, and Porphyry, in particular.[102] These two contradictory approaches converge in Laurin's study. In one place Laurin states that the work is directed mainly at the Jews, while in another he says that the main target is Porphyry, to whom Eusebius answers in every page of the *Demonstratio*! A similar contradiction is found in Sirinelli, who claims both that the *DE* was written specifically against Jews, and that it is replete with the anti-Phorphyrian polemic.[103]

It is true that specific charges by Jews against Christians, which Eusebius claims to answer, do appear in the *Demonstratio*. However, these seem to be few. In addition, he makes several references to the Jews' different exegesis of prophetic verses relating to the Mes-

---

[100] Rokeah, *Jews, Pagans and Christians*, pp. 74–76.

[101] See, for instance, E. des Places, *Eusèbe de Césarée commentateur: platonisme et écriture sainte* (Paris, 1982), p. 123. According to des Places, the *DE* was meant for Jews and was even destined to lead them to the Gospels through proof that the Messiah, incarnated and resurrected, was the one of whom prophets spoke.

[102] Barnes, for example, thinks that the *DE* is also part of Eusebius' systematic refutation of Porphyry. Indeed, according to Barnes the work reflects a Jewish threat to or rivalry with, Christianity in Eusebius' time, when, according to him, Judaism was still proselytizing. See Barnes, *Constantine and Eusebius*, pp. 178–179.

[103] J.R. Laurin, *Orientations*, pp. 370–373; Sirinelli, *PE, SC*, p. 28.

siah, and to Jewish criticism of the Christians' interpretation of the punishment of the Jews. Moreover, most of the Jewish charges against Christianity mentioned by Eusebius, or implied by the context of his words, are familiar to us from pagan polemical writings against Christianity. There are also places in the work that seem to reflect pagan arguments unfamiliar to us today but resembling those we do know. On the basis of the above analysis, it is my opinion that Eusebius' words should be accepted in all their complexity, i.e., his claim that he is also responding to the Jews should be accepted as more than a mere stylistic device. This view is based on the fact that it accords well with the principal anti-Christian pagan polemic, in which Christianity was attacked by the pagans for deviating from Judaism while claiming to adopt its sacred Scripture, and for misinterpreting biblical verses. Indeed—and this is beyond our scope here—Jewish anti-Christian arguments may have seeped into pagan circles and been used against Christians, but the extent of this phenomenon is not at all clear.

CHAPTER FOUR

THE CONCEPT OF CHRISTIAN PREHISTORY –
A CENTRAL AXIS IN THE POLEMIC

I. *Development of the Conception*

Eusebius conceived his apologetic *magnum opus* with a threefold purpose: (1) To shatter the foundations of pagan religion and philosophy (the negative dimension of his work). (2) To demonstrate that the Hebrew religion and philosophy preferred by Christians are superior in every way to pagan culture. (3) To explain how Christianity diverges from Judaism and is thereby superior. The last two objectives may be considered the positive aspects of the work, although the criticism of Judaism in the last has its negative aspect. It is against this background that Eusebius developed his distinctive concept of Christian prehistory as a central axis of his polemic.

At the very beginning of the *Praeparatio Evangelica*, Eusebius makes the important claim that Christians should not be regarded as mere deserters from paganism to Judaism. The Christians were a real people, independent and unique. They were not newcomers to history but constituted a nation with an authentic past and history.[1] Humanity was divided into three races or species: Greeks, representing paganism at large, Jews, and Christians. In this triple division—a variation on the familiar division of humanity between Hellenes and Jews—the Christians were the third race or nation.[2] This claim stems

---

[1] On the pagan charge against the Christians as innovators, see *PE* 4,1. Celsus also accused the Christians of "innovation" (καινοτομία); see *Contra Celsum* 3,5. On the importance attached to antiquity by the pagans, see Diogenes Laertius, *Lives of the Philosophers* (Pythagoras), 8,1,22, and Iamblichus, *Life of Pythagoras*, 8. On the negative view of the new and novel in the pagan religious outlook, see R. MacMullen, *Paganism in the Roman Empire* (New Haven-London, 1982), p. 3.

[2] *PE* 1,2,4; 5,12; *DE* 1,2; 10,8,111. Tertullian testifies that the Christians were called a third race or nation, after the Romans (and the Greeks) and the Jews, but he rejects this appellation (*Ad Nationes*, 1,8). A similar concept divided the world into four races: Barbarians, Greeks, Jews and Christians, as attested by the words of Aristides (*Apology*, 2). It seems that the division into four was rejected at an early stage in favor of the triple division. For the sources of the appellation "third race" (γένος) and its use in early Christian apologetics, see A. Harnack, *The Expansion of Christianity in the First Three Centuries* (New York, 1905), p. 300; J. Geffcken, *Zwei*

from Eusebius' aim to achieve honorable legitimacy for Christianity,[3] but it also becomes a fundamental assumption in the development of his concept of Christian and human history. This historical scheme prepares the ground for his weighty response to the twofold polemical charge underlying the work: the desertion of paganism and the deviation from Judaism. Eusebius transforms the earlier Christian polemical motivation to prove the antiquity and validity of Christianity through the antiquity and truth of Judaism, and to demonstrate that Christianity grew out of Judaism; he develops this with skill and sophistication in response to the complex polemical circumstances.

The conception of Christian prehistory appears in a rudimentary form already in the *Ecclesiastical History*[4]: even if the Christians and their name were new, their way of life and the ethical virtues of religious piety (εὐσεβείας δόγμασιν) were not recent inventions by them. These virtues existed from the dawn of humanity in the natural perceptions (φυσικαῖς ἐννοίαις) of those among the ancients who were the beloved of God. The nation of the Hebrews ('Εβραίων ἔθνος) was not new and was respected among people for its antiquity. The Hebrews possessed an oral tradition (λόγοι) and a Scripture telling of men of old who, while few in number, were distinguished in piety, charity and all the virtues. Some of them lived before the flood, some after. Distinguished among them was Abraham, whom the descendants of the Hebrews cherished as their ancestor. He who referred to those few who lived piously, from Adam to Abraham, as Christians—if not in name then in essence—did not invalidate the truth.[5] Eusebius goes on to note the moral content of the life of the

---

griechische Apologeten, p. 43; H.I. Marrou, *A Diognète, SC* 33, pp. 131–132; J. Sirinelli, *Les vues historiques*, p. 140, n. 5; Ulrich, ibid., pp. 125–130.

[3] Celsus claimed that the Christians had abandoned their traditional laws and were not a nation at all (*CC* 5, *33*).

[4] Sirinelli offers a general description of the concept of Christian prehistory that attempts to reconcile the various passages of *Hist.Eccl.*, *PE* and *DE*; see Sirinelli, *Vues historiques*, pp. 143–163. He did not perceive the complexity of this concept in Eusebius and barely recognized its apologetic-polemical context. Hence, Sirinelli's account is partial and somewhat simplistic. See also the critique of Sirinelli's book by M. Harl, "L'histoire de l'humanité racontée par un écrivain chrétien au début du IVᵉ siècle", *Revue des Études Grecques* 75 (1962), p. 529; For an analysis of this concept in the *HE* see also I. Krivouchine, "L'époque préchrétienne dans l'*Histoire Ecclésiastique* d'Eusèbe de Césarée", *Traditio* 51 (1996), pp. 287–294. For a general outline of the concept, mainly regarding *PE* 7, see Schroeder, introduction to *PE* 7 (*SC*), pp. 50–72; Kofsky, "Eusebius and the Christian-Jewish Polemic", pp. 70–83; Ulrich, ibid., pp. 57–68, 110–125.

[5] *HE* 1,4,4–6.

"Christian" patriarchs, in contrast to the life of Jews who lived according to the Law. The appellation "Christian" indicated that Christians, from their knowledge of Christ and his teaching, were distinguished by moderation, charity, restraint and virtues requiring courage, as well as by the religious awareness that God was one, unique and superior to all. The patriarchs were not concerned with circumcision, just as Christians did not bother with it. They did not distinguish certain foods from others, nor avoid eating certain foods. These laws had not been introduced until Moses established them for their descendants, much later.[6] Eusebius' conclusion in his pre-historical introduction, if it may be so called, to the *Ecclesiastical History* is that we should accept that the Gospel brought by Jesus to the Gentiles was the same ancient religion as the one revealed to Abraham, and the devotees of God who followed him.[7] We find here in a crude form the elements of the concept that identified the ancient patriarchs as Christians and their religion as Christianity, together with the distinction between Christianity as the religion of the patriarchs, and historical Judaism that began with the Law of Moses. Still in embryonic form, it may be viewed as an elaboration of Paul's brief words on Abraham in his *Epistle to the Romans*.[8] This becomes manifestly clear when Eusebius sets forth the content of Paul's claims. Of course, Paul did not call Abraham a Christian nor did he identify Abraham's faith with the Gospel of Jesus. The main point for Eusebius was that Paul said Abraham received the promise to inherit the world before he was circumcised. This was the proof that he was justified in his faith and not in the Law.[9]

Eusebius develops his concept into a detailed picture of Christian and Jewish history, especially in the seventh and eighth books of the *Praeparatio* and in the first book of the *Demonstratio*.[10] The discussion

---

[6] Ibid., 1,4,7–8.

[7] Ibid., 1,4,9–10.

[8] *Romans* 4,1–13.

[9] *HE* 1,4,11–14. A brief elaboration of Paul's concept may also be noted in the few words of Justin concerning the commandments and the fact that Christians did not observe them: the first human creatures, Adam, Abel, and Enoch were uncircumcised and were nevertheless loved by God. The Jews lived without the Sabbath until Moses' day (*Dialogue* 19,3–5), and even nature teaches that the commandments are redundant (ibid., 23,3).

[10] E.V. Gallagher even argues that the identification of Christianity with the religion of the patriarchs served as the organizing principle for the twofold composition (*PE–DE*). See E.V. Gallagher, "Eusebius the Apologist: The Evidence of the *Preparation* and the *Proof*", *Studia Patristica* 26 (1993), pp. 251–260.

fits into the general polemical framework mentioned above. The seventh and eighth books of the *Praeparatio* primarily respond to the second part of the accusation, namely, the Christians' abandonment of the traditions of their pagan ancestors in favor of weird barbarian religion and customs. From this point on, then, Eusebius will demonstrate the positive side of his argument. After proving that there is no truth in pagan religion and philosophy, he must show that religious, philosophical, and scientific truth resides in the "Hebrew" religion and philosophy. This is the place for a detailed idealization of the Hebrews in the spirit of Hellenistic Judaism, for proof of the antiquity of the Hebrews, and for the claim that the Greeks had plagiarized from the Hebrews on a vast scale, in the areas of religion, philosophy, and culture. The Hebrews were rational philosophers, but their thought was illuminated by the divine light of truth, not merely by speculative philosophy, hence their power of true prophecy. The Gentiles, however, worshiped a common demon under many different guises—like "a Hydra with many heads"—namely, pleasure, which to them was the supreme good.

Into this idealization of the Hebrews Eusebius weaves his new, evolving concept of a distinction between Hebrews and Jews. It gradually becomes apparent that his idealization of the Hebrews is nothing more than an idealization of the Christians and Christianity. If this does not yet amount to a full picture in the *Praeparatio*, it is clarified and supplemented in the *Demonstratio*. The religious and philosophical truth had been known to the ancestors of the Jews from olden times, long before Moses and the birth of Jewish nation. Therefore one had to draw a clear distinction (διαρθρῶσαι) between Jews, who did not exist in those early days, and their ancestors, who were Hebrew in name and character.[11] Here Eusebius explains the etymology of "Jew" and "Hebrew" as deriving from Judah and Ever, respectively. Moses was the first to legislate a constitution for the Jews. He taught them to observe the Sabbath for the study of the Law, to distinguish between different animals for food, about holidays, festivals and laws of purity. But the patriarchs, who had never heard of the Law of Moses, led unfettered lives unrestricted by their religion, maintaining a balanced way of life "according to nature" (κατὰ φύσιν). Thus they did not require laws to rule them, since their

---

[11] *PE* 7,6,1–2.

souls were free from passions and wantonness. This was why they received the true knowledge of the concepts concerning God (γνῶσιν δὲ ἀληθῆ τῶν περὶ θεοῦ δογμάτων).[12]

Moses himself was a "Hebrew of Hebrews". He was "the great theologian" (ὁ μέγας θεολόγος Μωσῆς Ἑβραῖος ὢν ἐξ Ἑβραίων). In other words, Moses was a Hebrew, but wrote his Law for the Jews. Drawing on his excellent knowledge and understanding of the exemplary lives of his Hebrew ancestors, he prefaced his holy laws with a description of the lives of these ancestors as models for a moral, pious, and virtuous life.[13] Eusebius next offers a hagiographic portrayal of these Hebrew ancestors in the spirit of allegorical interpretation. Under the title "ancestors of the Hebrews" or the "ancient Hebrews", he includes Enosh, Enoch, Noah,[14] and Melchizedek, who preceded Abraham.[15] Then he returns to the motif, by now familiar, that Abraham was justified by faith rather than by the Law. But now a new dimension is added to his words. The promises to Abraham—". . . for a father of many nations have I made thee" (Gen. 17:5), and ". . . and all the nations of the earth shall be blessed in him" (Gen. 18:18)—are regarded as being fulfilled by the Christians of Eusebius' own day.[16] The hagiographic account of the Hebrew patriarchs extends to include Isaac, Job, Jacob, Jacob's sons, and Joseph.[17]

After Joseph's time, the Hebrew people in Egypt greatly multiplied and the exemplary influence of their ancestors' lives began to fade. At the same time, the vile influence of the Egyptians and their customs increased to the point where the virtuous life of their Hebrew ancestors was completely forgotten. The people lived according to the customs and traditions of the Egyptians. It was at this wretched time that the Jewish nation was born,[18] and that God sent Moses to the people as leader and legislator. Moses gave them a constitu-

---

[12] *PE* 7,6,3–4.

[13] *PE* 7,7,1.

[14] It was before Noah's time that the art of sorcery (γοητεία) was invented (*PE* 7,8,12).

[15] Sirinelli ascribes special significance to the expansion of the concept of "Hebrews" to include their ancestors as far back as Enosh. According to him, this indicates a conscious decision by Eusebius to set the beginning of Hebrew-Christian history as close as possible to Adam and the dawn of humanity (ibid., pp. 151–152).

[16] *PE* 7,8,16.

[17] *PE* 7,8.

[18] *PE* 7,8,26. For Eusebius, the Egyptians were the most superstitious of nations (*DE* 5,4; 6,20), and Egypt was a symbol of corruption and degeneration (*DE* 9,2).

tion particularly suited to their precarious moral condition, when they were no longer able to live according to the model of the patriarchs. Moses included all the old truths in his Law, but some of them were now only hinted at in "symbols and shades" (σύμβολά τε καὶ σκιάς). He prophesied that his Law, with all its commandments, would survive only until the coming of Jesus Christ with his Law of the new covenant.[19] From here Eusebius goes on to examine the method (τὸν δογματικὸν τρόπον) of the Hebrews, that is, their theology according to the writings of the theologians Moses and the prophets,[20] and to prove that "the theology of the Hebrews" was superior to the theologies of all other philosophical schools. The prophets themselves, like their forefathers, were Hebrew theologians—unlike to the rest of the people of Israel, the Jews.[21] In his account of Hebrew theology, and especially in his presentation of the Logos-theology and the creation of the world, Eusebius draws on Philo and the Hellenistic Jewish writer Aristobulus,[22] whom he takes to be Hebrew theologians. In a similar context, he also refers to "Josephus the Hebrew."[23] It seems that, for Eusebius, Aristobulus, Philo, and even Josephus, were followers of the ancient Hebrews, like the prophets who preceded them. Although he takes Philo's work to represent the pure and original Hebrew doctrine that appeared in the Bible, in these chapters Eusebius actually expounds his own Christian theology as if it were the theology of the ancient Hebrews. Thus, he establishes that the Logos-theology and the Holy Trinity, which he conceives in terms of a subordinating hierarchy, are identical to Hebrew theology. The superiority of this Hebrew theology was the reason that Christians preferred it.[24] Eusebius also calls the apostle John a "Hebrew of Hebrews", whereas he labels Paul a "Hebrew

---

[19] *PE* 7,8,28–29.

[20] *PE* 7,8, 29–30.

[21] *PE* 7,11,7–11. Here Eusebius is forced to account for the style of Scripture—so different from that of systematic philosophical discussion—explaining that it is a didactic style (*PE* 7,11,1). The "crude" style of Scripture was attacked by pagans; see *CC* 4,50; 6,1; 6,2. Earlier apologetic writers felt a particular need to explain the inferiority of the literary style of Scripture; see Theophilus, *Ad Autolycum* 1,1; Clement, *Stromateis* 1,10; Minucius Felix, *Octavius* 16,6. This charge is reflected in a number of places in Eusebius' work; see *HE* 3,24,3; *PE* 12,4; 12,5; 12,20; 7,11. Pagan charges of this kind continued for a long time, as is attested by Jerome (*Epistle* 22,3) and Augustine (*Confessions* 3,5,9). This topic will be further addressed in Chapter 7 of this study.

[22] *PE* 7,12–14.

[23] *PE* 10,6.

[24] *PE* 7,15.

theologian". Thus a clear identity and continuity is established between
Hebrew and Christian theology.[25] Throughout the rest of the seventh book of the *PE*, he continues to examine the true doctrines of
Hebrew theology regarding angels, powers of evil, the creation of
man, creation *ex nihilo*, and the origin of evil.[26]

In the eighth book of the *PE*, Eusebius describes the Jewish civil
polity and its laws from the time of Moses. This is the second stage
in the history of religion peculiar to the Jewish nation. His purpose
here is to show, in the framework of the idealization of the Hebrews,
toward whom the Christians turned, that even the laws and regula-
tions of the state as set up by Moses were the most advanced among
the nations. These laws were unique to the Jews since Moses adapted
them for the Jews, and not for any other of the world's nations.
Moreover, these laws could not be kept by all men. Those living far
from Judea, like the Greeks or barbarians, were prevented from
observing them.[27] This book is composed almost entirely of quotations from the writings of Hellenistic Jewish authors. It is apologetic
and evinces a marked tendency toward idealization.

This second phase in the history of religion, the Jewish stage, is
also part of the divine scheme that was to presage the arrival of the
Redeemer of humanity. In this historical stage special importance
was assigned to the Septuagint. The translation of Scripture into
Greek was an act of preparation (προπαρασκευή) for the appearance
of Jesus, disseminating the biblical prophecies about him among the
nations and through public libraries. Without God's will and that of
Ptolemy, the Jews would have concealed the Scriptures through jeal-
ousy of the Christians, to whom the prophecies referred.[28] The long
list of citations that constitute the bulk of the eighth book is inter-
spersed with several short interludes in which Eusebius tries to tackle
a particular problem in his concept. Historical Christianity was born
out of later Judaism, and not directly from the patriarchs. In other
words, it grew out of the second, Jewish, stage of religion.

---

[25] *PE* 11,19.
[26] *PE* 7,16–22.
[27] *PE* 8,1.
[28] *PE* 8,1,6–7. For the positive preparatory role of the Law and Scripture in the
progress of humanity, see also *DE* 8, Preface, and *HE* 1,2,17–27. For the Christian accusation of the Jews as falsifiers of Scripture, see W. Adler, "The Jews as
Falsifiers: Charges of Tendentious Emendations in Anti-Jewish Christian Polemics",
in *Translations of Scripture: Proceedings of a Conference at the Annenberg Research Institute,
May 15, 1989* (Philadelphia, 1990), 1–27.

The solution to this problem lies in Eusebius' discovery that, in this second stage, the historical Jewish people were divided into two groups: between those who lived according to the literal meaning of the laws, and those who attained virtues and led virtuous lives. Moses exempted the latter from the literal meaning of the Law so they could devote themselves to philosophy and to understanding the inner meaning implicit in the laws. These were the "Jewish philosophers" (φιλοσόφων Ἰουδαίων γένος), who impressed so many with their ascetic life. Eusebius identifies the Essenes, described by Philo and Josephus, as such philosophers, adducing Philo's words as proof.[29] Eusebius thereby claims that Philo had already described Moses' division of the people into two, although in reality it is Eusebius' perspective. Philo does not seem to have exempted the extreme Jewish allegorists of his generation from observing the commandments.[30] Nonetheless, Eusebius proceeded to develop the idea of the historical continuity of the Hebrew proto-Christians from the patriarchs through Moses and the prophets, and to view Philo as a "Hebrew philosopher".[31] Here, too, lies the solution to another difficulty stemming from the fact that Christianity was, in fact, born out of later Judaism. Indeed, Eusebius states that he wishes to demonstrate that the theology of the "new" Jews is also a harmonious continuation of the theology

---

[29] *PE* 8,11. At the beginning of the ninth book of the *PE*, Eusebius ventures to show that even Greek historians mentioned the Jews and the Hebrews and their ancient philosophy. Indeed, the Greek writers did not make any distinction between Hebrews and Jews. They thought the Jews' way of life reflected philosophy and a practical morality based on philosophical concepts. The proof for this was Theophrastus' description of the Jews, quoted by Porphyry, as a nation of theological philosophers. Porphyry himself gave the example of the Essenes, whom he viewed as exemplifying a Jewish philosophical way of life. Here Eusebius adduces a proof from Porphyry to support his own view of the Essenes as Hebrew, and not Jewish, philosophers. This indicates that the Greeks, too, attested to the Hebrew character of the philosophers. Porphyry knew about the Essenes from Josephus, but Eusebius prefers, out of tactical considerations, to quote Josephus through Porphyry without mentioning him specifically, even though Porphyry himself refers to Josephus as his source and notes the titles of Josephus' works (Porphyry, *De Abstinentia* 4,11). Perhaps this is also why Eusebius avoids citing Josephus earlier, when he quotes Philo on the Essenes. At the end of the third chapter, after quoting Josephus through Porphyry, Eusebius says that this was Porphyry's testimony, taken from ancient sources, on the piety and philosophy of the Essenes (*PE* 9,1–3). It appears that this entire treatment is deliberate and stems from Eusebius' general tendency to prefer Porphyry as a source of proof. In the tenth book of *PE*, Eusebius sets out to demonstrate that not only did the Greeks know the doctrines of the Hebrews and praise them, but they also became enthusiastic imitators of them (*PE* 10,1).

[30] See Philo, *On the Migration of Abraham* 89–93.

[31] *PE* 8,10,10–11.

of Moses and patriarchs.[32] There was no contradiction here with his distinction between Hebrews and Jews, since the "Jewish philosophers" themselves were Hebrews who continued the tradition of their ancestors and the prophets, while living among the Jews. Eusebius' main example of this is Philo, the Hebrew philosopher who represented both the original Hebrew theology and philosophy, and the modern version,[33] that readily assumed Christian garb and could be adapted to the Christian theology of his day.[34]

At the beginning of the *DE* Eusebius delineates its polemical framework—the rejection of the charge that Christianity had deviated from Judaism. In order to reply in detail, Eusebius had first to sketch a portrait of the Christian religion. In so doing, he returns to the principal constituents of his doctrine. He then attempts to solve problems stemming from the identification of the religion of the patriarchs with historical Christianity. Eusebius repeats his claim that Christianity is not a form of Hellenism or Judaism, but an independent and unique religion. It was not a new creation, but an ancient one, a natural religion that had been known to the divine men who lived before the days of Moses. He goes on to repeat his definition of Judaism as the political entity founded according to the Law of Moses (τὴν κατὰ τὸν Μωσέως νόμον διατεταγμένην πολιτείαν) under the one omnipotent God, reiterating the triple division of humanity into Jews, Hellenes—including all Gentiles—and Christians. According to his definition, the ancients—Enoch, Noah, Japeth, the patriarchs, Job, and the others—were neither Hellenes nor Jews. They led lives of piety, holiness, and justice. He concludes therefore, that they lived according to the ideals of a different religion, which guided their life. This religion was a third religion, which stood in the middle (μεταξύ), between Judaism and Hellenism. It was the oldest religion and the most venerable philosophy. It was the religion heralded recently by the savior of all nations—Christianity. Therefore those who passed from Hellenism to Christianity did not join Judaism, and those who rejected the Jewish religion did not automatically become Hellenes. Rather, they ascended to the middle road, one that had been traversed by the holy men of old. This road was restored by

---

[32] *PE* 8,12,13–14.
[33] *PE* 8,12,14.
[34] For Philo's influence on ecclesiastical writers see D.T. Runia, *Philo in Early Christian Literature: A Survey* (Assen, 1993). For Philo's possible influence on Eusebius' theological and philosophical views see H. Berkhof, *Die Theologie des Eusebius von Caesarea*, pp. 24–29; Ulrich, ibid., pp. 88–100.

the redeeming Lord, according to the prophecies of Moses and the other prophets.[35]

Eusebius' argument here strives, somewhat more clearly than in the *PE*, to destroy the basis for the dual charge against Christianity, namely, of deserting paganism in favor of Judaism, and of deviating from Judaism while preserving its Scripture. In the *PE*, the main target was the idealization of Judaism and the presentation of its two historical phases, in order to answer the accusation of desertion in favor of a petty barbarian religion. Out of this presentation there also emerged the concept of a distinction between the religion of the patriarchs—ancient Christianity—and the historical Judaism of the Law, as well as the distinction between Hebrews and Jews. Here the main purpose is to demonstrate that the Christians have, in fact, advanced to the ideal religion, one that is distinct from Judaism. The picture that results is essentially similar, but the progressive structure of the work explains the repetition and the different emphases.

Eusebius seems to have sensed, however, that the idyllic picture he painted of the identity between the religion of the patriarchs and Christianity was not entirely adequate. The difficulty remained, since Christians accepted Scripture but did not act according to it. So here, in Book 1 of the *DE*, he offers a more realistic solution. Had Moses legislated a constitution more similar to that of the ancestors, he argues, it would have been possible for all nations to adopt it, i.e., all Gentiles would have followed Judaism, defined as a political entity where one lived according to the Law of Moses. However, from the start, Moses' polity was unsuitable for the nations of the world. It was suitable only for the Jews, and not even for all Jews, but only for the inhabitants of Judea. Hence the need to found a religion different from that of Moses, under which all nations would be able to live as followers of Abraham, and to share with him the divine promise.[36] Eusebius, then, does not entirely suppress the practical aspect of abrogating the demand of Gentile Christians to observe the commandments of the Law. He recognizes the difficulty, or impossibility, of adhering to this demand.

According to Eusebius' thesis, Moses' original intention was to limit his Law to those Jews living within the boundaries of the land of Israel. He finds support for this in the commandment to make a

---

[35] *DE* 1,2.
[36] *DE* 1,2,16.

pilgrimage to Jerusalem three times a year.[37] For those who did not
live in the vicinity of Judea, it was impossible to make such annual
pilgrimages. If this commandment could not be kept even by Jews
living far from the land of Israel, it was ill suited to nations dispersed throughout the world. To justify this claim, Eusebius goes on
to present the rules on sacrifices and purification that required one's
presence at the Temple. It was unreasonable to suppose that Moses
demanded compliance with these rules by Jews or Gentiles living far
away, even laying a curse on those who could not adhere to them.
His Law was difficult enough for the inhabitants of Judea to observe.[38]

The reason that Christians nevertheless accepted Scripture was
that they contained prophecies about the Christians and the coming of the "lawgiver of the Gentiles" (νομοθέτου τῶν ἐθνῶν), Jesus
Christ.[39] Eusebius finds prophetic verses that voice his main arguments. In the Psalm of King David, who was considered a prophet,
a distinction was made between the two covenants. The old covenant
was given as a law to the Jews when they had fallen away from the
religion of their forefathers, embraced the manners and life of the
Egyptians, and succumbed to the errors of polytheism and the idolatrous superstitions of Gentiles. It was intended to set them back on
their feet. Then came the new covenant, to start them on the road
to the promised kingdom of God. This was the law that would go
forth out of Zion to "all the nations", in the words of the prophet
Isaiah (Isa. 2:2,3). It was different from the law enacted by Moses
in Sinai. The Lord lived and taught in Jerusalem and on Mount
Zion. It was from there that the Gospel of the new covenant was
carried by the disciples to the whole world.[40]

---

[37] *DE* 1,3.
[38] *DE* 1,3. For P.W.L. Walker, Eusebius' claim that Moses limited Judaism to
the boundaries of Judea demonstrates Eusebius' rejection of the interest in Jerusalem,
the land of Israel, and holy places that characterized Judaism; see P.W.L. Walker,
*Holy City, Holy Places? Christian Attitudes to Jerusalem and the Holy Land in the Fourth Cen-
tury* (Oxford, 1990), pp. 58–59. For a discussion of Eusebius' complex attitude to
the holy places, see also R.L. Wilken, *The Land Called Holy* (New Haven & London, 1992), pp. 82–100. A generally similar argument, albeit with some differences,
was presented by Origen. The old Law was intended for a single nation sharing a
common tradition and customs, and was not suitable for all. Therefore it was impossible for all nations to live by it (*CC* 4,22). What appears to be the conclusion is
actually an assumption shared by Origen and Eusebius: it was impossible for all
nations to abide by the Law. See also Ulrich, ibid., pp. 154–160.
[39] *DE* 1,4,1.
[40] *DE* 1,4.

Thus the life and teachings of Jesus were the renaissance of the old religion of Abraham. This religion was suited to become the ideal of the new covenant for all nations, for any people or country.[41] Here Eusebius again invokes the idealization of the ancients, including Melchizedek and Job, according to the biblical verses.[42] The Christians shared the religion of the ancestors who, like the Christians, were worthy of knowing and witnessing the Christ-Logos. Christ was revealed to them and sojourned among them. This was a recurrent motif in Eusebius' work. On the various occasions that we are told that God, or the angel of God, revealed himself or talked to one of the ancients, the reference was not to God the omnipotent Father, but rather the "Second God", the Lord (τις δεύτερος, θεὸς καὶ κύριος ἀνηγορευμένος).[43] Thus in addition to the knowledge of God the Father, the ancestors and Christians shared a knowledge of Christ and a correct perception of the Son-Logos. Moreover, says Eusebius, there were many places in Scripture where the ancients were actually called Christians (Χριστοί)! That is to say, not only were they Christians but they were also called Christians.[44] They lived as Christians in an ideal sanctity which was not dependent on Moses' Law. They did not abstain from eating the meat of certain animals, and, like Christians, did not value circumcision. Before the

---

[41] Ibid., 1,5,1–2.

[42] The special status of Melchizedek in Christian tradition goes back as early as the *Epistle to the Hebrews*. Several studies were devoted to this topic in the Christian literature of the first centuries. Two central motifs characterize this figure: the emphasis on the superiority of the uncircumcised Melchizedek over the circumcised Abraham and his descendants, and Melchizedek's being the archetype of a priest to the supreme God—a priest who is not from Aaron's seed, and is in the image of Jesus. As a consequence of identifying the Hebrew patriarchs with the ancient Christians, in Eusebius' concept the proto-Christian figure of Melchizedek loses its original uniqueness; in fact, he is aligned with the ancestors of the Hebrew nation. At the same time, it seems that Eusebius was aware of devaluating the uniqueness of Melchizedek, and also of Job. It is possible that he wished to compensate for this by enlarging his discussion of these two figures, with a special elaboration of the second motif relating to Melchizedek, namely, the concept of the priesthood according to Melchizedek. However this topic goes beyond our limited scope. See J. Sirinelli, "Quelques allusions à Melchisédech dans l'oeuvre d'Eusèbe de Césarée", *Studia Patristica* 6 (1962), pp. 233–247. For previous studies on this topic in Christian literature of the first centuries, see his list, ibid., p. 233.

[43] Verses adduced to support this are given later in the chapter (*DE* 1,5), and throughout the *DE*. This is a recurrent theme in Eusebius' other writings as well (see, e.g., *Prophetic Extracts* 1,3; *HE* 1,4,4–6; *PE* 7,8,16); it was not common among earlier Christian writers, though it appears already in Justin, *Dialogue* 56.

[44] Eusebius adduces Ps. 105,12–15 ". . . touch not mine anointed" (μὴ ἅπτεσθε τῶν χριστῶν μου) as proof that the patriarchs were called Christians (*DE* 1,5,20).

Law of Moses there was a different set of divine commandments, the commandments of Christ, in which the ancients were justified. Moses himself testified to them. In his youth, he still lived according to the old laws, growing up in the house of the daughter of the king of Egypt, and partaking of Egyptian food without hesitation. The figure of Job is singled out as an ideal model of Christian piety in the time preceding Moses. According to Eusebius, Job lived two generations before Moses.[45]

The ancients were considered friends of God and prophets, and did not require Moses' laws, which were meant for weaklings and sinners.[46] The new covenant was both old and new. It was new in that, having been concealed since the days of Moses, it seemed to be reborn to new life through the teachings of the Savior. But the degeneration had begun earlier in Egypt, when the ideal of the new covenant was forgotten. The Law of Moses was introduced to nurse those childish souls. Or, to use a different image, it came as a physician, to heal a nation which had contracted the terrible Egyptian disease. Hence the Law had to introduce a less perfect way of life to the children of Abraham, who were too weak to follow their ancestors as a result of having adopted Egyptian customs, becoming idolatrous and, in fact, being like Egyptians in every way.

Moses was the first lawgiver in history to create a legal codex. But he adapted his laws to the defective condition of the people. He knew from the Holy Spirit that his Law was only temporary and would become superfluous when the new covenant was renewed by the Messiah and spread among the nations. That was why he limited its validity to one place. He did this knowing that there might come a time when the people would be denied its land, lose its national liberty and no longer be able to observe the commandments in a foreign country. Then the Jews would be forced to accept the new covenant heralded by the Messiah.[47] Here Eusebius repeats and develops the idea that Moses purposely limited the validity of his Law, thereby continuing his tendency of delegitimizing post-Jesus historical Judaism. Since Moses himself inserted into his Law a condition that would force Jews to accept the Gospel of the new covenant,

---

[45] See, especially, *DE* 1,6,13–17.

[46] Ibid. Krauss notes that Eusebius was aware of the rabbinic idea that the patriarchs had already obeyed the precepts of the Tora. See Krauss, "The Jews in the Writings of the Church Fathrers", p. 84.

[47] *DE* 1,6,31–38.

there was no justification for an ongoing Jewish phase in the history of the people and its religion. In this light, the Jews' refusal to accept Christianity was a rejection of Moses' will.

Moses predicted the renewal of the new covenant by the Messiah and the fulfillment of the terms that he set. Immediately after the coming of the Messiah and the promulgation of his teachings among the Gentiles, the Romans had besieged Jerusalem, destroying the city and the Temple. This spelled the end of Moses' Law and whatever remained of the old covenant. From then on, a curse had been placed on the heads of the Jews, who became lawbreakers (παρα-νομοῦντες) when they continued to observe the commandments after they were no longer valid and had been replaced by the new and perfect Law.[48] The Romans' destruction of the Temple and of Jeru-salem was therefore an integral part of the divine scheme. It nulli-fied any remaining validity in Moses' Law and the old covenant. From then on, those who continued to live according to the Law of Moses were lawbreakers. The new Law revealed with the com-ing of the Messiah was, in fact, the ancient Law by which the patri-archs lived.[49]

Eusebius finds support for his concept not only in Moses' words but also among the prophets.[50] He now repeats more figuratively the idea of the triple division of humanity, of which the prophets had already spoken. It was not merely a horizontal division but a verti-cal one as well. It reflected three stages leading to a recognition of religious truth: (1) those who were totally idolatrous in their poly-theistic error; (2) the people of the circumcision, who with the help of Moses, attained the lowest degree (βαθμός) in the ranks of holi-ness; and (3) those who had climbed the ladder of the Gospel's teach-ing (εὐαγγελικὴ διδασκαλία). From the perspective of progress in religious consciousness, Christianity stood above Judaism and Hel-lenism. From the perspective of religious and social reality, it stood in the middle. As noted, it does not follow from this triple division that those who seceded from Judaism or paganism in fact joined the other religion. The image that combines these horizontal and verti-cal divisions is that of Christianity standing on a high mountain ridge with Judaism and paganism occupying the deep valleys on either

---

[48] *DE* 1,6,39.
[49] Ibid., 1,6,40.
[50] Ibid., 1,6,41–61.

side. Christianity left behind Greek error and corruption, and the
useless Jewish commandments invented by Moses for the childish
and crippled Jews.[51] This graphic description is Eusebius' principal
response to the double charge against Christians. They had indeed
abandoned paganism, but not in favor of Judaism, rather to embrace
the third religion—the ancient Christian religion. At the same time
they had also rejected Judaism because they recognized the truth of
the revived ancient Christian religion. In Eusebius' dramatic description, personified Christianity stands at the summit of a high mountain declaring to humanity the new Law that befitted every nation
under the sun. It is a dramatic oration that includes verses from the
Gospel of Matthew and briefly summarizes the essence of Eusebius'
views. The speech ends with the promise of a reward to those who
deserve it—a land of milk and honey, and citizenship of the Kingdom of Heaven.[52]

II. *Major Conceptual Problems and Their Solutions*

The Life of Jesus according to the Law of Moses

Eusebius was aware of a particular difficulty inherent in his concept.
Jesus had brought a new law to the world. His advent abrogated
the validity of the Law of Moses. Jesus, however, is described as one
who lived according to the Mosaic law in all its aspects. The problem is transformed into a source of wonder—that Jesus, who was
about to be revealed as the new lawgiver of the new covenant, did
not rebel against Moses and did not oppose him. According to Eusebius, Jesus behaved in this manner for tactical reasons, not because
of his principles. Jesus had to be careful. Had he preached openly
against the Law of Moses, he would have served the purpose of the
heretics (αἱρεσιῶται) and supplied them with arguments against Moses
and the prophets. He would also have given the Jews grounds for
attacking him. For they already viewed Jesus as a rebel and a law-
breaker.[53] Eusebius' reply seems rather unconvincing. There is an
indirect admission of caution, even fear, on the part of Jesus. Such
caution and suspicion could not be explained by the usual response

---

[51] *DE* 1,6,62.
[52] *DE* 1,6,64–73.
[53] *DE* 1,6,7.

to the frequently repeated anti-Christian charges of cowardice on the part of Jesus, namely, by invoking the prophets' words that Christ would appear on earth in humility and wretchedness. Apparently, aware of this, Eusebius proposed another explanation. Jesus lived according to the Mosaic law. He did not transgress any command-ments, but rather brought them to completion (πληρωτὴν αὐτῶν γενέσ-θαι) and proceeded to establish the doctrine of the Gospel.[54] But this completion was apparently not to be found in Jesus' meticulous obser-vance of the commandments. Occasionally, Eusebius moves unwit-tingly from an ideological to a tactical explanation. Here he writes that if Jesus had violated the commandments of the Law, he would have been rightly regarded as abolishing the Law and proposing a new one in its stead. Likewise, if Jesus had transgressed the Law, it would have been impossible to have considered him the Messiah. Moreover, had he abrogated the Law of Moses, he could not have been viewed as the one whose coming had been prophesied by Moses and the prophets, and thus his new doctrine would have had no authority. Jesus, however, was the fulfillment (πληρότης) of the Torah and the prophets because he completely fulfilled the prophecies about himself (τὰς περὶ ἑαυτοῦ προρρήσεις εἰς πέρας ἀγαγών).[55]

The Numerous Progeny of the Patriarchs

The identification of historical Christianity, or even that of Eusebius' time, with the religion of the patriarchs raised further difficulties. The differences between the two were obvious and there were major discrepancies to be explained. For example, the family life, fertility, and many offspring of the patriarchs sharply contrasted with the Christian way of life. Eusebius held that abstinence and asceticism constituted the ideal Christian life. He thereby attested to the impor-tance of the ascetic ideal in Christianity even before its recognition of the monastic movement. But according to Eusebius, there were two paths to the Christian life, both anchored in the teaching of Christ. The elite were those who withdrew from the world and gave up property and married life. Out of heavenly love (ἔρως) they ex-changed normal lives for a life of service to God alone. They chose the first path, the perfect Christian way of life. For the rest of the

---

[54] *DE* 1,7,1.
[55] *DE* 1,7,14.

faithful, who lived with the weakness of human needs and desires, there was an alternative. This path allowed marriage in a state of purity, and procreation; administrative, government, and military service; work in agriculture and commerce, and other worldly occupations. For such people, there were regular, appointed times for the study of Scripture. Their religiosity was on a lower level (τις δεύτερος εὐσεβείας βαθμός). Eusebius implies that the elite did not need the above, and that both ways of life were part of the teaching of Christ.[56] The compromise regarding a Christian life for the majority was fully legitimate, despite its essential inferiority to the ascetic ideal. This was a far cry from the comfortable bourgeois way of life led by the Christian upper class of Alexandria, which was idealized by Clement of Alexandria, though of course he recommended moderation and restrictions.[57]

Eusebius notes the striking contrast between the patriarchs' preoccupation with marriage and procreation, and the ascetic ideal of Christianity. The latter might be interpreted as proof that Christians did not observe the ideals of the pristine religion.[58] He proposes three

---

[56] *DE* 1,8,4.

[57] *Stromateis* 3, 49–104; 7,12; *The Instructor* 2; *Who Is the Rich Man that Shall Be Saved?* 11, 16. He does not find any innovation in the Christian injunction to give up money and possessions to help the needy. However, the difference between Christians and others lay in the allegorical meaning of the reference in Luke 10:41–42 to abandoning money and possessions, namely, one had to divest oneself of passions (*Who Is the Rich Man*, 11). Ownership of wealth and property even had a positive religious Christian value, for it allowed one to help others. Without capital it was impossible to fulfill Jesus' commandment to aid and assist (op. cit., 14). The poor in spirit were free from the desire for money and possessions, rather than actually without. Money and possessions were of no consequence as far as values were concerned (op. cit., 16). Clement even interprets the Epistle to the Philippians 4:3 as meaning that Paul had a consort! (*Stromateis* 3,53). In fact, although Clement presents the ideal of married life as an antidote to the radical ideas of the gnostic sects, it also reflects his general approval of family life and comfortable circumstances. For a survey of ascetic tendencies in early Christianity and a discussion of Clement's position see H. Chadwick, "Enkrateia", *RAC* 5 (1962), cols. 349–365. Eusebius expresses a similar view elsewhere. Such opinions are at variance with the idealization of poverty and lack of possessions, and may have served to counter extreme expressions of the ascetic ideal. Eusebius speaks of the ideal, "golden mean" between wealth and poverty. Poverty itself was not ideal and could give rise to cruel pettiness (*PE* 12,35). Such statements recall Origen, who held in high esteem not poverty or the poor, but "the poor in spirit". Most of the poor had bad character! (*CC* 6,16). It is somewhat surprising to find such a marked absence of idealization of poverty in Origen.

[58] It is possible that underlying these statements is a problem on which Eusebius did not elaborate. Tatian, in particular, denounces the pagans' numerous progeny as proof of their licentiousness (*Address to the Greeks*, 34). This is an anti-pagan, Chris-

answers to this problem: (1) The patriarchs lived at the starting-point of humanity and had to be concerned with strengthening and enlarging its population, whereas Christians now lived at a time when the end of the world was approaching, and did not have to care about such matters.[59] (2) The ancients lived when physical conditions were simpler, and worldly concerns of subsistence and family life did not impede a full religious life. This was not true for the Christians. In Eusebius' time, worldly concerns distracted men from the religious life and led to evil thoughts. Such a statement contains an interesting variation on the classical motif of the diminishing generations. Eusebius adduces I Corinthians 7:29–35 as proof, for it notes the eschatological impulse as an important factor in justifying an abstinence from women—one of Eusebius' ideals, as we have noted.[60] (3) A further explanation for the intensive procreation on the part of the ancients, lies in a form of 'religious Darwinism'. The rest of the human race was mired in licentiousness and corruption. The ancients were thus obliged to preserve their superior seed (ζῶπυρον σπέρμα) and to bequeath to posterity the benefit of their learning and way of life. This could not have occurred had they lived a life of abstinence.[61] Furthermore, there was no need for Eusebius' contemporaries to bear numerous children, because many Gentiles were now flocking to the teaching of the Gospel. The many teachers who lived a life of abstinence could now engage in less mundane matters, and nurture the numerous believers as their spiritual children.[62]

The ancients and the patriarchs had, in fact, practiced a form of abstinence. Their children were born when they were young men, and later they refrained from fathering children. Enoch, Noah, Isaac, Joseph, Moses, and Aaron, exemplified such conduct. According to Eusebius, Melchizedek, Joshua, and many other prophets did not

---

tian argument. It also may have been used by the pagans as an anti-Christian argument, though it is not mentioned by Eusebius in this context.

[59] *DE* 1,9. Beyond apologetics, this reply may contain an authentic apocalyptic sentiment. Eusebius rarely expresses his eschatological beliefs. See his commentary on Luke, discussed in Chapter 2 of this study.

[60] *DE* 1,9, 1–7. See also Ferrar's note in his translation, p. 51. He remarks that it is interesting to find Paul's eschatological motivation for abstinence invoked as a justification for abstinence in the fourth century. In his opinion, an immanent eschatological sense played a more important role in the growth of Egyptian monasticism than had previously been thought.

[61] *DE* 1,9,8–13.

[62] *DE* 1,9,14–15.

have any children. He uses an *argumentum ex silentio* to prove his conclusions: if Scripture did not record the offspring of a particular
figure, then he had none. Eusebius refers the reader to a more comprehensive discussion of this question in a special work that he
devoted to the subject, entitled *On the Multiplication of Offspring amongst
the Ancients* (Περὶ τῆς τῶν παλαιῶν ἀνδρῶν πολυπαιδίας).[63] Prompted by
the growth of ascetic trends in Christianity, the anti-Christian critique, and the problems inherent in identifying the religion of the
patriarchs with that of historical Christianity, Eusebius explored this
subject at some length, devoting a monograph to it. The work has
been lost.[64] Eusebius closes his discussion on polygamy and numerous offspring with a recommendation to the clergy to refrain from
marital relations (γαμικὴ ὁμιλία) after ordination.[65]

The Problem of Sacrifices

Another major difficulty in identifying the religion of the patriarchs
with Christianity is the problem of sacrifices. The ancients gave sacrifices and offerings—a fact which must be considered further in a
polemical context. The polemical framework of Book IV of the *PE*
is the anti-Christian accusation that the Christians had greatly erred
in not honoring the divine powers and their cults. Their rejection
of the pagan cults and sacrifices to the gods constituted one of the
major arguments against Christians. The important issue of sacrifices had been discussed in the *PE* in the framework of the critique
of pagan religion in its the various forms. In this discussion, Eusebius manoeuvers between different opinions that Porphyry raises in
On Abstinence from Animal Flesh (*De Abstinentia*) (Περὶ τῆς τῶν ἐμψύχων
ἀποξῆς) and *On the Philosophy from the Oracles* (Περὶ τῆς ἐκ λογίων
φιλοσοπίας), in order to point out contradictions between the two
works. He also wanted to emphasize Porphyry's negative approach
in order to point out the futility of offering sacrifices and the inferior religious position that such a practice denoted.[66]

---

[63] *DE* 1,9,16–20. The name of the work is mentioned in *PE* 7,8,29. Here Eusebius describes the subject in general without naming it specifically (περὶ τῆς τῶν
πάλαι θεοφιλῶν ἀνδρῶν πολυγαμίας καὶ πολυπαιδίας).

[64] In fact, Eusebius states, in *PE* 7,8,20, that his monograph also described the
lives of the patriarchs in general.

[65] *DE* 1,9,21. This topic was discussed and rejected at the Council of Nicaea.
However, clergy was not allowed to marry after ordination.

[66] *PE* 4,8–10.

In *Philosophy from the Oracles*, Porphyry presents a symbolic interpretation of the various types of sacrifices, according to the respective gods.[67] *On Abstinence* gives expression to Porphyry's negative view of sacrifices. The idea of sacrifice undergoes a familiar spiritualization in Porphyry's works. The true sacrifice was service of the heart and silent prayer.[68] In order to rebut pagans, whose representatives equated Apollonius of Tyana—the well-known "enemy" of Christianity—with Jesus, Eusebius could also have adduced statements attributed to Apollonius. The *Life of Apollonius* has an approach similar to Porphyry's spiritualization of sacrifices.[69] According to his own testimony, Porphyry accepted the "historiosophical" concept of sacrifice articulated by Theophrastus, and viewed the development of sacrifice in the history of religion as a symptom of the degeneration of mankind.[70] Porphyry likewise pointed out the negative educational effect of offering sacrifices. When a child learned that the gods enjoyed expensive feasts of animal flesh, he would never prefer moderation and thrift. If he believed that the gods desired such sacrifices, he would inevitably think that he could do evil, in the certain knowledge that he could atone for his sin through such a sacrifice. The gods did not need sacrifices. They oversaw the moral behavior of men, and accepted a correct opinion of them as the greatest offering. From such a belief, man could act intelligently, righteously, and piously. Thus Porphyry concludes that "the most worthy sacrifice to the gods is purity of thought and a soul free of passions" (νοῦς καθαρὸς καὶ ψυχὴ ἀπαθής).[71]

Basing his argument on the above, Eusebius concluded that according to the Greeks and their philosophers, one could not sacrifice any living creature to the gods. Such an act was unholy, unjust, and damaging, to the point of being unclean and impure. This conclusion helps to shape his general approach to the phenomenon of sacrifices, which he views as a diabolical invention on the part of cruel demons identified with the gods of the pagan pantheon.[72] The culmination of this demonic scheme was human sacrifice, which persisted even up to the time of Jesus. Only through him, and the

---

[67] *PE* 4, 9.
[68] *PE* 4,11; *On Abstinence* 2,34.
[69] *PE* 4,12–13.
[70] *PE* 4,14,1–2; *On Abstinence* 2,11.
[71] *PE* 4,14,8.
[72] *PE* 4,14,9–10.

subsequent promulgation of the Gospel of salvation, was mankind
redeemed from the rule of demons, and human sacrifice virtually
ceased, though they actually continued at least until the reign of
Hadrian.[73]

Together with the cessation of human sacrifice, there was a sharp
decline in conventional sacrifices. Eusebius attests to the prevalent
neglect of pagan temples and cults, a fact which he invokes to refute
the argument that Christians did not participate in the cults. The
decline of pagan sacrifices was proof that God did not want them
and that the only acceptable offerings were the spiritual sacrifices of
the Christians.[74] Oracles, fortune-telling, and sacrifices in general
belonged to the demons who lured the public. Hence Eusebius' conclusion that anyone who sacrificed to demons in the past could not
be called intelligent or wise; the true philosophers, therefore, were
the Christians.[75] Demonstrating his skills as a polemicist, Eusebius'
final and definitive conclusion maintains, ironically, that Porphyry's
words were exemplified by the Christians.[76]

When Eusebius set out to solve the problem of identifying patri-
archal religion with Christianity, as concerns sacrifices, he began with
the polemical context. He endeavors to respond to the charge that,
whereas the patriarchs offered sacrifices, the Christians, who posed
as their successors did not sacrifice to God.[77] His primary aim is to

---

[73] *PE* 4,17. For the discussion on human sacrifice, see *PE* 4,15–20. In his discussion of the subject, Eusebius presents Porphyry's statements on human sacrifice
together with a number of historical examples from different peoples and countries.
Porphyry declares that human sacrifice existed in his own time (*PE* 4,16). When
Eusebius determined that human sacrifice had ceased under Hadrian, he probably
ignored Porphyry's statements, as they did not corroborate his own position. In
fact, Porphyry also claimed that human sacrifice belonged essentially to the past
(*On Abstinence* 2,56.) Eusebius' discussion on human sacrifice is actually based on
Porphyry, who quotes the Greek author Pallas' statement that Hadrian had forbidden human sacrifice and that it had all but ceased during his reign. In fact, he
adds that a form of human sacrifice continued even in contemporary Rome (*On
Abstinence* 2,56). Tertullian also claimed that the sacrifice of children to Saturn had
secretly continued in North Africa even in his own time (*Apology* 9,2). The cessation of human sacrifice was a direct result of the end of domination by the demons.
In a discussion on demons in another place, Eusebius also cites Plutarch on the
death of the demon during the reign of Tiberius. This event took place in the time
of Jesus, who liberated mankind from demons. Eusebius adduces it as definite proof
of the beginning of the demons' death, similar to the cessation of human sacrifice
(*PE* 5,17).
[74] *PE* 4,4.
[75] *PE* 4,19.
[76] *PE* 4,21.
[77] *DE* 1,10,1.

answer the key criticism that Christians did not offer sacrifices, and to point out that according to the Greeks, the ideal sacrifice was not necessarily an animal sacrifice. He briefly repeats Porphyry's statements, which he had cited in the *PE* in the spirit of Theophrastus. Primitive man neither sacrificed animals nor burned incense to the gods, but waved grass and burned leaves and roots as a sign of the creative power of nature. The second stage of human degeneration occurred when altars were defiled by animal sacrifices. The transgression was a serious one, because humans and animals had a similar, intelligent soul. Thus anyone who sacrificed a living soul was guilty of murder.[78]

Eusebius insists, however, that this concept of the cult practiced by the ancients differed from the accounts in Scripture, which said that man had worshiped God through animal sacrifices since the dawn of Creation. Thus the problem facing Eusebius was how to explain the cult of sacrifice among the early "Christians" in a manner that accorded with his idea of a Christian sacrifice. He wished to explain the question of sacrifices in Scripture in terms of a present-day theory. Ancient men recognized the fact that one had to atone for sins by paying a ransom to the source of life and of the soul, in exchange for deliverance. The most precious and valuable thing that they could sacrifice was their own life. But they offered animals as a substitute—life for life. They did not consider this sinful, because for them the souls of animals were not the same as the souls of men. They knew that the power of life was to be found in the blood. Thus there was proof that the ancients had always sacrificed animals, and that their concept of sacrifice was a theory of ransom.[79] Human life was the most precious thing and, therefore, most suitable for sacrifice. Animal sacrifice was the closest substitute for the ideal, i.e., human sacrifice.

This basic idea did not originate with Eusebius, who presents a variation on a Greek idea mentioned briefly by Dionysius of Halicarnassus in the framework of a lengthy discussion on human sacrifice.[80] Following his usual practice, Eusebius adduces biblical texts to prove this theory. In his explanation of sacrifices in the Bible, Eusebius has to counter Porphyry's opinion, in addition to the view

---

[78] *DE* 1,10,1–2.
[79] *DE* 1,10,3–7.
[80] *PE* 4,16,18.

that animals and humans share an identical soul.[81] Eusebius places
the former in the same category as plants and inorganic matter.
Hence eating meat was not wrong. Eusebius develops his idea of
sacrifice as an introduction, or a foundation upon which one should
add an additional floor. True ransom, the perfect and ultimate sacrifice, was Jesus Christ. The ancients were aware, through the holy
spirit, of the perfect sacrifice of Jesus, and they alluded to this in
the animal sacrifices offered as a ransom for their lives. They believed
that as prophets they had to offer his sacrifice symbolically (τὰ σύμβολα
τέως) as a prefiguration of the future (τὸ μέλλον προτυπουμένους).
Therefore, with the advent of the perfect sacrifice—the lamb of God,
according to the prophets—the previous sacrifices immediately ceased.[82]
The Christian sacrifice that commemorated the sacrifice of the blood
and body of Christ was the Eucharist.[83]

The lamb of God, however, took upon himself not only the sin
of the world, abolishing all sacrifices; he also took upon himself
Moses' curse upon the Jews, who continued to live according to
Moses' laws—as opposed to his words—and thus violated his Law.[84]
The Logos, the high priest of Creation, chose Jesus, the man, as a
sacrifice, casting upon him the sins of the world and the other curse
(κατάρα) of Moses concerning the man hanged on a tree ("the hanged
man accursed by God", Dt. 21:23), which had already been interpreted in the New Testament as the prophecy of Jesus' crucifixion.[85]
The conclusion was that the Christians of Eusebius' time offered sacrifices and burned incense in the form of prayers, in sanctity, and
with a broken heart. Through the prayers and hymns of the Eucharist,

---

[81] The question of the souls of humans and animals had been raised in the past
in pagan-Christian polemics, mainly with regard to Divine Providence. See *CC* 4,88;
4,97–99. According to Celsus, animals also recognized God and enjoyed prophetic
powers, and there was no room for the Christian anthropocentric concept of Divine
Providence. This issue was also a subject of debate between the different schools
of philosophy. Eusebius could very well have used the arguments of the Stoics who
pronounced animals devoid of reason. The debate with the Stoics on this question
occupies most of the third book of *On Abstinence*, which Eusebius knew well and
from which he quoted extensively.

[82] *DE* 1,10,11–14.

[83] Eusebius' statements seem to echo the practice of the daily Eucharist. See Ferrar's note *ad locum* (*The Proof of the Gospel*, p. 58, n. 1).

[84] *DE* 1,10,19.

[85] Epistle to the Galatians 3:13; *DE* 1,10,23. The brief theological formulation
on the Logos' election of Jesus, the man, as a sacrifice follows that of Origen (*CC*
2,9,20–25; *De Princ.* 2,6). See also the note by Ferar which presents Harnack's interpretation of the formulation of Origen's idea.

they sacrificed and burned incense in gratitude for their salvation. At the same time, they kept their bodies and souls unsullied by passions and sin, and worshiped God with the pure thoughts, honest intentions, and the correct belief that God desired more than sacrifices of fat, blood, and smoke.[86] Eusebius develops his argument on two levels. First, Christians offered sacrifices. Secondly, theirs was the true sacrifice, even according to the correct interpretation of the Greek philosophers. This was the perfect sacrifice of Jesus Christ, prefigured in the sacrifices of the patriarchs. Their sacrifice was offered daily in the sacrament of the Eucharist. Thus Eusebius refutes the two major arguments concerning sacrifices: that Christians did not offer sacrifices, and that they thereby contradicted their claim to follow the patriarchs. Thus, in addition to responding within the polemical context, Eusebius also resolved a basic problem posed by identifying historical Christianity with the religion of the ancient Hebrews.

The Christians' Indifference to the Sciences—Conceptual Difficulties and Polemical Problems; The Role of Socrates

Another difficulty in identifying Christianity with the religion of the ancient Hebrews arises from the fact that Eusebius—adopting the approach of Hellenistic Jewish apologists—presents it as an ancient philosophy from which the Greeks took many of their ideas. The Hebrews possessed philosophical truth from the time of Adam, and across the succeeding generations they kept it pure, with no theological changes made by either Moses or the Christian school.[87] For the most part, Hebrew philosophy was identical to Greek philosophy and dealt with the same issues. Eusebius, therefore, has to show that Scripture covered the various branches of philosophy, and to explain the paucity of "natural science" in the Bible. Herein lies an additional example of a circular response to the pagan argument that Christians had defected to "oracles", namely, to Hebrew Scripture. In so doing, according to Eusebius, they were following the great Greek philosophers who were enthusiastic imitators of the Hebrews.[88] But contemporary Christian sages were not interested in the scientific aspects of philosophy, notably physics. They were mainly

---

[86] DE 1,10,38–39.
[87] PE 14,3,1–3.
[88] PE 10,14,12–13.

concerned with ethics. While developing these ideas, Eusebius was
apparently unaware of this inconsistency; he recognized it later, when
he found it difficult to spoil the idealized picture he had painted
earlier. Eusebius solves the problem, but not in the definitive and
harmonious manner in which he had solved other difficulties encountered and recognized in the course of developing his concept. This
problem also has a distinctly polemical aspect, which Eusebius had
to address within its polemical framework—otherwise, it is possible
that the issue would not have been noted. For he refers to the anti-
Christian argument that Christians did not study the natural sciences
(physics), and therefore could not attain knowledge of God, being
like a herd of cattle.[89]

In Book XI of the *PE*, Eusebius shows the affinity between Greek
philosophy and the Hebrew "oracles" (λόγια), especially through Plato
and the Platonic school. He points out the tripartite division of philosophy among the Hebrews into ethics, dialectics (logic), and physics.[90]
He finds no difficulty in giving numerous biblical references in the
fields of ethics and dialectics. Moses, for instance, devoted much
attention in his teaching to cultivating a love of God through moral
behavior. According to his teaching, the purpose of life was religion
and companionship with God. The happy man was the friend of
God. The book of Proverbs was an ethical-philosophical work typical of the genre of *apophthegmata*.[91] The Hebrew religious philosophers
engaged in dialectics by means of divine illumination, and not by
indulging in sophistic arguments in the manner of Greek philosophers. This fact explained the non-philosophical language and style
of Scripture.[92] The book of Proverbs was not only an ethical tract,
but also a dialectic work.[93] Giving names to animals and people was
the specialty of the dialectician, because it was done according to
their nature and not according to a collective agreement. Moses was
the father of dialecticians. In Eusebius' works, Moses seems to act
through divine inspiration. But, as in the writings of Philo, he was

---

[89] *PE* 14,10,8.
[90] *PE* 11,3,6. On this division of philosophy in the *PE*, see E. dal Carolo, "La
filosofia tripartita nella Praeparatio Evangelica di Eusebio di Cesare", *Rivista di storia e letteratura religiosa*, 24 (1988), 515–523.
[91] *PE* 11,4.
[92] I will discuss later the criticism, which recurs several times in the double work,
of the poor literary style of Scripture, and its refutation by Eusebius.
[93] *PE* 11,5.

considered responsible for the arrangement, structure, dialectics, and details of the Torah.[94] Eusebius admits that there are difficulties with regard to physics. Theology, belonging to physics in the tripartite division of philosophy, presented no particular problems. Matters pertaining to the world of knowledge were available to everyone in the Holy Scriptures. But an understanding of the deeper reasons was granted only to a select few. Scripture, however, treated the natural sciences minimally. Eusebius' explanation for this is the simple fact that the Hebrews did not think it proper to present natural sciences to the masses in great detail. Actually, there was no problem in showing that subjects classified under physics were indeed dealt with in Scripture.[95] For example, Abraham was a meteorologist and astronomer.[96] Moses was a geologist, and Solomon a botanist and zoologist. In the opening verses of Ecclesiastes, Solomon explains the transitory nature of bodies and reaches a physiological conclusion that became the source of Plato's definition of the material world.[97]

In *PE* XIV, Eusebius confronts other philosophical schools with the intention of showing that Greek authors deviated from truth. In his discussion of philosophers engaged in "physics", which also includes theology, he points to the philosophers' argument that one cannot reach the truth without advancement in the sciences. At the same time, he sets out the anti-Christian argument that Christians did not study the natural sciences and therefore, could not attain a knowledge of God.[98] Eusebius seems to have taken seriously this double-edged argument and attempts to refute it in two places. His point of departure, however, is his acknowledgment of the fact that his Christian contemporaries did not study the sciences. The thrust of Eusebius' response is based upon pragmatic considerations. Many Greeks who studied the natural sciences neither attained a knowledge of God nor led a virtuous life,[99] while the barbarians excelled in religion and philosophy even without the sciences. The main proof

---

[94] *PE* 11,6. See Y. Amir, "Moses as the Author of the Torah in Philo", *Proceedings of the Israel Academy of Science*, 20, 6 (1980), pp. 83–103 (Hebrew).

[95] *PE* 11,7.

[96] *PE* 11,6. There is much material on astronomy in Scriptures (*PE* 11,7). See also Clement, *Stromateis* 6,11, where Abraham is an astronomer and a mathematician.

[97] *PE* 11,7.

[98] *PE* 14,10,7–8.

[99] *PE* 14,10,9.

of the insignificance and futility of engaging in the natural sciences actually came, in fact, from the paragon of Greek philosophy, Socrates. According to his disciple, Xenophon, Socrates hardly studied the natural sciences at all. He certainly knew the intricacies of geometry but claimed that they could occupy all of one's life and prevent one from studying other subjects. Socrates recommended that one should not waste much time in astronomical investigations.[100] Xenophon even intimates slight criticism of Plato's deviations from his master's teachings on this.[101] Therefore, since the study of physical philosophy was pointless, Moses and the Scriptures did not deal with it![102] It seems that when Eusebius wrote the above, he had forgotten his earlier statements. However, here the polemical context is not intended to prove that Greek philosophy derived from the Hebrews, but rather to justify the fact that Eusebius' Christian contemporaries did not study the natural sciences. Thus Eusebius justifies the Christians' neglect of scientific aspects of Scripture and Hebrew philosophy.

Furthermore, the disagreements among the philosophers on matters of cosmology vindicated Christian diffidence and reservations on the subject, and invalidated their opinions.[103] All the dissension among the philosophers pointed to the absence of truth and demonstrated the futility of studying the scientific area of philosophy, namely, physics.[104] Socrates himself had commented that the disagreements between physical philosophers was proof of the absence of truth among them and the futility of their efforts.[105] By his negation of, or contempt for, physical philosophy, Socrates emerged as a supporter of Christianity. With its focus on ethics, his approach resembled that of the Christian sages.[106] According to Eusebius, ethics were the only proper and beneficial realm of philosophy. Socrates was right, therefore, when he stated that, of those things which exist, some were beyond us and others had no meaning for us, because the secrets of nature were beyond us, and our existence after death

---

[100] *PE* 14,11.

[101] *PE* 14,12; Ps. Xenophon, *Epistle to Aeschines.*

[102] *PE* 15,8. Moses and the Hebrews do not deal with astronomy (*PE* 15,25).

[103] *PE* 15,32. Indeed, according to this principle, it is possible to justify a lack of interest in any controversial philosophical subject where opinion is divided between different schools of philosophy.

[104] *PE* 15,61.

[105] *PE* 1,8; 15,62.

[106] *PE* 15,61, as attested by Xenophon.

was meaningless. Only matters of human life concerned us.[107] In conclusion, Eusebius implies that there is no need to study physics,[108] and that the Christians abandoned the unnecessary study of natural sciences on the basis of intelligent deliberations.[109]

The role played by Socrates in the apologetic framework extends beyond the narrow polemical context described above. Eusebius does not often refer to him directly, but he features in the numerous quotations from the works of Plato and in passages comparing these with quotations from the New Testament. In this framework, Socrates exemplifies the best of the Greeks who accepted and lived according to the truths of early Christianity. Eusebius praises him and calls him "the admirable and marvelous (θαυμάσιος) Socrates",[110] a "great philosopher",[111] and "the wisest of the Greeks".[112] Socrates was aware of the great importance of living according to philosophical truth, and of the difference between a theoretical understanding and a practical moral application.[113] He viewed the purpose of human existence as the attainment of virtues, and therefore refused the gifts offered by rich friends and kings.[114] He recognized the great worth of those who were insulted but did not themselves insult or

---

[107] *PE* 15,62.

[108] Ibid.

[109] *PE* 14,13,6. Clement of Alexandria held an alternative Christian point of view, contrary to that of Eusebius. According to Clement, a true Gnostic (i.e., a Christian), studied all the sciences and benefited from them. Moreover, the study of the sciences was most important in order to defend the truth (*Stromateis* 6,10). Similar to Eusebius' is the attitude to the study of the sciences expressed by his contemporary, Arnobius. He admonishes the pagans that there is no point in investigating whether the sun is larger than the earth or whether its diameter measures only one cubit, or whether the moon receives its light from another source of light or shines with its own light. There was no advantage in obtaining such knowledge and one should leave such matters to God (*Adversus Gentes* 2,21). Lactantius expresses an opinion similar to that of Arnobius (*Div. Inst.*, 3,3,1–5). Grant's description of contemporary Christian interest in the natural sciences corroborates both the pagan arguments and Eusebius' admission of the facts. In fact, Grant notes a certain, albeit slight, difference between Latin and Greek Christians. According to Grant, the Christian lack of interest in science for its own sake reflected, for the most part, a general decline of interest in science. R.M. Grant, *Miracle and Natural Law in Graeco-Roman and Early Christian Thought* (Amsterdam, 1952), pp. 112–121.

[110] *PE* 1,8,15.

[111] *PE* 1,8,19.

[112] *PE* 15,61.

[113] *PE* 6,9,22. This was also the difference between the Christians and the Greek philosophers. Eusebius often returns to this issue and demands that the philosophers live according to their principles, even if not as Christians (*PE* 3,13).

[114] *PE* 8,14,21.

respond in kind. Thus he fulfilled Psalms 7:5 and the words of the New Testament,[115] thereby associating himself with the Old and New Testaments.[116]

His conduct during and after his trial serves as an important model of how to behave. Remaining steadfast in his moral virtues, Socrates faced the opinion of the crowd with equanimity and acted in the spirit of Jesus' words about seeking the honor of God rather than of man.[117] The death of Socrates was an example of preferring obedience to truth over life itself, resembling the New Testament statement that obedience to God took precedence over obedience to man,[118] and the words of Jesus on the ideal of martyrdom. One should not fear those who killed the body but not the soul.[119] Socrates is an example of a martyr on the altar of truth, as preached by Scripture.[120] The thinking of Socrates harmonized with Christian philosophy. Eusebius finds appropriate texts from the works of Plato. Alongside his correct theological concept of God, Socrates had believed in the anticipation of eternal life,[121] a trial after death,[122] and Paradise.[123] This belief had guided him throughout his life.

In addition, he took ideas of lesser importance from the Hebrews, such as the image of a midwife to describe his intellectual role in teaching, drawn from Isaiah 24:18.[124] The special connection between Socrates and his *daimon* derived from the influence of Hebrew angelology.[125] Socrates did not even hesitate to criticize pagan religion, and

---

[115] *PE* 8,7.

[116] According to Clement, Socrates even quoted from Hebrew Scripture (*Stromateis* 1,19).

[117] John 5:44; *PE* 13,6.

[118] Acts of the Apostles 5:29.

[119] Matthew 10:28.

[120] *PE* 13,10. Origen gives Socrates as an example of one who knew about his impending death and could have prevented it, but deliberately chose not to (*CC* 2,13). Clement saw him as a protomartyr (*Stromateis* 4,11). On Socrates as a protomartyr in early Christian literature, mainly in the works of Justin, Tertullian, and Clement of Alexandria, see E. Benz, "Christus und Sokrates in der alten Kirche: Ein Beitrag zum altkirchlichen Verständnis des Martyrers und des Martyriums", *Zeitschrift für die neutestamentliche Wissenschaft*, 23 (1950–51), pp. 195–224. According to Benz, the ideal of Socrates as a martyr had considerable influence on Christian martyrs!

[121] *PE* 11,27,10.

[122] *PE* 11,38,4.

[123] *PE* 11,27,16.

[124] *PE* 12,45.

[125] *PE* 13,13, in a quotation from Clement of Alexandria.

to express doubts regarding some of its tenets, especially the myths, which impaired the pure concept of God.[126] Socrates seemed, more than any other Greek, to come close to a proto-Christian figure, or to be a pagan parallel to the ancient Hebrews.[127] However, this was not Eusebius' intention. We have encountered his definitive declaration on the apologetic role of Socrates[128] in proving the Christian truths, whether through his criticism of Greek philosophy and religion, or through his acceptance of Hebrew-Christian philosophical truths, which he expressed in his thoughts and way of life. Although Socrates was close to perfection, he did not achieve it. His deficiencies, marginal as they were, sufficed to make it clear that he did not attain the level of perfection. He joined the masses in pagan celebrations, sacrificed a rooster to Asclepius, and had displayed a positive opinion of the Delphic oracle.[129] He could be accused of being, like the masses, susceptible to the error of pervasive superstition (τῆς δεισιδαίμονος πλάνης).[130] This was not the only way in which Socrates had failed. His greatest failure was the doctrine that he taught. His

---

[126] *PE* 8,4. Justin argued that in the past, out of fear and weakness, the pagans called the demons who had been revealed to them, gods. Socrates had tried to expose this deception and the demons had therefore plotted his death on charges of atheism and the introduction of new gods. A similar accusation of atheism was leveled against the Christians in his own time. Jesus Christ, through the Incarnation, played a role similar to that of Socrates (*First Apology*, 5). Elsewhere, Justin states that Socrates taught the condemnation of Homer and the expulsion of demons— namely, the Greek gods—with their mythological corruption (*Second Apology*, 5).

[127] Justin even declared that all those who, in the past, had lived according to reason, were Christians, even if they had been considered atheists in their time. Such Greeks included Socrates, Heraclitus, and others (*First Apology*, 46). The analogy between Socrates and the Christians may have been acknowledged by non-Christians, too; apparently, Celsus also likened the Christians to Socrates (*CC* 1,3).

[128] *PE* 15,61,12.

[129] *PE* 13,14,4. On the rooster, see also Tertullian, *Apology* 46,5. Origen remarked that, in addition to sacrificing the rooster, Socrates also prayed to Artemis, and argued that despite their accomplishments, philosophers such as Socrates and Plato persisted in their pursuit of vanities (*CC* 6,4). Tertullian went further, adding that, like Cato and others, Socrates had sinned because he gave his wife to his friends. Tertullian made allowance for the fact that Socrates and Cato had perhaps done so for purposes of procreation, rather than adultery. He could not say whether their wives had agreed or not, but, nonetheless calls Socrates and Cato pimps (*leno*)! (*Apology* 39,12). In addition, he condemns Socrates' homosexual tendencies (*Apology*, 46,10). Nevertheless, he praises him because Socrates swore upon an oak tree, a goat, and a dog, out of contempt for the gods (*Apology*, 14,7). He had, therefore, achieved a glimmer of truth (*Apology*, 46,5).

[130] *PE* 13,14,4.

teaching was ruined by the disloyalty, mutual disagreements, and moral decline of his disciples.[131] To these must be added the same factor that had brought about the decline of the Hebrews into Judaism, namely, the passion for Egypt and its teachings![132] In contrast to the disciples of Socrates, Eusebius emphasizes the harmonious continuation of the Hebrews' ideas by the Christians, and the latter's adherence to their way of life despite adversity and persecution.[133]

The General Concept of the Development of Pagan Polytheism and its Complementary Apologetic Role

Eusebius' particular concept of the ancient Hebrew-Christian religion is part of a general theory of the development of religions in history. This theory was intended to idealize the early Christianity of the Hebrews, as opposed to the gradual decline of the Gentiles to the point where they were trapped in the claws of demons. On the other hand, it was a concept that could explain why Jesus appeared so late in human history, a frequently repeated argument which Eusebius considers at length and discusses on numerous occasions in his double work. The general theory on the development of pagan polytheism was not fully consolidated in his work. Details emerge from brief statements in different parts of the *PE* and the

---

[131] *PE* 14,5,1–4. Justin remarked that philosophy had declined because of its disciples, the creation of the different schools (*Dialogue* 3,8), and the fact that the disciples of Socrates did not sacrifice themselves for the sake of his teachings, as the disciples of Jesus had done (*Second Apology*, 5). Eusebius gives a similar but more detailed account of the corruption of Plato's teachings by his successors, who distorted them by introducing alien doctrines. Immediately upon his death, the wonderful dialogues had ceased, and in the next generation there ensued conflicts and rivalries, which continued into Eusebius' lifetime. Thus the decline persisted, and the distance from Plato's truths increased. There was further deterioration from the time of Arcesilaus and the "Second Academy" with its emphasis on scepticism. Eusebius bases his argument upon Numenius' *On the Revolt of the Academics against Plato*, which was written as if designed to serve Eusebius' aims. Numenius defends Plato and describes how his successors in the Academy distorted, weakened, and deviated from the Platonic tradition (*PE* 14,3,5). Interestingly, this argument resembles Celsus' attack upon the Christians. According to Celsus, at first there was unity, and later, divisiveness and fragmentation (*CC* 3,10). The different Christian sects vilified each other and only the title "Christian" united them (*CC* 3,12). He charges that the contradictions and sharp divergences within Christianity invalidated it (*CC* 5,64).

[132] *PE* 14,12,1.

[133] *PE* 14,3,5. On the image of Socrates in the works of Eusebius and other fourth-century Christian writers, see A.M. Malingery, "Le personnage de Socrate chez quelques auteurs chrétiens du IV siècle", *Forma Futuri*, pp. 159–178.

DE, and these have to be combined into a single picture. From this we can obtain a fairly clear idea of Eusebius views.

Early in his work, Eusebius briefly presents the history of pagan religion as the antithesis of the antiquity of Hebrew wisdom and theology. In fact, men of ancient times had deviated from the true pristine religion of the patriarchs. Out of wonder and amazement they declared heavenly forces to be gods, and began to worship them. During this first stage, they neither built temples nor made statues in the form of human beings, but rather gazed at the skies. In subsequent generations, there was a sharp decline which even brought about the denial of the existence of God. The error of polytheism derived from the Egyptians and the Phoenicians, who then taught the Greeks.[134] In this early period the many male and female deities were not yet mentioned. Likewise, the mythology, mysteries, and superstitions of subsequent generations did not exist. Men did not yet revere demons. Religion was purely astral, and the cult of stars, which were considered gods, required no animal sacrifices.[135]

Elsewhere,[136] Eusebius describes a somewhat different prehistoric reality. At first, men lived like savages, without laws or government, and freely roamed the earth like animals. As far as religion and morality were concerned, many behaved as freely as animals, seeking the instant gratification of their physical needs. Others, however, felt a natural inclination to recognize the benevolent power of the deity, and sought him in heaven. But their search ended with the stars, which overwhelmed them with beauty and were regarded as gods. Others searched for god on earth, among men with great powers of body or mind, of authority and magic; these were recognized as gods either during their lifetime or after their deaths.[137] The qualities of natural religion were imbedded in human nature and guided man naturally towards God. God himself had planted the knowledge of God in every rational soul. Man, however, did not exploit this God-given reason or talent. With the exception of a select few among the Hebrews, man continued to err blindly, like a wild beast. Guided by their intelligence, the Hebrews attained a proper under-

---

[134] *PE* 1,6.
[135] *PE* 1,9.
[136] *PE* 2,5.
[137] According to the idea of Euhemerus, which Eusebius quotes from Diodorus Siculus (*PE* 2,2).

standing of God and the concept of his unity. But through ignorance
and error, most of humanity projected the natural concept of God
on men regarded as benefactors. Stricken by mental paralysis, they
lost their good judgment and sense of criticism. Thus the gods were
created before the establishment of norms of moral conduct and law,
while sin was considered a great accomplishment. Hence the myth-
ical gods appeared as loose, corrupt, and prone to lewdness and
murder. This decline even brought about the deification of the sex-
ual organs.[138]

According to Eusebius, the next stage in the development of pagan
polytheism was the great conspiracy of the demons. During the period
of a quest for God and the development of ceremonies and sacrifices around the cult of the dead, the demons saw that men were
straying and sensed a great opportunity to impose their rule upon
humanity. Through their sophisticated exploitation of innocent people, the demons turned the search for God and the cult of the dead
into a belief in demons as gods. They took advantage of human
suffering and credulity. They caused statues to move and created
illusions through oracles. As part of a devious tactic to encourage
man's dependence upon them, demons spread diseases which they
subsequently cured. Thus they greatly encouraged the error of polytheism. They made man believe in them and view them as heavenly forces and deities, or identify them with the souls of heroes who
had been previously deified. Polytheism grew and took hold. Demons
were considered to be the greatest deities. They continued to gain
strength by performing imaginary miracles; priests serving the gods
played a role in their machinations. The demons themselves taught
the priests to fool the public with various tricks.[139] Later, men learned
to distinguish between the various demons and to classify them into
different groups and hierarchies. The Greek pantheon developed in

---

[138] *PE* 2,6. The essence of this idea occurs already in Clement of Alexandria,
who held that the source of pagan religion derived from the adoration of natural
forces and heavenly bodies, from human feelings and passions, and from people
who were considered to be saviors (*Protrepticos*, 2). This view basically resembles that
of the *De Monarchia*, attributed to Justin, which states that monotheism is man's
original religion. Through negligence, man had transferred the names of god to
mortals. This despicable practice had become widespread; as a consequence, religion had become a cult of leaders and the true faith had been forgotten (*De Monarchia*, 1).

[139] *PE* 5,2.

this manner. At this stage, pagans transformed their unbridled desires and human activities into another form of gods of pagan theology.[140]

Although the Gentiles seemed to worship many demons, they actually worshiped the same demon—"a many-headed hydra"—in various ways, and pleasure was the supreme good.[141] The demons were

---

[140] *PE* 5,3. The idea of the demons' conspiracy appears briefly in the works of the early apologists. See Tertullian, *Apology* 22, 4–5; Athenagoras, *A Plea for the Christians*, 27; Tatian, *Address to the Greeks*, 18; Clement of Alexandria, *Protrepticos*, 3; Minucius Felix, *Octavius*, 26–27. The identification of the Greek gods with demons first appears in I Corinthians 10:10. For the most part, Eusebius' demonology is identical with that of the evil demons in Porphyry's *On Abstinence* (2,37–48), but he applies it to the entire pagan pantheon. See the summary of these brief chapters in Geffcken, *Last Days*, pp. 69–70. Apparently, it was Plotinus who opposed developing demonology too far in this direction. He attacked the Gnostics, and perhaps the Christians in general, for transforming pathology into demonology, namely, for attributing diseases to demonic beings, exorcising demons by charms, and publicizing these matters. In this way, magic had replaced medicine (*Enneads* 2,9,14). The positions of Plotinus and Porphyry differ somewhat, as the former writes in a polemical context, while the latter presents a general description. On the concept of demons and their activities in the works of Eusebius, see Sirinelli, *Vues*, pp. 312–326.

[141] *PE* 7,2. *DE* 4,8 has an astrological view that does not accord with the idea of the Gentiles being dominated by demons. The Gentiles were entrusted to different angels but they worshiped only heavenly elements, so that their religion was largely astral, not demonic. According to this view, Gentiles did not worship the forces of evil, but the heavenly elements which constituted the peak of creation and reflected the greatness of God. See also Chesnut, *The First Christian Histories*, pp. 70–71. This idea may be a variation on Eusebius' interpretation of polytheism, which relates to the state of pagan religion and the pronounced astrological aspect it had in his day. In *PE* 11,26, Eusebius interprets the Septuagint version of Deuteronomy 32:8. In its Greek form, the verse accommodates the concept of angels being designated for different peoples and countries—a concept that occurs as early as Justin (*Dialogue* 131,1) and Origen (*CC* 5,29). The idea of guardian angels for peoples, cities, and even individuals, also appears in the work of Clement (*Stromateis* 6,17). In *DE* 4,9, the Roman Empire emerges as part of Satan's program to oppose the ancient divine system of guardian angels. This uncharacteristic idea, which appears only here, is in direct conflict with Eusebius' view—to be discussed later— that the empire and the *Pax Romana* were part of the divine plan, a positive stage in preparing for the promulgation of the Gospel throughout the world. This view played a major role in his earlier writings and appears here as well.

Eusebius' view corresponds with the late pagan concept of the division of the world between the different gods, a concept that flourished under the influence of astrology. Celsus expresses this view as well. The administration of the world was given to "overseers" over regions and peoples. Each national tradition was adapted to its overseer; world order, therefore, should not be broken by abandoning ancestral traditions (*CC* 5,25). In fact, Celsus and Origen share identical views, but according to Origen and other apologists, all demons were wicked. Origen gives a negative definition of the term "demons", based on the Septuagint, where δαίμων always has negative connotation (*CC* 5,5). Thus the tasks which Celsus attributes to good

identified as fallen angels[142] who had descended to Tartarus. A few,
however, remained on earth and in the air in order to train the
"athletes of religious devotion" (τῶν εὐσεβείας ἀθλητῶν) in the trial,
temptation, and deception of man, thereby bringing about the error
of polytheism. Herein lies the positive role attributed to the demons
within the negative context of their existence.[143] They wished to
declare themselves gods, steal the titles of the gods, and set traps to
ensnare men through oracles and prophecies. In bygone times only
the ancient Hebrews had tried to escape them.[144] There gradually
emerges a general picture of the history of religion sliding into continuous decline. Far from the religion and philosophy of the patriarchs, mankind drowned in the chasm opened by the demons, and
became trapped in the net which they had spread. Only the Hebrews
withstood the demons owing to their knowledge of the one God;
moreover, the demons even played a role in strengthening them. On
the one hand, within the narrow context of his polemic, Eusebius
plays down such contrasts. On the other, within the wider polemical framework, he emphasizes the contrast between the ideal early
Christianity of the Hebrews, and the pagan polytheism that resulted
from ancient pagan error and demonic conspiracy, and forms the
basis of a general attack on all forms of pagan religion. The narrower polemical context was intended to explain the concept of poly-

---

demons as servants of gods—such as the overseers—are presented in Origen's works
as the tasks of angels and other divine ministers (*CC* 8,31). For more material on
the difference between angels and demons, see *CC* 3,37. Angels may also appear
in pagan demonology. In Iamblichus' demonological hierarchy, angels are gods who
are one degree below the great gods. Below the angels are good demons, and below
the latter, vengeful and evil demons (*On the Mysteries*, 2,7). Angels are not mentioned, however, in the description of demonology in Porphyry's *On Abstinence*. On
neo-Platonic pagan angelology, see F. Cumont, "Les anges du paganisme", *Revue
de l'histoire des religions*, 72 (1915), pp. 159–182. On the Jewish background of the
idea of appointed angels and demons, see J. Daniélou, "Les sources juives de la
doctrine des anges des nations chez Origène", *Recherches de science religieuse*, 38 (1951),
pp. 132–135; E. Peterson, "Das Problem des Nationalismus im alten Christentum",
in idem, *Frühkirche, Judentum und Gnosis* (Vienna, 1959), pp. 51–63. For rabbinic
sources see for example Lev. Rabba 29; BT Sukka 29a; Pes. Rabbati 21.

[142] According to Justin, demons are the offspring of fallen angels and women.
They received their names from their fathers, the angels, who fell to earth (*Second
Apology*, 5). Elsewhere, however, he states that they choose their own names (*First
Apology*, 5).

[143] On the positive role of the demons' destructive power, given by divine man-
date to return men to a good way of life or to strengthen them, see *CC* 8,31.

[144] *PE* 7,16. Demons also are identified with the biblical giants and mythological Titans (*PE* 5,5).

theism, and to adapt it as a riposte to the often repeated pagan question as to why Christ appeared when he did and not much earlier.[145] This question was frequently accompanied by another, namely, why Jesus had appeared in a remote corner of the world and among a wretched people.[146] The narrower polemical context gave Eusebius the opportunity to outline the subsequent stages in the history of polytheism, and the role of the Hebrews in its development.

Eusebius found Book VIII of the *DE* to be suitable for such a purpose. For the purpose of this book was to give testimonies as to the time of the Messiah's coming, which according to the prophets would coincide with the cessation of the three major hegemonies of the Jews—the kingdom, the high priesthood, and prophecy. The end of the Temple cult, the destruction of the Temple and of Jerusalem, and the subjugation of the Jews by their enemies—all this served as evidence that the Messiah had come in the appropriate time. The signs of the Advent were to be found in the simultaneous phenomena of the *pax romana*, the establishment of the Roman Empire, the abolition of other forms of government, the victory over polytheistic and demonic paganism, and the acknowledgment of faith in the Creator and supreme God. In order to explain why Christ had appeared at that particular moment in history, and not at an earlier date, Eusebius inserts into his introduction to *DE* VIII a brief excursus on the historical-religious development of mankind, within the narrow polemical context.

Primitive men first lived as savages without urban settlements or social organization, and without the knowledge of God. However, they had an idea of natural religion and formulated principles that led them to the conclusion that there was a divine authority, whom they called God and regarded as a beneficent power. But since they did not possess a proper understanding of the deity, their concept of a transcendent God deteriorated into a cult of images of dead kings and rulers, to whom they attributed divine power. Thus they sanctified their abhorrent and cruel practices as divine acts. The goodness and wisdom of Christ could certainly not have flourished in harmony with a humanity mired in evil. Before Christ, divine justice had to be carried out by means of flood, fire, war, massacre, and mutual siege, sent to punish man for obeying the demons whom

---

[145] *PE* 8, Introduction.
[146] This argument will be treated later.

they regarded as gods. Thus mankind lived without neighborly or
social relations, and without unity.[147] According to the Hebrew oracles, the few who lived a divine life encountered divine justice through
oracles and revelations, and were protected by the basic, though
beneficial, legislation of Moses. Here Eusebius depicts the law as
having a positive role, defending the ancient Hebrew faith. Indeed,
Eusebius views Moses and the prophets as successors to the ancient
Hebrews and distinct from the rest of the Jewish people. The Law
of Moses and the teachings of the prophets spread their sweet fra-
grance over the nations and moderated the savage nature of the
Gentiles. Later, other nations developed their own legal systems,
virtues, and philosophies. Here Eusebius articulates the broad issue
that he discussed in the *PE*, namely, the influence of Moses and the
prophets on the development of various aspects of Greek culture,
and the Greeks' emulation of the Hebrews. Thus the ground was
prepared and the time was ripe for the appearance of the perfect
heavenly teacher, the divine Logos, who would reveal himself at the
appointed time of the Incarnation.[148]

---

[147] *DE* 8, Introduction. This section contains some general theodicy, perhaps unin-
tentionally. Demons who brought about wars between men were acting according
to a general program of divine justice.

[148] *DE* 8, Introduction. The idea of the progressive development of humanity up
to the foundation of the Roman Empire as preparation for the advent of the
Redeemer has already appeared in *HE* 1,2,17–27. Grant tries to identify the sources
that influenced the progressive direction of this view, namely, Porphyry, *On Abstinence* and Bardesanes. See R.M. Grant, "Civilization as a Preparation for Christianity in the Thought of Eusebius", *Continuity and Discontinuity in Church History. Essays
presented to George Huntson Williams*, ed. F. Forrester Church and T. George (Leiden,
1979), pp. 62–70. The process of civilization is also the fulfillment of the biblical
prophecy in Isaiah 11:6–9. Interpreting these verses in the *Prophetic Extracts*, Eusebius said that human behavior had changed from "the depth of cruelty to gentil-
ity, through the appearance of our Savior" (*Prophetic Extracts* 4,8).

CHAPTER FIVE

PROPHECY IN THE SERVICE OF POLEMICS

According to Eusebius, biblical prophecy was perhaps the most convincing proof of the truths of Christianity. In fact, the greatest proof
of the Gospel's truth was based on prophecy. In the beginning of
the *PE*, Eusebius declares that the fulfillment of prophecy constitutes
the irrefutable answer to all opponents.[1] The general argument of
the *DE* is that the power of prophecy as proof derives from its continuous fulfillment throughout history. While biblical prophecies related
to human history as a whole, all events—from the New Testament
accounts at the inception of Christianity to the time of Eusebius—
actually comprised a chain of fulfilled prophecies. The fulfillment of
prophecies also proved the existence of divine Providence.[2] Hence
prophecies, and all of Scripture, therefore, were replete with historical allusions that covered the entire continuum of future history.
Indeed, Scripture could be understood only if one knew how to decipher and study it correctly. In his earlier work, *Prophetic Extracts*,
Eusebius had collected prophecies concerning Jesus and Christianity, and these may have served as a source for the *DE*. The main
purpose of the *DE*, however, was not to point out prophecies, but
rather to prove that every single issue in the New Testament, Christian dogma, and the development of Christianity had already been
set forth in biblical prophecies. Eusebius faced a two-fold task. First,
in the wake of Porphyry's campaign, he had to reassert the prophetic
status of the Holy Scriptures, particularly for the sympathetic pagan
public and for Christians of an enlightened pagan background. Secondly, he had to furnish detailed proof that prophecies could be fulfilled only through the life of Jesus and the history of Christianity
from Jesus to his own times, and thus contest the interpretation of
prophecies that contradicted Christian views—especially those of Jews,

---

[1] *PE* 3,8; *PE* 1,3. This chapter derives from my study "Prophecy in the Service
of Polemics in Eusebius of Caesarea", *Christianesimo nella storia* 19 (1998), pp. 1–29.
[2] In *PE* 4 Eusebius discusses at length the possible conflict between prophecy as
prescience on the part of the deity, and the concept of free will.

or pagans who used Jewish or heretical Christian material.[3] Occasionally, difficulties arising from the exegetical context of specific prophecies obliged him to develop his ideas accordingly.

Pagan Oracles and Hebrew-Christian Prophecy

In order to establish the uniqueness of Hebrew prophecy as a source and proof of the truths of Christianity, Eusebius had to differentiate it from pagan prophecy. For Eusebius, oracles were the main form of historical pagan prophecy. He devotes much attention, therefore, to refuting pagan oracles, describing them as diabolical conspiracies on the part of demons[4] who manipulated men in their service. The refutation of oracles was essential in order to establish the uniqueness of biblical prophecy as the only true oracle; it also had practical applications, for the various oracles and prophetic methods played a more significant role in pagan religion than the interpretation of religion and mythology by pagan authors and philosophers. In fact, Eusebius chose to concentrate his arguments within the framework of his criticism of the third kind of pagan religion—the official political (civic) religion and its ceremonies. Furthermore, a refutation of the oracles served the purpose of spreading the Gospel.[5]

In the contemporary political and polemical context, Eusebius' critique is noteworthy because interpreters of oracles and theurgists formed the hard core of opposition to Christianity. According to Eusebius, they had played a major role in the recent anti-Christian

---

[3] See Celsus' argument that prophecies could be interpreted as referring to others rather than Jesus (*CC* 2,28), and that there were Christian sectarians who did not consider Jesus the Messiah of biblical prophecies (*CC* 4,2).

[4] This concept is actually a variation on the views of pagan authors who tried to explain the decline of the oracles by the fact that God no longer spoke directly through them, but through demonic intermediaries. These demons suffered and even died. According to these writers, however, they were good demons, while Eusebius contends that they were diabolical, as there were no good demons. If good demons existed, they were angels. On Eusebius' distinction between the evil demons of Greek religion and the good demons, namely, the angels of Christianity, see *PE* 4,5; *PE* 7,5. The diabolical demons are identified with the gods of the pagan pantheon. For a pagan version, see H.W. Parke & D.E.W. Wormell, *The Delphic Oracle* (Oxford 1956), I, pp. 288–289. For a different assessment of the power of oracles, see P. Brown, *The Making of Late Antiquity*, (Cambridge, Mass., 1976), pp. 37–38.

[5] *PE* 4,1.

persecutions and they also belonged to the ruling circles in Antioch.[6] He reports that in their campaign against the Christians, pagans enlisted various oracles and soothsayers and asked them innumerable questions of an anti-Christian nature.[7] Such oracles proliferated in the pagans' effort to attain religious legitimacy and divine authority for their anti-Christian campaign. Eusebius makes several references to the extremely bitter public campaign in Egypt, where oracles and soothsayers played a major role, though he does not mention specific historical events.[8]

The refutation of oracles falls into the category of "negative" criticism and depends largely on internal Greek criticism. In fact, Eusebius adopts traditional Greek arguments in their original form, without elaborating on them. For this purpose, he quotes Plutarch, Diogenianus, Oenomaus, and Porphyry. The internal criticism is integrated into a general plan outlined by Eusebius, in which the oracles constitute the diabolical creation of demons who misled not only the masses, but also poets and philosophers.[9] In essence, all mythological poetry and oracular pronouncements were a man-made manipulative fiction. The miracles and wonders which impressed the masses had entirely natural causes. Eusebius admits, however, that this argument is not original and he even attributes it to others.[10]

Oracles that were clear and definitive owed this not to prior knowledge, but rather to coincidence or chance. The ambiguity of oracles drew upon ignorance and deception. The messages of the oracles were intended for foreigners, not for the local population. Eusebius reports his contemporaries' view that oracles were a fraud and a delusion, which people skillfully exploited. The Epicurean philosophers opposed the use of oracles, and despite his disagreement with their theological opinions, Eusebius expressed his appreciation and admiration for their negative and contemptuous attitude towards oracles. In fact, a leading critic, Diogenianus the Epicurean, developed his theories in order to refute the arguments of Chrysippus on fate according to oracles.[11] In addition, Oenomaus sharply attacks oracles

---

[6] *PE* 4,2. On this and on the influence of the oracle of Zeus in Antioch on Maximin's anti-Christian actions, see Eusebius, *HE* 9,3.

[7] *DE* 6,20.

[8] For example, see *DE* 6,20.

[9] *PE* 3,17.

[10] *PE* 4,1.

[11] Diogenianus apparently lived in the second century CE, during the debate of

in a satirical piece that presents them as absurd and ridiculous.[12] Eusebius simply took over these arguments. Emphasizing that his work was not just an academic exercise, Eusebius attempted to disprove oracles not only by means of scholarly arguments—largely unknown to the wider public—but also by citing commonly known oracular pronouncements. He thus created a tactical polemical advantage from the available material, such as Oenomaus' examples of well-known oracular statements.[13]

Oracles only recalled catastrophes and tragedies. Apollo caused death because of the vagueness of his replies.[14] Through the oracles, the gods sowed discord among men and brought about wars instead of making peace.[15] According to the oracles, the deity did not understand philosophy, but admired poets who, in Plato's view, were worthless.[16] Occasionally, the gods even combined in the oracles the myths of poets with the statements of philosophers. Thus the contrast between mythological themes and philosophical interpretation was traceable to the gods themselves—which constituted the height of absurdity.[17] Did we have to tread the depraved path of Archilochus in order to be worthy of the company of the gods?[18] Was popular acclaim or a banquet with tyrants a criterion for acceptance into the company of the gods?[19] Oracular statements in Homer were worthless and meaningless. His life resembled that of a beetle, as it did not matter from which pile of refuse it originated.[20] Oenomaus extended his critique *ad absurdum* by stating that an oracle could transform athletes, as well as poets, into gods—including Cleomedes, apparently a murderer of children. It would have been preferable to make asses, rather than boxers like Cleomedes, into gods. In fact, an ass was stronger than him. According to the oracle, boxing was a divine occupation. Therefore, the oracle should rather have been

---

the new academy against Chrysippus. See "Diogenianus", *OCD*, and *PE* 4,2–3. This shows how Eusebius derived his arguments from philosophical sources—in this case, Diogenianus.

[12] For the critique of Oenomaus the Cynic, see H.W. Attridge, "The Philosophical Critique of Religion under the Early Empire", *ANRW* 16,1 (1978), pp. 56–59.

[13] *PE* 5,18.

[14] *PE* 5,18–19.

[15] *PE* 5,26.

[16] *PE* 5,32.

[17] *PE* 3,15.

[18] *PE* 5,33.

[19] *PE* 5,33, according to the Oracle that spoke to Euripides.

[20] *PE* 5,33.

a sports instructor than a prophet, or perhaps it should have combined both roles.[21]

Eusebius bolsters Oenomaus' arguments with those of Porphyry—
a favorite source of contradictions.[22] Between his earlier work on
oracles and his later works, Porphyry's attitude to oracles undergoes
changes. Plotinus had a distinctive attitude towards oracles,[23] one
which Porphyry refined in *Philosophy from the Oracles*. This work showed
that Porphyry viewed oracles as sacred testimonies of pagan prophecy.
He even included theories of practical magic.[24] In his later works,
Porphyry's attitude was very negative. In his view, some oracles were,
at the very least, the lies of the gods, or even the lies of drugged
demons speaking out of ignorance or against their will, in order to
satisfy the wishes of those who made inquiries of the oracles.[25] Eusebius included the testimonies of several pagan authors who wrote
that oracles had declined and that many had ceased to function.
Plutarch testified that the end of demons and oracles actually coin-
cided with the Incarnation and the preaching of the Gospel.[26]

---

[21] *PE* 5,34.

[22] *PE* 5,36.

[23] On Plotinus' distinctive attitude towards oracles, see J. Geffcken, *Last Days*, p. 54.

[24] According to Geffcken, this work became a theurgic manual. He also thinks
that many oracles cited by Porphyry are actually neo-Platonic forgeries (Geffcken,
ibid., pp. 58–59). On the attitude to theurgy in neo-Platonic circles, see E.R. Dodds,
The Greeks and the Irrational (Berkley, 1951), pp. 283–291.

[25] *PE* 4–5.

[26] Plutarch, *The Obsolescence of Oracles*, 5 (*LCL*); Eusebius, *PE* 5,17. Plutarch does
not describe the end of oracles, but rather a decline in the scope of their activities. The Pythian oracle at Delphi continued to prophesy. However, whereas formerly there were three Pythian oracles, in Plutarch's time there was only one and
it served all needs. Furthermore, the metric form of the oracle had all but ceased
at that time. As a rule, he attests to the general decline of the Greek oracles. On
Plutrarch and the subject of oracles, see also J.R. Levison, "The Prophetic Spirit
as an Angel According to Philo", *Harvard Theological Review*, 88 (1995), pp. 189–207.
The philosophers themselves gave various reasons for the decline. The oracle at
Delphi underwent a renewal with the support of the Emperor Hadrian, and, later,
of Herodes Atticus. Local inscriptions attest to the renewal and rising popularity of
the oracle, which took place despite the literary critique by authors such as Oenomaus, Diogenianus, and Lucian. Later, oracles adapted themselves to the concepts
of astrology and eastern cults. Porphyry's early work on oracles attests to their existence in his time or shortly before. During the third century, however, many oracles fell silent, as did the remainder in the course of the fourth century. The last
oracle at Delphi was given to Julian. See Parke & Wormell, *The Delphic Oracle*, pp.
283–291. Therefore, we cannot fully rely on Eusebius' references to the cessation
of oracles. For example, he says that the oracles in Claros, Dodona, and Delphi
had ceased to function (*PE* 4,2,8). But those in Claros and Delphi continued to a
later date. On Claros, see Geffcken, *Last Days*, p. 120.

However, despite Eusebius' harsh refutation of oracles within the framework of his critique of different types of pagan religion, his attitude to oracular prophecy seems somewhat more complex. Various statements indicate that he did not completely deny the power of oracular prophecy, although he attributed it to demons. Furthermore, in his polemical campaign, he apparently used oracles as proof of the truth of Christianity. Despite the fact that he presented them as a diabolical trick on the part of demons and as a man-made manipulation, he did not hesitate to present their words as divine statements, in order to refute philosophical positions.[27] Elsewhere, he argued that one should prefer the words of the gods in the oracles to those of the philosophers.[28]

Such arguments appear somewhat contradictory and opportunistic in light of the definitive stance on oracles displayed by Eusebius previously. Thus we read once again that the words of the oracle of Apollo were intended to contradict statements made by Porphyry.[29] Furthermore, Eusebius used the oracles mentioned in Porphyry's work on oracles in order to prove the truths of the Hebrew Christians. Porphyry introduced an additional oracle, by Apollo, on the Hebrews. According to this oracle, the Hebrews knew religious wisdom and understood the wisdom of the heavens.[30] It is evident once again that Eusebius did not hesitate to use oracles that referred to divine knowledge, and to invest them with a positive prophetic value. Moreover, the major and decisive proof of the divine nature of Jesus, which would convince the last of the skeptics, derived from pagan oracles—even from the archenemy, Porphyry. Oracles attested that Jesus was a holy man whose soul had achieved immortality after death and dwelt in the Heavens.[31]

---

[27] In *PE* 3,14, the oracles appear to reject the physical, symbolic interpretations of mythology.

[28] *PE* 3,15.

[29] *PE* 5,6, and, likewise, *PE* 3,14.

[30] *PE* 9,10. On Apollo's positive oracle on the Hebrews, which Porphyry includes, and on Porphyry's ambivalent attitude to the Jews, see D. Rokeah, "Jews and their Law (Torah) in the Pagan-Christian Polemic in the Roman Empire", *Tarbiz*, 40 (1971), pp. 462–471 (Hebrew).

[31] *DE* 3, 6–7, quoting *Philosophy from the Oracles*. In fact, the oracle on Jesus, which Eusebius cites from Porphyry, includes negative statements about Christianity. Eusebius conveys only their positive conclusion. Augustine gives the complete statements. Jesus was condemned, and Christians were hated by the gods, because he gave Christians the "gift" of wallowing in error, namely, ignorance of the gods and the grace they bestowed. Jesus was the source of danger and imminent calamity (*City*

Eusebius attributes divine powers not only to the oracles but even, occasionally, to Plato. The martyrs of recent persecutions were the embodiment of Plato's ideal of righteousness, fulfilling the Platonic prophecy.[32] Elsewhere, Plato prophesied the passion and crucifixion of Jesus![33] According to Eusebius, the prophecy of Balaam (Numbers 24) could perhaps be regarded as a type of pagan prophecy. Eusebius interprets Numbers 24:15–19 as relating to events that transpired at the time of the Incarnation, and to the star that appeared at the time of the Nativity. The Magi were descendants of Balaam who had preserved the tradition of his prophecy. Apparently, Eusebius regarded the prophecy of Balaam as biblical prophecy, despite the fact that Balaam was a Gentile prophet; Balaam's descendants, the Magi, preserved prophetic tradition, although they were not an example of a pagan oracle.[34]

The above demonstrates Eusebius's ambivalent attitude to oracles.

---

of God, 19,23). On the differences between Augustine's more complete section from Porphyry and that which Eusebius includes in an apologetic context, see also P. de Labriolle, *La Réaction Païenne*, pp. 236–237. *Philosophy from the Oracles* also contained at least one further negative oracle on Christianity cited by Augustine. Someone asked Apollo how he could win his wife back from Christianity. The god replied that it was easier to write on water or to fly like a bird through the air than to restore to her senses a woman who had erred. It would be better to leave her to her vanities and dirges about a dead god who was condemned by wise judges and died a despicable death. According to Augustine, after quoting this oracle, Porphyry added that Apollo showed clearly that the faith of Christians was incurable and that the Jews upheld God more than the Christians (*City of God*, 19,23).

[32] *PE* 12,10. Lactantius expresses a similar, positive attitude towards the prophetic powers of Hermes and the Sibyls regarding Christianity (Lactantius, *Div. Inst.* 7, 18).

[33] *PE* 13,13, as quoted in Clement of Alexandria, *Stromateis*, 5,14.

[34] *DE* 3,9,1. Apparently, Eusebius relies on Origen for the prophecy of Balaam. In fact, the details of Origen's interpretation undergo changes in the work of Eusebius. According to Origen, Balaam prophesied the appearance of a star over Bethlehem, but the Magi were associated with demons. When Jesus was born, their strength diminished, and from this they understood that a king had been born, superior to any demon. Thus the major difference was Eusebius' omission of any reference to the Magi's demonic associations. Origen adds that the Magi were armed with the prophecies of Balaam (*CC* 1,59–60). On Celsus' and Origen's interpretations of oracles and prophecy, see M. Fedou, *Christianisme et religion païenne dans le Contre Celse d'Origène* (Paris, 1988), especially pp. 420–474. According to Clement, the Magi came from Persia (*Stromateis* 1,15). Balaam himself could be identified with Zoroaster. See H. Chadwick, *Origen, Contra Celsum* (Cambridge, 1953) p. 55, quoting J. Bidez and F. Cumont, *Les Mages héllénisés* (Paris, 1938), I, pp. 47–48. Basil thought that Balaam himself was a *magus*, see Chadwick, ibid. On Balaam and his prophecy in patristic interpretation, see J.R. Baskin, *Pharaoh's Counsellors: Job, Jethro, and Balaam in Rabbinic and Patristic Tradition* (Chico, 1983), pp. 101–113; G. Dorival, "Un astre se lèvera de Jacob. L'interprétation ancienne de Nombre 24,17", in *Annali di storia dell'esegesi* 13 (1996), pp. 295–353.

On the one hand, he was interested in the absolute refutation of their prophetic powers; on the other, he recognized their oracular worth. It is possible that the tradition of oracles, especially Delphi, and their power to prophesy the future, were too deeply rooted to be undermined. Perhaps the surrounding pagan world deposited a cultural and spiritual residue that persisted even in the soul of a Christian, finding expression in a positive attitude to oracular prophecy as the embodiment of pagan prophecy. Hence the two conflicting trends in Eusebius' attitude to pagan prophecies. Nevertheless, this tension enables him to exploit positive oracles for his polemical needs, either to counter Greek religious and philosophical concepts, or to adduce prophetic testimony of the truth of Christianity.

Furthermore, by evincing a positive attitude to pagan prophecy or, at least, by acknowledging its power, Eusebius could address the pagans and demand that they honor the Holy Scriptures, namely, the Hebrew oracles, as prophetic oracles; he could also let it be understood that respect for the Hebrew oracles had existed from the outset. Indeed, the above examples seem to indicate that, for Eusebius, oracles possessed prophetic power only when presented in a positive Christian context. This was not the case, however. Apparently anxious that he might have exaggerated the prophetic power of oracles, Eusebius is careful to distinguish between the prophetic power of pagan oracles and that of the Hebrew Bible. In the introduction to Book V of the *DE*, Eusebius establishes the status of the Hebrew oracles as a divine source attesting to the truth of the prophecies about Jesus in the Hebrew Bible. He takes the opportunity to elaborate upon the value of Hebrew, as opposed to pagan, oracles. Eusebius presents the Greek opinion that prophetic ability was given by the Creator equally to all peoples, including the Jews, who had no special advantage. Thus according to Eusebius, the Greeks validated the prophetic-oracular status of Hebrew scriptures. He concludes that, from this point on, one had only to prove that biblical prophecies indeed related to Jesus and Christianity—a claim which he had partially demonstrated in earlier books of the *DE*. On the other hand, by accepting this principle, he also legitimized the prophetic ability of the Greeks. In order to negate the latter, Eusebius inserts a brief summary from the *PE* refuting the value of all oracles with the exception of biblical prophecy.

Eusebius unwittingly supports the idea that pagan oracles had some truth, even though they were given by demons. Oracles were cor-

rect regarding trivial matters, such as discovering a thief or a rob-
bery, which came within the capability of less elevated spiritual beings.
Thus Eusebius reluctantly admits that oracles had prophetic power,
albeit derived from demonic forces.[35] This power, which Eusebius
rigorously limits, was nonetheless effective in various realms of life,
and was not restricted to an acknowledgment of the truth of Christianity or to supporting the Christian polemics against the pagans.
It seems that the difference between pagan and Hebrew oracles was
one of origin, not principle, deriving from the respective demonic
or divine source of the oracles. In a brief remark elsewhere, Eusebius states that the disparity between pagan demonic oracles and
Hebrew oracles, regarding the revelations and appearances of God
before the Hebrew Christians, lay in the continuing grace of God
who guaranteed the truth of the Hebrew oracles.[36] He expresses a
similarly ambivalent position in his discussions of pagan theurgy,
which, at one point, he rejects as the manipulation and deception
of the naive.[37] Elsewhere, he acknowledges the true pagan power to
activate demons and force them to comply by means of theurgic
incantations and prayers.[38] Eusebius concludes his reservations regarding the power of oracles by stating that they never uttered anything
of philosophical wisdom, or importance to the state, nor any intelligent item of legislation,[39] and that significant truth had never emerged
from a pagan oracle.

Another difference between pagan and Hebrew oracles lay in the
psychic state of their respective mediums. The demon was closest in
essence to darkness. Thus when he visited the soul of his medium,
he wrapped it in darkness and fog in dark places in the bowels of

---

[35] Elsewhere, Eusebius incidentally introduces another testimony to the relative
superiority of Hebrew oracles, and to the prophetic power that continued to exist
in Greek oracles. He argues that the antiquity of a prophecy—in this case, Isaiah
7:14 ("Behold a virgin shall conceive")—attested to its veracity (*DE* 1,7). Thus he
presents a further relative criterion for the truth of an oracle.

[36] *PE* 7,5. Theophilus recognized the presence of prophetic power among the
pagans. He found it in the Sybil, whom he viewed as a pagan parallel to the
prophets (*To Autolycus* 1,9). Unlike Eusebius, Origen did not cast any doubt on the
oracular power of demonic oracles, despite being unaware that they were proph-
esying about Jesus and Christianity. In fact, he saw them as the product of a conspiracy between demons and spirits hostile to humanity (*CC* 7, 3–4).

[37] *PE* 4,1.

[38] *DE* 3,6; *PE* 5,8. I shall come back to this in my treatment of the accusations
of sorcery, magic and fraud leveled against Jesus.

[39] *DE* 5, Introduction.

the earth. The demon placed the medium under his influence as if a corpse (τὸν ὑπ᾽ αὐτὸ οἶα νεκρόν), whose powers of intelligence departed. As a consequence, he did not know what he was saying or doing; he was unconscious and acted like a lunatic. Hence this state was called "prophecy" (μαντεία), from the word "lunacy" (μανία). In short, pagan oracular prophecy emerged from a mental state characterized by a of loss of the senses, or, at least, a paralysis of the powers of reason resembling an epileptic fit.

In contrast, the nature of the divine spirit was like that of light. It shed a new and bright light upon its medium and purified the soul and mind. Thus one was in a state of supra-sobriety and had the strength to understand and interpret prophetic words (θεσπιζόμενα) emanating from him, as in the case of the Hebrew prophets to whom the Holy Spirit had granted an accurate knowledge of the present and the future. Hebraic-Christian prophecy was manifestly superior to other forms of prophecy using birds, living creatures, movements of the water, inspection of the entrails of sacrifices, and the blood of snakes and moles.[40] The different mental state of the medium, in pagan and Hebrew oracular prophecy, respectively, explained the superiority of the Hebrew oracles. Eusebius' explanation for this difference seems to lie in the nature of the force that activates this state—a demonic force or the Holy Spirit.[41]

---

[40] *DE* 5, Introduction, 26–30. On the possibility of a theurgic, divine inspiration that is activated via the faculty of imagination and does not paralyze the powers of reason, see Iamblichus, *On the Mysteries*, 3,14.

[41] Perhaps Eusebius' statements on the different psychic circumstances of oracular and divine prophecy are an elaboration of Origen's ideas in *Contra Celsum*. Origen speaks of the Pythian priestess who receives the spirit in her womb, indicating the impure nature of the spirit. She enters into a state of ecstasy and unconsciousness, which, according to Origen, is inappropriate for receiving the divine word. Only demons and evil spirits that enveloped the mind of the priestess with darkness could bring about a loss of self control and the power of reason (*CC* 7, 3–4). According to Chadwick, the distinction between divine and demonic inspiration in this instance, is based on Plato (*Timaeus* 71; *Phaedrus* 244), who held that divine inspiration purifies, and does not excite the mind (Chadwick, *Contra Celsum*, p. 397, note 2). Origen also thought that in the case of the biblical prophets and Jesus, visions and revelations were an internal, not a physical, matter. A select few had the special, divine sense that enabled them to undergo spiritual experiences involving all their senses, as if they were in an objective state of mind (*CC* 1,48). Origen also indicates that the practice of bribery associated with oracles was a further reason for their inferiority to biblical prophecy (*CC* 8,48). Cumont states that the interpretation of dreams was the only type of prediction of the future that was not rejected by Christianity (F. Cumont, *Lux Perpetua*, Paris, 1949, p. 92). Origen held that methods of predicting the future according to animals, derived from

An important question remains as to whether the pagan Greeks recognized the oracular dimension of the Holy Scriptures as deriving from divine authority, whose intimations of divine truth had to be accepted unequivocally. A slightly different question is whether Eusebius thought that pagans viewed or accepted the Holy Scriptures as an oracular source. Apparently, he believed that some pagans had always considered Hebrew Scriptures as an oracle. All his efforts in the *PE* prepare the ground for and lead to the universal recognition of the Holy Scriptures as the sole oracular source of truth. But Eusebius also acknowledges the problematic aspect of pagans relating to Scripture as oracle. He certainly was aware of the difficulty to find such a belief in anti-Christian pagan circles. However, he had no particular problem with assuming that the truth of Christian theology could be proved by presenting all the biblical phrases that expressed this theology. Thus in Eusebius' view the Greeks acknowledged that the Bible contained oracles bearing the word of God.[42]

We may infer that, according to Eusebius, many Greeks recognized the oracular value of the Scripture and therefore had to accept it as proof of the truths of Christianity, providing it has proved that Christianity was indeed the subject of biblical prophecies. The problem facing Christianity, therefore, was to arrive at a correct interpretation of Scripture, which was open to a variety of interpretations. Eusebius knew that it was hard to convince pagans of the power of biblical prophecy. But he was optimistic. If the pagans could accept that prophecies had in fact been fulfilled, they would remove the doubts from their hearts and acknowledge the truth of these prophecies, and, indeed, of all Scripture, of Christianity, and of the Hebraic-Christian dogma. Even those pagans who were fighting Christianity could discern these truths by the powers of reason.[43]

Nevertheless, Eusebius apparently understood that his view was more optimistic than realistic. In replying to specific anti-Christian, pagan arguments, he admitted that the prophetic oracles were intended for believers, who accepted the oracular authority of Scripture. It is not clear if he was referring only to Christians, or also to pagans

---

demons who gave them signs in order to entice men to into error and thus prevent them from seeking God. He also correlated the different forms of demons with the different animals that performed prophetic tasks (*CC* 4, 92–93).

[42] *DE* 5, Introduction.

[43] *DE* 1,1,12.

sympathetic to Christianity and others who viewed biblical prophecies as oracles. In order to convince those who did not believe in the prophets, one had to present different types of arguments.[44] Apparently, Eusebius thought that many pagans tended to view the prophecies in the Hebrew Scriptures as a type of oracle, like the pagan oracles and prophetic writings. He did not expect staunch opponents of Christianity to share this attitude. Refutation of their arguments had to take a different point of departure, one that would bring opponents to the preparatory stage of acknowledging the prophetic oracular authority of the Holy Scriptures; then they would assert that prophetic oracles spoke of Christianity and proved its truths.[45]

The Actualization of Biblical Prophecies

Oracular prophecies in the Holy Scriptures encompassed all of human history and were fulfilled with regard to specific details, individual figures, and world history. They contained prophecies pertaining to the histories of different peoples before Christ, as well as prophecies that described the history of Jesus and the events recounted in the New Testament. Several prophecies related to events that occurred in the course of the history of Christianity and humanity, from the time of Jesus up to and including Eusebius' time. Other prophecies described future events in subsequent generations.[46]

Prophecies that had been fulfilled in the past, before the advent of Jesus, and those that related in detail to Jesus and the New Testament, were well known from Jewish and Christian literary traditions. In fact, even the many prophecies dealing with details of events in the New Testament and with Eusebius' view of Christian theology, receive unprecedented elaboration in the *DE*.[47] Apparently, there was particular interest in the fulfillment of prophecies relating to the

---

[44] *DE* 3,2.

[45] See *DE*, ibid.

[46] *DE* 1, Introduction.

[47] Eusebius' intense preoccupation with the interpretation of prophecy in the *DE* makes it an important testimony of his biblical exegesis. In his study of Eusebius' biblical exegesis, C. Sant gives many examples from the *DE*, see C. Sant, *The Old Testament Interpretation of Eusebius of Caesarea* (Malta, 1967). In later commentaries on Isaiah and Psalms, Eusebius included interpretations of verses from the *DE*. For examples of parallels between *DE* and the commentary on Isaiah, see Des Places, *Eusèbe de Césarée commentateur*, p. 117, n. 26, and on parallels with the commentary on Psalms, see ibid., pp. 87–98. On Eusebius' polemical tendencies in the com-

history of Christianity from the post-apostolic period to the time of Eusebius, and to events that occurred during his lifetime. One example was Isaiah's prophecy (Isa. 6), which was seen as referring to the Bar Kokhba revolt, the establishment of Aelia Capitolina, and the ban on the entry of Jews into Jerusalem. The verses of Isaiah 7 showed the devastation of the land and of the Jewish people, the acts of the apostles and the spread of the Gospel. They spoke of the founding of Christian communities and churches, and even described the ecclesiastical hierarchy. This prophecy went on to portray in detail two types of Christian disciples—neophytes, who had not yet been baptized, and those who had been baptized recently.[48] Psalm 84 included a prophecy on the holiness of Sunday, the Lord's day, when Christian communities all over the world would gather together.[49]

Many prophecies predicted the great historic success of Christianity and its expansion throughout the world.[50] This subject features prominently in the works of Eusebius, who often cites the success of Christianity as proof of its truth. He certainly considered this an extremely important argument, one that in his view was based on historical fact. For example, Isaiah 44:18–19 foretold the use of the sign of the cross, the sign of Christ's salvation, at baptisms and other rites.[51] The prophecy in Isaiah 19:1–4 spoke of quarrels, riots, and conflicts on religious issues between pagans and Christians in Egypt during Eusebius' lifetime.[52] Isaiah 7:18–25 related to the internal hierarchical division in the Church.[53] The prophecy of Zechariah (14:1–10) envisioned the schisms and heresies that took place in the Church throughout its history.[54] Psalm 108:1–8 described how Jewish contemporaries of Eusebius cursed Jesus, even in synagogues—a phenomenon predicted by the prophets.[55] The prophecies of Micah spoke of the persecutions in Eusebius' time and the ongoing campaign against the Christians.[56] The verse, ". . . Zion shall be

---

mentary on Isaiah, see M.J. Hollerich, "Eusebius as a Polemical Interpreter of Scripture", in Attridge & G. Hata (eds.), *Eusebius, Christianity, and Judaism*, pp. 585–615.

[48] *DE* 2,3.
[49] *DE* 4,16.
[50] *PE* 1,3; *DE* 1,1; *DE* 2,3.
[51] *DE* 6,25.
[52] *DE* 6,20.
[53] *DE* 7,1. On prophecies that include specific instructions for the ecclesiastical hierarchy, see also Clement, *The Instructor*, 3, 12.
[54] *DE* 6,18.
[55] *DE* 10,3.
[56] *DE* 2,3.

ploughed as a field; Jerusalem shall become a heap of ruins, and
the mountain of the house a wooded height" (Mic. 3:12), had been
fulfilled even in Eusebius' lifetime. He attests to having seen on the
Temple Mount a Roman farm, a sown field and oxen plowing. They
were proof of the words: "Zion shall be ploughed as a field". "Jerusalem shall become a heap of ruins" could be interpreted according to Aquila's translation, namely, that "Jerusalem shall serve as a
source of stones for building" (Ἰερουσαλὴμ λιθολογηθήσεται). The fulfillment of the prophecy indeed followed Aquila's translation, for
Eusebius reported that stones from the ruins of Jerusalem and the
Temple were used to build temples and houses of entertainment in
the pagan city.[57]

Jesus the Prophet

Prophecies in the Hebrew Bible spoke of Jesus who had come to
fulfill them. Jesus, however, also was a prophet. He was the prophet
of whom Moses spoke (Deut. 18:15), who was destined to fulfill the
promise given to Abraham.[58] His prophecies were fulfilled in his own
lifetime and in subsequent generations, up to the time of Eusebius.
They were testimony and proof of Christian belief in Jesus.[59] Indeed,
Jesus had foreseen the history of the apostles and the subsequent
history of Christianity.[60] Eusebius recalls a work in which he collected all the prophecies of Jesus and showed how they were fulfilled in history, thus proving beyond all doubts the truth of Christian
views on Jesus.[61] In this work—since lost—which may have resembled the *Prophetic Extracts*, he collected and organized prophecies

---

[57] *DE* 8,3.

[58] *PE* 1,3,12; *DE* 1,3. In *DE* 9,11 Eusebius addresses the question as to why the
prophecy envisions a prophet and not a divinity as in the case of the Incarnation.
This poses a real problem, for in the major prophecy on Jesus, the verse speaks
only of a prophet. Eusebius' response is that the Logos which speaks in Deuteronomy 18:18, predicted Jesus' advent as a prophet on account of the weakness of
mankind, which was unable to comprehend his greatness.

[59] *PE*, ibid. The role of Jesus as a prophet is well known and occurs in early
apologetics without particular emphasis. Justin argued that his prophecies were being
fulfilled in his own times and that some would be realized in the future (*Dialogue*
8,35); likewise, Clement (*Stromateis* 7,15) and Origen (*CC* 2,13). According to Clement,
the apostles were also prophets (*Stromateis* 5,6).

[60] *DE* 3,5. According to Clement, he also foretold the disputes that would take
place within the Church (Matt. 13:28; *Stromateis* 7,15).

[61] *PE* 1,3,12.

according to their order of appearance in the Gospels. The work may have been similar to many chapters in the *DE* dealing with prophecies and their interpretations.[62]

Indeed, Eusebius does not interpret the prophecies of Jesus extensively, referring only occasionally to the Gospels and Epistles in order to prove his statements and the truths of Christianity. His general tendency, in fact, is to keep to a minimum the testimonies and proofs of Christianity taken from Christianity itself.[63] The same is true with regard to Christian writers and the New Testament. Proof of Christianity from Christianity itself was not forceful enough for a non-Christian. Proof had to be taken from the Old Testament, namely, from the oracle itself, which was not perceived as specifically Christian by a non-Christian. Despite the prophetic-oracular status of Jesus' words, the Gospels and the Epistles were usually used to reinforce a given proof, but not as proof in their own right.[64]

The Vague Language of Prophecy

The formulation of prophecies that truly predict the future is vague. True prophecy cannot be clear. If it were formulated in clear language it could turn out to be false in the future. An ambivalent and vague articulation allows all manner of interpretations and allows for the

---

[62] Lightfoot suggested that this work formed the basis of the fourth book of Eusebius' *Theophany*; likewise, Gressmann (Lightfoot, "Eusebius", p. 331; H. Gressmann, *Theophany*, p. 20).

[63] In fact, the marginal place that Eusebius accords to the prophecies of Jesus in *DE*, does not sit well with his declaration at the beginning of *PE*, that the fulfillment of the prophecies of Jesus, especially during the time of Eusebius, was more persuasive proof than any words in the endeavor to silence aggressive enemies. Eusebius' main focus was the prophecy that Christianity would spread among Gentiles throughout the world, strongly withstanding its enemies and the challenges it faced (*PE* 1,3,12). Here he mentions the specific work in which he collected the prophecies of Jesus and demonstrated their fulfillment in history. In context, it seems that the brief section on the importance of the prophecies of Jesus and their fulfillment—together with proof of the Church's strength vis-à-vis its enemies and death—is based on this earlier work. Perhaps it explains the inclusion of such statements at the beginning of *PE*, whereas in *DE*—which is largely devoted to prophecy—the proof of this fulfillment of Jesus' prophecy is relegated to a marginal place, unless Eusebius put this subject in the second, lost half of *DE*, due to the numerous prophecies of Jesus regarding the future of Christianity. Perhaps, one can assume that, although he saw this as important proof, he preferred to minimize it for the methodological, tactical reasons that I have noted.

[64] See Eusebius' statements in *DE* 7,1.

fulfillment and validation of the prophecy. This explains the significance of the oracle's enigmatic language. Prophecy is formulated in
clear and unequivocal language only when it relates to the past,
vaticinia ex eventu. Of course, this view was not held by Eusebius,
despite his knowing that Porphyry was of such an opinion, as we
have shown. A prophecy relating to the past, such as Daniel's, can
also be formulated in vague language because it was intended to
appear as true prophecy. This follows from Porphyry's argument,
although it is not certain he himself drew this conclusion. According to Eusebius, vagueness was an intrinsic feature of pagan oracles.
It could not, however, characterize a divine Hebrew oracle.

The voice of true divine prophecy had to come forth loud and
clear. In the cases of vague prophecies (according to Eusebius, not
all were vague), there had to be one or more reasons for the different formulation of the prophecy. Eusebius clearly states that prophecies had to be examined carefully. If they were vague, there had to
be a reason for their vagueness. Prophecies regarding the Jewish people were intentionally vague and ambiguous from the outset. For,
had they been written in clear language, and had the Jews known
their true meaning, they would have destroyed such prophecies.
Prophecies of this kind included the Incarnation and Ascension, the
Advent of the Savior, and his activities among the Jewish people, as
well as his rejection by the Jews, and their final destruction. All the
above related to the bitter fate of the Jews. God hid the fact of the
Jews' final destruction in order to enable them to preserve the Holy
Scripture for the Christians! Had the prophets openly foretold the
destruction of the Jews and the success of the Gentiles, the Jews
would have destroyed their own prophetic books.[65] Therefore, the
prophets themselves, who were persecuted and vilified by the Jews,
obscured their own prophecies. Clearer prophecies spoke of spread-

---

[65] *DE* 6, Introduction, 3; *DE* 7,1. This is a distinctly apologetic motif. Justin
argued that if the Jews had understood all the hints at Jesus in the prophecies, they
would have deleted them. In fact, he genuinely believed that the Jews destroyed
certain Christological passages. However, the sections to which Justin refers are
Christian interpolations and are not original (*Dialogue* 120,5). Similarly, Clement
argued that the prophets spoke about the Lord in enigmatic language so as not to
be considered blasphemers by the masses, who had different ideas. For prophets
were persecuted and killed when they spoke about Jesus (*Stromateis* 6,15). Irenaeus
wrote that the Jews would have not hesitated to burn their own writings had they
known of the future existence of the Christians, whose biblical proof promised them
everlasting life. By contrast, the Jews, who were proud to be "the house of Jacob",
would no longer inherit the grace of God (*Against Heresies*, 21,3).

ing the Gospel to the Gentiles, and of their redemption.[66]

Occasionally, there are other issues that could be regarded as problematic within a limited exegetical context. For example, Isaiah 7:18–25 speaks of events occurring with the advent of the Messiah. The Roman conquest and destruction of Jerusalem and the Jews eventually fulfilled this prophecy. Eusebius had to explain why the Romans are not mentioned by name in all the biblical prophecies that refer to them, and why some prophecies refer to them as Assyrians. Eusebius states that this prophecy regarding the Romans was veiled in signs and riddles in order to lend it the vague character of an oracle, and to thus avoid offending the rulers of the empire with unflattering prophecies. For in the future, the prophetic books would be published in Rome and throughout the empire, together with Jesus' Gospel. Such statements also held true for the prophecy regarding the Romans in the book of Daniel.[67]

Here, Eusebius clearly states that biblical and oracular prophecies both have an enigmatic, oracular character, even though he sees a need, in the above example, to explain the vagueness.[68] In fact, all prophecy that can be understood only symbolically or allegorically, should be regarded as ambiguous. The attitude of Eusebius to the method of allegorical interpretation is somewhat problematic. We must remember that Porphyry attacked the radical Christian allegorical method of Origen,[69] and Eusebius rejected the philosophical-allegorical interpretations of mythology and pagan religion. Apparently, he was aware of a problem in this regard. On every possible occasion, he makes superb use of the different Greek translations of the Bible and of the corrected Greek version of Origen's *Hexapla*, in order to find a textual source for his preferred interpretation.[70] Often,

---

[66] *DE*, ibid.

[67] *DE* 7,1.

[68] Eusebius' interpretation expresses respect for the empire. This attitude is consistent and is occasionally given a theological foundation, which will be discussed later.

[69] Porphyry, *Against the Christians*, Harnack, F. 39. Celsus also attacked the Christian allegorical method. As a devoted user of this method, Origen could not abandon it. He only partly censured pagan allegory, and at one point even asked that philosophical allegory be treated as fairly as Christian allegory, for an attack on the allegorical interpretation of Bible stories could serve as a double-edged sword, which could be turned against pagan allegory (*CC* 4,38).

[70] On Eusebius' keen selection of quotations from the different translations in order to suit his interpretation, see also Wallace-Hadrill, *Eusebius*, p. 87, and D. Barthelemy, "Eusèbe, la Septante, et 'les autres'", *La Bible et les Pères* (Paris,

however, Eusebius had no alternative to allegory, and this required an apology on his part. For if an allegorical interpretation were not used in some cases, we would be left with inconsistent and absurd mythology![71] In fact, the latter argument had always been put forward by the Greek allegorical commentators of Homer and of mythology. Here Eusebius again shows that one cannot become completely detached from one's cultural world, even when attempting to destroy and invalidate it. Nevertheless, it was Eusebius' belief, it seems, that biblical verses which can be understood only through allegory were intentionally written as such.[72] This was not the case regarding Homer and Greek mythology, upon which philosophers forced their absurd interpretations. According to Eusebius, therefore, allegorical interpretation was valid in those sections where Scripture could only be understood allegorically,[73] though he does not follow this principle consistently. Thus Eusebius offers an apology for allegorical interpretation. However, despite his extensive use of allegory, when compared with other Christian commentators he can be considered a moderate allegorist. At times he even voices opposition to the prevalent practice of extreme allegorization among Christian writers.[74]

Many prophecies concerning Jesus and Christianity were to be found in Psalms. The *DE* is full of verses from the Psalms which Eusebius interprets as prophecies, where the Logos frequently speaks from the mouth of the divine poet. In fact, one could say that in the *DE*, the Psalms are presented as the Christians' foremost prophetic book! For example, Psalm 22 even included a theological oration in first person, given by Jesus on the cross before his death![75] As we have noted, King David was considered a prophet alongside the patriarchs and other prophets. But in Eusebius' time, there were

---

1971), pp. 52–55. In the different works of Eusebius, the same biblical text sometimes receives different interpretations. See Des Places, *Eusèbe de Césarée commentateur*, pp. 157–188.

[71] *DE* 2,3.

[72] Origen applied this rule to the entire corpus of Scripture, all of which, he believed, was written with an allegorical purpose, including the "historical" books of the Bible (*CC* 4,49).

[73] *DE*, ibid.

[74] See Sant, *The Old Testament Interpretation of Eusebius*, p. 42. According to Des Places, Eusebius was never extreme in his allegorical interpretation of the Bible, maintaining a middle ground between the Alexandrian and the Antiochene schools of interpretation, just as Caesarea itself was located between the two cities (Des Places, *Eusèbe de Césarée commentateur*, p. 194); cf. Hollerich, *Commentary*, pp. 94–102.

[75] *DE* 10,8.

apparently those who contested the prophetic status given to the Psalms by the Christians. He relates to such arguments, referring to those who regarded the Psalms as simply a book of sacred hymns rather than a book of prophecies. Christians were accused of vainly searching the book of Psalms for predictions of the future. However, Eusebius does not indicate the target of his refutation—Jews, Christians, or heretics, or even, perhaps, Porphyry. He sets out to prove that the Psalms were indeed a book of prophecy,[76] by showing that the prophecies in Psalms had been fulfilled. His intention was to prove the fulfillment of prophecies, not with regard to Christianity, but rather as proof of their intrinsic truth. Once again, it was preferable to demonstrate this from Jewish and general history, not from Christian history. The fulfillment of prophecies not pertaining to Christians would prove the truth of prophecies about Christians.[77] This issue touches on the more basic question of whether one can discover prophecies anywhere in the Bible, and if not, which non-prophetic biblical books might contain prophetic words. Eusebius, however, does not elaborate on this beyond relating to arguments against the prophetic status of the book of Psalms.

An Example of Apologetic Interpretation of Prophecy

I shall present only one example of Eusebius' detailed interpretation of prophecy as it appears in the framework of the *DE*. Jacob's blessing to his sons, especially to Judah (Gen. 49:8–12), is understood as a prediction of the future.[78] The apologetic-polemical framework for the interpretation of this prophecy stems from the need to explain the historical circumstances of the advent of Jesus Christ and its timing, due to the anti-Christian argument regarding the late appearance of Jesus in history—an argument often linked to critical

---

[76] Apparently, Eusebius had a special regard for the book of Psalms as an all-encompassing work. He maintained that the book of Psalms contained everything mentioned by Plato (*DE* 12,21). On Eusebius' relative allegorism and the interpretation of Psalms as a sort of breviary of Scripture, see C. Curti, "L'esegesi di Eusebio di Cesarea: Caratteri e sviluppo", in *Eusebiana, I: Commentarii in Psalmos* (Catania, 1987), pp. 195–213.

[77] *DE* 10,1.

[78] Justin's understanding of this blessing as a prediction of the future (*First Apology*, 32) may have served as a basis for Eusebius' wider interpretation. See also Hippolytus, *On Christ and Antichrist* 8–13; Irenaeus, *Against Heresies* 4,10; Origen, *Commentary on Matthew* 10,21; *CC* 1,53; Archelaus, *Disputation with Manes* 43–44.

comment on his appearing to a despised and barbaric people in a remote corner of the world. Eusebius deals with this argument in a polemical context, within the framework of the historical concept that he had developed.[79] Here, the interpretation of prophecy is seen as important proof of the truth of the prophecy, which it describes and explains.

Perhaps Eusebius viewed the blessing of Jacob as a special prophecy. He states, though not explicitly, that it had to be understood as including all the important events related in the New Testament and in the history of Christianity, particularly the marvelous birth and death of Jesus.[80] In other words, Jacob's words constituted a major prophecy containing the main points of Christian history. Eusebius does not make this claim in his interpretation of other prophecies, even if they include many details of the history of Christianity. In fact, the entire, lengthy first chapter of Book VIII of the *DE* is devoted to Jacob's blessing to Judah.

The novelty of Eusebius' unprecedented and complex exegetical efforts becomes apparent when compared to the earlier patristic exegesis of such authors as Justin, Clement, Irenaeus, Hippolytus, and Origen. In Justin and Hippolytus one finds the beginning of a systematic interpretation of Jacob's blessing to Judah, but it is still rather basic and undeveloped. Nonetheless, it is also evident that the interpretation of these biblical verses had become an apologetic-polemical convention by the time of Eusebius, who employed some of the exegetical motifs of his predecessors—as will be further indicated—and incorporated them into his elaborate scheme.

Before his death, Jacob assembled his sons in order to find out which of his descendants would be the ancestor of Jesus Christ, the bearer of the Gospel and Redeemer of mankind![81] Jacob did so in the knowledge of God's promises to his grandfather Abraham and his father Isaac, and even to him, regarding the mission to the Gentiles. After he had scolded his three eldest sons because of their sins, he told them that fulfillment of prophecies would not be achieved through them due to their evil deeds.[82] When Judah's turn came, Jacob prophesied and spoke of the oracle that had been given to

---

[79] *DE* 8, Introduction, 12; *DE* 1,9,1–13.
[80] *DE* 8,1,63.
[81] *DE* 8,1,6.
[82] *DE* 8,1,1–5.

him: "A company of nations shall come from you, and kings shall spring from you" (Gen. 35:11), as referring to the descendants of Judah. It is a well-known fact that the royal family came from the tribe of Judah.[83] In his prophecy, Jacob indicated the historic time of its fulfillment, and the fulfillment of the promises to the Gentiles. Thus the verse, ". . . until Shiloh comes and to him shall be the obedience of all peoples" (Gen. 49:10) is interpreted as referring to the Messiah and the Gospel, and to the Gentiles. Jesus Christ who was the "Shiloh", could not precede the fulfillment of the condition in the first part of the verse, "the scepter shall not depart from Judah;" only when political power was removed from the Jews, would the Messiah be revealed.[84] Before he could prove the fulfillment of the prophecy in the historical circumstances relating to the time of Jesus' appearance, Eusebius had to show that the historical precondition of the prophecy had been fulfilled—namely, that the tribe of Judah had ruled over the people with a supremacy that went back to the very beginnings of a Jewish political entity in the land.

Here he embarks on an exegetical undertaking, collecting verses and fragments of verses that attest to the primacy of the tribe before the reign of King David. For example, even during the period of the Judges, when there were judges from different tribes, the tribe of Judah led the people. The same held true for the period of the return to Zion, led by Zerubbabel of the tribe of Judah. According to Eusebius, there was additional proof that the tribe of Judah had enjoyed superior status from the days of Moses and Joshua until the destruction of the First Temple. This lay in the fact that the author of the book of Chronicles had placed Judah first in the genealogies of the twelve tribes (I Chron. 2). While less was known about the Second Temple period, it was established that the leaders did not come solely from the tribe of Judah. Even then, as in the period of Judges, Judah had hegemony until the time of Augustus and Herod (who was of foreign origin), when the Jews lost their autonomy and the Redeemer was born.[85] Thus political rule by the Jews did not cease until the fulfillment of the hope of the Gentiles, i.e., the advent of Jesus Christ. The Septuagint version of Genesis 49:10, "and to him shall be the obedience of all peoples", was "hope of the Gentiles"

---

[83] *DE* 8,1,7–10.
[84] *DE* 8,1,18–20. See also Justin, *First Apology* 32; *Dialogue* 52 and 120.
[85] *DE* 8,1,11–17.

("αὐτὸς προσδοκία ἐθνῶν"). He, Shiloh, was the hope and anticipation of the Gentiles, the promise given to Abraham and his descendants.[86] This prophecy bound the two signs together and thus identified
the time of the advent of Jesus.

Eusebius tried hard to show that the prophecy made to Judah
spoke of the tribe of Judah, in general, as leader of the people from
the times of Moses, and not of Judah himself or the individuals who
led the tribe. The prophecy could not be taken as applying to rulers
from the tribe of Judah, because many leaders prior to King David
were not from this tribe. Furthermore, it did not apply to kings from
the house of David because they could not fulfill the condition of
continuous rule ("the scepter shall not fall from Judah"); for the most
part, they ruled over only three of the tribes.

To argue his case, Eusebius used the Septuagint and the translations of Theodotion and Aquila. From the return to Zion until the
birth of Jesus, the people were ruled by an aristocracy (πολιτεία ἀρισ-
τοκρατική) and by high priests who were not of the tribe of Judah.
Eusebius apparently included the Hasmoneans in this plan.[87] He concludes that the prophecy had to be understood, therefore, as referring to the tribe of Judah in general, and not to individual rulers
who arose from its midst. This point could be proved by the name
of the country, Judah, and the name of the people, the Jews. Thus
"the scepter shall not fall from Judah and the ruler from between
his feet" referred to the hegemony of the tribe. Here Eusebius was
assisted by the translation of Symmachus, who translated the passage as "the power of sovereignty shall not fall from Judah" (οὐ περι-
αιρεθήσεται ἐξουσία ἀπό Ἰούδα), and linked it with Aquila's translation
which stated that the "scepter" was the sign of royalty.[88]

Eusebius proposes a neat parallel to strengthen his interpretation
of the prophecy as relating to the entire tribe. The parallel is between
the Roman Empire in his time, and Jewish history up to the Roman
conquest. One can see the apologetic intention underpinning such
a proposal. Not all the rulers or high officials were Roman or descendants of Romulus and Remus, but were nonetheless called "Romans".
Likewise, in the Jewish state, the tribe of Judah served as the name

---

[86] *DE* 8,1,25. See Justin, Dialogue 52; 120; Hippolytus, *On Christ and Antichrist* 9;
Origen, *CC* 1,53; Archelaus, *Disputation* 44.
[87] *DE* 8,1,25–32.
[88] *DE* 8,1,33–34.

for the entire people, despite the fact that kings and rulers came from different tribes. Eusebius' entire exegetical effort may have been directed at demonstrating the fulfillment of the ancient prophecy of Jacob, father of the nation. The first part of the prophecy may also have come under virulent attack. In order to sustain the interpretation that the prophecy was fulfilled in Jesus, it was first necessary to prove the earlier condition that constituted the first part of the prophecy. The exegetical purpose of Eusebius was to present the tribe of Judah as the ideal tribe, for Christ descended from it. Thus the prophecy included praise of the tribe of Judah as the ideal tribe. Eusebius further elaborates on the condition of the prophecy, namely, that when "the ruler will depart from Judah", i.e., when Jewish rule ended in Judah, Christ would appear. The fulfillment of this condition began when Herod was appointed king by Augustus and the Roman senate. The rule of the high priestly dynasty also ceased with the reign of Herod, who was the first outsider to be made king over the Jews.[89] His time saw the birth of Jesus, the destruction of the kingdom of the Jews, and the fulfillment of the prophecy "the scepter shall not fall from Judah . . .". Hence, Luke's testimony that Jesus' activity began under Tiberius and Pontius Pilate, with the end of Jewish rule, and the testimony of Matthew that, on the birth of Jesus, came the call to the Gentiles with the appearance of the three wise men (Magi) from the East.[90] In light of the above, Jacob's message to his sons, "Gather yourselves together, that I may tell you what shall befall you in days to come" (Gen. 49:1), was easy to understand. "The days to come" were the end of the days of Jewish rule over the people and the land, namely, the time of the birth of Jesus. Or, as Eusebius also puts it, these were the final days of the existence of the Jewish people as a national entity (τὰ ἔσχατα τῆς συστάσεως τοῦ Ἰουδαίων ἔθνους), when the political existence of the state would cease, the land and the people would be destroyed, and the rule of Christ would be established over the Gentiles.[91] This was the meaning of the words: "and to him shall be obedience of all peoples".

Genesis 49:8–9 describes the hegemony of the tribe of Judah over

---

[89] *DE* 8,1,38–45. Eusebius conveys the tradition that Herod's father, Antipater, was the son of a temple servant in the temple of Apollo in Ascalon, who married an Arab woman named Cypros. See also *HE* 1,7,11. See also Justin, *Dialogue* 52.

[90] *DE* 8,1,46–48.

[91] *DE* 8,1,48–49.

the people, and its past glory. Perhaps the most problematic words in the prophecy are "until Shiloh comes". In the Septuagint, the passage appears as "until comes what lies for him in the future", (ἕως ἂν ἔλθῃ τὰ ἀποκείμενα αὐτοῦ); the Septuagint seems to have translated the Hebrew שילה (Shiloh) as if it were שלו, meaning "his". The problem of the verse on Judah was solved by showing that, in the Bible, the Messiah had many names, among them, Jacob, Solomon, David, and even Judah. Thus we should understand the verse as referring to the things awaiting the Messiah, and not Judah. A complementary interpretation of the earlier passages had now been established.[92]

Thus the Messiah was the subject of the verses "Judah, your brothers shall praise you; your hand shall be on the neck of your enemies; your father's sons shall bow down before you. Judah is a lion's whelp; from the prey, my son, you have gone up. He stooped down, he couched as a lion and as an old lion; who shall rouse him up?" (Gen. 49:8–9). The verses included the praise of his brothers, conquest of his enemies, and admiration by the sons of his father; they were fulfilled in Jesus, who was admired by his brothers—his apostles and disciples. Moreover, Eusebius discerns a growing awareness of the true essence of Jesus on the part of the apostles and disciples. This progressive awareness was hinted at in the prophecy. At first, they regarded him as an extraordinary person and a prophet because of the miracles he performed. However, once they realized the magnitude of his wondrous miracles and saw how he overcame the great enemy, namely, death, ruler of the world, and his demonic forces, they immediately believed in him and worshipped him as divine. This was the meaning of "your hand shall be on the neck of your enemies; your father's sons shall bow down before you".[93]

"Your hand shall be on the neck of your enemies" was also understood as the Messiah's pursuit of the demons fleeing from him on his descent to Hades, and their turning their backs on him after

---

[92] For a comprehensive survey of the use of Genesis 49:10, "until Shiloh comes", and its identification with Christ in Christian biblical exegesis, see A. Posnansky, *Schiloh: Ein Beitrag zur Geschichte der Messiaslehre*, I (Leipzig, 1904). This verse is interpreted as a prediction of the Messiah also in rabbinic literature, "shiloh" interpreted as the Messiah's name. See e.g., BT Sanhedrin 98b; Targ. Ps. Jon. Gen. 49:10.

[93] *DE* 8,1,52–59. Here Eusebius inadvertently expresses two unconventional opinions: that the apostles only gradually recognized the divinity of Jesus—a sober view of the Gospel account, and that the recognition of divinity took place because of the greatness of Jesus' miracles.

acknowledging his divinity.[94] However, the words "your hand shall be on the neck of your enemies", could also be interpreted as referring to the time of Eusebius, namely, the end of the persecution of the Christians and the failure of their enemies. The phrase, "your father's sons shall bow down before you", referred to Christians all over the world who acknowledged God the Father, and God, Christ, the Word. The words, "Judah is a lion's whelp", attested to the birth of Jesus from the royal seed of David. "He stooped down, he couched as a lion" tells of the death of Jesus. In the Septuagint, the word "couched" is translated as "fell asleep" (ἀναπεσὼν ἐκοιμήθης ὡς λέων), and Eusebius may have interpreted sleep as death. As for the phrase, "And as an old lion who shall rouse him up", the Septuagint reads "who shall awaken him" (τίς ἐγερεῖ αὐτού), which signals the resurrection of Jesus. For if Jacob said "who shall awaken him?", he was certain that he would be aroused. And who would rouse him, if not the father of the universe? Here Eusebius uses the translated versions of Aquila and Symmachus, whose language accords with his interpretation of the verses on death and the descent into Hades, likening this to a prison, and the escape from there, to flight from an animal trap. This was the meaning of the words: "from a prey my son, you have gone up". He interprets Symmachus' translation of the phrase, "he stooped down, he couched". While the Septuagint reads "you have fallen down, you have gone to sleep" (ἀναπεσὼν ἐκοιμήθης), Symmachus translates the phrase as "you have stooped down, you have stood up" (ὀκλάσας ἡδράσθης). Eusebius regarded Symmachus' translation as hinting at the unique death of Jesus. His soul stood up, and was not dragged and removed as the souls of other people after their death.[95]

The subsequent verses relating Jacob's blessing to Judah (Gen. 49:11–12), are interpreted in terms of Jesus and the apostles, and events or expressions mentioned in the Gospels. In "Binding his foal to the vine and his ass's colt to the choice vine", the vine was the divine power of the Redeemer, as attested by Jesus himself in John 15:1 ("I am the true vine"). "His foal" was the group of apostles

---

[94] *DE* 8,1,60. *DE* 10,8 contains a longer section on the descent into the netherworld (Hades), which includes several traditional themes closer in spirit to the *Gospel of Nicodemus*. See Ferrar's note to his translation of the *DE*, part 2, p. 112.

[95] *DE* 8,1,64–69. In the continuation of his statements, Eusebius seems to suggest that the apostles and his disciples recognized the divinity of Jesus only after his Resurrection.

and disciples. The "choice vine" was the doctrine of the Logos, by means of which he bound the ass's colt, namely, the new people from among the Gentiles. They were the descendants of the apostles. The fulfillment of the literal meaning of Jacob's prophecy was Jesus' entry into Jerusalem upon a colt as related in the New Testament (Matt. 21:2). Jacob's prophecy also hinted at the coming of the Messiah on a donkey colt, as the prophet Zechariah had envisioned (Zech. 9:9).[96] "He washes his garments in wine and his vesture in the blood of the grape", is the prophecy of the suffering, the passion of Jesus. Wine was the symbol (σύμβολον) of the blood of Jesus, with which he purified the clothing, that is, the bodies of the believers baptized to his death.[97] The new covenant, contained in the bread and the wine, concluded the prophecy.

The verse, "his eyes shall be red with wine; and his teeth white with milk", alluded to the mystery of the new covenant. The Septuagint translates "his eyes shall be red with wine", as "his eyes sparkle from wine" (χαροποὶ οἱ ὀφθαλμοὶ αὐτοῦ ἀπὸ οἴνου). Eusebius understood this as the eyes expressing the happiness of the mystical wine (μυστικοῦ οἴνου) that Jesus gave his disciples at the Last Supper. "And his teeth white with milk" referred to the brightness and purity of the mystical food (τὸ λαμπρὸν καὶ καθαρὸν τῆς μυστηριώδους τροφῆς). Jesus gave his disciples the symbols of his divine essence when he commanded them to make these the image of his body (τὴν εἰκόνα τοῦ ἰδίου σώματος ποιεῖσθαι). Here the symbolic and mystical meaning of the bread and the wine is clear, as Eusebius actually calls the bread the symbol of the body of Jesus.[98] The concept of sacrifice is presented as the antithesis of the animal sacrifices that repelled Jesus. The purity of the sacrifice is acknowledged by the bread, a simple and pure food. This was the meaning of "his teeth white with milk". Thus Jesus commanded his disciples to make an image of his body by means of the symbols which he had placed in their hands, namely, bread and wine. However, Eusebius states

---

[96] For this traditional interpretation in early patristic exegesis and variations, see Justin, *First Apology* 32; *Dialogue* 53; Clement, *The Instructor* 1,5; Hippolytus, *On Christ and Antichrist* 10.

[97] For the interpretation of this verse on Christ's passion, see Justin, *First Apology* 32; *Dialogue* 53; Hippolytus, *On Christ and Antichrist* 11.

[98] On the symbolic interpretation of the bread and wine at the Last Supper, see also Clement, *The Instructor*, 1,6. For a different interpretation of this verse, see Hippolytus, *On Christ and Antichrist* 12–13.

that these issues were complicated and required profound discussion, which he could not undertake in this framework. He had to continue with the testimony of the prophets regarding the time of Christ's appearance, within the apologetic-polemical framework of his detailed and lengthy commentary on the prophetic aspects of Jacob's blessing to Judah.[99]

Conclusion

For Eusebius prophecy in scripture is one of the great polemical proofs, perhaps the greatest, of the truths of Christianity. The fulfillment of the prophecy is the ultimate answer to every provocation, and the force of prophecy as a proof stems from its fulfillment in history. This is the general perspective of the *Demonstratio Evangelica*. The prophecies in holy scripture envision the whole of human history, but the main proof is that everything told in the New Testament and all events in the history of Christianity up to the very days of Eusebius actually constitute a single chain of fulfilled prophecies. The fulfillment of the prophecy is at the same time a proof of the existence of divine providence. The prophecies and indeed entire scripture become a book full of historical clues entailing the entire scope of future history. We could read it if we only knew how to decipher and study it with proper eyes. Eusebius faces a double task. He must reestablish the prophetic status of scripture following the assault of Porphyry. This is true especially with regard to sympathetic pagans and to Christians coming from an educated pagan background. But he must also demonstrate in detail that the prophecies are fulfilled only in the life of Jesus and in Christianity after him. In order to establish the uniqueness of Hebrew prophecy as source and proof for Christian truth Eusebius must distinguish it from the manifestations of pagan prophecy. For him the main form of pagan historical prophecy is oracular prophecy, and in the *Praeparatio Evangelica* he dedicates long pages to the refutation of pagan oracles. The need to refute the oracles is not only a theoretical matter. Oracles and various arts of divination were an important part of pagan

---

[99] *DE* 8,1,72–81. Eusebius develops the parallel between Jacob's blessing on Judah, and the prophecy of Balaam (Numbers 24), insisting on their similarity (*DE* 9,3). It provided additional proof that Jesus fulfilled the biblical prophecies. As the realization of one prophecy had been verified, another, similar one would be fulfilled.

religious behavior. Furthermore, oracular and theurgical circles were strongholds of pagan resistance to Christianity. Eusebius does not deny the prophetic powers of the oracles altogether but asserts their inferiority to Hebrew "oracles". His complex view of the oracles enables him to exploit certain positive pagan oracles for his polemical purposes. He also believes that many pagans regard the holy Hebrew scripture as an oracular source. All his efforts in the *Praeparatio* are aimed at preparing the ground for the universal recognition of Scripture as the sole oracular source of truth.

CHAPTER SIX

MIRACLES: A MAJOR SUBJECT
IN EUSEBIUS' POLEMICS

Eusebius' Ambivalent Attitude To Miracles

Miracles were always an integral part of Christian apologetics. In the context of Christian-pagan polemics, miracles performed by Jesus played a particularly important role, as proof both of the truth of his Gospel and of his divinity.[1] As polemics developed, several problematic aspects became evident, notably the subsequent comparison and rivalry between "Christian" and "pagan" miracles. We have noted that such a comparison soon became a major theme in polemics. Pagan critics argued that miracles performed by Jesus and the apostles were no more special or unusual than the wonders attributed to gods, heroes, and men with exceptional powers. Christians did not have a monopoly on miracles. Moreover, pagan miracle workers did not pretend to be gods. While not denying their validity, Hierocles attempted to depreciate Jesus' miracles and to show that those performed by Apollonius were greater. Porphyry belittled the particular significance that Christians attached to miracles. For him, the ability to perform miracles was a universal human characteristic whose importance should not be exaggerated. Miracles could not be of such consequence if they were performed by simple apostles. Egyptian magicians performed many miracles to counteract those of Moses, and Apollonius also performed numerous miracles.[2]

Pagan critics acknowledged magical powers and thus had no difficulty in recognizing Jesus as a wonder worker. But the fact that Jesus

---

[1] According to Justin, miracles were proof of the truth and the divinity of Jesus. The miracles of Jesus and those which continued to take place in his name were proof of his divine perfection (*Dialogue* 7,3; *Dialogue* 35,8). Miracles and exorcisms still performed in the name of Jesus constituted ongoing proof of his divinity (*Dialogue* 85,3).

[2] Harnack, F. 4. According to his own testimony in *Philosophy from the Oracles*, Porphyry also exorcised demons at least once. See Bidez, *Vie de Porphyre*, p. 49. According to Geffcken, pagans exorcised demons as eagerly as Christians did (*Last Days*, p. 57), but this is not corroborated by literary evidence.

was viewed as an ordinary miracle worker detracted from the special status and divine power of the miracles as proof of the truth of Christianity. Christian apologists replied that the nature of Jesus' miracles, which were more astounding, evinced their divine origins, while pagan miracles were the result of demonic machinations. This argument dated from the time of Justin Martyr.[3] For Christian apologists, comparisons with pagan wonders gradually reduced the appeal of miracles as evidence of the truths of Christian doctrines. They began to focus more on the content of Christianity and the moral character of its teachers, in order to imbue miracles with authority and authenticity. The appeal to moral perfection may have derived its strength from the Christians' moral standards, which were greatly superior to those of pagan society, a fact acknowledged by Christians and pagans alike. An attenuated version of this view can be found in Justin,[4] and occasionally it is stated more explicitly in Origen.

This line of thought is fully developed in Eusebius.[5] In the context of their treatment of other issues, both J. Sirinelli and G. Lampe have argued that Eusebius avoided basing his arguments on miracles in his apologetic-polemical writings. According to Sirinelli, miracles play a marginal role in Eusebius' historical-apologetic writings.[6] Sirinelli and Lampe base their arguments on negative evidence: in his historical and polemical works Eusebius devotes relatively little space to the subject of miracle, and thus one can conclude that he accords it marginal importance. However, with the exception of a brief remark on Eusebius' refutation of criticism directed at Jesus and the apostles that was intended to discredit his miracles, neither Sirinelli nor Lampe study those sections of Eusebius' work where miracles are presented as substantial proof of the divinity of Jesus and the truth of the Gospel. Apparently, each scholar chose, in his own way, to minimize Eusebius' statements, to the extent of totally ignoring them.[7] Sirinelli tried to discern Eusebius' general attitude to

---

[3] See Justin, *First Apology*, 14. In fact, this argument may have parallels in pagan literature. For example, Iamblichus (*Life of Pythagoras* 28), states that the wonderful tales about Pythagoras and his miracles attested to his divinity. Iamblichus goes on to note that Pythagoras was worthy of being called divine because of his moral teachings (ibid.).

[4] Ibid.

[5] For a general view on miracles in early apologetics, see G.W.H. Lampe, "Miracles and Early Christian Apologetic", *Miracles: Cambridge Studies in their Philosophy and History*, ed. C.F.D. Moule (London, 1965), pp. 205–218.

[6] Lampe, ibid., p. 214; Sirinelli, *Vues*, p. 373, p. 380.

[7] Sirinelli adapts his view to his belief that Eusebius had a strong tendency to

miracles outside an apologetic-polemical context, particularly in the
HE and the *Martyrs of Palestine,* and claimed that Eusebius acknowledged the truth of Christian miracles. Eusebius stated that he saw
miracles performed[8] and was present at exorcisms, and he may have
performed an exorcism himself.[9] But his attitude to miracles was generally circumspect, and in this he resembled Porphyry. He was not
carried away by descriptions of miracles and did not use them extensively.[10] He viewed Christian miracles largely as part of a totality
encompassing the Old and New Testaments, and contemporary Christian miracles. For example, the miracle experienced by Constantine
at the battle of the Milvian Bridge resembled the drowning of Pharaoh
and his horses in the Red Sea.[11] One miracle actually enhanced the
other, the more recent confirming the truth of the earlier one, and
this demonstrated the principle of divine intervention.[12] Later, we
shall see that this is in fact an apologetic-polemical concept that takes
its place in the framework of arguments attesting to the truth of miracles in the *DE.*

According to Sirinelli, Eusebius' reservations concerning miracles
derived both from his reaction to the skeptical attitude of critics of
Christianity towards Christian miracles—especially the more recent
ones—and from the prevalence of magic in his day. Sirinelli holds
that despite his belief in miracles, Eusebius was not interested in
their "miraculous" character and sought to neutralize this aspect. He
also states that Eusebius shrank from the very personal revelations
of divine power that took the form of miracles.[13] Even if Sirinelli is

---

rationalize miracles. Such a tendency is to some degree evident. But one can get
the impression that Sirinelli shrinks from the possibility that Eusebius related to
miracles as significant occurrences though not to their fantastic aspects. Sirinelli also
was influenced by a strong desire to emphasize the historical dimension of the miracle—that sacred Christian history was an ongoing miracle that dwarfed miracles
in their classical sense. In his opinion, each individual miracle takes its place in the
grand design of Providence, the grand design of the sacred history of the Gospel.
Thus continuous historical processes can be interpreted as miracles. The great ongoing miracle was the entire history of Christianity, in which individual miracles lost
their uniqueness (Sirinelli, *Vues,* p. 387). Lampe may have chosen to ignore explicit
statements by Eusebius that interfere somewhat with the general thesis of his article; however, the complexity of Eusebius' standpoint is indicative of its multifaceted
nature rather than of any contradictions in its overall perception.

[8] *Martyrs of Palestine,* 4;9;11.
[9] *Against Hierocles,* 4.
[10] Sirinelli, *Vues,* p. 377.
[11] *HE* 9,9,3. On miracles in *HE,* see Sirinelli, ibid., pp. 379–380.
[12] Sirinelli, ibid., p. 375.
[13] Sirinelli, ibid., pp. 379–380.

right as regards Eusebius' reserved attitude to miracles in general,[14] perhaps the strength of his contemporaries' belief in magic and miracles gave added force to arguments and proofs based on miracles. Thus historical facts could serve as an excellent basis for his ambivalent attitude. First, the miracles of pagans and heretics were the creation of demons. Hence his negative attitude to pagan miracles. This could also explain his reservations regarding Christian miracles, when these were equated by pagan polemicists with pagan miracles. Secondly, the major Christian miracles were proof of the truth of Christianity precisely because the belief in miracles was so strong. Even if Eusebius attempts to perceive a miracle in rational terms and to minimize its fantastic dimension, this does not negate the great importance that he attributes to miracles as proof of divine power. This is the heart of the matter. The power of the miracle, and not its external aspects, indicates the divine power behind it. If Eusebius' somewhat ambivalent attitude to miracles derives partly from a reaction to the pagan writers' critique of Christianity, this demonstrates the way in which the literary context prevails over the social-religious reality in his writing. Perhaps in the heyday of Iamblichus and the late neo-Platonists, the challenge facing Christian apologists did not lie in a reluctance to believe in the authenticity of miracles. The critiques by Celsus, Porphyry, and Julian had no epistemological basis in the prevalent consciousness, even among pagan intellectuals of that generation. Thus the true difficulty for Christian apologists lay in the distinction that had to be made between Christian miracles and pagan magic, and not in the question of authenticity of the miracle itself.[15] Perhaps this can explain Eusebius' distinction between anti-Christian pagans who accepted Jesus' miracles as a fact, and those who rejected them. Those who rejected them seemed to be, for the most part, active enemies of Christianity, including authors such as Celsus and Porphyry. In fact, even if the enemies of Chris-

---

[14] I shall include only two examples from *DE* which show Eusebius' tendency to rationalize miracles. In *DE* 1,3, he states that Isaiah 11:6 ("And the wolf shall dwell with the lamb") teaches us about the transformation of savage nations, who live like wild animals, into a social, moderate, and holy way of life, with the coming of Christ. Here he presents an historical rationalization for a miraculous eschatological prophecy. In *DE* 9,12, Eusebius interprets Job 9:7–8 ("... and who trampled the waves of the sea") as Job's prediction of the miracle of Jesus' walking on the water. To this he adds allegory and symbolism: the sea serves as an arena for the struggle between the forces of Satan and God.

[15] See R.M. Grant, *Miracle and Natural Law*, pp. 214–215.

tianity viewed the miracles of Jesus as authentic events, they could attack their credibility for tactical reasons. Eusebius' generally ambivalent attitude to miracles may have been influenced by the works of Origen, who expressed similar opinions.[16] Eusebius' attempts to invest miracles with rational characteristics were not intended as an interpretation of such miracles in terms of the laws of nature, as was the case in later patristic literature, particularly the school of Antioch.[17] In other words, there is no phenomenology of miracles deriving from their rationalization. For Eusebius, the possibility of miracles was axiomatic. They did not pose a problem that had to be explained in terms of the prevailing view of natural law. The apologetic-polemical framework did not require a discussion of such problems. Pagan critique did not undermine the principle that a miracle was an extraordinary phenomenon, intervening in the processes of nature. The very existence of miracles was never questioned, even if they had to be explained in terms used for unusual natural phenomena. Christian miracles were attacked only because they were thought to be fictitious and false, or because they were alleged to be proof of the divinity of Jesus, and hence to be in themselves divine. We have noted exceptions such as the Incarnation and resurrection of the dead, which were virulently attacked as logical and theological absurdities. In fact, as we shall see, Eusebius' attitude to these last two tenets was problematic.

The two apologetic-polemical themes coexist in the work of Eusebius. On the one hand, miracles are a crucial foundation for proof of the truth of Christian doctrines. On the other, within the narrow

---

[16] For Origen's ambivalent attitude to miracles, see Grant, *Miracle and Natural Law*, pp. 197–208. Despite Origen's ambivalent attitude to miracles, as Grant has shown, he does not hesitate to make use of miracles in the context of his polemic against Celsus. Although the nature of this work does not allow for the development of this theme, suffice it to say that Origen's statements in various works have a cumulative weight. In reply to Celsus' claims, Origen several times uses the apologetic argument that seeks to prove the divinity of Jesus and the truths of the Gospel from miracles performed in the past and in the present, too, in the form of healing, exorcism, and the historical success of Christianity (*CC* 1,67; 2,9; 2,33; 2,35; 2,79; 3,33; 8;9). Furthermore, even pagan magicians used the name of Jesus in order to exorcise demons. The power of the name was so strong that even evil men, charlatans, and impostors could use it (*CC* 1,6; 2,49). Thus not only Christian miracles proved the divinity of Jesus, but pagan miracles, too. However, as shall be seen, Origen is not satisfied with such arguments, needing the moral argument, too, which features only marginally and remains relatively undeveloped.

[17] For this approach, see Grant, *Miracle and Natural Law*, pp. 210–220.

polemical context of refuting specific anti-Christian arguments, the uniqueness of Christian miracles is proven by the moral character of Jesus, the apostles, martyrs, and other Christian believers throughout the generations. We shall consider both themes; from Eusebius' treatment of them there emerges a composite picture of the issues in question.

Miracles play an important role in the framework of Eusebius' apologetic-polemical argument, as evinced by their prominence in the *DE*, particularly in Book III. As we have noted, Eusebius views Book III as the real beginning of the *DE*, the first two books serving as a kind of introduction or foreword (προλεγόμενα) to the main part (ὑπόθεσις) of the *DE*.[18] The major subject of the *DE*, namely, proving the truth of prophecies relating to the theology of the person of Christ, could be treated only after his divinity had been proved to those who did not initially accept prophetic arguments as proof. This emerges in the polemical context as a direct reply to the anti-Christian comments on Jesus and the apostles, which resemble Porphyry's arguments, if they are not actually his. Elsewhere in the *DE*, and on occasion in the *PE*, Eusebius relates briefly to specific points that are linked to the major theme, and thus shed further light on his general attitude towards this question.

Miracles as Proof of the Divinity of Jesus and the Truth of the Christian Faith

Eusebius categorically states that the miracles performed by Jesus are proof of his divinity (τοῦ σωτῆρος ἡμῶν τὰ πολυύμνητα τῆς ἀρετῆς θαύματα, ταῦτα τῆς ἐν αὐτῷ θεότητος τὰ τεκμήρια). The miracles were proof of the divinity within Jesus.[19] Moreover, Christians accepted miracles as proof of the divinity of Jesus, miracles through which the Lord still revealed signs of His power to those whom he viewed as worthy of such revelation. They upheld this proof after meticulously examining the facts behind it, testing it by more logical means, in debate with those who totally rejected belief in miracles, or with those who acknowledged miracles as no more than magic, sorcery, deceit, and charlatanism, designed to mislead the beholder as jug-

---

[18] *DE* 3, Introduction.
[19] *DE* 3,4,30.

glers frequently do.[20] Thus Eusebius argues that Christians put the miraculous proof of the divinity of Jesus to an objective test that met the logical criteria of Christianity's critics. But miracles performed by Jesus were not just one more proof of the divinity of Jesus. Elsewhere Eusebius states that they are the strongest proof of the divine power of the Redeemer. The proof of his divine power was found not only in the miracles he performed in the past, but in the continuity of the divine power animating the world and the miracles that occurred even in Eusebius' own time. This power was revealed in the victory over all obstacles to, and enemies of the Gospel, in the crowds of believers it drew throughout the world, and in the healing of souls.[21] The decisive proof of the divine power of Jesus, therefore, was the fact that he lived, existed, and was active throughout the entire world up to the present day. This power was expressed by the triumph of the Church. The divine Christ determined the course of history.

Apostles and disciples gradually learned to acknowledge the true essence of Jesus. At first, it seemed that he was simply an extraordinary individual and a prophet, as indicated by his miracles. However, they had not yet realized the full wonder of his miracles. Later, when this became evident, they acknowledged his divinity![22] In fact, the apostles could perceive the divine power of Jesus from the beginning. For Eusebius writes elsewhere that walking on the water proved his true power to his disciples.[23] Apparently, however, Eusebius hints that the final acknowledgment on the part of the apostles and disciples came only after the ultimate miracle of his Resurrection from the dead.[24] Likewise, many Gentiles recognized the divinity of Jesus after seeing his divine power through his wondrous and great miracles (τῆς ἐνθέου δυνάμεως αὐτοῦ χάριν κύριον ὁμολογοῦντα).[25] Eusebius goes even further, stating that without the wondrous miracles, a belief in Christ on the part of many Jews and Greeks would have been inconceivable. "For by what other means, could he have attracted

---

[20] *DE* 3,4,31.
[21] *DE* 9,13.
[22] *DE* 8,1.
[23] *DE* 9,12,4.
[24] *DE* 8,1. Apparently, Origen held a similar view regarding the gradual development of awareness on the part of the apostles (*CC* 2,45). He half-heartedly admits that the disciples needed the revelation of Jesus after his Resurrection in order to strengthen their faith once again (*CC* 2,39).
[25] *DE* 3,2,32. See also *HE* 1,13,1 and 1,13,7.

the Jewish and Greek masses, if not by miracles and wondrous deeds"
(πῶς γὰρ ἂν ἄλλως προσήγετο τοῦ Ἰουδαϊκοῦ καὶ τοῦ Ἑλληνικοῦ πλείους,
εἰ μή τισιν θαυμαστοῖς καὶ παραδόξοις ἔργοις).[26]

Eusebius viewed the *Testimonium Flavianum* as an external testimony
that confirmed his statements, for it attests to the miracles performed
by Jesus (ἦν γὰρ παραδόξων ἔργων ποιητής) and to the masses of Jews
and Greeks attracted to him. Josephus does not state that they were
attracted by the power of the miracles, but Eusebius infers this from
the words of Josephus.[27] In conclusion, despite the problems posed
by pagan comparison with non-Christian miracles, Eusebius persisted
in his claim that one could acknowledge the divinity of Jesus only
through recognition of his divine acts, namely, miracles. In retrospect,
such divine feats demonstrated the fulfillment, in him, of prophecies
regarding the Messiah. However, polemics still required proof that
the acts of Jesus were by nature divine.

Miracles also constituted proof of the veracity of the faith. The
wonder of the miracles attested to the truth of religion and to the
belief professed by those who performed these miracles. Thus miracles were actually necessary for man because of the weakness of
humanity. Miracles also served as a sign of the truth of religion and
of the entire Gospel, as in the case of the miracles performed by
Moses and Jesus.[28] The same was true of miracles of the apostles.
The apostles astonished their audiences, primarily through their miracles. The wonders encouraged people to take an interest in and
inquire after him in whose name and power the apostles acted. When
they subsequently taught the Gospel, they discovered that the faith
of their audience had preceded the study of the Gospel. Thus divine
acts or miracles possessed greater power of persuasion than words.[29]
For it is related that some even thought that the apostles were gods
and wanted to sacrifice to them.[30] The major proof of the truth of

---

[26] *DE* 3,5,108.

[27] *DE* 3,5,104–108.

[28] *DE* 3,2,8.

[29] To paraphrase, one miracle is worth a thousand words.

[30] Acts of the Apostles 14:12. Origen shares a similar view on the fundamental
importance of miracles in persuading non-believers and spreading the Gospel. The
miracles performed by Jesus and the apostles were necessary for the purpose of
persuasion (*CC* 1,46). Jesus himself was assisted by miracles in persuading those who
did not accept his arguments (*CC* 2,39) and those who needed proof of signs and
miracles (*CC* 2,52). During the initial stages of Christianity, miracles played a more
important role than sermons or preaching. It was difficult to suppose that many

Jesus' miracles and of the Gospel lay in the miracles performed by his apostles and disciples, who acted in his power. Proof of the miracles of Jesus, particularly the miracle of faith, was not through words—which could not be proved—but through the ongoing action of the divine miracle-working power. Such activity proved that Jesus was still alive.[31] In other words, present-day miracles constituted the decisive and ultimate proof of the truth of the Gospel. Miraculous deeds nullified the paradox inherent in belief, especially the paradox of belief in Jesus' Resurrection. This was true not only for the generation of the disciples and apostles, but as a guiding principle. Even for Eusebius, in his time, the only way to accept the paradoxical belief in the miracle of Resurrection was through observing how the divine power brought about the historic wonder of Christianity's great conquests.[32] The miracle of the spread of Christianity in Eusebius' time attested to the truth of the great miracle of Jesus, which was beyond reason. This answered the question as to how and with what power the disciples of Jesus spread the Gospel and persuaded their Greek and barbarian followers to believe in Jesus as the word of God.[33]

---

joined the Christian fold without the motivating force of miraculous events (*CC* 8, 47). Tertullian put forward a similar argument regarding miracles performed by the prophets, which were designed to foster belief in their divine authority (Tertullian, *Apology* 18,5). MacMullen accepts the word of Christian authors, stating that the major cause of the pagans' conversion to Christianity, especially before Constantine, was their experience as witnesses to the miraculous forces—in exorcisms, healing, and the deaths of martyrs. Both pagans and Christians regarded the miraculous force as the sole testimony to the truth. According to MacMullen, it is the only way to explain the fact that millions of pagans became Christian during the first centuries. To prove his point, he quotes the testimonies of converts who describe a particular miracle they witnessed, after which they converted to Christianity. He is also convinced that miracles were the key factor determining conversion from one cult to another within the pagan world. He cites Iamblichus on the Pythagoreans, who spoke of miracles in order to convince their audience that Pythagoras was not an ordinary man but a more exalted being (Iamblichus, *Life of Pythagoras*, 28;143; MacMullen, *Paganism*, pp. 95–96; 135). This subject is a major theme in his book on the spread of Christianity throughout the empire, and it recurs throughout his entire work. See R. MacMullen, *Christianizing the Roman Empire (AD 100–400)* (New Haven-London, 1984), pp. 4, 27, 30, 36, 40.

[31] *DE*, 3,7,25–27.
[32] *DE* 3,7,22–23.
[33] *DE* 3,7,28–29.

The Difficulty of Proving the Divinity of Christ
on the Basis of Miracles

Depending as they did on the evidence of Jesus' miracles, Christian apologists were open to two critical approaches: 1. The miracles stories were fictitious and Jesus, the apostles, and the evangelists were swindlers and charlatans. 2. The miracles were authentic, but as acts of magic and sorcery, not divine power. Quadratus, a contemporary of Hadrian and possibly the first Christian apologist, was apparently aware of the first argument. He replied that the miracle stories were transmitted by a first-hand source, by eyewitnesses, or even by those whom Jesus had healed, who were still alive in Quadratus' day. He did not know them personally and had little information about them.[34] This argument, however, was feeble even then, as Quadratus was not acquainted with anyone who had witnessed Jesus' miracles. Eusebius would definitely not have overlooked such testimony had he found it in Quadratus' work.

Origen on Miracles

Origen admitted that the actual value of Jesus' miracles as proof had declined. But their credibility was enhanced by the fact that they had been predicted by Old Testament prophecies.[35] However, this claim recapitulates the argument that the power of prophecy upheld the truth of a miracle story, whereas previously the miracle served as proof of the truth of prophecy. Without first proving the truth of a miracle, one had to assume the truth of prophecy, and thus the premise of the argument based upon miracles falls apart. Nevertheless, as we have noted, when the exigencies of polemics required it, Origen did not hesitate to use miracles as weighty evidence attesting to the divinity of Jesus and the truth of the Gospel.

Another consequence of the difficulty in proving the credibility of the miracles of Jesus and the apostles was the gradual shift in emphasis from the physical miracles of Jesus in the remote past, to the ongoing miracles of Christianity as proof of the active power of Jesus in the present day, which verified all that had been related about

---

[34] *HE* 4,3,2.
[35] Origen, *Commentary on John* 2,34.

past miracles.[36] This gradual shift is already noticeable in Origen's *Against Celsus*. Of the seven statements in which he uses miracles as a polemical argument, three involve miracles which Jesus performed and which prove his divinity.[37] Elsewhere, Origen recalls contemporary Christian miracles, such as healing, exorcism, and the conversion of the masses to Christianity in his own day. Such miracles attested to the divine power of Jesus working in the present, and to the truth of the great miracles in the past.[38]

Relying on the miracle-argument was problematic, given the polemical context of Origen's statements. Celsus was forthright in his anti-Christian claims that Jesus was a magician and miracle maker, who did not differ essentially from similar pagan figures and actually may have been their inferior.[39] Celsus even argued that Jesus himself admitted that his miracles contained nothing of a divine nature, and that his successors would perform similar acts.[40] Given the background of such an argument, which presents the miraculous power of Jesus in relative terms, the argument that miracles denoted divinity could be a double-edged one, applicable to pagan miracle workers as well, as Celsus had shown.[41] Thus, on several occasions Origen resorts to the moral argument as proof of the truth of Christian miracles, and as a factor distinguishing them from pagan miracles. Although his statements are not fully developed, their direction is clear. Jesus was a man of impeccable moral character who acted out of religious-educational motives. This was the essential difference between Jesus and the pagans, who engaged in magic.[42] It was the educational, moral, and religious purpose of the act that distinguished miracles from magic, or to use later terminology, "white" from "black" magic. The superiority of Jesus over the various pagan figures who performed miracles and were reputed to have divine powers, such as Aristeas and Cleomedes, could be found in his moral purpose and its great success. The supreme expression of this success was the readiness of his disciples to sacrifice their lives upon the altar of this

---

[36] See also M.F. Wiles, "Miracles in the Early Church", *Miracles*, ed. C.F.D. Moule (London, 1965), p. 225.
[37] *CC* 2,9; 2,35; 8,9.
[38] *CC* 1,2.
[39] See *CC* 1,68; 2,8; 2,45; 3,22; 3,24; 3;26; 3,33; 3,36; 7,55.
[40] *CC* 2,49.
[41] *CC* 3,26; 3,32; 3,33; 2,45.
[42] *CC* 1,68.

purpose.[43] Even a thief and a traitor such as Judas Iscariot possessed a modicum of decency and honor because of the strength of Jesus' teaching, and this was solid proof of its might and truth.[44] Readiness to die for Christianity in every generation was decisive proof of the truth of the Christian faith.[45] However, the truth of the divine power of Jesus was proven in the far-reaching moral transformation that took place among his followers throughout the history of Christianity. Origen made this point in his refutation of Celsus' argument that Jesus deceived his disciples and followers. The moral transformation was proof of the moral stature of Jesus, which eliminated any thought of fraud or fiction.[46] Origen repeats that the great moral accomplishment of the Gospel, and its moral influence on the lives of the masses, was of major benefit to Christian communities.[47] Celsus pursues his argument: even if one accepted that Jesus became a god after his death and departure from the body, how did he differ from Greek gods? Origen responds that the decisive proof lies in the moral superiority of Jesus, which led to the moral improvement of many people.[48] Perhaps the two arguments are used in different ways. On the one hand, miracles did indeed offer proof of the divinity of Jesus and the truth of Christianity. On the other, in response to arguments comparing Jesus to pagan figures, the greatness of the miracles could serve as proof only after their uniqueness had been distinguished from pagan miracles by means of the moral argument, namely, that moral purpose is proved by moral success. As we have noted, Origen's statements are not fully developed, at least within their polemical context, and the synthesis that we have proposed is based on his short answers in different parts of *CC*.

Eusebius on Miracles

The theme beginning with Origen reaches its full development in the polemical context of Book III of the *DE*. Eusebius makes a point

---

[43] *CC* 3, 32–33, and similarly, *CC* 1,26, where Origen states that readiness to die for Christianity is proof of the truth of the faith. Martyrdom as proof of the truth of Christ and the Christian faith appears as early as Justin, *Dialogue*, 121,2.

[44] *CC* 2,11.

[45] *CC* 1,26.

[46] Ibid.

[47] *CC* 1,64.

[48] *CC* 3,42.

of answering a battery of arguments leveled against Jesus and the apostles with the aim of undermining their authority as founders of the Christian religion. He explains his method in his anti-pagan polemic refuting these points, and sees this as a prerequisite for consolidating his arguments based on prophecy, which form the essence of the *DE*. He states that he will begin his statement on the Messiah by asserting the Messiah's humanity. After presenting proof that Jesus was superior to all mortals throughout history, Eusebius discusses his divine nature and seeks to prove that Jesus' power did not derive only from his humanity.[49] Namely, he proposes that had Jesus been the most perfect human being in all of human history, this alone would have sufficed as evidence that his uniqueness derived from divine power. The basic issue, therefore, was not the existence of Christian miracles, but the divine power behind them, in other words, the humanity and divinity of Jesus in a polemical context. Eusebius immediately indicates the specific polemical context of his statements. In the past, many non-believers called Jesus a magician, a sorcerer, a swindler, and various other insulting names. They continued to do so even in Eusebius' time, and they were not few in number (τῶν ἀπίστων οἱ πλείους γόητα καὶ πλάνον ἀποκαλοῦντες καὶ μυρίαις ἄλλαις κατηγορίαις βλασφημοῦντες αὐτὸν οὔπω καὶ νῦν παύονται).[50] He would not answer them on his own but with the teachings of Jesus.

Chapter 3 of *DE* III briefly considers Jesus in terms of conventional human nature and powers, and proves that, on important issues, the words of Jesus were identical to those of the prophets and the ancient Hebrew wise men. It presents Jesus as the most exalted human figure in this chain of patriarchs and prophets. The chapter itself is aimed at those who viewed Jesus as a swindler (πλάνος). The moral issue is raised from the beginning. It was not possible for a swindler to be a teacher and the embodiment of modesty, purity, and all the noble qualities of character, in the eyes of those who were his dupes. Could he who forbade men to look lustfully at women, who taught philosophy in its most elevated form, who taught his disciples to share their property with the needy, and who championed diligence and charity, be called a swindler? Could he who roused the simple masses and taught them to enjoy Scripture, be a

---

[49] *DE* 3,2,78.
[50] Ibid.

fraud? He was remote from all falsehood and placed truth before
everything, and was cautious in taking oaths. Briefly, the moral ideal
that he radiated obliged all lovers of truth and those who adhered
to the truth[51] to admit that he was not a swindler at all, but a somewhat divine man (τινα θεῖον) and the author of a divine and holy
philosophy (θείας καὶ εὐσεβοῦς φιλοσοφίας εἰσηγετήν).[52] He revived the
divine way of life of the ancients and spread it among countless
Greeks and barbarians.[53] This was the ethical aspect of his teaching. Jesus could not be accused of fraud with regard to his major
teachings. In the *PE*, Eusebius proved the extent of the influence of
Hebrew philosophy on the Greek savants, and quoted the testimony
of Greek oracles concerning Hebrew wisdom.[54] Moreover, Jesus made
the theological and philosophical truths accessible to a large public,
whereas in the past such knowledge had been in the possession of
a select few.[55]

Eusebius proposed that Jesus may have been considered a swindler
due to the fact that he did not demand animal sacrifices and incense
as part of the worship of God. Thus Eusebius once again, albeit in
a different context, rejects the criticism that Christians did not offer
sacrifices, and seeks to demonstrate that the Christian attitude derived
from a valid theological concept that was shared by Greek philosophers. To support this view, he includes statements by Porphyry and
Apollonius relating to sacrifices—already cited in Book IV of the
PE—which featured above in our discussion of sacrifices within the
concept of Christian pre-history.[56] Similarly, the cosmological concept held by Jesus and the ancient Hebrews was identical to that of
renowned philosophers. Jesus taught that the world was created
(γεννητὸς ὁ κόσμος). Therefore one should not worship heavenly beings,
but their creator. Jesus also preached the destruction of the world
and its transformation into something better—a vision shared by
Plato.[57] His statements on other major issues, such as the superiority
of human souls over those of animals, the Day of Judgment, reward
and punishment, immortality, the kingdom of heaven, spirits and angels,

---

[51] Perhaps an ironical reference to Hierocles and his work, "Lover of Truth."
[52] *DE* 3,3,2.
[53] Ibid.
[54] *DE* 3,3,6.
[55] Ibid.
[56] *DE* 3,3,8–11.
[57] *DE* 3,3,14–15.

demons and evil forces, and other teachings, were identical to the religious concepts of the prophets and the Hebrew wise men of antiquity. It was therefore impossible, Eusebius concludes, that a teacher of holy doctrines that were philosophical, beneficial, and valuable, be called a swindler. Having thus far discussed only the human power, spirit, and nature of Jesus, Eusebius next proceeds to examine his divine aspect.

Chapter IV is a summary of the major miracles that Jesus performed in his lifetime, and at his death, Resurrection, and afterwards. According to Eusebius, the miracles were unique and evinced their divine origin, proving the divinity of Christ, as has been noted above. The chapter establishes the uniqueness of Jesus' miracles. From Eusebius' point of view, the challenge is twofold: to prove the truth of the stories about Jesus and the apostles, in order to verify the greatness of the miracles, and to respond to claims that Jesus' miracles were attributable to magic, which placed him within the ranks of pagan wonder-workers. In the immediate polemical context of the chapter, Eusebius divides the critics of Jesus and his disciples into two groups—those who did not believe what was written about Jesus, and those who, even partially, accepted the accounts but viewed the miracles as acts—of magic, for example—that did not transcend human capabilities. The moral argument is introduced in order to solve these two problems. First, it serves as proof of the authenticity of the narrative. By proving the truth of Scripture, the major proof based upon miracles becomes self-evident. Secondly, the moral argument serves as a response to the problem of attributing miracles to magic and human capabilities, thus invalidating the uniqueness of Jesus' miracles. Like Origen, Eusebius introduces the moral argument in order to distinguish between Christian and pagan miracles, that is, between magic and miracles, or between black and white magic. The strength of the moral argument lay in its totality. But although such an argument could be effective in the polemic against the pagans, it invited comparisons with other biblical figures and their miracles, notably Moses.[58]

Eusebius was apparently aware of this difficulty, though he did

---

[58] Parkes claims that there may have been two major Jewish arguments in Jewish-Christian polemics which were not reflected in works of the *Adversus Iudaeos* genre, and which had to be sought elsewhere: 1. Old Testament miracles were superior to those mentioned in the New Testament. 2. The figure and personality of Jesus were inferior to those of the Old Testament prophets (Parkes, *The Conflict of the*

not consider it a real problem in the immediate polemical context
of *DE* III. His statement that, as far as human qualities were concerned, Jesus was the most perfect person in all human history, comes
after a detailed comparison between the figures of Moses and Jesus,
proving the superiority of Jesus over Moses in every way. The comparison and parallel between Moses, the first redeemer, and Jesus,
the final redeemer, did not require a narrow polemical context, but
grew from the roots of early Christianity. God's words to Moses in
Deuteronomy 18:18: "I will raise them up a prophet from among
their brethren like unto thee . . ." were naturally interpreted as referring to Jesus. Eusebius himself devoted some exegetical effort to proving that only Jesus could have fulfilled this prophecy. The phrase
"like unto thee", however, had particular significance. The fact that
the prophet who would arise would resemble Moses in every way,
would have to be proved.[59] In *DE* 3,2, Eusebius develops the parallel between Jesus and Moses with regard to major issues, and by
comparing them, demonstrates that Jesus' actions and teachings were
superior to those of Moses. The criterion of this superiority was the
universal scope of Jesus' activity and his teaching. Whereas Moses
limited himself to the Jews, the Land of Israel, and life in this world,
Jesus was a universal legislator, who conquered paganism throughout the world and overcame demons.[60] Our interest here lies not so
much in the general parallel and comparison between Moses and
Jesus, as in the comparative view of their miracles. Eusebius hopes

---

Church and the Synagogue, p. 114). Such arguments may have been used by pagans
as well.

[59] There is a further problem unrelated to the parallels between Jesus and Moses,
namely, that this prophecy speaks of a prophet and not a Messiah. Eusebius deals
with this issue elsewhere and it will be discussed later.

[60] On the superiority of Jesus over Moses as a universal legislator possessing
greater divine power, see *DE* 9,11. The parallel between Jesus and Moses in *DE*
3,2 is the subject of a brief study by J.E. Bruns, "The 'Agreement of Moses and
Jesus' in the *Demonstratio Evangelica* of Eusebius", *Vigiliae Christianae* 31 (1977), pp.
117–125. Bruns attempted to identify a particular literary source for Eusebius' parallel and proposes that it comes from the lost work of Amonius, *On the Harmony
between Moses and Jesus* (Περὶ τῆς Μωυσέως καὶ Ἰησοῦ συμφωνίας) mentioned by Eusebius in *HE* 6,19,10; cf. Ulrich, ibid., pp. 172–176. Jewish traditions about the similarity between Moses and the future Messiah (e.g. Koh. Rabba 1,28; Targ. Ps. Jon.
on Deut. 33:5) may have also influenced these harmonies between Moses and Jesus.
These harmonies were a powerful weapon against Marcionite tendencies. For a
Jewish polemical comparison between Moses and Jesus, proving the superiority of
Moses, see S. Pines, "Judaeo-Christian Materials in an Arabic Jewish Treatise", in
The Collected Works of Shlomo Pines, Volume IV, Studies in the History of Religion (Jerusalem,
1996), pp. 301–303.

to prove the superiority of Jesus' miracles. Moses employed miracles in order to prove his professed religious truths. Similarly, Jesus was assisted by miracles in order to plant faith in the hearts of beholders. Moses freed the Jews from slavery in Egypt; Jesus freed all mankind from the tyranny of the demons. Moses promised the chosen land of Judea; Jesus promised the kingdom of heaven. Throughout his comparison, Eusebius presents a miracle of Moses followed by a parallel miracle of Jesus. Before each of Jesus' miracles, he reiterates that Jesus performed these miracles on a greater scale, and in a more powerful, divine manner.[61]

On Those Who Reject the Authenticity of Jesus' Miracles

In the continuation of Chapter 4, Eusebius addresses the attack on the credibility of the Gospels. He directs his statements at those who do not believe the disciples' account of the Redeemer's miracles. We have noted that pagan critique was aimed not only at Jesus, but also—and more emphatically, perhaps—against the apostles and the evangelists, in order to undermine the fundamental texts of Christianity. Eusebius had to refute the claim that Jesus did not perform the miracles witnessed and related by his disciples, and that these were simply distortions and inventions. We have encountered these charges in Porphyry's criticism, and, in simpler from, in Celsus'

---

[61] *DE* 3,2,6-30. See also *DE* 9,13 which states that the power of Jesus' miracles was completely different from that of the most superior men, such as Moses and the prophets, since he was God, and as such gave power to his apostles. These matters were introduced as part of the content of Isaiah 35:3. Moses was known among pagans as a miracle-worker with magical powers. This strengthened the possibility that pagan criticism could target the miracles of Jesus from the vantage point of Moses' miracles as well. On the figure of Moses as a performer of magic and miracles, see *CC* 1,26, and J.G. Gager, *Moses in Graeco-Roman Paganism* (Nashville-New York, 1972). In *PE* 9,8, Eusebius presents Numenius' testimony concerning the great miracles performed by Moses, and the fact that Moses was beloved of God. Origen drew a brief comparison between Moses' and Jesus' miracles. He found parallels between the miracles of Jesus and his disciples, and those of Moses, in contrast to the miracles of impostors, which resembled those of the magicians of Egypt and the Antichrist. Thus he discusses the issue in the framework of the distinction between Christian and other miracles (*CC* 2,50). Elsewhere, he offers a different explanation from that of Eusebius for the superiority of Jesus' miracles to those performed by Moses. He states that Jesus' miracles were greater and more divine because they had the power to divert people from Judaism (*CC* 2,52). Furthermore, Origen put forward an altogether surprising argument. The reason for Jesus' appearance among the Jews was that they were accustomed to miracles; they

polemic as well.[62] Eusebius attempts to prove the truth of the disciples' accounts by extrapolating from the nature of their relationship with their master. He applies here the ethical argument we encountered earlier: a moral character can evince the truth of the miracle stories. The disciples taught and handed down only the teachings that they heard from their teacher. These focused on the philosophy and practices of ascetic ethics. If one truly studied the teachings of Jesus, his apostles' and disciples' purity of character, and their devotion to the truth, it was inconceivable that the disciples should have conspired to fabricate the deeds of their master. Their large numbers would have prevented them from maintaining secrecy. No argument could undermine the credibility of so many who based their lives on piety and the fear of God.

At this point, Eusebius adopts a rhetorical tactic drawn from pagan arguments. If the moral and religious teaching of Jesus was nothing but a fabrication, let us imagine, for a moment, that Jesus taught the opposite. Let us suppose the absurd, says Eusebius, that Jesus was a wizard and magician who preached sin, crime, corruption, and hypocrisy. If that were the case, would his followers have united in a life-and-death struggle to exalt him by concocting a harmonious web of lies? And all this, after his wretched death. Did they wish to share his fate? If he were honored as one of this band of crooks, why should they continue to admire him—even more—after his death, especially since it was said that while he was alive, they aban-

---

were therefore capable of comparing the miracles of Jesus to those of his predecessors and could acknowledge their superiority! (*CC* 2,57).

[62] Celsus argued that the evangelists made up verses and stories (*CC* 2,10). The disciples themselves initiated the claim that Jesus knew and prophesied all that would happen to him in advance (*CC* 2,13). The inventions of the disciples were designed to justify and explain events in the life of Jesus (*CC* 2,16). Celsus extended his criticism to include Christians of his own day. He claimed that Christians changed the versions of the Gospels to resolve problematic issues (*CC* 2,27). He even argued that some of the forgery and fabrication went back to Jesus himself, and that it was he who made up the story of his virgin birth and granted himself the title "God" (*CC* 1,28). Jesus was a swindler and liar (*CC* 2,7–8) and his disciples were tricked into believing that he was God (*CC* 2,26). A similar claim was apparently directed at Pythagoras, perhaps as part of an anti-Pythagorean polemic. According to the Pythagorean tradition, Pythagoras descended into Hades during his life-time. On his return, he could relate all that had happened in his town during his absence. According to this charge, he had made up the entire story as part of a plot he concocted with his mother. In fact, he had gone into hiding with her help, and she had informed him as to what had happened in the interim. The success of this fraud had led many to believe that Pythagoras was a divine being. See Diogenes Laertius, *Lives of the Philosophers: Pythagoras*, 8,1,41.

doned him and denied him? But behold, after his death, they themselves preferred death to renouncing the testimony which they had fabricated. How could they attest to the glory of their Lord through their deaths, if during his lifetime he did not display any quality that enriched them spiritually, but only cruelty, fraud, and public deception. For they could have continued to live quietly and peacefully in the comfort of their homes with their loved ones. How could a band of crooks and swindlers deem it proper to die for the sake of a man who was their mentor in evil and did not enhance their lives. Men of that kind, slaves to a life of desire and hedonism, would not be capable of taking upon themselves the punishment of their friends and relations, much less so, the punishment of other criminals. Hence it was inconceivable that the disciples should acknowledge their mentor as a swindler and a wizard, and then, cruel-hearted as they allegedly were, that they should endure every kind of insult, humiliation, and punishment at the hands of their people, only so as to uphold their testimony about him. Such was not the nature of crooks and criminals.[63]

Eusebius adopts a further rhetorical device. He juxtaposes one pagan argument with another, in order to negate the first. If the apostles and evangelists were, in fact, a band of swindlers, then they were also common people, barbarians, uneducated and unschooled in foreign languages, with the exception of Aramaic, their spoken language.[64] How therefore, asks Eusebius, could they have spread

---

[63] *DE* 3,4,1–43. In the different editions of *DE*, confusion reigns on the question of chapter divisions in Book 3, Chapters 4–5. In his edition, Heikel dispenses with the problematic division and combines Chapters 4 and 5, numbering their sections consecutively. I follow his enumeration. The division in Ferrar's English edition differs slightly.

[64] We have mentioned the familiar, long standing pagan argument regarding the inferior origins of the apostles. It was based not only on the Gospels, but also on the statements of many Christians who accepted the lowly origins of the apostles as a fact. The basis of this claim can be found in Acts of the Apostles 4:13, "that they were uneducated, common men". According to Justin, the apostles were illiterate (*First Apology*, 39). Theophilus thought that some of the prophets, at least, were illiterate and unschooled (*To Autolycus* 1,35). Celsus argued that Jesus' apostles were wretched, of humble origins, and few in number (*CC* 1,62; 2,46). He put forward a similar view on the humble origins of Jesus (*CC* 1,28). Origen accepted this as a fact. He admitted that the apostles were inarticulate and lacked rhetorical and dialectical skills. However, he viewed this as an advantage. Their selection by Jesus was a tactical measure. He deliberately chose them as his apostles in order to prevent Christians being identified with a particular philosophical school! If divine truth had been clothed in Greek literary garb, it might have misled people, and might not have been identified! (*CC* 1,62). This reply also rebutted the pagan criticism

their words through the entire world? And whence did they acquire
the considerable understanding necessary for so daring a plan? What
enabled this enterprise to succeed? Perhaps they could have deceived
their own countrymen. But the spread of the Gospel throughout the
entire world, from the British Isles to India,[65] could not have been
the activity of swindlers and magicians (πλάνους καὶ γόητας); there
must have been a superhuman force active in them (ταῦτα οὐκ ἔτ'
ἔγωγε ἡγοῦμαι κατὰ ἄνθρωπον εἶναι).[66] Thus according to Eusebius, the
great undertaking of the apostles, with their humble background,
obliges one to acknowledge the divine force that worked among
them. Elsewhere he says that the humble background of the apostles was in fact proof of the greatness of Jesus' enterprise. He deliberately chose peasants, simple folk, to carry out the impossible. This
was further proof of the divine will and power that acted through
them and came from the power of Jesus.[67] The apostles' work derived
from the magical power of the name of Jesus.[68] In addition, the fact
that the apostles knew only one language, Aramaic, demonstrated
the vastness of their undertaking to spread Christianity through all
the countries of the world, among the speakers of seventy languages.[69]
Eusebius naturally accepted as historical fact the legendary traditions
according to which the Gospels had been promulgated throughout
the world by the apostles. He goes on to ask how they could have
coordinated different versions to fabricate a story about their master, "the charlatan", and yet produced a story that was so coherent—with all the apostles saying the same things in their testimonies.[70]

Eusebius repeatedly stresses the uniformity and harmony in the
Gospel testimonies on Jesus. In so doing, he may have intended to

---

regarding the poor literary style of Scripture. Moreover, the apostles possessed divine
power which derived from Jesus (*CC*, ibid.). Origen adds that apostles, who did not
learn sophistry and rhetoric, could not have made up the Gospels. Therein lay
another reason for Jesus choosing them, to allay suspicions of sophistry! Furthermore, the naivete of the disciples and the gift of divine power had accomplished
much more than any literary sophistication or logical argument (*CC* 3,39).

[65] In *HE*, traditional accounts of the apostles' promulgation of the Gospel in different countries are found mainly in *HE* 3,1.

[66] *DE* 3,4,45.

[67] *DE* 3,7,5–7. Achieving this through philosophers would have been easier, and
thus less remarkable.

[68] *DE* 3,7,12–13.

[69] *DE* 3,7,9–12.

[70] *DE* 3,4,46. For a discussion of Eusebius' treatment of the apostles' conspiracy
see also F. W. Norris, "Eusebius on Jesus as Deceiver and Sorcerer", in Attridge
and Hata (eds.), *Eusebius, Christianity, and Judaism*, 527–536.

counter the charge that there were contradictions and discrepancies between parallel traditions. From the unity and concurrence of the independent testimonies, he could deduce the truth that they conveyed. Harmony and agreement were indicative of truth, while contradictions and disagreements attested to error and falsehood. This principle runs through the entire apologetic undertaking of Eusebius, and, as we have seen, it is an argument used by pagans against Christianity. From this point of departure he can use a *reductio ad absurdum* to turn pagan claims regarding a conspiracy on the part of the apostles, into farcical absurdity. He argues that the only alternative explanation for the coordination and uniformity of the testimonies was indeed that they met secretly for the purpose of conspiracy (συνωμοσία), coordinating their false versions and fabrications of events that never took place.[71] Thus if the Gospel accounts were an ingenious forgery, there must have been a conspiracy to plan every detail in advance. Eusebius ridicules this notion in rhetorical terms and describes an imaginary sermon delivered at a plenary meeting of the conspiratorial alliance.[72] In his farce on the great conspiracy, he uses the testimonies as historical documents, despite his acknowledged intention to prove them true as independent accounts, and to refute the claims that they were a forgery. For his immediate purpose, he chooses to overlook temporarily the charge of inconsistency and contradiction in the Gospels.

The chief of the apostles and leader of the band of conspirators, writes Eusebius, delivered a sermon describing the program of the conspiracy. All the assembled were witness to the character of the arch-swindler. He appeared before the masses as a saint in order to serve his selfish ends, and did nothing of worth. All his teachings were a fabrication. He was not at all worthy of resurrection. At this point, the conspirators had to make an alliance, then invent and publicize a corroborated story concerning his miracles, which the conspirators had neither seen nor heard. His unfortunate end and death were widely known and could not possibly be hidden, but the conspirators could overcome this difficulty by fabricating reports that he had appeared after his Resurrection, and had eaten and spent time with them. The strongest testimony would be their determination that only death would separate them. It was no shame to die

---

[71] *DE* 3,4,47.
[72] *DE* 3,4,48–5,59.

for a foolish purpose. They would invent tales that would help no one, not even themselves, or the leader whom they elevated to a god. They would spread the fabrication all over the world. Furthermore, for every nation they would make laws that ran counter to all ancient customs and traditions. The conspirators would declare war on their gods and destroy their influence, not by words or arguments, but by the power of their crucified Lord. They had to march enthusiastically towards torture, wild beasts, prison, corporal punishment, and death itself. For there was no higher goal than to make men and gods into enemies for no reason and for no profit, but simply for the sake of swindling. The act was the great prize, going against everyone to proclaim that their Lord who was crucified before their eyes was God, and to present him as the Son of God for whom they were prepared to die, with the clear knowledge that they had not learned anything true or useful from him. For evil and truth are one and the lie is the opposite of evil (κακὸν γὰρ ἴσως ἀλήθεια, τὸ δὲ ψεῦδος ἔχει τοῦ κακοῦ τὸ ἐναντίον). Let them say, therefore, that he revived the dead, cured lepers, exorcised demons, and performed many additional miracles, knowing full well that he did none of these things. They would invent anything and cheat anyone they could.[73]

After rhetorically inflating pagan accusations of the apostles' fabrications, charlatanism, and fraud into an absurd balloon of universal conspiracy, Eusebius returns to juxtaposing the pagan arguments. Now the absurdity of the pagan argument was to be exposed in all its ludicrousness, at least to the sympathetic audience. Could anyone believe that poor and ignorant people were capable of fabricating such stories and conspiring against the Roman Empire? Or that human nature, which inclines to self-preservation, could deliberately invite death, for no purpose.[74] This last argument raised in the conspiracy speech also appears in reverse form elsewhere in Eusebius' work, and, to a lesser degree, in apologetic writing before his time. Namely, the death of Christian martyrs attested to truth of their faith and divinity of the Messiah. The assumption was that voluntary death could only be as a sacrifice for a higher purpose.[75]

---

[73] *DE* 3,5,58–59.

[74] *DE* 3,5,60.

[75] We have encountered this argument in the works of Justin and Origen. Eusebius used it in other works, too. See also, *DE* 9,13, where Eusebius explicitly states that martyrdom was testimony to the divine acts and divinity of Jesus. In effect, the argument of Christian truth based on martyrdom constitutes an extreme exam-

Another absurd possibility was that the disciples reached such a level of insanity that they invented a web of lies and were prepared to die for them. Here, Eusebius' opponent—anonymous, and perhaps imaginary—argues that the disciples did not suspect that they would suffer at all, even slightly, and were thus not at all afraid to go out into the wider world. Eusebius replies that it was only reasonable for someone who proclaimed to Romans, Greeks, and barbarians the uprooting of their god, to expect and be prepared to suffer on behalf of his Lord. And behold, written testimony clearly described how they conspired against the apostles, who were arrested by the conspirators and even put to death shortly after the death of Jesus.[76] Here Eusebius does not hesitate to use the words of the New Testament as historical testimony, despite the fact that the arguments refuted in his polemics are those that deny its credibility as an authentic historical source. He bases his statements on the Acts of the Apostles; this is perhaps why he differentiates between Acts, which has a more historical tone, and the Gospels. According to Eusebius, if the apostles had conspired, it would have been extraordinary if they had managed to uphold their uniform, coordinated versions of the texts right up to their deaths, with none faltering when he learned of the death imposed on his fellow-conspirators, and thus revealing the conspiracy and plot. And it was most incredible that insidious and ignorant people who spoke only their native tongue, should not only dare to go to the ends of the earth, but even succeed in their plot. Here the argument suddenly changes: the claim of conspiracy gives way to a testimony of the great wonder of the apostles' promulgation of the Gospel. Eusebius has cleverly manipulated the reader. The argument of conspiracy, placed in the mouths of the pagans, led them, as it were, in a dialectical-paradoxical manner to acknowledge the great marvel of the apostles' consistent and uniform accounts of the acts of Jesus, and their readiness to die for this truth.[77] Here Eusebius uses a rhetorical tactic, as if the reader has forgotten the point of departure—the pagan charge of forgery that was inflated to conspiracy—and now beholds in openmouthed astonishment the pagan admission of the great wonder of the apostles. Eusebius

---

ple of the moral argument, as we have noted in the parallel between Socrates and Jesus regarding their readiness to die for the truth.

[76] *DE* 3,5,60–62.
[77] *DE* 3,5,66-69.

summarizes the pagan argument in all its absurdity. This absurd
logic could also be applied in the case of Moses; when he says:
"Thou shalt not murder. Thou shalt not commit adultery. Thou
shalt not steal. Thou shalt not bear false witness against thy neigh-
bor", he could be accused of speaking fraudulently and ironically.
In other words, he had actually intended his audience to murder,
commit adultery, and act in violation of his teaching. He simply
chose to appear before them in the guise of a holy man. By likewise arguing fraud and forgery, it was possible to denigrate and belit-
tle all the testimonies concerning Greek philosophers, to argue that
their way of life directly contradicted their written teachings, and
that their choosing a philosophical way of life was simply preten-
tious hypocrisy.[78]

After refuting the pagan argument and determining the historical
validity of the New Testament stories, Eusebius could again use them
as an historical source for the rest of his polemic and thus refute
other arguments against the apostles. He subsequently begins to examine the veracity of the Gospels regarding the character of Jesus' disciples. Indeed, he now confronts the argument of the apostles' lowly
origins and ignorance. He acknowledges, as his predecessors did, the
historical fact of their humble background and lack of education.
However, he paints an idealized picture of the transformation that
came over their lives with their acceptance of their mission. They
fell in love with the philosophical and holy teachings and the exemplary ascetic way of life—fasting, abstinence from meat and wine,
and other physical strictures, accompanied by prayer and supplica-
tion to God. They also maintained a strict purity of body and soul.[79]
Thus they were virtually monks, or neo-Pythagorean ascetics, like
Apollonius. Eusebius continues to idealize the apostles in a language
resembling Philo's description of the Therapeutae in *The Contempla-
tive Life*.[80] Through their divine philosophy, they detached themselves
from married life, were indifferent to money and property, and were
not lured into the complications that ensued from sensual desire; nor
were they enslaved by the wish to have children and descendants,

---

[78] *DE* 3,5,71–72.
[79] *DE* 3,5,75.
[80] In fact, Eusebius views the *Therapeutae* as proto-Christian monks and nuns, and
states that Philo attested to the existence of an ascetic philosophical group whose
members were among the first in Egypt to receive the Gospel from Mark (*HE* 2,16).

since their souls longed for eternal spiritual, and not mortal, descendants.[81] Eusebius evokes the solid moral character of the apostles,
based on accounts describing them and Jesus. They did not shrink
from physical suffering and did not pursue pleasure. Christ himself
planted in them his way of life, and announced to them unequivocally the suffering that awaited them in their struggle for the sake
of his name—suffering that derived from the very fact that they
would be called Christians,[82]—which during the persecutions in Eusebius' time was sufficient reason for harsh corporal punishment.[83] The
proof of these virtues derived from a painstaking examination and
literary analysis of the Scriptures as well. Matthew did not hide his
dubious past as a tax collector, thus becoming his own prosecutor
and inculpating himself. Out of humility, he revealed his former life
and did not try to hide it. Even when presenting himself as the part-
ner of Thomas, he placed himself second (Matt. 10:2–3), despite the
fact that he was greater, according to Luke, who made Matthew
precede Thomas and did not refer to him as a tax collector.[84] Likewise John omits mention of his own name in his letters, and does
not refer to himself as an elder (πρεσβύτερος), an apostle, or an evan-
gelist (εὐαγγελιστής). Despite the fact that the Gospel described John
as the one loved by Jesus, he did not refer to himself by name.[85]
Peter did not permit himself to write a Gospel, out of deference
(εὐσέβεια). His friend and companion, Mark, wrote what he heard
about Jesus from Peter. However, Peter did not tell his own praises
to Mark, as told by Jesus (Matt. 16:17–20). Therefore, Mark chose
not to mention them. However, Mark did not hesitate to present
the weaknesses of Peter, which the latter had demonstrated. This
proved that the apostles not only avoided praising themselves and
spreading their own glory, but even recorded pejorative statements
about themselves, which they could easily have concealed from the
world. It was evidence of their selflessness and loyalty to the truth,
for they gave a simple and faithful description, a testimony to their

---

[81] *DE* 3,5,75–76.

[82] Likewise Tertullian, who states in *Apology* 2 that the very mention of the title
"Christian" sufficed to persecute someone.

[83] *DE* 3,5,79. Here he states that during the persecutions it was enough to declare
oneself not to be a Christian, to obtain immediate release, even for a convicted
criminal (*DE* 3,5,80).

[84] Luke 6:13. *DE* 3,5,81–87.

[85] *DE* 3,5,88.

love of truth.[86] To those who denigrated Christianity with accusations that the apostles were frauds, charlatans, and clever sophists,
Eusebius declares that they themselves should become the butt of
jokes and teasing, for they were evil and jealous men, enemies of
the truth.[87] The pagan argument, however, could be upheld by claiming that the Gospels combined a mixture of truth, falsehood, and
half-truths, that not everything was fabricated by the apostles and
the evangelists, who nonetheless invented and forged the text when
necessary. At this point, Eusebius tries to formulate a general rule.
He cites an unknown Christian source that states: "one must believe
completely in the disciples of Jesus, or not believe in them at all"
(πάντα χρὴ πιστεύειν τοῖς τοῦ Ἰησοῦ μαθηταῖς, ἢ μή), and if one did not
believe them, then one could not believe any author who had ever
written anywhere.[88] Eusebius embarks upon ruling out the possibility that the Gospels contained a combination of truth and fabrication. As far as logic was concerned, it was impossible for the evangelists
to present truth and falsehood at the same time. Nor was it possible that the detailed description of the wretched passion, crucifixion,
and death of Jesus was just a fiction. If, in fact, the aim of the apostles was to invent and then to exalt their master through lies, they
could not have written the Gospels in this manner, with its description of Jesus' passion and deliberations. They would not have mentioned that they had abandoned him, and that Peter, the first apostle,
had denied him. Future generations would not have been able to
prove that they had left out such events.[89] The evangelists could have
lied by saying that after Judas Iscariot had betrayed Jesus with a
kiss, he had turned to stone, or that the hand of the person who
was about to hit Jesus had withered, or that the high priest Caiaphas,
who had conspired against Jesus with false witnesses, had lost his
sight. Furthermore, they could have related that nothing had happened to Jesus, and that he laughed when he vanished after his
arrest, while they thought that he was present and continued to work

---

[86] *DE* 3,5,89–95. The general line of argumentation appears in Origen, *CC*, without detailed development. The fact that the evangelists also included inappropriate
material was, he claimed, a sign of their truthfulness. Thus Celsus had to believe
in "divine stories" related in the Gospels (*CC* 1,63). If the disciples had made up
the stories, they would not have recorded Peter's denial of Christ (*CC* 2,15).

[87] *DE* 3,5,96.

[88] *DE* 3,5,96.

[89] *DE* 3,5,97–101.

against him.[90] Moreover, they could have described him as not being mortal at all, but rather a divine being who had descended to earth to sort out human affairs through his divine power, and then returned to his divine glory in heaven.[91]

Eusebius' reply is not simply a piece of rhetoric. Behind it, apparently, lies the pagan polemical argument that dwells on the real difficulty of presenting Christian dogmas to the pagan public and persuading it to accept them. In Chapter 7, he discusses the question of how and to whom the apostles spread the Gospel. Here he chooses to overlook the claim that they had initially worked among the ignorant and naive, such as slaves, maidservants, and children. His statements reflect the pagan argument that apostles and other missionaries played down the less flattering descriptions in the Gospels and silently passed over Jesus' suffering and humiliation, and his miserable death, which was a difficult issue for pagans. The apostles spoke only of great events, miracles, and his divine teachings. For thus it was certainly easier to win over the hearts of his audience. According to this argument, they may even have refrained from mentioning problematic dogmas such as the Incarnation and Resurrection, which were very difficult concepts as far as belief was concerned. The argument reflected here, therefore, is that it was not the evangelists but the missionaries, who evaded problematic issues.[92]

---

[90] This seems to combine the story of Apollonius and his miraculous disappearance at his trial, with Docetic explanations. We have observed that Apollonius' disappearance figured prominently in the favorable comparison of the latter with Jesus. In his polemic, Celsus argues that in order to prove his divinity, Jesus should have vanished from the cross at once. Origen used the argument that the apostles could easily have written that Jesus disappeared from prison; the fact that they did not proved the truth of their testimony (*CC* 2,68).

[91] *DE* 3,5,102.

[92] D. Flusser has proposed a similar argument in principle for early Christian apologetics in general. As in the case of Judaism, Christian apologetics tried to win adherents by arguing that the new religion was acceptable to the simple mind, and that Christology did not, therefore, have a prominent place. See D. Flusser, "The Jewish Origins of Christianity", in idem., *Jewish Sources in Early Christianity* (Tel Aviv, 1979), p. 433 (Hebrew). This argument is less valid in the case of Eusebius' apologetics, which have a relatively large measure of Christology, although theology does not figure prominently. Christology receives greater attention in Christian theological works, and in internal debates or arguments against heretical views. In essence, this argument has a parallel in modern theories on the development of Christian art. For apologetic reasons, early Christian art was not considered unique because of the desire to downplay more problematic dogmas and less impressive stories. In contrast, it tended to emphasize the common, unifying themes of Christianity and the general culture found in art. See L.W. Barnard, "Early Christian Art as Apologetic", *Journal of Religious History* 10 (1978), pp. 20–31.

According to Eusebius, however, the apostles hid nothing and related the wondrous and almost incredible events of the Incarnation and Resurrection. The doctrine of resurrection from the dead was the main obstacle for Paul's audience in the Areopagus (Acts 17:31–32), and would remain so for future generations. Belief in resurrection was a joke among pagans, as attested by many apologists,[93] and as we saw in the sharp words of Porphyry. Eusebius points to the pagans' difficulty in accepting Christian dogmas even in his own time, because of their inherent irrationality. Who could believe that the disciples saw Jesus rise from the dead, while during his lifetime he could not protect himself? Who could believe ignorant men who preached that one should despise one's ancestral gods, and instead put one's trust in these men and in the crucified one, because he was the only and beloved son of the most high God. Such words indicate the force of the pagan argument. For here, in a moment of truth, Eusebius admits the irrationality of the dogma: "When I ponder these things sincerely, I must admit that I cannot find in it any power of persuasion, honor, or credulity, and even no particular likelihood that could persuade even one among the most simple people."[94] Here, he gives an answer indicated earlier in this study: the proof of the truth of these statements, even for him, is *post factum*, i.e., from the great conquests of Christianity through the power of the Logos.

The ultimate proof of the Gospels' truth was the miracle that nullified all paradoxes, including the paradox of the miracles that formed the basis of the dogma. Doctrines that seemed absurd at first were actually a historical wonder that could be understood in terms of divine power. This divine power was manifest in miraculous deeds in the past, and was still active. Although he does not state this explicitly, Eusebius seems to distinguish between miracles, in general, and miracles that underlie teachings such as the Incarnation and Resurrection. These miracles were difficult to accept even in a world that believed in miracles. Here, Eusebius exhibits a dialectical ten-

---

[93] See Athenagoras, *A Plea for the Christians*, 36; Tatian, *Address to the Greeks*, 6; Minucius Felix, *Octavius*, 11; Origen, *CC* 2,16; 2,55; 5,14; 8,49.

[94] *DE* 3,7,21. Such statements recall the diametrically opposite view of Tertullian. He hoped to propose Christianity as the challenge or alternative to philosophy; reducing it to neat logic would mean disregarding its supernatural character. Thus his ultimate Christian confession is the paradox that "one must believe because it is absurd (*ineptum*)" (*De carne Christi*, 5).

sion between his rational tendencies and his belief in miracles. Indeed, this tension also appears when he is dealing with dogmas within the framework of apologetic writing; it could be viewed as apologetically motivated, but it may reflect a fundamental position that also finds expression in the apologetic work. Perhaps the basic skepticism of a literal understanding of the dogmas makes it difficult for Eusebius to deal with them in an explicitly apologetic-polemical context. In his extant apologetic-polemical writings, he does not venture to defend the dogmas as such, beyond pointing out that they also exist among Greek philosophers in one form or another, and that from early on they were part of the pristine Christian lore of the patriarchs and the prophets, as attested by the many prophecies he cites. For example, he admits that the Incarnation and Virgin Birth are difficult concepts for Christians too, but other miracles in the life of Jesus that were not inferior to the miracle of the nativity, compel us to accept that miracle.[95] This is precisely the distinction (which I have pointed out) between more "reasonable" miracles, as it were, and intractable miracles, which cannot be upheld by reason, such as the Incarnation and the Resurrection. Paradoxically, though, Eusebius determines that it is precisely those intractable wonders that underpin the dogmas, constituting the great and formative miracles. In fact, he states that all miracles follow on from the great miracle of the nativity, which serves as the founding miracle.[96] He presents a similar argument in his interpretation of Isaiah 7. Because details of the prophecy had been fulfilled, as he had shown in other verses, one also had to accept the prophecy of Virgin Birth (Isa. 7:14). Hence the fulfillment of the other parts of the prophecy meant that this part would also be fulfilled.[97]

From the brief statements regarding the Incarnation, presented in the polemical context, it is not clear whether his audience was Christian, pagan or Jewish. Eusebius expresses a Christological view that borders on Docetism and approaches Monophysitism, aspiring to preserve the divine perfection of Jesus, and in effect negating all human nature in Jesus despite his appearance on earth in human

---

[95] *DE* 7,1,92.

[96] Ibid.

[97] *DE* 7,1,94. Justin argued that there was no rational basis for the Incarnation. Had other prophecies not been fulfilled, such as those concerning the destruction of Jerusalem and the conversion of the Gentiles to Christianity, it would have been impossible to accept the Incarnation! (*First Apology*, 53).

form. He stresses that one should not be deterred by the idea of the Incarnation, for the pure was not made impure by the body, just as the rays of the sun did not become polluted by their contact with various bodies. Moreover, the body itself had undergone a transformation through the Incarnation, and through the Logos it had changed from a corrupt to a holy and eternal state.[98] Hence, even the acceptance of the dogma as a dictate of faith solely maintained by divine power is not a final statement. In the polemical context one can see how this idea reduces problematic aspects of the belief in the Incarnation. It is possible, however, that we have here a considerable residue from Origen's opinions. Likewise, the symbolic interpretation of the Eucharist, and the allegory relating to the miracle of walking on the water, are imbued with Eusebius' rationalizing instinct. In a brief account of the problem of creation *ex nihilo*, Eusebius offers a solution as if by magic, in a neo-Platonic tone indicating that he may not have believed in creation *ex nihilo* in the first place.[99]

Eusebius summarizes his principal refutation of the argument that the Gospels blended truth and falsehood, as follows. Since the apostles and the evangelists had not been tempted to gloss over embarrassing or somber events in their descriptions, then the text was certainly stamped with the seal of literary truth. The seal of truth was indivisible. If it were recognizable in one part, one could infer from this to the other parts of the whole, and so view the testimony regarding the miracles of Jesus as true.[100] The moral argument, intended to rebut attempts to undermine the credibility of the apostles as witnesses—and thus discredit Jesus' miracles as proof of his divinity and the truth of the faith—grew and developed from an examination of arguments against the apostles. Finally, the moral

---

[98] This is a further example of Eusebius' view that the body of Jesus was not identical to ours. See also *DE* 6,20. It was Origen's belief that the body of Jesus was not like a human body. For example, see *CC* 6,77. Nevertheless, his view was not completely identical to that of Eusebius. In *CC* 4,15, Origen expresses a concept of the Incarnation which borders on Docetism: that the Incarnation existed for human beings who were not able to look at the bright light of the divinity. In addition, the concept of resurrection of the body was given a more complex interpretation. During the process of resurrection, the body underwent a transformation and was not identical to mortal bodies in this world, becoming a spiritual body (*CC* 2,62; 5,19; 7,32). Methodius vehemently opposed this view. Eusebius voices a similar opinion in *Theophany* 1,72.

[99] *DE* 4,1. For a discussion of Eusebius' understanding of creation and *creatio ex nihilo* see Lyman, *Christology and Cosmology*, pp. 95–96.

[100] *DE* 3,5,102–103.

argument completes its circular course. Inherent in it is testimony concerning the reliability of tradition. The pagan opponents had to admit that this had a minimum of truth. Logic would then oblige them to concede that the testimony of the disciples and the evangelists was true as far as miracles of the Redeemer were concerned. The independent report by Josephus is adduced as historical proof of the veracity of the Gospel account of Jesus' wondrous miracles, the prime importance of the miracles for Eusebius, and the argument that developed from the internal examination of the testimony contained in the Gospels. To this, Eusebius adds the testimony of the Acts of the Apostles. This may be another indication that Eusebius views Acts as a work whose historical value is less controversial.[101] Thus Eusebius' response to pagan arguments against the apostles, disciples, and evangelists consists of an internal examination of their testimony, the development of the moral argument as a validation of their testimony, and the presentation of the independent historical proof as an objective indication of the inherent truth of that testimony. The exposition of these issues falls within the framework of his reply to the first type of denigrators, those who do not believe in the miracles of Jesus.[102] One angle of pagan critique was to target the miracles of Jesus through those who disseminated accounts of them, namely, the apostles, disciples and evangelists. The purpose was to undermine and demolish the foundations of the Christian faith, in which miracles were regarded as the supreme manifestation of the divine powers of Jesus. There ensued fundamental struggle as Eusebius adopted the tactics dictated by pagan arguments. First, he had to refute them in order to re-establish the credibility of the testimonies concerning Jesus, by proving the perfect loyalty to truth on the part of the apostles. Once restored, this foundation could be viewed as proof of the truth of the miracles, thus validating once more the proof of the divine power of Christ and of the truth of the faith. Next, Eusebius had to address the second group of detractors, those who conceded that Jesus had performed miracles, but claimed that he did so by deceptive magic or spells, as a soothsayer.[103]

---

[101] *DE* 3,5,104–108.
[102] *DE* 3,5,109–110.
[103] *DE* 3,5,110.

On Arguments that Miracles Depend on Magic and Sorcery

The pagan claim that Christian miracles were authentic but were nonetheless acts of magic, presented the apologists with an even greater problem. Justin was aware of this type of pagan argument. Jesus was a man who performed magic and miracles, and may only have seemed to be the Son of God.[104] He dismisses this argument with the general principle that magic, as opposed to miracles, comes from demons.[105] Celsus repeated this argument in different versions, with some effect, it seems. On the one hand, Celsus had hoped to refute the traditions about Jesus; on the other, he was prepared to acknowledge that Jesus' miracles took place, but considered them acts of magic. Thus he attacked on two—albeit contradictory—levels. Perhaps this is not so much a tactical move to attack on all fronts, but rather a testimony to the acceptance of magic as a natural part of the world picture, and even as part of the range of man's natural powers. In fact, he relates to magic as an inferior occupation unworthy of philosophers. According to Celsus, magic had no effect on philosophers or anyone who studied philosophy. Sorcery acted only on the ignorant, uneducated, and morally corrupt.[106] Thus the array of arguments that presented Jesus as a magician, and the Christians as being misled by magic, served Celsus as more than just a negation of the Christian idea that the uniqueness of Jesus' miracles was proof of his divine status; it was another facet of Celsus' overriding purpose to present Christianity as an inferior religion for boors and ignoramuses. He argued that the Christians were led by the magic of Moses and Jesus.[107] Jesus found his way to Egypt where he learned magic.[108] His miracles were the results

---

[104] *First Apology*, 29. He was acquainted with the Jewish background of this argument as it appears in *Dialogue* 69,7, where the Jews accuse Jesus of magic and charlatanism.

[105] *First Apology* 14.

[106] *CC* 6,41. Likewise, see Plotinus, *Enneads* 4,4, 43–44.

[107] *CC* 5,51.

[108] *CC* 1,28. On Egypt as the birthplace of magic, see also the Babylonian Talmud, *Kiddushin* 49b. On the Jewish origins of the argument that Jesus studied magic and witchcraft in Egypt, and on the adoption of this argument by Celsus, see D. Rokeah, "Ben Stara is Ben Pantera", *Tarbiz* 39 (1970), p. 17 (Hebrew). Josephus describes a false prophet and wizard (γόης) who misled many and caused their deaths at the hands of the Procurator Felix (*War* II, 261–263; *Antiquities* XX, 172–196). The charges leveled against Jesus of practicing witchcraft and being a tool in the hands of Beelzebub—the minister of the demons, who enabled him to

of his studies in Egypt. Celsus compares his miracles to the conventional magic that derived from the active force of the evil demon.[109] Thus he also attributes magic to evil demonic forces. Celsus presents Jesus as an ordinary magician not fully sure of his power, who has to threaten and curse at weak moments. This demonstrated his inability to convince his audience. Such curses and threats were inappropriate for intelligent people, let alone a god.[110] It was his desire to thwart competition and prevent any erosion of his status that led Jesus to warn against magical acts performed by others, with the excuse that they were merely wizards, magicians, charlatans and imitators.[111] In his miraculous appearance before his disciples after his death, Jesus merely gave the impression of having physical wounds.[112] Celsus compares the figure of Jesus to a long series of pagan figures, and his miracles to pagan miracles, in order to prove his claim that Jesus was inferior even as a magician, and to destroy his pretense of being a god.[113] Here, the magic attributed to famous pagan figures at least partially contradicts the distinction formerly made between magic and philosophy. According to Celsus, lies and fiction were part of magic, in general, and of the magic of Jesus, in particular.

His arguments against Jesus resemble those leveled at the apostles

---

perform miracles—are placed in the mouths of Jews in the Gospels (Matt. 12:24; 9:34; Mark 3:22; Luke 11:15). It is possible that this reflected Jewish views at the time of the evangelists, and perhaps later too. The Talmud includes accusations of sorcery against Jesus (BT *Sanhedrin* 43a), and a comparison with Balaam as a magician (BT *Sanhedrin* 106a–b). See also Rokeah, ibid.; Baskin, *Pharaoh's Counsellors*, 75–100.

[109] *CC* 1,68.

[110] *CC* 2,75.

[111] *CC* 1,6.

[112] *CC* 2,61.

[113] *CC* 3,22–24; 3,26; 3,32–33; 3,36. Pythagoras appears among Celsus' figures (for example, *CC* 2,55). Fantastical legendary traditions surrounded the figure of Pythagoras, including a halo of holiness and divinity, in an entire branch of quasi-hagiographical works about Pythagoras of which very little remains. This trend later reached its climax in neo-Pythagorean and neo-Platonic circles, and found full expression in the hagiography by Iamblichus, the *Life of Pythagoras*. Several traditions regarding the miracles and divinity of Pythagoras could have served as proof of his superiority to Jesus, as I shall discuss later. Celsus, however, avoids such traditions, which may not have been prevalent in his times. On Pythagoras' prophetic skill, see Porphyry, *Life of Pythagoras* 25; 28; 29; Iamblichus, *Life of Pythagoras* 28. Regarding his gift of instant translocation, see Iamblichus, ibid. On his power and mastery over natural forces, see Porphyry, *Life of Pythagoras* 28. For traditions regarding the birth of Pythagoras from Apollo, and on Pythagoras as the incarnation of Apollo see Diogenes Laertius, *Lives of the Philosophers* 8,1,11; 8,1,21 (Pythagoras); Porphyry, ibid., 2; Iamblichus, ibid., 2; 19; 28.

and the evangelists. He claims that some of the fraud and deception could be traced to Jesus himself. For it was he who made up
the story of the Virgin Birth and gave himself the title of God.[114]
He lied and cheated,[115] and his disciples were duped into believing
that he was in fact God.[116] In conclusion, the image that Celsus
sought to convey was that of a mortal, a magician, a swindler, and
a charlatan.

Origen responds to Celsus' various arguments and determines principles regarding magic. We have seen the importance he attaches to
miracles as proof of the divinity of Jesus and the truth of the Gospel.
At the same time, however, he tends to attenuate the miraculous
aspect and emphasize the symbolic value of the miracle. Thus although
the miracle preserves its basic power as proof and a means of persuasion, there also emerges a parallel trend towards the allegorical
spiritualization of the concept of miracles. This trend derive from
polemics, or it may be an expression of Origen's general inclination
towards the spiritualization of concepts and doctrines. In any case,
by downplaying the miraculous aspect, Origen could present arguments regarding Jesus that essentially resembled those relating to the
apostles. The truth of Jesus' miracles was confirmed by their few-
ness. He revived only three people. A fabrication would have included
more such acts, and would have required him to revive not only
those who had died recently, but also the long-dead, in order to
enhance the impression of the miracle. Only those whom the Logos
considered suitable were resurrected. The miracles of resurrection
were also precursors of great deeds that the apostles would perform
according to Jesus' promise. Greater than any physical miracle was
their spiritual miracle, which opened the eyes and ears of the soul
so that it could eagerly hear about God.[117] Here the tendency towards
the allegorical spiritualization of miracles is manifest. While preserving their authenticity, the miracle stories also acquire the status
of parables.

Origen had to distinguish between Christian and pagan miracles,
between "black" and "white" magic. The Egyptians performed miracles similar to those of Moses, but they used trickery, whereas Moses

---

[114] *CC* 1,28.
[115] *CC* 2,7–8.
[116] *CC* 2,26.
[117] *CC* 2,48.

worked by divine power. Likewise, the miracles of false prophets and impostors, like those of the Egyptian magicians, were lies intended to deceive, while the miracles of Jesus and the apostles, like those of Moses, led to redemption.[118] Thus Origen acknowledged the real power of the pagans' magic and conceded that, from a phenomenological point of view, acts of miracles and magic were one and the same. It was the force behind a specific act dictating its purpose that determines whether it was a miracle or merely magic. Divine power acting behind a miracle directed it towards a good purpose; demonic power behind magic made it fraudulent. This principle included further proof of the real existence of divine miracles. For when something evil pretended to be good, it made the point that good was the antithesis of evil. Hence magic was proof of the actual existence of divine miracles.[119] For magic was an act that pretended to be divine and well-intentioned, whereas it was in fact a human act performed by those who were animated by demonic powers, aided by Satan and his son the Antichrist, for the purpose of fraud and deception.[120] The criterion for distinguishing between magic and miracles, or between pagan and Christian miracles, was therefore the moral character of those involved, and the consequence of the miracle. The activity of Moses and Jesus was divine, as evinced by the results of their actions. Moses established a nation; Jesus taught about life according to the Gospel.[121] An essential difference between Jesus and the magicians was that Jesus worked towards an educational-religious goal.[122] Proof of the truth of Jesus' miraculous resurrection lay in the exemplary lives of the disciples![123] Origen presents the contradiction between magic and ethics as if the very concept of magic was antithetical to ethics. If Jesus engaged in magic, why did he bother himself with moral teachings that were not relevant to the activities of a magician?[124] A man who wanted to nurture morality among people could not be a magician.[125] Thus Origen shares the position of Celsus that magic involves charlatanism and

---

[118] *CC* 2,49–50.
[119] *CC* 2,51.
[120] *CC* 6,45.
[121] *CC* 2,51.
[122] *CC* 1,68.
[123] *CC* 2,51.
[124] *CC* 1,38.
[125] *CC* 1,68.

moral corruption. On the other hand, he rejects the separation between magic and philosophy—which contains a distinct polemical element. He strives to show that the philosophers had a propensity for magic and believed in it. The outstanding example was Apollonius, who inclined towards magic and convinced other philosophers to acknowledge magical powers.[126]

The moral criterion was fundamental to identifying and distinguishing between miracle and magic. Beyond the polemical context, however, Origen had to make clear distinctions for another reason. In his time, Christians used magic for spells, amulets, and exorcising demons, in a manner basically identical to pagan practice. Furthermore, Origen himself was curious and knowledgeable about both pagan and Christian manifestations of magic, as *Against Celsus* amply demonstrates.[127] In fact, the leaders of the Church sharply condemned Christians who dabbled in magic, thereby strengthening our impression that the phenomenon was more widespread than appears in the literature.[128] Tertullian argued that Christians did not resort to astrology, fortune telling, or magic—skills that humans had learned from fallen angels. God forbade such techniques.[129] However, rather than reflecting reality, his statement apparently derived from an external polemical need and the desire to take a strong and unequivocal position for internal Church purposes.[130] Origen also states that Christian doctrine forbade magic, and it was thus absurd to claim that the disciples of Jesus engaged in it.[131] Likewise, he claims that magic was not prevalent among Christians. However, his intentions differ from those of Tertullian. Although demonic pagan magic was not to be found among Christians, miraculous Christian magic—activated by divine power and the name of Jesus—was alive and well, claims Origen, even among simple and ignorant Christians.[132]

---

[126] *CC* 6,41.

[127] See *CC* 1,22; 1,24; 1,25; 4,33–34; 5,9; 5,46; 7,69; 8,58; 8,61. On the interest in magic shown by Origen and Julius Africanus, see also Grant, *Miracles*, pp. 109–110.

[128] See Grant, ibid., p. 121.

[129] *Apology* 35,12.

[130] A similarly extreme attitude towards anything associated with pagan practices appears in his work, *On Idolatry* (*De Idololatria*).

[131] *CC* 1,38.

[132] He claims that it was mostly uneducated Christians who engaged in exorcism. He explains that invoking the name of Jesus was sufficient against the weakness of the demons and that exorcism did not require an educated man versed in doctrinal proof (*CC* 7,4).

In Chapter 6 of *DE* III, Eusebius seeks to respond to the second category of detractors, namely, those who concede that Jesus performed miracles, but that he did so by deceptive magic, as a magician or a sorcerer. This exposition is relatively brief because he does not use all of Origen's points, basing his main argument on the moral criterion, as he did in his response to charges against the apostles and disciples. However, Eusebius further develops and consolidates the moral criterion as a basis for truth, and introduces a number of secondary arguments not encountered in Origen. As we have noted, Eusebius does not deny the actual power of magic and theurgy, despite the fact that on occasion he negates them, in the general framework of a rejection of all forms of pagan religion.[133] In *Against Hierocles*, Eusebius does not deny the magical power of Apollonius, but rejects attempts to clothe magic in the robes of divine wisdom. He acknowledges the power of magical formulae and pagan theurgic adjurations that control demon-gods and compel them to appear and to act.[134] Celsus argued for a separation between magic and philosophy, presenting magic as inferior and immoral. In contrast, Porphyry expressed the prevalent view that magic was a gift of the gods to humans, enabling them to liberate themselves from the fetters of fate.[135] It was virtually the only way left for man to extricate himself somewhat from his cruel destiny, which was governed by astrological and deterministic powers.[136] Therefore, magic could exist within the framework of philosophy and possess a positive meaning.[137] Here Eusebius saw a polemical opportunity to juxtapose and contrast magic and true philosophy, and thus emphasize the superiority

---

[133] See *PE* 4,1.

[134] *PE* 5,8.

[135] *PE* 6,4, according to *Philosophy from the Oracles*, and, likewise, Iamblichus, *On the Mysteries*,10, 4–5.

[136] On this concept of magic in late antiquity, see Cumont, *Astrology*, p. 88.

[137] Porphyry took this position in his early work, *Philosophy from the Oracles*. For a reconfirmation of this as one of Porphyry's early works, see A. Smith, *Porphyry's Place in the Neoplatonic Tradition* (The Hague, 1974), pp. 132–133; *ANRW* II.36.2 (1987), pp. 731–737; T.D. Barnes, "Scholarship or Propaganda", p. 59. For a different opinion see R.L. Wilken, *The Christians as the Romans Saw Them*, pp. 134–137. Later, in his *Letter to Anebo*, Porphyry opposed theurgy and various forms of divination. The letter has been reconstituted mainly from quotations, especially from Eusebius, Theodoretus, and Iamblichus. See the edition by A. Sodano, *Porfirio, Lettera ad Anebo* (Naples, 1958). For an analysis of the letter, see also Bidez, *Vie de Porphyre*, pp. 80–87. The work of Iamblichus, *On the Mysteries*, answers the critique of his teacher, Porphyry.

of Christian philosophy from another aspect.[138] The basic difference between a magician or charlatan, and Jesus, was the purpose underlying the miracles each performed—in other words, the moral criterion. Eusebius employs a rhetorical stratagem similar to the one used regarding the apostles. If we assumed the pagan argument as a point of departure, and called Jesus a magician and charlatan, how could he have been the source of the moral teachings that spread throughout the world; magicians and wizards were naturally corrupt and acted from base and obscure motives. Thus Jesus' moral pronouncements and his moral image in the New Testament made it impossible to accuse him of magic and sorcery. Once he had proven their credibility, Eusebius could freely rely on the testimony of the Gospels. He could also use the opposite argument deriving from the proof of the apostles' credibility. How could they have conveyed the moral teachings of Jesus if they had seen that their lord was avaricious and behaved in a manner that contradicted his teachings? They would have left him immediately in disgust if they had thought that he had a double moral standard, for himself and, for them. In other words, they would have left him had they discovered that the legislator did not behave according to his own laws.[139] The aim of magicians was to enjoy forbidden pleasures, such as casting magic spells on women and seducing them, whereas Jesus was pious and ascetic.[140] They aspired to honor and renown, while Jesus distanced himself from all fame and display. From then until now, Christians who had followed him eschewed magic, as befitted their master's example, and occupied themselves instead with philosophical matters. Jesus was "the senior philosopher and the teacher of the devout fearers of God" (φιλοσόφων ὁ πρώτιστος καὶ εὐσεβῶν ἀνδρῶν διδάσκαλος).[141] As he was a philosopher and a devout man (εὐσεβής), he could perform miracles from the strength of his piety and divine power; so, too, could the apostles and their Christian disciples in subsequent generations.[142] Proof lay in the fact that Christians did not

---

[138] *PE* 6,4. Here is another example of Eusebius' talent for exploiting the different views expressed by Porphyry in his various works. Eusebius knew the *Letter to Anebo* and cites it in *PE* in order to present Porphyry's critique of pagan religion.

[139] *DE* 3,6,1–3.

[140] *DE* 1,6,4.

[141] *DE* 3,6,8.

[142] See also *HE* 2,1,10–12. When Eusebius first mentions Simon Magus, he explains his tricks as magic, whereas the miracles of Philip derived from divine power.

allow even the sick to be assisted by such ordinary magical means as spells on leaves or amulets, magical poems, incense, or similar methods. Eusebius presents a general argument similar to that of Tertullian. Christian doctrine forbade the use of magical techniques and, in his time, Christians did not need amulets or magical formulae.[143] In fact, though, as we have noted, literary and epigraphic evidence indicate otherwise.[144] Additional proof of the moral greatness of Jesus and the impossibility of his being a magician or a wizard was to be found in the character of his disciples. Eusebius argues for the principle that, in all branches of learning, a pupil testifies to the excellence of his teacher—a somewhat optimistic view of student attitudes to those who teach them. Thus the best testimony for a magician was that of his followers.[145] This argument enables him to present the pagan claim as if put to an historic test. Across the years, Christians had been forced to undergo investigation and torture designed to elicit information about their religion. And behold, since Jesus, not a single Christian had been convicted as a magician! Not one had admitted to engaging in magic, despite the fact that doing so would have gained him release; all he had to do was to offer sacrifice to the gods. If this were true regarding Christians in post-apostolic generations, it was all the more so for the apostles themselves. Therefore, in light of this argument, it was clear that their master could not have been a magician.[146] This reasoning is distinct from the moral argument, and for Eusebius it has an objective historical value quite unconnected to the distinction between magic and miracles. Eusebius likes to display, as it were, generosity and magnanimity in his polemic. He concedes that perhaps this argument is not based upon historical documents, in which case he is prepared to produce proof from written and documented history as well (ἵνα δὲ μὴ ἐξ ἀγράφων ὁ λόγος ἡμῖν ὁδεύοι, δέχου τὰς ἀποδείξεις καὶ ἀπὸ ἱστορίας ἐγγράφου).[147] And what is this recorded history, if not the

---

[143] DE 3,6,9–11.

[144] See Ferrar's note, Eusebius, The Proof of the Gospel, pp. 146–147. On the use of magic among Christians in the fourth century and subsequently, see also MacMullen, Christianizing the Roman Empire, p. 77. Geffcken held that magic had particular importance for the survival of paganism among the general public, and even among neo-Platonic philosophers who adopted popular beliefs. Christians had adopted such magic and popular beliefs, and preserved them in various forms (Geffcken, Last Days, p. 13).

[145] DE 3,6,12.

[146] DE 3,6,13.

[147] DE 3,6,14.

Acts of the Apostles![148] In other words, Acts was an historical work
that had to be accepted as such by the opponent in the polemic.
We have noted how Eusebius tends to differentiate between the
Gospels and Acts, regarding the latter as a text that could be used
in polemics because, for the pagans, its historical credibility was
somewhat less suspect. In fact, it is possible that he invokes the historical veracity of Acts after earlier proving the credibility of the testimony of the apostles and disciples, and that from this point on
Acts has to be accepted unequivocally as an historical document.
The work relates that many magicians, astounded by the teachings
of the apostles, transformed their lives completely and threw their
forbidden books into the fire.[149] Conceivably, if there were magicians
among the disciples of the apostles, even these magicians—so the
book informs us—underwent a transformation and their hearts were
purified. If this held true for the disciples, then it was also for their
teacher.[150]

Eusebius was able to expand the moral argument, giving it greater
strength and importance on the basis of the historical reality of contemporary Christian society—which differed from that of Origen's
day—namely, the growth of the ascetic movement in Christianity in
the generation that preceded the flowering of monasticism as a mass
movement. Eusebius describes a widespread movement comprising
many men and women who followed that way of life for the sake
of their leader, Jesus. Such pronouncements indicate that he did not
mean monks. His description is reminiscent of Philo's idealized view
of the Therapeutae.[151] In fact, in the past, there had been examples
of such a lifestyle among the Greeks, but these were few and exceptional, whereas thousands of Jesus' disciples, contemporaries of Eusebius, had sold their possessions and distributed them among the poor.
Thus the results of the teachings of Jesus could be noted not only
in words but in deeds.[152]

The masses of Greeks and barbarians who acknowledged the truth
of monotheism and, as a result of Jesus' teaching, abandoned polytheistic misconceptions, were proof of the truth of the Christian faith.[153]

---

[148] *DE* 3,6,15.
[149] Acts of the Apostles 19:19; *DE* 3,6,15–16.
[150] *DE* 3,6,18–19.
[151] *DE* 3,6,20–21.
[152] *DE* 3,6,22–23.
[153] *DE* 3,6,24.

Such proof, based on the continuity of historical success, could serve either side of the polemic on different occasions. However, it was not necessary to use this argument although Eusebius repeatedly resorts to proof based on historical success, for even Plato had acknowledged the most high God.[154] In this case, Eusebius understood the theological concept of Plato as a monotheistic philosophical concept. But unlike Jesus, Plato had had neither the power nor the courage to spread his teachings, as Eusebius noted with regard to the *Timaeus*. More precisely, he did not have the power of holiness, unlike the disciples of Jesus, who enjoyed the support of their master.[155] Here Eusebius refers to Plato as a religious personality, hence the apparent ease with which he compares the latter to the apostles.

Eusebius' polemic has a personal dimension. He addresses his anonymous opponent in a friendly manner,[156] using rhetorical techniques. He toys with the pagan charge that Jesus was a magician and founder of a new charlatanism, and in the course of this pleasantry, uncovers a pagan admission of the divinity of Jesus! He asks whether Jesus himself founded the doctrines of magic and charlatanism that he preached, or whether one had to search for the sources that influenced him. For if one claimed that no one had taught him, and that he discovered and invented everything, we had to regard him as divine. Otherwise, such a wonder could not be understood. For even a simple laborer required a teacher, a guide and mentor to train him, as he was not born with the knowledge of his craft, teachers of literature and rhetoric, or physicists, not withstanding.[157] Therefore, ostensibly relying on logical arguments, Eusebius makes his pagan opponent concede the divinity of Jesus from the supposition of his own argument. He had to acknowledge, therefore,

---

[154] Ibid.

[155] *DE* 3,6,24–25.

[156] *DE* 3,6,26. He uses the second person singular, in the present tense, as if arguing with a personal rival. This form of address, and the direct pagan arguments that his opponent is made to voice—arguments to which Eusebius provides answers and which are known to us from Celsus and Porphyry—may strengthen the assumption that he is engaged in a direct debate with Porphyry, even if this is not stated explicitly. A substantial section of the third book is constructed as answers to specific arguments, in contrast to most of *PE* and *DE*, which constitute a response to a number of fundamental arguments underpinning the work. Later, however, Eusebius makes it difficult to identify his anonymous opponent with Porphyry, as we shall see.

[157] *DE* 3,6,26–27.

that Jesus who was the teacher of a true religion (εὐσεβείας ἀληθοῦς διδάσκαλος) and performed great miracles, was born with divine power and did not need the teachings of the ancients or the instruction of teachers; he thus transcended humanity.[158] This argument progresses as follows: having established that the divinity of Jesus was a logical consequence of the pagan argument—on the pagan assumption that Jesus had invented a new form of magic and charlatanism—Eusebius introduces the premise that Jesus was unique as a Christian teacher of religion and morality, whose truths had been proved and who had therefore, by inference, proved his divinity.

The personal debate with the anonymous opponent, whom he repeatedly addresses in second person continues. Following the previous argument and his own reply, Eusebius puts in the mouth of the pagan, as an answer to his rejoinder, the familiar pagan claim that Jesus had teachers in magic and sorcery. He asserts that Egyptian magicians had instructed Jesus in the tradition of the secret wisdom of their ancestors.[159] This is rejected with the argument that we do not hear of any magicians, wonder workers, or teachers of magic, who had surpassed him, either in Egypt or elsewhere. We had heard neither of them nor of their reputation. No one celebrated their fame in the manner that Christians praised Jesus. Here Eusebius repeats his previous arguments. Historically speaking, no magician had trained as many disciples, or established laws and doctrines, as the Redeemer had. Who had associates and witnesses to his deeds who would follow him through every test and become martyrs, spilling their blood and dying for his sake (καὶ τέλος διὰ τοῦ ἰδίου αἵματος τὰ περὶ αὐτοῦ μαρτυρηθέντα αὐτοῖς πιστωσάμενοι)?[160] The truths of Jesus had been tested through fire, like gold, by his disciples, the martyrs.

Afterwards, Eusebius includes somewhat well-worn arguments. No magician in history had thought of establishing a new nation named after him. Surely the fulfillment of such an idea was beyond human

---

[158] *DE* 3,6,27. Eusebius could have included traditions relating to the childhood of Jesus, and to the fact that he did not need teachers, as related in the *Infancy Gospel of Thomas*. From *DE* 9,4, it appears that he knew of such traditions. Perhaps he was disinclined to rely on them because of his tendency to reject the tradition of miracle stories from Jesus' childhood.

[159] *DE* 3,6,28.

[160] *DE* 3,6,29–30.

strength. No wizard could have planned to proscribe idolatry, against the dictates of kings, ancient lawgivers, poets, philosophers, and theologians. No magician of former times had invented or undertaken any such daring and revolutionary plan, as required by the argument that Jesus had learned from and been assisted by others. Once again we had to admit that no one was like him and no one had influenced his character. This was the proof that a strange and divine being had sojourned on earth (ξένην τινὰ καὶ θείαν φύσιν ἐπιδεδημηκέναι τῷ βίῳ). Unprecedented acts had been performed by Jesus, and recorded. His essential uniqueness in history was proof of his divinity.[161]

Eusebius concludes his treatment of the pagan arguments against Jesus' divinity by attacking his anonymous rival. Had he ever heard of wizards and magicians who did not require the external assistance of libations or incense, or the presence of *daimons*? These were never needed by Jesus, his disciples, or Christians to the present day. For Jesus opposed all gods as demons and forces of evil, and it was, therefore, absurd to assume that he was their protégé Christians used his name even today to exorcise demons; they trembled upon hearing it, out of fear of punishment and torture, and so left the bodies that they had entered.[162]

It is the moral argument that once again closes the circle. Eusebius identifies magic with all that is scandalous, low, atheistic, unjust, and impious. If Jesus, as a magician, sinned in all these areas, how could he have been a teacher of religion, moderation, and acknowledgment of God and His justice? Should he not have commanded the opposite, namely, to deny God, and His providence and justice, and to disparage morality and faith in the immortality of the soul? If someone had testified that the Lord and Redeemer was indeed of such a character, the argument would have been irrefutable. However, if the contrary was proved true, then one had to conclude that he did not perform his miracles by magic, and that they derived from an ineffable power, namely divine power (μηδὲν μὲν ἡγεῖσθαι κατὰ γοητείαν αὐτὸν τῶν παραδόξων πεποιηκέναι, δυνάμει δ' ἀπορρήτῳ καὶ ὡς ἀληθῶς ἐνθέῳ).[163]

Eusebius closes the circle and returns to his point of departure.

---

[161] *DE* 3,6,31–33.
[162] *DE* 3,6,34–37.
[163] *DE* 3,6,37–38.

He sought to prove the uniqueness of the miracles as proof of the divinity of Jesus, for the benefit also of those who acknowledged them but only as acts of human magic. After proving their uniqueness by means of various arguments—notably the moral argument— Eusebius advances his proof of Jesus' divinity by invoking the greatness and singularity of the miracles. A superb tactician, Eusebius saves the decisive proof against his rival for the last moment. The wary opponent may have refused to heed the force and consistency of logical arguments, but Eusebius finally presents the supreme proof that would silence the last of the skeptics, proof that derived from the gods themselves, namely, the demons. This was the proof from the oracles, attesting to the holiness of Jesus, his wisdom, and his ascension to heaven. And what greater proof did we have than that which was written by our enemy (τοῦ καθ᾽ ἡμῶν πολεμίου), Porphyry?[164] This last passage may support the assumption that Eusebius is not debating directly with Porphyry, or at least, that he did not intend his anonymous disputant to be identified as Porphyry. For he distinguishes between the anonymous opponent addressed in the second person, and Porphyry, whose testimony he quotes as evidence against that very same anonymous opponent. This distinction supports the general impression that, despite the fact that Porphyry occupies a central position in this work and even constitutes the main reason for its composition, he is not presented as the direct target of the polemic. Eusebius intends to give his work a general tone beyond the narrow confines of a polemic against Porphyry. Later we shall discuss the role of Porphyry in this work.

Eusebius goes on to discuss briefly several other issues in Chapter 7, thus completing Book III. As we have noted, he regarded this book as the true beginning of the *DE*, an essential introduction to the essence of the dual composition. After proving his basic assumptions, he continues with the mysterious theology of Christ, and discusses the nature of the one who performed miracles through the manifest humanity of Jesus.[165]

---

[164] *DE* 3,6,39.
[165] See *DE* 3,7,40.

On Arguments Alleging Jesus' Weakness,
Wretchedness, and Cowardice

The pagan critique of the divine, miraculous power of Jesus included a series of arguments that indirectly undermined his status in this regard. The figure of Jesus that emerged from the Gospels was one of weakness, wretchedness, and inferiority, inconsistent with his presentation as a person possessing such wondrous powers. Ancient apologists hardly mention such arguments, but Celsus gives them substantial attention,[166] and they appear in Porphyry's critique as well. It is difficult, however, to assess their importance for him from the fragments that comprise only a small part of his work against the Christians. Similar arguments occur in the work of Hierocles, as well. But it seems that Eusebius did not view this type of critique as inseparable from the critique of the miracles of Jesus and the apostles. Such arguments do not appear in the detailed discussion in Book III of the *DE*. However, various arguments of this kind are to be found throughout the *DE* in the context of other issues. The general impression is that, even if Eusebius did not attach great importance to the

---

[166] Previously Celsus' arguments addressed different chapters in the biography of Jesus. Herod sought to kill Jesus as a king-messiah. When Jesus grew up, why did he not become king, instead of living in misery (*CC* 1,61)? Jesus fled and hid from his pursuers (*CC* 2,70). How could he be considered a god when he attempted to flee and hide, and was even betrayed by his friends (*CC* 2,9)? He acted out of weakness, endured insults, and did not use his power to take revenge (*CC* 2,35). He was not able to prevent his own suffering (*CC* 2,24) and could not free himself from arrest. This fact clearly indicated the limitations of his power (*CC* 2,34). Origen states that some viewed Matt. 26:39 as a sign of the cowardice of Jesus (*CC* 7,55). Celsus also argued that as a god, his body had to have some distinctiveness. Origen partly accepted this. Celsus simply did not understand the nature of such uniqueness. According to Origen, this uniqueness was the ability to appear in different forms according to the needs of those with whom he was in contact. The great revelation of this was the regular appearance of Jesus, as opposed to his single appearance at the transfiguration (*CC* 6,77). (Eusebius also adhered to the concept of the uniqueness of Jesus' body.) Most of the criticism was leveled at his wretched death. His death on the cross was a stark demonstration of weakness and misery (*CC* 7,56; 2,16). In order to prove his divinity, he should have vanished from the cross (*CC* 2,68). Jesus' behavior before his death was inferior to that of Anaxarchus and Epictetus before their deaths; the Christians should rather have chosen them as a god Jonah or Daniel, who behaved heroically in the face of death (*CC* 7,55). It would have befitted the Christians to have turned to someone else who died a noble death and made for himself a halo of a god, figures such as Heracles, Aesclepius, Orpheus, and Anaxarchus (*CC* 7,55). And if Jesus had been resurrected, he would have had to demonstrate his divine power by appearing before all, as he had during his lifetime, and not only before his disciples (*CC* 2,16).

possibility of such arguments undermining the divine status and miraculous power of Jesus, he found it necessary to relate to them, albeit not as separate issues worthy of detailed discussion. An examination of the context in which Eusebius relates to such arguments directly or implicitly gives a distinct picture of their relative importance in the framework of the anti-Christian critique. Eusebius' replies to the different arguments are somewhat dependent upon the immediate context of those arguments.

In several places, he offers general, fundamental responses; elsewhere, he relates to specific arguments. The general criticism of Jesus' wretchedness was supported by a further argument, namely, that this image clashed with the figure of the Jewish Messiah in Scripture. In reply, Eusebius posits the duality of the relevant verses, which relate to the first appearance of Jesus in humility and the Second Coming in glory. Herein lay the root of the error made by the Jews, who interpreted in a literal sense all verses on the coming of the Messiah. For they confused the second appearance with the first. Hence Eusebius' answer to the argument regarding the wretchedness of Jesus, which he views as stemming from a misunderstanding of the prophecies.[167] Elsewhere, Eusebius states the above in explicit terms. The appearance of Jesus in a state of humility and misery formed part of the divine plan envisioned by the prophets, particularly in Isaiah 53.[168] Another basic response is that the advent of Jesus in humility was proof of his participation in the humanity of man. It was proof of compassion, not of weakness.[169] Furthermore, the unbroken tradition of humility from Jesus and the apostles through successive generations of Christians, was the external expression of

---

[167] *DE* 4,16. For an interpretation of messianic prophecy on both appearances, and the confusion between them, see also *DE* 9,17. The prophecy of Zechariah 9:9–10 speaks of Jesus' entry into Jerusalem on a donkey—his first appearance in humility. The prophecy of Daniel 7 speaks of the *parousia*, the second heroic coming of Jesus in glory. Eusebius knew that both passages were interpreted by Jews as first appearance of the Messiah (see also BT Sanhedrin 98a), and he presents to the Christians the contradiction between them, namely, between riding on a donkey and riding on heavenly clouds, in response to Jews or to pagans presenting Jewish arguments. The duality of messianic verses had already been noted by Justin (*Dialogue* 14,8; 110,2). However, he proposes it not as a refutation of the argument of Jesus' wretchedness, but rather to counter the claim that Jesus was not the Messiah mentioned in Scripture; cf. Ulrich, ibid., pp. 160–172.

[168] *DE* 3,3.

[169] *DE* 9,17.

a great moral ideal, the principle of countering evil with good. This ideal was shared by Plato and the Holy Scriptures. It was the ideal of exalted moral achievement.[170] Eusebius speaks of similar humiliation on the part of the prophets, and presents the ideal of the suffering righteous man. Plato also acknowledged this ideal in his description of the suffering of the righteous. According to Eusebius, a truly righteous person was one who, constantly humiliated, performed righteous deeds for their own sake and not for his personal honor.[171] Thus quite apart from the messianic prophecies in Scripture, humility and suffering still constituted a great moral ideal, which Jesus and his Christian successors embodied perfectly.

The words of Eusebius in *DE* 9,4 reflect the argument as to why Jesus did not defend himself despite having divine power. Eusebius also alludes to a specific argument, namely, if Jesus had had divine power from birth, why did he not use it to act against Herod? Here Eusebius embarks on a defense of the accepted account of the life of Jesus, as opposed to traditions or claims regarding miracles he had performed as a boy, such as those related in the *Infancy Gospel of Thomas*.[172] According to Eusebius, it was not fitting that Jesus should have performed miracles as a child before his designated time, nor that he should have prevented Herod's chosen path of cruelty. Here, Eusebius could present himself both as a rationalist and as an orthodox Christian, which suited his general tendency to reduce the fantastical dimension of miracles so as to deflect anti-Christian arguments. Thus he arrives at a general principle. Jesus' miracles were neither directed against his enemies nor used in self-defense, but only as aid to those who were suffering. Jesus often preferred to maintain modesty and discretion regarding his miracles, lest they be made public. Herein, perhaps, lay the reply to the argument that, notwithstanding his miracles and the revelation of his power, Jesus had behaved like a coward and avoided confrontation, despite his strength. Eusebius finds support for the above in Isa. 42:1–7, which seemed to have been written expressly against that argument.[173] Furthermore, it was in order to postpone their punishment to the Day of Judgment

---

[170] *PE* 13,7.

[171] Ibid.

[172] Perhaps the statements of Justin (*First Apology*, 35) reflect the query as to why no one had heard of Jesus during the period between his childhood and adulthood.

[173] *DE* 9,15.

that Jesus had submitted to such insults and not opposed his enemies, despite his great power.[174] Eusebius explains Jesus' "fear and trembling" before his death as the final struggle of the powers of Satan against him.[175] We should also recall Porphyry's argument concerning the state of agony and the supplications of Jesus in Gethsemane. Jesus, however, cast off the spirit of fear of death, as an athlete throws a discus.[176]

Eusebius' statements reflect the way in which the enemies of Christianity made a point of deriding the passion, humiliation and crucifixion of Jesus.[177] The pagan argument regarding the miserable death of Jesus on the cross was extremely important. Many Christians found this death difficult to accept, as attested by various Docetic concepts. Eusebius interprets the entire text of Psalm 88 as relating to Christ, his passion, the Church, and the derision of the foes of Christianity.[178] Psalm 22 is interpreted as a grand reply to those who disparaged the crucifixion and the total helplessness of Jesus. The title of the Psalm included the miracle of Resurrection, which was the main issue! Eusebius starts with a Jewish interpretation (apparently derived from Aquila's Greek translation) of the verse, "My God, my God, why have you forsaken me?" (Psalms 22:2), claiming that this referred to the power of God, and should be read as: "My strength, why have you forsaken me?" For at the time of the crucifixion the divine power in Jesus left his body,[179] a concept already encountered in Eusebius. In this case, there is a theology of surrender and sacrifice together with a measure of apologetics and rationalization. The crucifixion could not have taken place without the departure of the power of God. Furthermore, the cry "My God, my God . . ." had didactic significance. It was intended to make us ask why God abandoned His Son. The answer was that He forsook him as a blood ransom for all of humanity, so that it could be delivered from the worship of demons.

In order to attain the greatest possible humility, Jesus had to be literally transformed into a worm, as in the words, "But I am a worm,

---

[174] Ibid.
[175] *DE* 10,2.
[176] Ibid.
[177] *DE* 4,16.
[178] Ibid.
[179] In this exegetical context, it is not stated explicitly that the Logos leaves the body, but rather the divine power in general, which derives from the Father.

and no man . . ." (Ps. 22:7). The latter draws on a biological concept dating from Aristotle, that worms were born from decomposed
corpses. In a speech before his death, Jesus speaks of his humiliat-
ing death on the cross and the degradation he witnessed among
those surrounding him on the cross.[180] It is as if he replies in advance
to the pagan arguments. The Father abandons Jesus on the cross as
a sacrifice, but the sacrifice is Jesus' triumph over the demons in the
netherworld. He is abandoned in order to enhance his independence
and the magnitude of his victory over the demons. Hence his words
on the cross, "My God, my God . . .". He becomes aware of the
fact that he is alone in his struggle against the forces of evil. The
descent into the netherworld is the final step in the contest of Christ
against the forces of evil. God the Father organizes and judges the
competition. Jesus is the outstanding athlete. On the cross, through
his divine eyes, Jesus sees the demons dancing around him. Eusebius relates that dancing demons waiting to seize his soul, apparently thought that his soul was human, like any other. It seems that
Eusebius thought the soul of Jesus was not human.[181] This was a
common proto-Apollinarian view.[182] We have noted that Eusebius
also held that the body of Jesus was not human like other bodies.
Demons had no authority over souls that did not belong to mortals.
In conclusion, Eusebius' answers to these arguments, scattered throughout the text and assembled here in order to consider their importance within the larger work, are intended to negate the pagans'
basic purpose of undermining the idea that Jesus possessed divine
power, as manifested in his ability to perform wondrous miracles.

To summarize, we might say that Christian apologetics discovered
that appealing to miracles as proof of the divinity of Jesus and the
truth of the Gospel, could be problematic. Arguments based on miracles could become a double-edged sword. It was often necessary to
defend important miracles in the Gospels. No longer was it possible
simply to base the Christian argument on miracle tales. For miracles to be believed, Jesus' teaching, and more especially, his personality as described in Scripture, had to have a greater impact.
Miracles could serve as proof for Jesus. First, however, Jesus had to

---

[180] *DE* 10,8. For a discussion of the christology of this passage see Lyman, *Christology and Cosmology*, pp. 119–121.
[181] *DE* 10,8.
[182] See Lyman, *Christology and Cosmology*, pp. 117–118.

serve as proof for the miracles. It was not enough to ask people to
believe in the divinity of Jesus because of his miracles. Perhaps they
could accept the miracle tales because they first acknowledged his
divinity. However, herein lies the paradox. For one was hardly likely
to accept Jesus' divinity without its being revealed through miracles.
Hence the tendency to turn to his character and personality in order
to prove the authenticity and the divinity of the miracles. In a world
where divine men such as Apollonius and Apuleius performed miracles, there was no reason to view the miracles of Jesus as extraordinary. Hence, the differentiation between magic and miracles according to the moral criterion guiding them. There is greater emphasis,
on the one hand, on the continuity of miracles in Christian history,
which persisted because the power of Jesus acted through his disciples
and their successors, and, on the other hand, on the moral perfection of Jesus' followers and the scale of an ascetic movement, which
attested to the sublime moral perfection of Christianity's founder.
This proved the divinity embodied in the Gospel, which enabled it
to spread throughout the world. We have encountered the full development of these ideas in the work of Eusebius. Less than a hundred
years after him, the prevailing attitude among Christian writers
changed course. Chrysostom and later authors inclined to the view
that the era of miracles had passed, that they belonged to the first
phase of the Gospel and were destined to cease after a certain time.
Their purpose had been to give an initial impetus to the Gospel
until it gained enough momentum to advance by itself. In their own
day, they asserted, miracles had ceased since the Church could get
along without them.[183]

---

[183] See Lampe, "Miracles and Early Christian Apologetic", p. 215.

CHAPTER SEVEN

MINOR APOLOGETIC-POLEMICAL ARGUMENTS AND ISSUES

This chapter will consider several topics of an apologetic-polemical nature that are not central to the *PE* and the *DE* (*PE-DE*), but arise in the course of discussing other subjects and pagan arguments, besides the major pagan arguments that formed the basis of Eusebius' great apologetic undertaking. As we have stated, Eusebius constructed his double composition as a general response, and not as specific answers to a series of anti-Christian arguments, as in Origen's work or in his own earlier piece against Porphyry. Nevertheless, several arguments appear throughout *PE-DE*—in either direct or indirect form—most of which were familiar from pagan-Christian polemics. This enables us to discover more about the polemical aspects of his statements and to discuss a number of his arguments that are pertinent, though not central, to the work.

The Roman Empire and the Incarnation

Attributing significance to the simultaneous establishment by Augustus of the Roman Empire and the Pax Romana, on the one hand, and the Advent of Jesus and the beginning of the Christian Gospel, on the other, constitutes an historical-apologetic concept. Both E. Peterson, who investigated its roots,[1] and subsequently Sirinelli, have explored the subject extensively.[2] In the framework of this study, therefore, it will be treated briefly, for the purpose of comment and addition. The motif of this simultaneity appears in Hippolytus[3] and in Melito of Sardis,[4] albeit not as part of a providential plan whereby the empire is assigned the role of paving the way for the Gospel's

---

[1] E. Peterson, "Der Monotheismus als politisches Problem", in idem, *Theologische Traktate* (Munich, 1951), pp. 83–94.

[2] Sirinelli, *Les vues historiques d'Eusèbe*, pp. 388–411.

[3] Commentary on Daniel, 9,4.

[4] See Eusebius, *HE* 4,26, 7–8; Peterson, "Der Monotheismus",, p. 86; Sirinelli, *Les vues historiques d'Eusèbe*, pp. 388–389.

dissemination. Origen had noted that the Pax Romana of Augustus prepared the ground for the Gospel by removing barriers between peoples and making them the subjects of a single ruler, which facilitated the work of the apostles. Before Augustus, men had to serve in the numerous armies of the different states, and this fostered a militaristic spirit that ran counter to the pacifist message of Jesus, hence the delay of the Advent! This idea appears once in a polemical context in *Against Celsus,* as a sign of the fulfillment of the prophecies of the Incarnation and the Christ.[5] Eusebius develops this idea more extensively, with varying emphasis, in his different works. The Pax Romana was the universal peace prophesied in Scripture and brought to the world by Christ.[6] The establishment of the empire and of peace was one more in a series of signs attesting to the coming of the Messiah in fulfillment of the prophecies,[7] which maintained that the Roman Empire, together with Christ's teaching, would gain strength.[8] The Pax Romana was established in order to facilitate the apostles' freedom of movement and to instill in its subjects the fear of a strong government. For without central authority, the persecution of the Christians would have been greater.[9]

On the basis of statements in the *DE,* the *Life of Constantine,* and *In Praise of Constantine,* Peterson attempted to construct a political theology grounded in Eusebius' particular interest in the political rule of Constantine. He claimed that eschatological theology had gradually been transformed into a political utopia. Thus he proposed the parallel between the concept of the empire and the peace of Constantine, and the idea of Christian monotheism, which was first realized with the rule of Augustus. Peterson lends great significance to Eusebius' statements in the *DE.* For our purpose, his theory is of no particular consequence. Sirinelli accepts it and goes on to argue that the historical circumstances of the persecutions and their cessation caused Eusebius' to develop his ideas beyond the *Prophetic Extracts* to the *HE* and the *DE.* With Christianity's new status in the empire at the end of the persecutions, Eusebius developed a positive, conciliatory attitude, imbuing the empire with religious and moral content

---

[5] *CC* 2,30.

[6] *DE* 7,2,22; 8,3; 8,4,12; 9,17,13.

[7] *DE,* 8, Introduction.

[8] *DE* 9,3, as an interpretation of the prophecy in Numbers 24:3–9.

[9] *DE* 3,7,30–35. Perhaps there is a reflection of the changing historical reality up to the time of Constantine.

and making it the embodiment of peace and order within the framework of a sacred history of God, going back to the early days of the Gospel.[10] The empire also created a new political order that abolished the old one which had come from the rule of the demons. Therefore it participated in the victory over them.[11]

Sirinelli identified two problems that occupied Eusebius: (1) Recognition of the moral progress of society and a desire to link such progress with Christianity. Before creating a connection between the empire and Christianity, he had first attributed this progress to the spread of the Law and philosophy of the Hebrews among the nations. (2) The need to understand the new status of the Empire vis-à-vis Christianity.[12] The development of this idea was explored in solid and impressive theses by Peterson and Sirinelli. But they seem to have overstated the importance of this concept in Eusebius' works, at least those written before 324. They tended to discover later ideas in earlier works. Neither the *PE* nor the *DE* gives any major significance to this concept, which appears briefly several times as an argument in a narrow polemical context. In fact, we have noted the converse in the *DE*, which points to the empire as a tool of the devil, although it also fully articulated, for the first time, the positive concept of the empire as a prerequisite for the effective promulgation of the Gospel. Likewise, emperors were both messengers of the devil and messengers of God.[13] In the religious-historical excursus in the introduction to *DE* VIII, human progress, as we have noted, was regarded as deriving from the progress of the Gentiles; the growth of political order and philosophy had been influenced by the spread of the Law of Moses and the teachings of the prophets, which laid the groundwork for the coming of the heavenly teacher. Neither the Pax Romana nor the empire played a role. It was Christ who brought about the Pax Romana, the peace which made it possible for the Gospel to be disseminated throughout the world.

Eusebius' statements on the empire and the Incarnation are made in the polemical context of a discussion of the great miracle of the Gospel's promulgation by the apostles, as noted in the previous

---

[10] Sirinelli, ibid., pp. 393–394.
[11] Sirinelli, ibid., p. 404; cf. Hollerich, Commentary, pp. 188–196.
[12] Sirinelli, ibid., pp. 394–395.
[13] For Eusebius' presentation of Roman emperors see Grant, "Eusebius and Imperial Propaganda."

chapter of this study.[14] The great historical miracle of the subjugation of most peoples by the empire, under the sole rule of Augustus, was an event unprecedented in human history. The divine plan
was to synchronize this miracle with Christ' Advent and the Gospel,
in order to remove the great obstacles faced by the apostles and disciples in propagating the Gospel among peoples who were at war,
living under different regimes, or scarcely known to each other. God
facilitated their travels (τὴν πορείαν αὐτοῖς προεξευμαρίσαντος) by breaking down the barriers that separated peoples,[15] and by subjugating
the proud spirit of those in the different countries who believed in
superstitions (τοὺς θυμοὺς τῶν κατὰ πόλεις δεισιδαιμόνων) to the fear
of a strong authority.[16] For without a central authority to check the
polytheistic error inimical to the teaching of Jesus, there would have
been revolts, wars, and persecution.[17]

Eusebius sensed the problems inherent in the concept of the Pax
Romana as a divine instrument for spreading the Gospel. Such an
idea could have detracted from the great miracle of the Gospel's
promulgation by the apostles and disciples. Moreover, it could be
argued that Christianity thrived in the wake of official tolerance and
owed its success to human counsel and not to divine power. A historical examination of the persecutions resolved this problem. If, on
occasion, there were rulers under the influence of evil forces that
opposed the word of Christ, God enabled them to act as they wished
and to persecute the Christians, so that the success of Christianity
could not conceivably be attributed to the sympathetic attitude of
Roman rulers. Likewise, the persecutions gave Christians the opportunity to act as "athletes" in order to demonstrate their holiness.
Nevertheless, rulers were fully punished by torture and disease, and

---

[14] *DE* 3,7,30–35.

[15] Until this point, the idea resembles what we have seen in Origen.

[16] Peterson saw this as Eusebius' innovation; in his opinion, it was the essence
of Eusebius' theological history (ibid., p. 89), and of the parallel between the empire
and peace, and monotheism (ibid., p. 90).

[17] The idea of the empire as a restraining factor in the service of Christianity is
also included in the prophecy of Isa. 19 (*DE*, ibid.). The historical concept of the
time preceding the Advent of Jesus, the Pax Romana and Augustus—one of diverse
nations under different governments, instability, and continuous wars—also appears,
briefly, in *DE* 7,2. In fact, in the introduction to *DE* 8, wars and schisms between
peoples were the result of demonic activity which, as part of the program of divine
justice, was intended to "thin out" humanity and enable men to accept the good
influence of the teachings of the Hebrews who, in turn, prepared the ground for
the Advent of Christ.

finally admitted their crimes against Christ. The persecutions served as a test and edification for all believers, and allowed the splendor of the Gospel of redemption to shine more brightly. During the persecutions, Christians also fought against invisible demons floating in the air.[18] In dealing with the problem raised by the empire as an instrument of providence, Eusebius seems to provide theological justification for the persecutions. We shall return to this subject later.

Although the PE and the DE do not devote much attention to the synchronization of the empire and the Pax Romana with the Incarnation, they include several brief statements on the Romans and display a rather positive attitude towards the Roman people and its authority. The Romans were a tool in the hands of Providence, and not only for the role they played in changing the political order of the world and establishing world peace. For along with the abolition of other regimes and governments, came the abolition of the autonomous authority of the Jewish people as well. We have noted that, according to Eusebius, the fact that the Jewish people continued to exist, unchanged, after the Advent of the Redeemer, constituted a crime against the Law of Moses. In the war of destruction, the Lord Christ fought alongside the Romans during the siege of Jerusalem as the supreme commander of all its forces.[19] Eusebius' respect for Roman authority is plain from his assertion that the Romans were not mentioned by name in biblical prophecies so as not to offend them.[20] In the context of his critique of mythological religion in PE III, he also deals with Roman religion. He flatters the Romans and praises their ancestors for ignoring the Greeks' myths and contrived commentaries.[21] He prefers to present the Romans as rejecting the allegorical interpretation of mythology, rather than being ignorant of the subject or unable to develop a similar, independent philosophical interpretation. He presents the relative poverty of Roman mythology as a great advantage. In his description of Roman religion, Eusebius chose to cite Dionysius of Halicarnassus, an ardent admirer of the Romans, whose work was a great encomium to Rome.[22]

---

[18] DE 3,7,35–40.
[19] DE 6,18; 8,3.
[20] DE 3,7.
[21] PE 3,7.
[22] PE 3,8.

The Persecutions

The persecutions posed a problem for Christian apologetics. How could they be explained and reconciled with the concept of Providence and a Logos active in history? How could the persecutions be justified as part of the conduct of the Christian God of history? Eusebius deals with this problem mainly in the *HE*, where it is added as an afterthought to the descriptions of persecutions in various periods. E. Keller, and subsequently, Sirinelli, analyzed the various aspects and elucidations of this motif, which do not present a unified or coherent picture in the *HE*.[23] I have referred to the subject in the brief discussion on the *HE* in Chapter 2 of this study. Here, as in the previous section, I shall outline the issue, then present some comments and clarifications.

The detailed discussions undertaken by the two above-mentioned authors do not cover the polemical aspect of the persecutions. The persecution of Christians has served as an argument against the Christian faith. Celsus, for example, claimed that Christians were persecuted and crucified without help or vengeance on the part of the Son of God.[24] God did not assist Christian victims past or present,[25] and their persecutors did not suffer during their lifetime.[26] This charge may explain Eusebius' emphasis on the terrible punishment endured by the persecuting rulers, even though this did not conform with his general concept of persecutions, as will be shown. Clement of Alexandria refers to the pagan argument that the persecution and death of Christians proved that God did not protect them.[27] Tertullian and Minucius Felix mention similar arguments.[28] Clement replies that persecution had to be considered as the fulfillment of part of Jesus' prophecy; furthermore, it served to strengthen the faith.[29] In addition, the fact that the Gospel withstood the ordeal of persecution proved its divine origin and truth.[30] Tertullian argues that only evil emperors had persecuted Christians. Good and right-

---

[23] E. Keller, *Eusèbe: historien de persécution* (Geneva, 1912); Sirinelli, *Les vues historiques d'Eusèbe*, pp. 412–448.
[24] *CC* 8,39.
[25] *CC* 8,69.
[26] *CC* 8,41.
[27] *Stromateis* 4,11.
[28] Tertullian, *Apology* 5, 5–6; Minucius Felix, *Octavius* 27,1; 9,36.
[29] *Stromateis* 4,11.
[30] *Stromateis* 6,18.

eous emperors never initiated persecution.[31] Furthermore, Christians aided and guaranteed the existence and well-being of the empire as a whole. During Marcus Aurelius' war against the Germans, the prayers of Christians brought rain, thus ending the drought and thirst that had nearly brought about the defeat of the army.[32] Like Clement, Minucius Felix argues that persecution was an ordeal by which God tested the faithful and refined them, like gold in fire.[33] Elsewhere, he presents an opposing view, namely, that demons caused the persecution of the Christians.[34] Replying to Celsus, Origen argues that Christians were persecuted only with God's permission to Satan. For the most part, however, God preserved the peace of the Christians even in a hostile world. Thus, Origen gives a theological explanation for the sporadic nature of the persecutions up to his time, and for the relatively small number of Christian martyrs. Here, perhaps, is the germ of an idea which later appears in Eusebius—that persecutions could only have taken place with God's permission. The brief statements noted above form part of a broader and somewhat more complex picture.

The first seven books of the *HE* contain several explanations for the persecutions, as follows:[35] (1) The persecutions were the result of the general hard-heartedness and personal cruelty of the emperors. (2) The foolish and arbitrary behavior of the local governors and populace contributed to the persecutions. (3) Persecutions originated in the imperial court as a specific, premeditated policy. Emperors, however, were occasionally misled by bad advice, and their counselors, by irrelevant issues. Sometimes persecution was the result of internal conflicts within the empire. Such arguments do not offer any political or theological explanation for the phenomenon of persecution in general, only partial explanations for individual instances, with persecution regarded as a random and transient occurrence. (4) On occasion, the *HE* presents the persecutions as the acts of demons, but without elaboration.

HE VIII suggests that the persecutions were part of a providential plan, though the idea is not pursued or fully developed. The

---

[31] *Apology* 5,5.
[32] *Apology* 5,6.
[33] *Octavius* 9,36.
[34] *Octavius* 27,1.
[35] The detailed and lengthy expositions of scholarly studies are presented here in a very abbreviated form.

persecutions took place in order to punish the Christians for their internal divisiveness, corruption, and hypocrisy.[36] However, God's action was indirect and sporadic. He gave rulers a free hand to act against his elect, then stopped them and reversed their policy, allowing them to be kind to Christians after the latter had suffered enough, and to extinguish the fire of persecution. Several details in *HE* VIII are not compatible with the general concept of the persecutions, and may derive from later editing and interpolations on the part of Eusebius.[37] The theory that the empire suffered as a result of the persecutions presents its earlier prosperity and security as the antithesis of the chaos that followed.[38] Order could be restored only once there was peace with the Christians. This seems to be linked to Tertullian's idea that the peace of the empire was dependent on the tranquillity of the Christians. Unlike evil rulers, good sovereigns were sympathetic to Christianity; they were instruments of providence.[39] The punishment of individual rulers accompanies that of the empire as a whole. Their repentance and the cessation of the persecutions is another motif that we have encountered. Such motifs do not entirely accord with the concept of the persecutions as part of a divine scheme. For if the empire and its rulers were an instrument of God, why did they have to be punished? The answer may be that they acted arbitrarily, as well. Even if they played the part of messengers in a wider scheme, there was still evil in their deeds. The messenger inflicting evil had to be punished and divine justice had to be seen. Eusebius was, in fact, aware of the problem,[40] hence his somewhat hesitant tone. *HE* 10,4,14 presents the idea of the demon being responsible for the rulers' persecutions, as part of his war on God and the faithful. However, Eusebius does not specify

---

[36] The *Martyrs of Palestine* includes a reference to the idea, which appears later in *DE*, that God allows persecution, torture and martyrdom in order to strengthen the Christians and to grant them greater reward (*MP* 8, 9–10). It is a more positive variation on the theme. See also *HE* 10,4, 33–34; Sirinelli, *Les vues historiques d'Eusèbe*, p. 445.

[37] See Sirinelli, ibid., p. 431.

[38] This idea appears clearly in the *Martyrs of Palestine* 3,5.

[39] On the apologetic trait of presenting emperors as sympathetic to Christianity, see Chapter 2 of this study, and Linder, "Ecclesia and Synagoga".

[40] See also Sirinelli, ibid., pp. 438–439. According to Sirinelli, Eusebius did not attribute great significance to the concept of divine punishment and vengeance against rulers who persecuted Christians, and did not see it as an integral part of his general thinking of persecution.

whether the demon acted in accordance with a divine plan that fitted the general concept.

The *PE-DE* hardly mention the persecutions—only in one passage is there a brief discussion![41] Apparently the subject was not of major apologetic interest, though it might be mentioned incidentally when arguing the truth of Christianity on the basis of historical success. For—as Clement also put it—on its road to success, Christianity had to overcome enormous obstacles, among them, the persecutions. As we have noted, *DE* 6,20 states that one of the roles of the empire was to control and restrict pagan forces opposed to Christianity. Eusebius remarked that greater persecutions would have occurred had there been no empire and no central authority.[42] The concept of the positive historical role of the empire posed certain difficulties as far as the persecutions were concerned. Hence the contrived explanation that the persecutions took place so as to counter the view that the Gospel had spread because of the generosity and tolerance of the emperors. Thus on occasion, God allowed rulers to persecute Christians when they wanted to, or when they were under the influence of demons. This explanation brings in another positive motif noted in the *Martyrs of Palestine*—the uplifting value of the "athletes of the faith", which was worthy in itself and not simply a by-product of the persecutions. The persecutions occurred in order to prove to all that the victory of faith was not simply the result of human action, but of divine power.[43] Thus the empire and the persecutions were harmoniously intertwined in a providential plan that might appear to the uninitiated as an unfathomable and convoluted scheme fraught with contradictions. We can discern the apologetic dimension of this concept, a concept that—as presented in the *DE*—accords with Eusebius' generally positive attitude towards the empire, and may have reflected the new relationship between the Church and the empire in the years following the persecutions.

---

[41] *DE* 3,7, 35–39 (noted in the previous section). Sirinelli considered this brief discussion as the first articulation of a definite and consistent theory of the persecutions.

[42] *DE* 3,7, 35–39.

[43] Ibid.

On Arguments Concerning the Late Date
and Geographical Remoteness of Jesus' Appearance

This argument, especially the first part, has figured in earlier discussions. The apparent delay in the coming of the Redeemer helped
determine Eusebius' concept of the development of human history.[44]
Within this framework, Eusebius presented his major response to the
argument. But the historical refutation did not answer its main point,
namely, that the late advent of Jesus may have denied redemption
to earlier generations. Jesus' appearance before a small and barbaric
people in a remote corner of the world was problematic in that it
did not correspond with the concept of a divine Christ who had
come to redeem all of humanity. He should have appeared in the
center-stage, both globally and historically, before peoples who represented the height of cultural achievement and their great leaders.

Justin was acquainted with the pagan argument that Jesus had
been born not long previously, during the administration of Cyre-
nius, and that those who lived beforehand were not responsible for
their actions, as they were predestined not to be redeemed.[45] Irenaeus noted briefly the late appearance of Jesus in history but did
not develop a historical concept.[46] The argument of a historical delay
in the appearance of Jesus and of Christianity is to be found in the
Letter to Diognetus.[47] Both parts of the argument are integrated, for
the first time, in Celsus. Did God fall asleep, he asks sarcastically,
and only later remember to redeem mankind? Did He not care
about it previously? If so, why did He send his spirit (Logos) to a
single corner of the world? For according to Stoic theology, he could
have inspired many other bodies and dispersed them throughout the
world. Moreover, it was ridiculous to assume that the Son of God
would be sent especially to the Jews.[48] Porphyry developed and refined
this argument, as we have seen in Chapter 1.[49]

Justin replied that the Logos had indeed been sent in previous

---

[44] *DE* 8, Introduction, and Chapter 4 of this study.
[45] Justin, *First Apology*, 46.
[46] *Against Heresies* 38,1.
[47] *Epistle to Diognetus*, 1.
[48] *CC* 4,7; 6,78. On the argument that Jesus had come to redeem mankind only
in "one corner of the world", see also *CC* 4,4.
[49] *Against the Christians*, Fragments 81–82. See also Rokeah, *Jews, Pagans and Christians*, pp. 143–144.

generations, albeit for brief periods, to those who were deserving, namely, to the patriarchs and prophets.[50] But this does not really answer the question regarding the late appearance of Jesus and of Christianity. Origen repeated Justin's statement. The Logos descended to earth, to holy men of every generation, and made them "friends of God" and prophets.[51] Moreover, the place and the time were not wrong, for Jesus had to appear before a monotheistic people who had learned about his coming from Scripture. Strangely enough, Jesus had appeared before the Jews because they were accustomed to miracles and could appreciate the greatness of his miracles. He had to appear at a time appropriate for the dissemination of his teaching from that corner to the entire world.[52] There was no need for a multiplicity of *logoi* resembling Jesus in order to illuminate all of humanity with his teaching. On the contrary, the one Logos had sufficient divine power to light up the entire world from one corner of Judea, in order to reach the hearts of all those ready to receive it.[53]

As we have noted, Eusebius presented his major refutation of this argument in the framework of his historical concept. But various aspects are also addressed briefly at several points in piece-meal fashion, without extensive development. Hence the relative importance of this secondary pagan argument among those that feature in *PE-DE*. Early in the *PE*, Eusebius appears to echo Origen's argument regarding the appearance of Jesus in a remote corner of the world.[54] For Eusebius also compares Jesus to the sun of reason whose rays illuminated the religious darkness of humanity. The claim concerning the remote corner is thus insignificant. It is clear that both Origen and Eusebius derive their image from the first chapter of the Gospel of John. Here the polemical context may indicate a link with Origen. Eusebius' response serves more as the basis for a brief excursus on the state of the entire pagan world prior to the appearance of Jesus and Christianity, than as a rejoinder to the specific argument as in Origen.[55]

---

[50] Justin, ibid.
[51] *CC* 4,3.
[52] *CC* 6,78. Here, he is referring to the establishment of the empire which facilitated the promulgation of Christianity.
[53] *CC* 6,79.
[54] This argument is also reflected in Eusebius' statements in *HE* 1,4,2; 10,4,19.
[55] *PE* 2,5.

Eusebius developed his historical scheme in order to refute the argument of the late date and geographical remoteness of Jesus' appearance. First, however, Jesus had to address the Jews in order to accomplish the literal fulfillment of the biblical prophecy, "I will raise up for them a prophet like you from among their brethren", (Deut. 18:18). Only after his rejection by the Jews could he have ordered the apostles to turn to the Gentiles, as had been prophesied.[56] In this instance, Eusebius appears to address the question of why Jesus appeared before the Jews—a small, uncultured people that did not belong to the dominant cultural nations of the empire—outside the context of the historical scheme.

Although the historical reply attempted to explain the late date, it did not solve the fundamental question concerning the redemption of previous generations. The claim that emerged was that the spirit of Jesus, or his divine element, left his body before death and descended to the netherworld to conquer it and rescue the souls of previous generations.[57] This may have answered the charge that his late appearance prevented the salvation of previous generations, a salvation noted, of course, in Scripture.[58] A slightly different response proposes that Jesus atoned for the past sins of humanity and thus also saved previous generations;[59] it was to be noted, moreover, that the prophecies actually spoke of a delay in the coming of Jesus.[60]

In *DE* 2,7 there is a relatively lengthy discussion of the town of Bethlehem as the birthplace of the Messiah. This emphasis could be a reaction to arguments disputing the town's claim to be the birthplace of Jesus—either because of its remoteness or because rival claims cited Nazareth or another Galilee location—or, like Porphyry's, assailing the contradictions between Matthew and Luke regarding the genealogy of Jesus. Eusebius searches for all possible evidence to link Jesus to Bethlehem and to enhance the town's stature. To his discussion of Bethlehem he adds an interesting comment on the town of Nazareth. This apparently reflects an apologetic tendency to praise the sanctity of the wretched village of Nazareth, whose poverty was

---

[56] *DE* 9,11.

[57] *DE* 4,12.

[58] Ps. 107; *DE* 6,7.

[59] *DE* 8,2.

[60] Hab. 2:3–4; Zech. 14:7. Eusebius rejects the argument that the prophecy refers to the reign of Antiochus Epiphanes (*DE* 6,18; commentary on Zechariah 14:1–10). He does not reveal whether the argument is of Jewish or pagan origin.

recalled in the New Testament, "Can anything good come out of Nazareth?" (John 1:46). Although not born in Nazareth, Jesus spent most of his life there.

Eusebius' unusual interpretation can be summarized as follows. He comments on the name "Nazareth" and the epithet of Jesus, "Nazoraios". There was a link between the word, "Nazirite" (Lev. 21:12) and the Hebrew נֵזֶר (crown). He interprets the name Nazareth as testifying to the inherent holiness of the town, predating the time when Christ and his family lived there. Its sanctity had been established in Scripture. Its name was linked to the high priesthood (Heb. נֵזֶר שֶׁמֶן, "a crown of oil"), and high priests—who were called Nazirites, or men of Nazareth—were suggestive of Jesus, the high priest. Eusebius' exegetical purpose is served by his excellent knowledge of the various Greek translations. The commentary on the name has a direct affinity with Matthew 2:23, "And he went and dwelt in a city called Nazareth, that what was spoken by the prophets might be fulfilled, 'He shall be called a Nazarene'", and with Isaiah 11:1, "There shall come forth a shoot from the stump of Jesse and a branch (Heb. נֵצֶר) shall grow out of its roots".[61]

On Criticism of the Literary Style of Scripture, and Contradictions between the Old and New Testaments, and between the Gospels

Porphyry's great onslaught on Christianity focused primarily on undermining the sacred, prophetic status of Christian Holy Scriptures—the Old and New Testaments—and uprooting the foundations of Christianity in the New Testament by attacking its authors and discrediting them. Porphyry, however, did not overlook any weak points, and also attacked beliefs, matters of style, contradictions, and inconsistencies. Against the background of this campaign, Eusebius formulated fundamental answers, mainly in the *DE*. Occasionally, however, *PE-DE* contain echoes of pagan arguments against specific issues in Scripture, such as the frequently reiterated criticism that the literary style was barbaric, naive and crude.

Prior to Porphyry, pagan-Christian polemics contained sporadic arguments against Scripture that were not as systematic or well-formulated.

---

[61] Jerome opposed this interpretation, as he did the linguistic affinity between crown (Heb., נֵזֶר) and branch (Heb., נֵצֶר) in Eusebius' work. See Ferrar's note on this passage.

Christian authors with a Greek literary education felt somewhat uncomfortable with the simple and non-philosophical style of Scripture. This reaction was not necessarily connected to pagan arguments on the subject. It is difficult to judge the degree to which style actually hampered pagan intellectuals interested in Scripture, or indeed Christians.[62] Apologists, in particular, saw a need to explain and justify a literary style perceived as inferior. To this end, they emphasized and developed a motif from the classical literary tradition, one which had been stressed by the Stoics. Reason was at its clearest with a style that was unsophisticated and adorned, supported only by truth. The apologists stressed the ambiguity and deception of rhetoric.[63] Clement presented the simplicity and stylistic beauty of Scripture as an advantage; thus its voice and the Gospel emerged harmonious and enormously persuasive.[64]

To demonstrate the inferior style of Scripture, Celsus compares it with that of Plato in passages that expressed similar ideas.[65] Origen attests to the fact that others had voiced similar views on the impoverished style of Scripture,[66] and he offers several replies to Celsus. His main argument is essentially pedagogical, namely, that the Scriptures were written in a way that matched the simple minds of the unlearned masses. Origen expounds on the contrast between the literary style of Plato and the popular simplicity of Epictetus, who was admired even by the simple folk. (Here, he conformed with the Stoic argument mentioned above.) This contrast was presented to show the importance of the simple style of Scripture, which actually improved the lives of the masses.[67] Origen uses a similar argument regarding the uneducated apostles. The truth of their teaching could be perceived more clearly on its own merit than through a persuasive rhetorical style, and that was why God had chosen them.[68] The naivete of the disciples and the gift of divine power achieved much more than rhetorical sophistication or logical arguments.[69] The cri-

---

[62] Pagan criticism of the language of Scripture continued long afterwards, as attested by Jerome (*Epistle* 22,3) and Augustine (*Confessions* 3,5,9).

[63] See, for example, Theophilus, *To Autolycus*, 1:1; Clement, *Stromateis* 1,10; Minucius Felix, *Octavius*, 16,6. On the classical and Stoic tradition of this argument, see the lengthy note of G.W. Clarke on *Octavius* 16,6 in his edition.

[64] *Protrepticus* 8.

[65] *CC* 6,1.

[66] *CC* 6,2.

[67] *CC* 6,2; 4,50.

[68] *CC* 1,62.

[69] *CC* 3,39.

terion for judging the value of literature was not its style but its benefit to mankind.[70] In fact, Origen presents a twofold argument. The Greek style of Scripture may have been poor, he says, but the original Hebrew possessed artistic style, adhering to the literary rules of the language of the prophets.[71] However, Origen did not consider this particularly important—for he understood that it did not advance his pedagogical argument—and although he mentions it briefly in the course of his discussion, he emphasizes immediately afterwards that the true value of the Scriptures lay not in their style but in their benefit to man.[72]

Celsus also raised the issue of contradictions between the Law of Moses, the Old Testament, and the teachings of Jesus, but he did not discuss it at length or develop it. Origen refuted the point by arguing that Celsus had interpreted Scripture literally, without penetrating its deeper meaning.[73]

Eusebius' statements echo the pagan criticism that the Scriptures were empty and their form—with the New Testament parables and tales—infantile. Like Origen, he emphasized the style's educational and didactic purpose. By integrating parable, legend, and fantasy, but yet including grains of truth, the style of the Scriptures was designed to attract children and prepare them for absorbing absolute truths. Plato also stressed this educational principle, but the Hebrews had taught Scripture to children simply and easily through legends and parables long before Plato's time. More advanced students could be taught the deeper concepts of Scripture, through commentaries on the texts (δευτέρωσις), that were not known to the masses.[74] Plato proposed that an ideal education for children began with carefully selected parables and stories. The Hebrews had done so before him. Moreover, through entertaining and calming children by singing them selected tales and morals from Scripture, which were parables of educational value, parents and carers would prepare them to receive the truth of religion in their adulthood.[75] Plato recommended educating young children—who could not cope with too much seriousness—through songs, rhymes, and plays, which spoke to the soul of

---

[70] *CC* 7,59.

[71] Ibid.

[72] *CC* 7,59.

[73] *CC* 7,18.

[74] *PE* 12,4. The argument regarding the crude style of the New Testament appears in *HE* 3,24,3, where Eusebius feels it necessary to justify and briefly explain its use.

[75] *PE* 12,5; Plato, *The Republic* 2, 377B.

the child. Eusebius says that in his day Christian children were educated through songs and hymns as an easy and pleasant way of instill-
ing them with truth. They sang hymns and verses from Scripture,[76]
written with a didactic purpose.

Eusebius felt the need to justify the style of the Creation story—
essentially a chapter of cosmology and cosmogony worthy of philosophical discussion and analysis—because it differed from that of
systematic, philosophical discussion. He presented the style as one
that was learned and didactic.[77] True secrets were not given to the
masses who could not understand, and might ridicule them—a principle discerned also by Plato. Proof could also be adduced from the
New Testament.[78] In making these points, Eusebius may also have
been alluding to the claim that Christianity appealed only to children, women, slaves, and ignoramuses, all of them uneducated and
petty-minded. The story of Eve's temptation by the serpent, their
exchange, and the serpent's power of persuasion, may also have been
a target of pagan critics, who ridiculed the notion of conversation
between men and animals. Mindful of this, Eusebius felt obliged to
explain the likelihood of such a conversation by quoting a parallel
from Plato. The Greek philosopher had recognized such a possibility in the myth of the sons of Kronos, who exploited their ability
to converse with animals in order to increase their wisdom and their
knowledge of creatures and of the world, namely, in order to learn
philosophy.[79]

The use of anthropomorphisms in referring to God also emerges
as a didactic method. Lies were told for educational purposes, says
Eusebius, to those who needed such instruction. Here he may be
alluding to pagan criticism of the anthropomorphic concept of the
deity held by Jews and Christians.[80]

Celsus and Porphyry assailed the contradictions between the Old
and the New Testaments, and between the different Gospels. Through-

---

[76] *PE* 12,20; Plato, *The Laws*, 659C–660E.

[77] *PE* 7,11.

[78] *PE* 12,7; Plato, *Letter II*, 313E; Matthew 7:5.

[79] *PE* 12,14. Plato, *Statesman*, 272B. Legendary traditions according to which
Pythagoras possessed the gift of conversing with animals, were also the object of
ridicule. See Iamblichus, *Life of Pythagoras*, 13.

[80] *PE* 12,31. Clement, Origen, and the pseudo-Clementines confirm the existence
of such ideas among Christians. See Chadwick's note to *CC* 6,63. Origen may have
been attacking the view of Melito of Sardis that God was corporeal, like man who
was made in His image. See Chadwick, *Early Christian Thought*, p. 164, note 67.

out *PE-DE*, however, Eusebius repeatedly emphasizes the complete accord between Moses, the prophets, and the apostles on all issues and doctrines. This unanimity reigned not only in Old and New Testaments, but also among the apostles themselves.[81] The emphasis on unity and harmony is a central motif that is adduced as conclusive proof of the truth it represents, as opposed to the contradictions and disputes among Greek authors and philosophers. Eusebius tackles the problematic contradictions—which Porphyry attacked—between the different versions, in Matthew and in Luke, of Jesus' genealogy. However, he does not write about such topics at length, so as not to be diverted from the continuum of the *DE*. He directs the reader to a specific work devoted to this question, entitled *Questions and Answers on the Genealogy of the Redeemer*.[82] Julius Africanus had previously discussed the problem of contradictions in the genealogies.[83] Apparently it continued to vex Christians even before Porphyry's attack. Eusebius dealt with it at length in *HE* 1,7, which cites Africanus, and again, briefly, in his description of Africanus in *HE* 6,31,3. The problem of tracing Jesus' genealogy from Joseph in the New Testament was apparently discussed by Christians at a relatively early stage, as an internal Christian issue arising from the belief in the Virgin Birth. For why would the evangelists describe the genealogy of Joseph if Jesus were not his son? Likewise, it was necessary at this point to prove Mary's link with the Davidic line in order to show that Jesus was a descendant of David. Eusebius states that he has dealt with both parts of the problem in the first book of a special work. The problem was also noted briefly in *HE* 1,7,17.

The special work, entitled *Questions and Answers Regarding the Genealogy of the Redeemer* (εἰς τὴν γενεαλογίαν τοῦ σωτῆρος ἡμῶν ζητήματα καὶ λύσεις), was apparently the first part of a book entitled *On the Discord between the Gospels* (περὶ Διαφωνίας Εὐαγγελίων). Attributed to Eusebius, it is mentioned by Christian authors and has survived in a partial, abridged form, and as short fragments of *catenae* of commentaries.[84] Thus Eusebius devoted a special volume to the resolution

---

[81] See the conclusion of *PE* 12, *PE* 12,52. The subject of contradictions between the Gospels also appears briefly in *HE* 3,24,12–13. Eusebius illustrated the problem by presenting the contradictions between the opening passages of John's Gospel and the Synoptic Gospels, respectively, and offers short paradigms for solving the problems.

[82] *DE* 7,3,18.

[83] See *Letter to Aristides*.

[84] *PG* 22, 879–1006. See Lightfoot, "Eusebius", p. 338.

of contradictions not only in the genealogies, but throughout the
Gospels. It is not clear whether internal Christian matters were the
backdrop to this work, or if Eusebius was motivated by pagan critiques like that of Porphyry. Ostensibly, he addresses the questions
and difficulties pointed out by Stephanus and Marinus, whose iden-
tities are unknown. Was this, then, an internal Christian commentary or an apologetic-polemical tract? Lightfoot tends to view it as
a commentary.[85] According to Laurin, it may have been a supple-
mentary, detailed refutation of Porphyry's arguments concerning contradictions in the Gospels. Laurin notes that from the genealogical
point of view, Eusebius concentrated not on Luke but on Matthew,
in response to Porphyry's attack on Matthew. He also maintains that
the arguments, presented anonymously, were written by Porphyry himself or one of his close circle, and that they reflected authentic anti-
Christian arguments rather than serving simply as a literary device.[86]
The issue is problematic, as many questions are attributed to Stephanus and Marinus. Lightfoot believes that the anonymous questions formed part of the editorial style of the abridged version.[87]

From the abridged version, we learn that the work comprised
three books. Book I, dedicated to Stephanus, dealt mainly with the
details of the differences between the genealogies and the various
attempts to synchronize them,[88] the human condition of Jesus,[89] and
his place of residence during his early years.[90] Book II apparently
treated other questions and contradictions between the Gospels. However, the abridgment does not provide us with much information.
Book III, dedicated to Marinus, discussed discrepancies between the
Gospel accounts of the Resurrection of Jesus. It is relatively short,
with four chapters. Eusebius' method of presentation consisted of
proposing alternative answers to problems without deciding between
them. Later authors borrowed heavily from this work in their attempts
to harmonize the Gospels. Jerome included much material from this
book in his epistles dealing with the problems of the Gospels.[91]

The questions-and-answers formula was well known from Greek

---

[85] Lightfoot, ibid.
[86] See Laurin, *Orientations maîtresses des apologistes chrétiens*, p. 339.
[87] Lightfoot, ibid.
[88] Chapters 1–13.
[89] Chapters 14–15.
[90] Chapter 16.
[91] See Lightfoot, ibid.

literature. Philo had also used it extensively. But Eusebius was apparently the first Christian author to make systematic use of this particular genre,[92] which continued to develop in fourth-century Christian literature, especially apologetics.[93] Perhaps it suited apologetic literature because rival pagan works, especially that of Porphyry, were arranged as a series of specific arguments on various subjects.

On Prophecy in the Book of Daniel

For Christians, Daniel 9:20–27 constitutes a pivotal text, presenting a historical prophecy with an exact chronology of major events before the start of Christianity. Like Jacob's blessing to Judah, it is a key prophecy. Eusebius' commentary on the blessing of Jacob has been discussed in Chapter 5 of this study.

The Daniel prophecy plays a central role in *DE* 8,2, where it is the subject of a lengthy commentary intended to improve upon that of Julius Africanus. We have noted Porphyry's decisive attack on the prophetic status of the book of Daniel. This may have prompted Eusebius' relatively extensive discussion, for he attempts to address several problems relating to the interpretation of Daniel's prophecy that had not been solved by Africanus. Eusebius had to improve upon Africanus' commentary because Porphyry had denied its validity. In addition to references to the Messiah and the Jewish people, the prophecy also outlined the historical stages of the decline of the Jewish people. Africanus' problem was that his interpretation of the seventy weeks, mentioned in Daniel, did not end with Jesus. He had proposed beginning with Nehemiah.

Eusebius suggests two possible interpretations. According to the first, the reader begins counting from Cyrus; the second would begin the period in the second year of the reign of Darius, and end with Augustus. According to Eusebius, the latter was correct, but he offers a combination of both interpretations, starting the reckoning with Cyrus, and thus overcoming the problem arising from the first suggestion, which did not span the years up to Jesus' time.

The final week, when the remaining events described in the prophecy took place, referred to the Herodian period and the decline

---

[92] See Laurin, ibid., p. 385.
[93] See Labriolle, *La Réaction Païenne*, pp. 487–508.

of the high priesthood. The prophet spoke of Hyrcanus, the last of
the Hasmonean high priests who was killed by Herod, and of the
Herodian dynasty, which, with its compliant, appointed high priests,
achieved the historic task of corrupting the Jewish people.

The prophecy also related to Jesus and the New Testament. The
period of Jesus' activity was determined by Eusebius in accordance
with the prophecy of three and a half years, namely, half a week.
This interpretation follows the Gospel of John. Eusebius states that
after the Resurrection, Jesus remained with his disciples for the same
amount of time, namely three and a half years! However, elsewhere
in *DE* 3,4, he mentions only a short period, when Jesus appeared
to them for forty days as described in the first chapter of Acts. Perhaps Eusebius wished to solve the problem of the last week of the
prophecy by relating it entirely to Jesus. But he could only have
proposed this interpretation, if it was generally accepted that Jesus
spent more time with his disciples after the Resurrection.[94] He tried,
however, to maintain the forty days, consistent with Acts 1:3. During the three and a half years that Jesus spent with his disciples after
the Resurrection, he appeared to them in only forty days. The
prophecy continued to be interpreted as relating to Jesus, the apostles and disciples, and other faithful among the Jews.

The end of temple worship and the abomination of desolation
began at the same time as the Passion and the tearing of the cur-
tain in the Sanctuary. Eusebius had to suit the historical facts to the
interpretation of the prophecy. Thus we find that despite the abysmal
decline among the people during Jesus' time, there still was prophetic
power in the Temple, where prophets such as Anna and Simeon
(Luke 2:25–39) could be found. Otherwise, Jesus could not have
joined the multitudes in pilgrimage. Eusebius had to explain the
anomaly of Temple worship continuing several decades after Jesus.
He maintained that although the worship continued outwardly, it
was not the will of God and was not performed properly. He found
confirmation of the latter in the prophetic verses. This interpretation conformed with the historic scheme of Eusebius, according to
which—as we have seen—from the time of Jesus, both the Law and
the Temple service were directly opposed to the Law of Moses.[95]

---

[94] The *Apocryphon of James* refers to a duration of 550 days after the Resurrection. See *The Nag Hammadi Library in English*, ed. J.M. Robinson (San Francisco,
1977), p. 30.

[95] *HE* 3,7,8–9 gives another explanation for the forty years from the death of

Jesus was the ultimate sacrifice, marking the end of all previous sacrifices and annulling their power and validity. The new sacrifice was given to mankind in the form of the sacraments of the new covenant on the occasion of the Last Supper. The sacraments were symbols of this covenant with which God replaced the former covenant. Henceforth, all Temple sacrifices were the offerings of profane men in a desecrated place. The Temple would remain in ruins until the end of the world. Eusebius presents various Jewish interpretations for the time-calculation of Daniel in order to reject them. The total destruction of the city and the Temple, and the prophecy of the abomination of desolation, continued to be fulfilled, as this abomination was found on the Temple Mount even in Eusebius' time.[96] Jews still lived in blindness, darkness, and obstinacy as Isaiah had prophesied (Isa. 6:9).[97]

We have mentioned Porphyry as a possible catalyst for the lengthy interpretation of the prophecy of Daniel, summarized above. But nowhere does Eusebius relate to Porphyry's sharp critique and incisive argument; its forcefulness may explain why Eusebius chose to ignore the critique rather than publish it, although it was undoubtedly reflected in his commentary, especially in the additions and emendations to Africanus, which were probably influenced by Porphyry's specific criticism. A remaining fragment of *DE* 15 dealt with Daniel's prophecy, and possibly attests to Eusebius' recurrent and detailed preoccupation with Daniel in the wake of Porphyry's critique.

Other Implied Arguments

Both the *PE* and the *DE* contain echoes of pagan anti-Christian arguments that Eusebius does not discuss. Behind these statements there may lie pagan arguments not considered relevant for his exposition. As I have noted, Eusebius constructs his work around several

---

Jesus to the destruction of the Temple. The apostles and disciples who continued to live in Jerusalem until the outbreak of the revolt granted the city its final grace, as the last of the righteous in Sodom, hoping that the Jews would repent. This explanation more closely resembles Origen's reason for the gap between the Crucifixion and the punishment of destruction. Such was the time required for the repentance of the Jews and the acceptance of the Gospel through the signs and wonders performed by the apostles (*Homilies on Jeremiah*, 14,13).

[96] This may refer to the location of Roman worship on the Temple Mount.

[97] For a brief commentary on Daniel 9: 24–27, see *HE* 1,6,11. For a brief commentary that adduces Daniel 7 as proof, see *DE* 9,17.

major arguments that are integrated into the didactic thrust of the dual composition. I shall briefly present a list of the pagan arguments not yet noted in this study, and others possibly implied in his work. Discerning the latter is a question of interpretation, especially as regards those arguments without parallels in Christian and pagan literature. In addition, Eusebius makes references that seem to reflect unstated pagan arguments. These will be presented in the order of their appearance in the *PE* and the *DE*.

PE 3,14 notes the pagans' derision of Christians and their claim that Jesus was not divine, but born of a mortal, human mother—a well-worn argument against the anthropomorphism of God in the Incarnation, which was also expounded, at length, by Celsus.[98] Eusebius' brief response was that the Greeks had many gods who were born of women.

PE 4,1 presents the pagan argument that Christians created problems through their love of innovation. The pagans justified the death penalty against Christians on such grounds. Christians were also charged with establishing laws that contravened the laws of the nations and their gods.

In *PE* 7,15, Eusebius concedes that although Christians believed in mediating entities, the latter served only as part of the hierarchy. His words may have been intended to refute the charge that Christians worshiped angels and intermediary beings—a charge that was usually leveled by Christians and pagans against the Jews, not against Christians.[99] The context of Celsus' words cited by Origen may indicate that, in this instance, the claim was directed at Christians as well. Elsewhere, Celsus voiced other arguments based on the assumption that Jesus himself was an angel.[100]

In *PE* 12,1, Eusebius declares unequivocally that his work serves also as a defense against attack and derision. It seems that Book 12 was even constructed as a series of replies to prevailing arguments against Christianity (although Eusebius does not state this explicitly). To demonstrate this fact, I shall present all such arguments—some of which have been mentioned in the course of this study.

---

[98] *CC* 1,69–70.

[99] See Epistle to the Colossians 2:18; Aristides, *Apology*, 14; *CC* 1,26, and other parallels in Chadwick's edition of *CC*, note, p. 26. For a short discussion of this topic see M. Simon, *Verus Israel*, pp. 345–347.

[100] *CC* 5,52. See also *CC* 5,2.

PE 12,1 mentions that faith takes precedence over investigation and understanding, thereby rebutting, it seems, the frequent claim that Christianity was accepted naively, without examination or rational critique.

PE 12,3; 12,5, and 12,20 relate to the crude style of Scripture, and to the formulation of the pedagogical, didactic reply and its Platonic parallel, noted in this chapter.

PE 12,7 states that true secrets are not divulged to the masses, who cannot understand them and only would view them derisively. This may echo a refutation of the well-known argument that Christianity was directed towards children, women, slaves, and ignoramuses.

PE 12,9 has a brief apology on the religious value of Christians' eschewing positions of leadership and power, possibly a reference to the argument that Christians evaded government and military service.

PE 12,10 presents an apology relating to the humility of the prophets, the Platonic ideal of the suffering righteous and its realization by the martyrs. The motive behind these apologetics seems to be the argument that the humiliation and insults suffered by Jesus attested to his lack of divine power.

In *PE* 12,14, Eusebius includes a discussion on Eve and the serpent which may reflect the charge, noted in this chapter, that the concept of such a discussion was absurd.

PE 12,31 comments on the didactic use of anthropomorphism concerning God, apparently reflecting pagan criticism of the anthropomorphic concept of the deity.

In *PE* 12,32, Eusebius writes about the basic equality between women, men and people in general, and about Christian attitudes to equality—possibly in response to the argument that Christianity appealed to women and slaves.

PE 12,33 stipulates that one should not learn about Christians in general from specific groups among the Christians. In *DE* 10,8, Eusebius says that the pagan enemies of Christianity derived their views of Jesus and Christianity from heretical Christian groups. Apparently, he is responding to anti-Christian arguments that held true only for radical heretical groups. Such statements also refute pagan claims that the truth of Christianity was invalidated by the multiplicity of disputes,[101] an argument which Eusebius often used against Greek

---

[101] Celsus proposes such an argument (*CC* 2,74) and similar pagan charges are mentioned by Clement (*Stromateis* 2,26,2) and Tertullian (*Apology* 47,9; 47,11).

authors. By way of contrast, he points to the complete harmony with-in Christianity as proof of its truth.

PE 12,36, describes respect for parents and the elderly, perhaps with reference to the argument that Christianity encouraged the rebel-lion of sons and daughters and the rupture of families.

PE 12,52 asserts the above-mentioned harmony between Moses, the prophets, and the apostles.

Above-mentioned are the secondary arguments, both implicit and overt, that appear in *PE* 12; this book contains more such argu-ments than any other in *PE-DE*.

In *PE* 13,6, Eusebius acknowledges that Christians do not take into account the views of the pagan masses. Here he finds a paral-lel in the works of Plato, which state that one should heed the opin-ion not of the masses, but of the expert. The Christian parallel was to listen to the will of the one God. Eusebius is possibly alluding to the pagan claim that Christians were misanthropic and unsociable.

In *PE* 13,12, the Christian veneration of saints and martyrs is compared with the admiration for mythological heroes who had undergone an apotheosis into demons, as described by Plato. This may be intended as an answer to the pagan argument that Chris-tians worshiped human beings and engaged in a cult of the dead. In *HE* 8,6,7, Eusebius mentions a similar charge which claimed that Christians related to saints and martyrs as if they were gods.

In *PE* 13,19, Eusebius briefly compares the cruel laws that treated slaves as inferior human beings, as in Plato, with the noble and human laws of Moses. This may allude to the claim that Christianity appealed mainly to women, children, and slaves.

DE 4,5, apparently relates to the pagan criticism of the fact that Christians assumed only one force was active in creation. Eusebius asks why Christians should not accept this single divine force behind creation rather than a number of forces.

In *DE* 9,1 Eusebius deals with events that took place during the Incarnation, and the star that appeared at the birth of Christ in ac-cordance with the prophecy of Balaam (Num. 24:17). (We have noted declarations that the Magi were descendants of Balaam who preserved the tradition of his prophecy.) Eusebius was perhaps responding to the claim that the birth of other important figures was also marked by the appearance of a special star or meteor. Since this was a popular belief, Eusebius had to prove that the star of Jesus was unique. It was new and strange, he stated, and appeared directly above Judea, hence the Magi's hurried journey to Palestine, to seek the king whose birth had been heralded by the star. The reason for the appearance of the strange new star, the star of Bethlehem, was its mission to announce the new light shining on humanity—the divine Christ. The star's location—vertically above Judea—derived from the astrological concept of the vertical position of the planets at the time of birth of the horoscope's subject. Eusebius was acquainted with this concept, presenting it in detail in a quotation from Origen's commentary on Genesis in the framework of a discussion on Providence and free will, and during a refutation of astrological determinism in *PE* VI.[102] This again demonstrates Eusebius' failure to detach himself totally from pagan beliefs and opinions; indeed, he even adopts them in order to prove his statements. Here he uses a clearly astrological concept, despite his endeavors, in *PE* VI, to undermine the foundations of astrology.

Eusebius' statements on the star were apparently drawn from Origen. He combined the general astrological concept found in Origen's commentary on Genesis with Origen's pronouncements on the Magi and the star in *Against Celsus*, responding to Celsus' critique of the story of the Magi. Origen interpreted the star as a new star.[103] But this was not enough, for it had to be shown that this was completely different from other stars, belonging to a rare group of stars that appeared at dramatic turning points in human history. Origen's problem was that the appearance of such stars was apparently regarded as a sign of disaster and calamity, and only rarely as a good omen. So he turned to Chaeremon to seek proof that the special star could also augur good events such as the birth of new dynasties.[104] In Origen's discussion in *Against Celsus*, the astrological concept of the vertical position of the planets at the time of Jesus' birth is absent. In fact, Origen did not offer a full solution to the problem confronting Eusebius. For in Origen's opinion, although the star of Jesus was special, it was one of several similarly distinguished stars. Eusebius, however, wished to prove that it was unique. He chose to ignore Origen's apologetic statements regarding the fact that the star usually foretold calamities, but could also presage blessed events. In

---

[102] *PE* 6,11.
[103] *CC* 1,58. The idea that the star was new was not original; it can be found in Ignatius and Clement of Alexandria. See Chadwick's edition of *CC*, note, p. 53
[104] *CC* 1,59, and Chadwick's note.

Eusebius' view, the special stars usually appeared before events such as the birth of important and famous people, or at the time of unusual occurrences. The negative aspect of this astrological phenomenon was suppressed. In order to lend weight to the words of Origen in *Against Celsus*, Eusebius combined them with the astrological concept of the vertical position of the star above Judea at the moment of Christ's birth. In Origen, this features as part of the internal development of the discussion, and not, it seems, as a response to a specific argument on the part of Celsus. Thus the words of Eusebius are not perhaps directed at any specific pagan arguments, but rather at resolving problems posed by the concept itself even before its exploitation by a pagan opponent. This is a further example of the way Eusebius occasionally handles his sources without direct reference to them.

DE 9,5, focuses on the figure of John the Baptist, perhaps reflecting polemical issues, such as why John went to preach in the desert and not in cities or even in Jerusalem. This recalls the criticism of the fact that Jesus' birth-place and forum of activity was a remote corner of the world and not a major location, among leading world figures. Eusebius emphasizes the fact that John did not perform miracles—as if to refute a possible comparison between John and Jesus. The uniqueness of John the Baptist lay in his ascetic way of life in the desert. John the Baptist was also a Nazirite, by Jewish definition. He had a divine countenance and for long periods could survive without food. His contemporaries viewed him as possessing superhuman qualities and even as an angel of God. Eusebius does not say whether he also thought John to be the messenger in the prophecy, "Behold, I send my messenger before thy face" (Mal. 3:1; Mark 1:2). In *DE* 9,11, he again relates briefly to John the Baptist. John was a prophet but not the prophet of Moses' prophecy (Deut. 18:18). Moses was referring to the Logos, the Christ who would appear to humanity in the garb of a prophet. It was clear, therefore, why the Jews investigated John the Baptist, to ascertain whether he was the prophet about whom Moses had spoken (John 1:21). These comments may have provided the answer to a claim that the ancient prophecy referred to John and not to Jesus. We have encountered attempts to explain the difficulty posed by the prophecy that spoke not of the Messiah, but of a prophet.

CHAPTER EIGHT

TACTICS, RHETORIC AND THE ROLE
OF PORPHYRY IN THE DUAL COMPOSITION

I. *Tactics and Rhetoric*

In previous chapters of this study we have encountered various aspects of Eusebius' rhetorical technique. This chapter will discuss other salient features of his literary style and method of composition, with particular emphasis on rhetorical devices. Analysis of this kind can offer insights into other aspects of his writing.

Early in the dual composition, Eusebius claimed it to be a unique work,[1] one that differed from traditional Christian apologetics. Eusebius' method—to which he refers on several occasions—was to attack pagan religious groups and philosophical schools by citing pagan authors. He allows pagan testimony to speak for itself rather than quoting evidence from the Scriptures, so as to avoid raising the suspicion of being biased in favor of Christianity. Thus, he could not be accused of making false statements, and he presents himself, from the start, as an objective judge.[2] In the introduction to the last book of the *PE*, he reminds his readers of his dialectical skills and announces his objectivity. The purpose of this approach was to negate pagan religious and philosophical concepts by studying pagan sources and exposing the contradictions they presented in every field.[3] Such discrepancies invalidated the pagan claim to truth, an argument emphasized in specific books of the *PE*. For example, at the beginning of Book XIV Eusebius declares his intention to present the philosophers' deviations from the truth, on the basis of the testimony of Greek authors.[4] We have noted that for his critique of pagan religion and philosophy, Eusebius had a well-stocked arsenal in the form of pagan arguments against religion and the different philosophical schools. The principle of this method was not new; it was used by

---

[1] *PE* 1,3.
[2] *PE* 1,5; 1,6,8; *PE* 3, Introduction.
[3] *PE* 8; 2,6,8; *PE* 2,8.
[4] *PE* 14,1.

both pagan and Christian authors and it appears in pagan-Christian polemical literature on both sides.

Celsus had argued that Christian Scripture provided sufficient material for refuting Christianity and that there was no need to add external testimonies.[5] Porphyry raised Celsus' argument to a new level of detail and sophistication. A similar pagan charge based on the internal contradictions within Christianity was applied to the disagreements between Christian groups. Clement of Alexandria invokes the argument that one could not accept Christianity owing to the disagreements between the various groups.[6] Celsus regarded sectarian doctrines as representing Christianity as a whole, so that the contradictions existed not between different groups but within one school. Tertullian gives the pagan argument sharp expression by asserting that pagans who compared the divisions within Christianity with the different schools of pagan philosophy were disparaging both on similar grounds, but to the advantage of philosophy. For if there was no essential difference between Christian groups and pagan philosophical schools, their pagan background decided in favor of the latter.[7] Tertullian adds that the divisiveness within Christianity created many complex ramifications from the same point of departure, and that this contributed to the comparison between Christian groups and philosophical schools, and to the condemnation of a divided Christianity that could not claim to possess the truth.[8] Here it is worth noting Tertullian's claim that the origins of Christian heresies lay in philosophy and the various philosophical schools, and in attempts to distort the New Testament by interpolating philosophical opinions.[9] In addition to that Eusebius argues that the enemies of Christianity derived their opinions on Jesus and Christianity from misleading and heretical Christian groups.[10] He presents the apologetic argument that one cannot generalize about Christianity as

---

[5] *CC* 2,74.

[6] *Stromateis* 7,15.

[7] *Apology* 47,11.

[8] *Apology* 47,9.

[9] Tertullian, *De praescriptione haereticorum*, 7. This was also the view of Hippolytus. In fact, his *Refutation of All Heresies* was written mainly in order to prove that heresies originated in the philosophical schools and were dependent upon them. See, in particular, the introduction to the work. Later, Plotinus put forward similar arguments regarding the Gnostics. He regarded Gnosticism as a distortion of philosophical ideas (*Enneads* 2,9,6).

[10] *DE* 10,8.

a whole from specific Christian groups.[11] His statements seem, in part, to confirm the argument; anti-Christian claims were valid only where referring to extreme heretical groups. Nevertheless, his statements provide a response to the pagan claim that the absence of truth in Christianity was manifest in its divisiveness.

Apologetic authors used the very same argument against philosophy. Justin argued that the purpose and true nature of philosophy had eluded the philosophers, as their divisiveness demonstrated. Philosophy had become a hydra with many heads.[12] His disciple, Tatian, pointed out the contradictions between philosophers,[13] and even announced that he would undertake to prove, through Greek sources acceptable to them, that their disagreements indicated a lack of historical truth in their statements.[14] In fact, he wrote a brief exposition of this theory. Theophilus also states briefly that one can find contradictions and differences not only among philosophers but also in the writings of a single philosopher.[15] A work attributed to Justin declares that one cannot learn about the true religion from philosophers because of the confusion and contradictions among them.[16] Athenagoras attacked contradictions found in the diverse allegorical-symbolic methods of explaining the Greek pantheon.[17] Clement also adduces conflicting statements by Greek authors to argue against philosophy, in the manner formulated by Tatian. He stresses the need to address the pagans in a manner and language comprehensible to them, namely, to make use of pagan texts and subjects, philosophers, authors, and poets. It was necessary to use a method that dealt with pagans on their own terms.[18]

Eusebius was well acquainted with the earlier apologetic tradition. He cites Tatian's statements that he used Greek writings in argumentation against the pagans, and employs the same apologetic-polemical tactics.[19] Nevertheless, after a brief reference to earlier apologetic traditions, he declares that the method he uses is his own. Such statements should be understood in context. For although the

---

[11] *PE* 12,33.
[12] Justin, *Dialogue* 2,1–2.
[13] *Address to the Greeks*, 25.
[14] Ibid., 31.
[15] *To Autolycus* 3,7.
[16] *Cohortatio ad Graecos*, 4.
[17] Athenagoras, *A Plea for the Christians*, 22.
[18] *Stromateis* 1,16,12.
[19] *PE* 10,10.

principle of this method had been known for a long time, no one had applied it on a large scale in any comprehensive work before Eusebius. He constructed a weighty, systematic piece of writing (the *PE*), largely through the broad and unprecedented implementation of this method. The new kind of work that he created owed its proportions to this radical approach. Eusebius had a conscious desire to accumulate testimonies and proof, and to present them in full; the more numerous the testimonies, he argues, the stronger the confirmation of the truth.[20] Furthermore, he sought to demonstrate the scope of his knowledge of philosophy and pagan religion in order to refute the prevalent claim against Christians that they preferred the Hebrew oracles because of their ignorance of Greek culture.[21] He also makes use of this method, in a different form, in much of the *DE*. Here, however, Hebrew sources, namely Scripture, take the place of pagan sources, and they are presented not in order to contradict and undermine the argument, but to prove and bear witness to the truth.

The strength of this technique—introducing pagan sources in order to prove his arguments—lay mainly in the persuasive effect of negative testimony regarding pagan religion and philosophy. Eusebius, however, wished to apply this same principle to ancient Judaism. In this case, pagan testimonies had their limitations: the positive ones were scarce and many were negative, or even "antisemitic". In the case of Judaism, Eusebius claims to have consulted the opinions of outsiders, many of whom were apparently Jews.[22] Proof of the truth of Christianity was gleaned from Scripture. As we have often noted, Eusebius invokes the writings of the New Testament mainly in order to support or strengthen proof, but not as proof in itself, and uses them both as negative evidence against pagan concepts and as positive evidence for matters pertaining to Christiainty. We have noted in Chapter 6 how Acts of the Apostles was apparently given separate status as a historical work. The main proof for Christianity had to come—as far as possible—from the Old, not the New Testament, namely, from the Hebrew oracle. For this purpose, the Old Testament is viewed as external prophetic testimony for Christianity, despite

---

[20] *PE* 10,9.

[21] *PE* 14,2. In *PE* 3,13, Eusebius states that his lengthy interpretations of Greek mythology and Egyptian religion were intended to show that Christians were well acquainted with the principles of Greek and Egyptian religions and acknowledged that they were guilty of abandoning them.

[22] *PE* 8,14.

the fact that the Logos-Son spoke from the mouth of the prophets. Thus Eusebius adheres to the recognized principle that the most effective negative criticism stems from within, while praise and proof of the truth are stronger when taken from an external source.

Eusebius claims to be fair and objective throughout this dual composition. He likes to present himself as a magnanimous and noble opponent who eschews pettiness. He expresses respect and admiration for philosophers and great men of the Greek tradition. He generously compliments philosophers and philosophical schools, and even apologizes to them for the fact that he has to assail them. His words, however, bear no trace of personal animosity,[23] and we have noted his particular regard for Socrates and Plato. While his respect was genuine, his noble gestures were also a characteristic stratagem. On several occasions he does not hesitate to attack, or to treat philosophers with sarcasm and derision. At one point, Eusebius magnanimously deflects personal attacks on Aristotle and his way of life, and claims to concentrate only on refuting Aristotle's philosophical method from the standpoint of "objectivity". However, in presenting Aristocles' defense of Aristotle, he enumerates all the slanderous accusations against the latter and thus contributes to mocking him—clearly a rhetorical tactic.[24] In his descriptions of Christian concepts, Eusebius often uses Platonic or Stoic philosophical terminology.[25] Thus his writing is not without rhetorical devices and a tendency to deride the opponents' position—features that characterize Eusebius' style of polemical one-upmanship.

So far we have noticed a great deal of Eusebius' literary rhetoric. Several additional examples regarding both his general methods and minor rhetorical devices will now be discussed. As a rule, Eusebius refutes a pagan concept in a direct manner. The second stage in this process consists of presenting himself as a magnanimous polemicist. At this point, he may even assume that the concept about to be refuted is correct, only to then show that it lends itself easily to contradictory interpretation, thereby indicating its inferiority.[26] On numerous occasions, when Eusebius decides, for the purpose of debate, to give generous credit to the concept about to be refuted, it quickly

---

[23] See for example *PE* 14,1–2.

[24] *PE* 15, Introduction.

[25] See, for example, *PE* 3,6, for Stoic philosophical language describing the theology of the Gospel of Jesus.

[26] See, for example, *PE* 3,6.

becomes apparent that this credit is rather limited. While attacking the metaphysical-symbolic concept of paganism, he is prepared to accept and discuss it on its own merits, but only in order to round on the idea and dismiss it as a manifestation of metaphysical polytheism. Thus he chooses to ignore the monotheistic-philosophical principle embodied within this concept, despite later admitting that he is aware of this principle.[27] At this point, one should ask whether Eusebius intentionally distorted the symbolic concept; or perhaps he was unwilling or unable to grasp the fact that the philosophical concept virtually emptied pagan religion of its contents or, poured the religion into a new mold. Occasionally it seems that Eusebius intentionally distorts the original intention of the philosophers.[28] In *PE* 10,9, in his treatment of the complex question of the chronology of Moses, he even admits to glossing over inherent difficulties. Elsewhere he argues that his refutation is clear and perfect, where it is, in fact, partial and superficial.[29]

Another method was to appear to accept the opposing view, and then to present it as ludicrous in its own terms. In *PE* 3,10, Eusebius magnanimously accepts a philosophical concept, only to refute it later on. But he combines the philosophical interpretation of mythological motifs with the motifs themselves, thus making the philosophical concept appear ridiculous. He goes on to juxtapose mythological motifs and symbolic interpretation in a deliberately absurd manner.[30] He also presents the gods as rejecting the physical-symbolic interpretation of mythology.[31] At one point, he points to contradictions between the declarations of the gods through the oracles, and the words of the philosophers, and determines that the former should be preferred. This, despite the fact that elsewhere, the very same gods were evil demons, and the pronouncements of the oracles were merely the product of human manipulation.[32] Occasionally, the gods are made to introduce poetic myths together with philosophical interpretations, and the ludicrous contradiction between them goes back to the gods themselves, taking the absurdity to a new height.[33] A further example of this caustic style can be found

---

[27] *PE* 3,13; 6,7; 10,2.
[28] For example, *PE* 2,6,7.
[29] For example, *PE* 3,8.
[30] *PE* 3,13.
[31] *PE* 3,14.
[32] *PE* 3,15.
[33] *PE* 3,15; 3,17.

in the remarks against the recurrent pagan argument that Christians betrayed the traditions of their ancestors. Eusebius replies that if that were the case, pagans should continue their forefathers' practice of human sacrifice lest they be considered apostates.[34]

In their critique of pagan beliefs and practices, many apologists, including Eusebius, tend to ignore the contemporary aspects, notably the religious tenets and opinions of the educated classes. Eusebius frequently refers to early types of pagan religion that, by his time, barely existed outside literature. However, he also criticizes contemporary interpretations of pagan religion, primarily through his critique of Porphyry as the leading figure and representative of the new philosophers, particularly in Book III of the *PE*. In *PE* 3,7, Eusebius states his intention to address the contemporary neo-Platonists led by Porphyry, and to reject their didactic symbolism. However, as we shall demonstrate, Eusebius does not attack the content of Porphyry's statements directly, but instead uses rhetorical devices to find contrasts, contradictions, and absurdity in the latter's various works. Similarly, in Book VI, he attacks the astrological determinism prevalent in contemporary pagan religion. On the other hand, Eusebius testifies that mythology continued to flourish in his own times, to a greater degree than is commonly thought. It is difficult, however, to accept his statements at face value.[35]

We have noted Eusebius' characteristic and decisive assaults on pagan concepts; he did not hesitate, however, to make use of them according to his apologetic-polemical needs. This practice cannot be explained merely as a rhetorical feature, for its roots lay deep in the shared pagan culture common to Christians and pagans alike. Thus despite the fact that the *PE* attacks pagan allegory, Eusebius wishes to approve and defend Christian allegory because rejection of the allegorical interpretation of certain parts of Scripture would leave nothing but an inconsistent and meaningless mythology.[36] Likewise, in Book VI of the *PE*, where Eusebius attacks astrology, he does not hesitate to introduce explicit astrological concepts in order to interpret the prophecy of Balaam.[37] The same holds true regarding oracles: Eusebius attempts to undermine oracles as a major revelation of pagan prophecy, but does not hesitate to present oracles as testifying

---

[34] *PE* 4,20.
[35] *PE* 15, Introduction.
[36] *DE* 2,3, discussed at length in Chapter 5.
[37] See Chapter 7.

to Jesus and the truths of Christianity, or as refuting various manifestations of pagan culture.[38]

We have encountered several other rhetorical tactics in our discussion of Book III of the *DE*.[39] In his presentation of the conspiracy of the apostles in *DE* 3,5, Eusebius elevated rhetorical strategy
to a consummate art through his use of *reductio ad absurdum*. Another
device used in the same chapter was the juxtaposition of two pagan
arguments in order to discredit one of them—in this case, the contradictory claims against the apostles, one stating that they were
swindlers, the other, that they were common, ignorant, uneducated
men. Another tactic applied in this chapter is to use the pagan claim
like a boomerang against the pagans themselves: the charge that the
evangelists had forged the texts of the Gospels could also be leveled
at the Greek philosophers. Yet another rhetorical move consists of
admitting the basic assumption of the pagan criticism, but giving it
a positive significance, for example, the humble origins of the apostles. In *DE* 3,6, we saw how Eusebius manipulates the pagan claim
that Jesus was the founder of charlatanism, and by reversing it makes
it yield a pagan acknowledgment of the Christian dogma on the
divinity of Jesus. In fact, when he addresses a particular pagan argument and develops his reply to it, he sometimes ignores another that
could jeopardize the very answer he has formulated.[40]

The interpretations of prophecies are not without some rhetorical
elements that lie outside typological, allegorical, analogical, and symbolic interpretation. Below are three brief examples that illustrate
this point. In *DE* 6,12 we find the following interpretation of I Kings
8:27–28. In his wisdom, King Solomon prophesied that the Son of
God would descend to earth. The rhetorical question in the verse:
"But will God indeed dwell on the earth?", invites a negative reply
in the context of that passage, but Eusebius turns it into a prophetic
question whose answer is positive, namely, the Incarnation. He dismisses the rest of the verse which does not suit his purpose (". . . how
much less this house which I have built").

A further technique was the interpretation of prophecy by negation, which proved that biblical predictions were fulfilled solely by

---

[38] See Chapter 5.
[39] See Chapter 6.
[40] See, for example, the discussion in *DE* 3,7 of how, and to whom, the apostles spread the Gospel; and also Chapter 6 of the study.

Jesus.[41] For example, *DE* 8,4 speaks of Zechariah's prophecies regarding the signs of the Advent of the Messiah, the call to the Gentiles, and the final destruction of Jerusalem. In his interpretation of such prophecies, Eusebius often asks when, before the Advent of Jesus, the events described in detail in those prophecies took place. If such events did not transpire before the Advent, we had to conclude that the prophecies were fulfilled only in the time of Jesus.

Another rhetorical method typical of Eusebius' resourcefulness is the selective use of different Greek translations of the Old Testament. When interpreting a particular verse, if the Septuagint version does not correspond to his interpretation, he uses other translations. If the other translations accord with each other on a specific point and differ from the Septuagint, all the better![42]

Although some rhetoric is evident in *PE-DE*, the unique structure of this work does not leave much room for rhetorical manoeuvering. It seems that this was not a priority for Eusebius. As he declared on several occasions, it was important for him to appear as an objective judge of the issues so as to strengthen the conviction of those in his audience who were not devout followers. Thus ridicule and derision do not characterize the work as a whole, but are found only in those sections where Eusebius is openly attacking a particular pagan concept or directly responding to a pagan anti-Christian argument. Other rhetorical devices are relatively inconspicuous; some are camouflaged or even invisible. Thus in contrast with the sharp, incisive language of Celsus, Hierocles, and Porphyry, Eusebius apparently tried to maintain an impression of fairness within the framework of the prevalent style of polemics, for the benefit of his audience, particularly for sympathetic readers who may not have been fully convinced of the truth of Christianity.

The discussion below of the role of Porphyry in the double composition will offer further opportunity to consider Eusebius' rhetorical methods.

---

[41] *DE* 7,2.

[42] For an example, see *DE* 10,8. On Eusebius' choice of quotations from the various Greek translations, and the interplay between them for purpose of interpretation, see Wallace-Hadrill, *Eusebius*, p. 87, and Barthelemy, "Eusèbe, La Septante et 'les autres'", pp. 52–55.

II. *The Role of Porphyry in the Dual Composition (PE-DE)*

My study began with the argument that Porphyry's *Against the Chris-tians* was a decisive factor in motivating Eusebius' apologetic-polem-ical writing. We may recall that Eusebius replied to his great pagan opponent with a detailed apology encompassing 25 books. *PE-DE* frequently mentions Porphyry and he is extensively quoted. Major pagan arguments in the apologetic work are similar to, if not iden-tical with, Porphyry's arguments. This feature has led several schol-ars to assume that Porphyry's polemic filled the pages of *PE-DE*,[43] and that throughout writing it, Eusebius was haunted by Porphyry.[44] As we have noted, Stevenson goes so far as to propose that Book III of the *DE* was taken from Eusebius' lost work against Porphyry.[45] While such views are plausible, they have not been subjected to close scrutiny and remain problematic, for nowhere does Eusebius state that *PE-DE* constitutes a grand reply to Porphyry. In fact, although he directly challenges Porphyry in several parts of the book, Euse-bius' target is not the views expressed in *Against the Christians*, but the religious and philosophical opinions in Porphyry's other composi-tions. Even when Eusebius is apparently responding to an argument from *Against the Christians*, he does not mention it as such.[46] Fur-thermore, Eusebius directly quotes from *Against the Christians* only three times. His purpose in these instances is not to present an anti-Christian argument and the response to it, but to find in Porphyry's statements a positive testimony on Christianity, as will be shown shortly. The question of the polemic against Porphyry in *PE-DE* is, it seems, highly complex. Perhaps, as Harnack has suggested, one may detect arguments by Porphyry between the lines of Eusebius' statements.[47] Perhaps, in addition to those views of Porphyry that are adduced either as testimony or as meriting refutation, Eusebius relates to other, unidentified opinions held by Porphyry. Tracing such references in Eusebius' work is a matter of educated guesswork and need not concern us.

---

[43] See Chapter 3.
[44] See Sirinelli, *Les vues historiques d'Eusèbe*, p. 287, note 1.
[45] See Chapter 2.
[46] According to Barnes, Eusebius does not mention Porphyry by name when responding to his arguments because he intended not only to refute Porphyry's views but also to eliminate his name as an opponent (*Constantine and Eusebius*, p. 179).
[47] *Against the Christians*, p. 91. See also Chapter 1 of this study.

Porphyry and Eusebius were remarkably similar in many respects. Both were extremely learned, to the point of pedantry. In their literary polemics, this learning took the form of an erudite polemic based on a detailed study of the opponent's sources. They both tended to be punctilious on minor details and had a predilection for quoting and naming sources. Their manners of polemicizing show definite parallels. Both were quick to pounce upon every contradiction, real or imaginary, in the opponent's statements or writings. Each disallowed his opponent that which he permitted himself.[48] Each rationally criticized the other but did not allow the other to criticize him using the same rational methods. A noteworthy example of this is their respective attitudes toward allegory.[49] While Porphyry's attitude to allegory undergoes a certain development, Eusebius remains circumspect. Both thinkers display a spirit of asceticism and moral abstinence.[50] On concepts such as demonology, they have much in common—for example, the demonology of Eusebius is basically identical to the demonology of the evil *daimons* in Porphyry's *On Abstinence*. Eusebius, however, applies it to the entire pagan pantheon.[51] An analysis of religious and philosophical parallels in the writings of Eusebius and Porphyry, to reveal differences and similarities and thus determine the significance of neo-Platonic philosophy—and, in particular, the importance of Porphyry—in the formation of Eusebius' spiritual world, would constitute a major subject in its own right. In any case, it is clear that Eusebius was well acquainted with the writings of Porphyry. In *PE-DE*, Eusebius names seven of Porphyry's works and quotes directly from them. These are *On Abstinence*, *Philosophy from the Oracles*, *On Images of the Gods*, *Letter to Anebo*, *To Boetus on the Soul*, *A Philological Discourse*, and *Against the Christians*. Most of the quotations come from the two first works, for reasons

---

[48] On this parallel in pagan-Christian polemics, see Geffcken, *Last Days*, p. 65.

[49] On the similarity of their criticism of allegorical interpretation, and the way in which each uses the same arguments to favor his own allegorization and discredit his rival's, see Rokeah, *Jews, Pagans and Christians in Conflict* , p. 107.

[50] In the case of Porphyry, this feature is particularly noticeable in *On Abstinence* and the *Letter to Marcella*.

[51] For a brief summary of demonology in *On Abstinence*, see Geffcken, *Last Days*, pp. 69–70, and, Rokeah, *Jews, Pagans and Christians in Conflict*, pp. 148–151. Sirinelli even speculates that the theology of Eusebius is constructed largely around the polemic against neo-Platonic philosophy, and that as a result, it developed both against Porphyry and under his influence (Sirinelli, *Les vues historiques d'Eusèbe*, p. 287, note 1).

discussed later.[52] Eusebius is the only extant source for quotations
from Porphyry's lost works, *On the Soul* and *A Philological Discourse*,
and the main source for fragments from the non extant works, *Philosophy from the Oracles* and *On Images of the Gods*. Porphyry is quoted
directly some forty times in the *PE* and five times in the *DE*, a tally
second only to quotations from Plato.[53] He also is the latest philosopher quoted by Eusebius.

Eusebius does not hesitate to mention Porphyry by name or by
some other unmistakable title. His name is given before or after most
of the quotations, usually without any additional title.

In addition, Eusebius mentions Porphyry by name in the list of
chapter titles that prefaces each book, and at the head of each chapter. Occasionally, however, he refers to Porphyry using a particular
word or epithet, together with a comment. Sometimes the epithets
occur without specific mention of Porphyry, but it is clear that they
refer to him, and his name may appear subsequently. The epithets
can be classified into two types: those describing Porphyry as an
enemy of the Christians, and those that—with heavy sarcasm—praise
him. The first group of epithets usually precede the quotation and
do not mention his name, although the reference is obvious. After
inserting a passage from Porphyry, Eusebius mentions him by name.
In *PE* 1,9,5, he is called, "our contemporary who is well known for
defaming us" (καθ' ἡμᾶς γεγονὼς αὐτὸς ἐκεῖνος ὁ ταῖς καθ' ἡμῶν λαμ-
πρυνόμενος δυσφημίαις). Similarly, in *PE* 1,9,20, he is called, "our
contemporary who has written a plot against us" (ὁ καθ' ἡμᾶς τὴν
καθ' ἡμῶν πεποιημένος συσκευήν). At the end of the quotation, Eusebius calls him "Porphyry the philosopher"[54]. In *PE* 4,6,2, he refers
to Porphyry as "that friend of the demons, our contemporary who
became famous through his false arguments against us" (τὸν δαιμόνων
φίλον αὐτὸν ἐκεῖνον, ὃς δὴ καθ' ἡμᾶς γεγονὼς ταῖς καθ' ἡμῶν ἐλλαμπρύνεται
ψευδηγορίαις). Likewise, in *PE* 5,1,9, Eusebius calls him "the contemporary advocate of the demons" (ὁ καθ' ἡμᾶς τῶν δαιμόνων προή-
γορος) who wrote a plot against us.[55] In *PE* 10,9,8, the epithet expands
into a brief description: "the most daring and bitter enemy of both

---

[52] For a brief inventory-survey of quotations from these works in *PE*, see Des
Places, *Eusèbe de Césarée commentateur*, pp. 60–68.

[53] See Chapter 3.

[54] *PE* 1,10,27. He constantly repeats the phrase, "the author of the plot against
us". For additional examples, see *PE* 5,1,7; *PE* 5,5,10.

[55] The epithet "defender of the demons" also appears in *PE* 6, Introduction.

the Hebrews and the Christians. The contemporary philosopher who, in his strong hatred, published his plot against us, in which he defamed not only us, but the Hebrews, Moses, and subsequent prophets as well."

On occasion, Eusebius' sarcastic praise appears to contain elements of real esteem for Porphyry. In *PE* 3,7,4, he concludes a long quotation from Porphyry with the wry phrase, "the wonderful philosopher" (ὁ θαυμαστὸς φιλόσοφος). Similarly, in *PE* 3,13,8, Eusebius refers to him sardonically as "the most wise" (ὁ σοφώτατος) and, in *PE* 5,14,3, as "the noble philosopher of the Greeks, the admirable theologian, the initiate into the mysteries" (ὁ γενναῖος Ἑλλήνων φιλόσοφος, ὁ θαυμαστὸς θεολόγος, ὁ τῶν ἀπορρήτων μύστης). After the laudatory superlatives, he proceeds to mock the theology of the passage just quoted.

Eusebius states explicitly that he hopes, above all, to adduce Porphyry's writings as testimony both for and against pagan philosophy and religion. He notes that he made a point of choosing Porphyry in his refutation of pagan religion and theology. The pagans could thus be beaten by means of their own weapons, using one who was perceived as devoted to his religion and a friend of the gods, one who had examined their religion meticulously.[56]

The numerous quotations from Porphyry, and Eusebius' subsequent comments, may be roughly divided into two categories: (1) Testimony against various aspects of pagan religion and philosophy. (2) Porphyry's statements on a number of subjects pertaining to religion and philosophy, to be criticized and exposed as contradictory and fallacious. The two categories occasionally merge. The following is a brief examination of these passages according to the two categories and the role played by Porphyry in Eusebius' work.

Porphyry as Supporting Testimony

In *PE* 1,4, Eusebius includes Porphyry's statements from *On Abstinence* 4,21 as evidence of the cruel barbaric customs common among peoples in the distant past. In fact, the section quoted from Porphyry describes the cruel practices of specific peoples, some of whom are mentioned by Herodotus.[57] Eusebius, however, does not note this

---

[56] *PE* 5,5,10.
[57] E.g. the Massagetes and the Scythians described in his first book.

fact despite his knowledge of Herodotus, which is evident from a
brief look at the index of the *PE*.

In *PE* 1,9, he quotes from *On Abstinence* on the historical development of the practice of sacrifice, and on the pure, pristine concept
of that practice. Here Porphyry's statements, as he himself declares,
are based on Theophrastus, and Eusebius does not attempt to hide
this fact.

According to Eusebius' concept of human history and the development of religion, the polytheistic error originated among the Phoenicians and Egyptians and subsequently spread to other peoples, as
attested by the ancient historians of those nations. The Phoenician
historian Sanchuniathon, whose words were preserved in the Greek
work of Philo of Byblos, gave evidence on Phoenician religion and
customs. Eusebius cites Porphyry (*PE* 1,9,15–17) as proof of the antiquity of the Phoenicians, and of the historical credibility of Sanchuniathon and Philo of Byblos. Thus he uses Porphyry to lend authority
and credibility to his statements and those of Philo of Byblos. This
direct quotation is taken from Book IV of *Against the Christians*, which
is mentioned by name in only three places in the *PE*. In this particular case, however, Eusebius' use of the quotation has no connection whatever with its original context in *Against the Christians*,
namely, the presentation of the accounts by the historians Sanchuniathon and Philo of Byblos, of the true history of the Jews, as
opposed to the version in Scripture.

After the quotations from Philo of Byblos, Eusebius repeats that
Sanchuniathon's statements were translated by Philo and confirmed
as a true testimony by "Porphyry the philosopher"[58]. Perhaps Porphyry's testimony and his confirmation of Phoenician traditions is
given greater weight by his possible "Phoenician" origins and acquaintance with these traditions. Eusebius, in fact, declares that the ancient
religious customs, the names of the gods and their mythologies, still
prevailed in the towns and villages of Phoenicia.[59]

Porphyry's testimony was important because Eusebius emphasized
the authenticity and significance of existing ancient traditions as a
testimony of the truth. The fact that Phoenician religious traditions
were still in existence precluded the claim that Eusebius' words were
unimportant or anachronistic. Eusebius himself may have been aware

---

[58] *PE* 1,10.
[59] *PE* 1,10, 36–37.

of the problems inherent in criticizing the forms of ancient religion, and so stressed that such practices were alive and well in his own day.

In *HE* 3,4, Eusebius introduces Porphyry's statements in the *Letter to Anebo* as testimony on Egyptian religion. In addition to a factual description, the letter included a critique of theurgy and of various techniques for predicting the future. However, in the framework of his negative description of Egyptian religion, and his refutation of it—as part of a general attack on different manifestations of polytheistic error—Eusebius adduces Porphyry's factual description, which was not originally negative.

In the course of his condemning the third form of religion, "political religion", Eusebius attacks the practice of sacrifices. Here the words of Porphyry (*On Abstinence* 2,54) provide useful testimony against sacrifices in general. The passage quoted deals with the practice of human sacrifice in the past among pagans, and peoples in different countries. Moreover, Porphyry's statements attest to the practice of human sacrifice during his own time.[60] Two further sections from *On Abstinence* (2,43; 2,52) are adduced as evidence regarding demons. Eusebius uses Porphyry's testimony to prove the superiority of human intelligence, which forbade sacrifices to evil *daimons*, over the demongods. In fact, Eusebius applies Porphyry's statements, originally intended only for the evil *daimons*, to the gods in general. Porphyry strengthens Eusebius' argument by stating that evil *daimons* never attacked pure souls.[61] Later Eusebius proves that, according to *Philosophy from the Oracles*, even Apollo was a demon-god who demanded sacrifices. Here Eusebius points to contradictions between *On Abstinence* and *Philosophy from the Oracles*. These were noted in our discussion on sacrifices in Chapter 4 and we shall return to the subject later. This is linked to Eusebius' reply to the argument that Christians were traitors to their ancestral tradition. If that were the case, he declares, then pagans should continue their ancestors' practice of human sacrifice.[62] Perhaps this was also an oblique response to Porphyry's insistent claim that Christians betrayed tradition—a claim which largely determined the writing of the *PE*.

Eusebius' provocative conclusion is that the negative approach to

---

[60] *PE* 4,16, and see the discussion on sacrifices in Chapter 4.
[61] *PE* 4,18–19.
[62] *PE* 4,19–20.

sacrifices reflected in Porphyry's *On Abstinence*, is actually realized by
the Christians.[63] Moreover, Porphyry admitted that poets and philosophers were trapped by the machinations of the demons.[64] Eusebius
finds in Porphyry's words pagan affirmation of his belief that poets
and philosophers were misled by demons and that they, in turn, misled the masses into thinking that the demons were gods.

In *PE* 4,23, Eusebius quotes Porphyry's *Philosophy from the Oracles*
as evidence of pagan demonology. Serapis and Hecate dominate the
evil *daimons* whose symbol—the three-headed dog—represents the
cruel *daimon* in the three elements: earth, water and air. In a brief
paragraph that mentions Jesus, in Porphyry's *Against the Christians*,
Eusebius finds proof of the weakness of the demons with the Advent
of Jesus.[65] In this instance, there is an obvious polemical element. It
is noteworthy that Eusebius finds proof of the defeat of paganism
and of the power of Jesus in Porphyry's polemical work. This is a
polemical device that Eusebius combines with a general critique of
gods and oracles. He chooses to relate only to Porphyry's seemingly
positive testimony regarding Christianity in the cited passage. In it
Porphyry lashes out sharply against Christianity, blaming it for the
current plague in Rome. The plague was able to rage for a long
time because Asclepius and other gods no longer were present in
the city. For, ever since people had begun to revere Jesus, no one
felt the care of the gods any longer.[66] Thus Eusebius does not attempt
to refute Porphyry's accusation against the Christians regarding the
plague; instead he makes positive use of the testimony—implied in
Porphyry's statements—that Jesus had the power to chase away
demons. Eusebius proceeds to outline the pagan charges that Jesus
was a mortal and a charlatan. He relates to these claims only briefly,
to reinforce his argument: namely, if Jesus were simply a mortal and
a charlatan, why had Asclepius and the other gods not overcome
his power, and how had he brought about the flight of the gods?

In the *Letter to Anebo* and *Philosophy from the Oracles* Eusebius finds
passages that prove the limited power of the gods. The sections he
quotes discuss the mythological "tasks" of the goddesses. From Porphyry's description, Eusebius concludes that such tasks did not fit
the elevated concept of "divinity", as it was also understood by Por-

---

[63] *PE* 4,21.
[64] *PE* 4,22, a long quotation from *On Abstinence* 2,38.
[65] *PE* 4,1,7–8.
[66] See Chapter One of this study.

phyry. Porphyry's remarks attested to the limitations of the gods' powers and to the coercive force of prayers and adjurations addressing them.[67] Appearing to base himself on Porphyry's statements, Eusebius then asserts that gods who were subject to theurgy were not really gods.[68] Thus, according to his needs, he exploits Porphyry's critique of theurgy in the *Letter to Anebo* while taking advantage of Porphyry's previously positive attitude to the subject in *Philosophy from the Oracles* to adduce evidence of the limited power of the gods. For Eusebius, Porphyry's statements in *Philosophy from the Oracles* also attested to the decline of the oracles. To reinforce Oenomaus' argument against oracles (noted in Chapter 5), Eusebius includes Porphyry's statements in *Philosophy from the Oracles*, not as critical testimony but as an objective description supporting his claims, despite the fact that they originally reflected the author's positive attitude to oracles.[69]

At the beginning of his polemic against astrological determinism, in Book VI of the *PE*, Eusebius comes out against fatalistic determinism regarding both demons and humans. In Porphyry's description and in the oracles from *Philosophy from the Oracles*, he finds support for his assertion that even demons made divinations according to heavenly bodies and the movement of the stars, and that they therefore lacked intrinsic power. The demon-gods who predicted the future according to astronomy were no more powerful than human beings. By believing in fate, they also destroyed human freedom of will. In the oracle of Apollo cited by Porphyry, Eusebius finds support for the argument, prevalent among apologists, that the gods did not even have the power to protect themselves, namely, their temples, from natural disasters such as lightning and fire. Prayers addressed to them were therefore worthless, for everything was subject to fate, which even the gods feared.[70] In fact, from the oracle in Porphyry quoted by Eusebius (*PE* 6,3), it appears that the fates were subject to the rule of Zeus as supreme god, a point which weakens Eusebius' argument. Thus he continues to argue by *reductio ad absurdum*, against the background of the gods' weakness, that sacrifices and honors were worthless and that supplications had to be addressed to fate. Alternatively, he was prepared to accept the words of the oracle that Zeus was the universal ruler and master of the fates. But here he

---

[67] *PE* 5,7–8.
[68] *PE* 5,9.
[69] *PE* 6,1–3.
[70] *PE* 6, Introduction; *PE* 6,3.

tries to reverse the oracular words. For if Zeus was indeed the universal ruler and master of the fates, why not simply acknowledge him as the sole benificent and providential God? One had to turn to Him and liberate oneself from the shackles of fate. In this seemingly logical development, Eusebius disregards the weakness of his previous argument, because the fates in the oracle were also an expression of the will of Zeus, which could not be circumvented. In *Philosophy from the Oracles*, Porphyry declares that magic was a gift of the gods to liberate humanity from the shackles of fate. Here Eusebius sees an opportunity to attack Porphyry as representing the magical-astrological concept. For, if Porphyry's declaration were true, why could the god not save himself, namely, his temple, from fate? Eusebius went on to present the oracle and Porphyry as encouraging the use of magic and theurgy, as opposed to exhorting for philosophy. This contrast does not exist in the statements of the oracle or the remarks of Porphyry presented by Eusebius. It is a rhetorical addition on the part of Eusebius.[71] In this case, it is convenient for Eusebius to overlook Porphyry's negative attitude towards theurgy in the *Letter to Anebo*, upon which Eusebius bases his earlier statements. Porphyry's exposition in *Philosophy from the Oracles* was also adduced as proof that the gods lied; certain *daimons* lied inadvertently, owing to insufficient knowledge, in order to please their supplicants.[72] Eusebius seized upon such words and declared that the divinity, by contrast, never lied. Furthermore, no decent man related his lie to the force of fate and the orbits of the stars.[73]

Eusebius faithfully repeats the statements of Theophrastus—as quoted by Porphyry in *On Abstinence* 2,26—as external evidence that the Jews were a nation of philosophers and theologians.[74] Eusebius juxtaposes this with a quotation from Porphyry about the Essenes exemplifying the philosophical way of life of the Jews.[75] For tactical reasons, it seems, Eusebius chose to cite Josephus[76] through Porphyry[77] rather than directly and by name, as he usually did, even though Porphyry gives Josephus as his source and even mentions by name the

---

[71] *PE* 6,5.
[72] *PE* 6,5, and see Chapter 5 of this study.
[73] *PE* 6,6.
[74] *PE* 9,2.
[75] *PE* 9,3.
[76] *BJ* II, 8, ii–xii.
[77] *On Abstinence* 4,2.

texts in which the Jewish historian describes the Essenes.[78] Tactical
reasons may also help explain why he refrains from quoting Josephus earlier, while including the statements of Philo of Alexandria
on the Essenes.[79] At the end of the chapter, after concluding Porphyry's quotation from Josephus—without mentioning Josephus by
name—Eusebius declares that such was the testimony of Porphyry,
apparently from ancient sources, regarding the Essenes' devotion to
philosophy. Is this tactical sophistry on the part of Eusebius, who
knew the works of Josephus well, or had he perhaps failed to identify the quotation from Josephus, despite Porphyry's clear mention
of his name? Apparently, the omission of Josephus' name was deliberate, for Eusebius wished to adduce Porphyry as proof, in accordance with his stated strategy. He was intent on introducing Porphyry,
wherever possible, as negative testimony on the pagans and as positive testimony on the Hebrews and the Christians wherever possible—which Eusebius found in the oracles of *Philosophy from the Oracles*.
Porphyry includes the oracle of Apollo which mentions the Jews,
interpreting it as meaning that the Greeks—and not the barbarians,
such as the Hebrews—were misled in their approach to the gods.
Another oracle of Apollo spoke of Hebrews who were acquainted
with the wisdom of religion and understood the wisdom of the heavens.[80] As we have noted, Eusebius does not hesitate to use oracles
as a manifestation of divine knowledge when they support his position.

Porphyry also played an important role as witness to the philosophers' plagiarizing from barbarians and the Hebrews, and from other
Greek philosophers. In his typically generous manner, Eusebius cites
the pagan authors directly, not satisfied with the testimony of a Christian author such as Clement of Alexandria, despite the latter's use
of quotations from pagan authors. In keeping with his usual methods and tactics, Eusebius gives priority to Porphyry. He includes a
lengthy passage from Porphyry's work *Philological Discourse* (Φιλολόγος
Ἀκρόασις), of which little remains.[81] The quoted section deals with
the subject of literary plagiarism and gives many examples from
Greek literature; even Plato does not emerge innocent of the charge
of plagiarism. Porphyry enumerates many Greek works that discussed

---

[78] *On Abstinence* 4,11.
[79] *PE* 8,12.
[80] *PE* 9,10.
[81] *PE* 10,2–3. Eusebius interprets it in the subtitle, and not in the body of the
chapter.

the issue of plagiarism, especially on the part of specific authors. Beyond the four passages quoted by Eusebius, nothing remains of this work. Its contribution to our knowledge of plagiarism in ancient Greece is thus considerable.[82]

Porphyry's statements contain important testimony concerning the problems of the chronology of Moses. Eusebius says that he will adduce evidence of the antiquity of Moses based on the work of Porphyry, "the most bitter and audacious foe of Hebrews and Christians alike. The contemporary philosopher, who, in his vehement hatred, published a libelous tract against us which slanders not only us but the Hebrews as well, including Moses and the subsequent prophets." For, the most decisive proof of the truth was to be found in the testimony and consensus of the enemies of Christianity. The passage quoted above is the third in the *PE* that cites *Against the Christians* by name.[83] It is another extract from Porphyry's discussion of the ancient Phoenician historian, Sanchuniathon, as the most reliable source for the true history of the Jews. Eusebius uses it here as well because of the positive testimony it offers regarding the antiquity of Moses, and not in response to criticism by Porphyry. In fact, the chronology of Porphyry differs from that of Eusebius, but the latter's main purpose here is to present a convincing argument for dating Moses very early. The disagreement between the two chronologies is inconsequential; indeed, Eusebius admits that he elegantly glosses over the difficulties.[84] According to Porphyry, as cited by Eusebius, Moses lived some two thousand years before the Christian era![85]

---

[82] See E. Stemplinger, *Das Plagiat in der griechischen Literatur* (Leipzig & Berlin, 1912), pp. 40–57. According to Porphyry's *Life of Pythagoras*, 53, the Pythagoreans argued that Plato and Aristotle plagiarized from the early Pythagoreans, and presented this as their own creation. Later, Plato and his disciples presented slanderous fabrications as Pythagorean teachings.

[83] *PE* 10,9,8.

[84] *PE* 10,9,11.

[85] *PE* 10,9,12. Eusebius says that Porphyry fixed the date of Moses 850 years before the Trojan War (*PE* 10,9,20–22 = Harnack, *Against the Christians*, F. 41). It seems that in this instance Eusebius used his sources with considerable license. Porphyry placed Moses in the time of Queen Semiramis, on the premise that she lived shortly before the Trojan War. Eusebius, however, knew that she was born about 800 years before. He stated therefore that this was the date that Porphyry had determined for Moses! See the analysis by R. Goulet, "Porphyre et la datation de Moïse", *Revue de l'histoire de religions* 184 (1977), pp. 137–164.

Books XI–XIII of the *PE* deals with the influence of the Hebrews' philosophy on Platonic thought, the congruence between the two, and Plato's rare deviations from Hebraic wisdom. Eusebius presents Porphyry's statements as an explanation of Plato's concept of the soul, in order to show the compatibility that existed between Plato's and Moses' respective theories of the psyche.[86] These statements are taken from the lost work *For Boethus, On the Soul* (Πρὸς Βόηθον Περὶ Ψυχῆς). After a lengthy discussion on Plato, Book XIV of the *PE* sets out to settle accounts with the heirs of Plato and the other philosophical schools. In Chapter 9, Eusebius attempts to examine philosophers who deal with "physics", a category that included theology. He states his intention to discover whether their comprehensive studies included the acquisition of theological truths from the sages of previous generations; but then he immediately rejects the need to probe this matter. For if previous generations had possessed a knowledge of divine matters, he argues, it would not be necessary to have "human philosophy", and in any case, neither innovation nor dissension would have ensued. There would have been no need to wander among the barbarians in order to acquire knowledge. For it would have been possible to learn from the gods or from commentators on religion. Similarly, if ancient peoples had possessed the truths, why had they not adopted them and preserved them in harmony?

Thus, according to Eusebius, once it was proved that philosophers did not learn anything from their predecessors, and that they required innovations and speculations of their own, they had to admit that ancient theology contained nothing beyond what Eusebius had discussed in the earlier books of the *PE*. At this point, the definitive testimony comes from the prosecutor himself, from Porphyry's *Letter to Anebo*.[87] Eusebius' task is thus simplified: if he can prove that Greek philosophy was the product of speculation, controversy, and error, then he can also prove his earlier arguments. But it seems that he sought to present the limitations of human knowledge in contrast to revealed truth. He continues with quotations from the *Letter to Anebo, On the Soul,* and *Philosophy from the Oracles*.[88] Eusebius' purpose is well served by Porphyry's assertion, in the short passages he quotes, that most philosophers simply engaged in speculation and

---

[86] *PE* 11,28.
[87] *PE* 14,9.
[88] *PE* 14,10.

that the impossibility of absolute knowledge was a human limitation. Therefore, all "philosophical truth" was questionable or doubtful. Porphyry also speaks of the error of the Greeks. Apollo himself attested to this error and to the discovery of the truth by the barbarians, including the Hebrews. Porphyry praises the barbarians and the Hebrews who found the winding and tortuous path to God. After these quotations from Porphyry, Eusebius reiterates the pagan accusation that the Christians had abandoned the Greeks in favor of the Hebrews. The answer he provides, with support from Porphyry is: What can one learn from philosophers whose knowledge is entirely based on speculation and controversy, and whose arguments are easily dismantled because of their heavy reliance on sophistic language? We were right, therefore, to leave the Greeks for the Hebrews. Here again Eusebius does not attribute the argument to Porphyry, but it is possible that the juxtaposition of these statements is not coincidental. In the last book of the *PE*, Eusebius quotes Porphyry's *On the Soul* to reinforce his critique of Aristotle's concept of the soul,[89] and to refute the Stoic concept of God.[90]

Unsurprisingly, the *DE* has few direct quotations from Porphyry. These are confined to the first three books, as the remainder deal mainly with adducing proof from Scripture. In *DE* 1,10, Eusebius explores the polemical context of the question as to why Christians did not require sacrifices or the burning of incense. Eusebius gives Porphyry's opinion, as he did in the *PE*—but here without mentioning his name—quoting *On Abstinence*, in which Porphyry rejects the significance of sacrifices. In light of his explanation of sacrifices in Scripture, Eusebius then has to reject Porphyry's opinion, which he had previously praised, and likewise, the latter's view that animals had souls similar to humans. Later Eusebius uses Porphyry to support his reply to the pagan criticism that Jesus did not demand animal sacrifice and incense in honor of God. In this case, the leading representative of paganism and great prosecutor of Christianity replies as if he were on the opposing side. Here Eusebius again quotes from *On Abstinence*, expressing Porphyry's negative view of sacrifices—a view similar to that encountered in *PE* 4,14.[91]

Definitive proof of the holiness, miracles, and divinity of Jesus,

---

[89] *PE* 15,11.
[90] *PE* 15,16.
[91] *DE* 3,3.

and of the truth of all the reports concerning him, which would suffice to convince the last of the skeptics, comes from the oracles themselves, as testimony written by the archenemy Porphyry. "And what testimony could be more deserving of trust than that which is written by our enemy in Chapter 3 of his work, *Philosophy from the Oracles*."[92] There follows the famous oracle on Jesus as a saint and as immortal.[93] Ironically, the greatest accuser, Porphyry, provides the key response to those calling Jesus a wizard and magician. The passage is presented in an abridged form appropriate to the apologetic context, whereas Augustine reproduces the entire section, including the oracle's negative statements on Jesus and Christianity.[94] Moreover, taking advantage of the rhetorical potential, Eusebius draws the far-fetched conclusion that Jesus was able to perform miracles only because of the divine power within him—this, on the basis of Porphyry's words! The quotation from Porphyry and the statements by Eusebius suggest that he is not arguing directly against the pagan philosopher here or elsewhere in Book III of the *DE*. At the very least, he has no intention that his anonymous opponent be identified as Porphyry. For he clearly distinguishes between the two, and adduces Porphyry's statements to counter that same rival, thereby reinforcing the general impression that although Porphyry plays a major role in the double composition, the work is not directed specifically against him. In this case, apparently his opponent serves as a straw man representing all pagan enemies of Christianity. This explanation also suits Eusebius' overall intention of attributing a general significance to his work beyond the narrow polemic against the arguments of Porphyry.

Eusebius' approach to Porphyry's testimonies may be summarized thus: he uses them as extensively as possible, as negative testimony on pagan religion and philosophy, and as positive testimony on Christianity. Porphyry's statements carried great weight, since he was the major spokesman for paganism, an important representative of philosophy in his generation, a commentator on the different forms and concepts of pagan religion, and the leading opponent of Christianity. The testimonies appear throughout the *PE* and in the first part

---

[92] *DE* 3,6.
[93] *DE* 3,7,1.
[94] *City of God* 19,23. On the differences between the two passages, see Chapter 5 of this study.

of the *DE*. Eusebius took texts originally written by Porphyry as a
positive description of pagan religion, such as *Philosophy from the Oracles*, and used their emphasis on the ceremonial and cultic elements
of religion to support his own critical view of the religious concepts
involved. Furthermore, he seized upon statements written in the spirit
of deliberation and internal criticism of pagan religion, and motivated by a desire for religious reform, or as philosophical commentaries that did not correspond to a literal understanding of mythology
and religious tradition, as in *On Abstinence*. When necessary, Eusebius
singled out the statements of one work as if they alone represented
Porphyry's overall view, disregarding any divergent views on the
same subject in another work—although elsewhere, such views became
the basis of Eusebius' argument. In those instances when Porphyry's
statements were not critical, Eusebius integrated them into his own
critique by removing them from their original context, or by select-
ing only those parts that suited his purpose. Thus Eusebius enlisted
positive and neutral statements to serve his negative critique. Likewise, he honed Porphyry's positive comments on Christians while
ignoring their generally negative context. On several occasions, as
we have seen, Eusebius used Porphyry's words to draw conclusions
that were unconvincing and even, perhaps, illogical. For Eusebius,
such conclusions became integral to Porphyry's thought; he could
project his own needs onto Porphyry's text and interpret it accordingly. The boundary between rhetoric and autosuggestion is not
always discernible. His strong desire to present Porphyry as a major
witness, may explain why Eusebius used his quotations of famous
authors rather than citing and naming those authors directly, and
also why he states that Porphyry based himself on "ancient sources".
The three places where he quotes *Against the Christians* were not
adduced in order to deal with Porphyry's anti-Christian arguments,
but to transform his statements into positive testimony on Christianity. The polemic against an unnamed opponent in Book III of
the *DE* is not aimed specifically against Porphyry, although he may
have been the source of the major arguments to which Eusebius
responds.

A Critique of Porphyry's Views and Inconsistencies

In the framework of his critique of the prevailing polytheism in
Egypt, Eusebius also criticizes Porphyry's interpretation of "Egyptian theology". He also targets the contemporary cult of the sun and

of astrology,[95] though the main thrust of such criticism is to be found in Book VI of the *PE*. Eusebius quotes Porphyry's *Letter to Anebo* and *On Abstinence* 4,9. His purpose in introducing Porphyry is not only to criticize him; Eusebius uses Porphyry's description as a positive account of Egyptian religion. His basic criticism is that, despite Porphyry's idealization, Egyptian religion had to be considered a form of polytheism. Later, Eusebius opposes the idea that the souls of animals and humans were essentially the same, as Porphyry describes in his idealization of Egyptian religion.[96] Eusebius further develops his critique of this concept in his discussion of sacrifices, as we have noted.

From this point in *PE* 3, 6–7, Eusebius focuses his critique on the new generation of contemporary philosophers—the neo-Platonists led by Porphyry, who is mentioned by name. He also assails their theology and their interpretation of mythology, which combined the Creative Reason and the Platonic Ideas with ancient theology (mythology). Here he quotes Porphyry's *On Images*. This critique of the neo-Platonic interpretation of religion, directed at Porphyry as the major spokesman of this school, continues sporadically up to Book VI of the *PE*. However, as we shall see, the comprehensive criticism is not directed against the contents of Porphyry's statements, even though Eusebius wants to give that impression. In fact, he rejects the didactic symbolism of Porphyry as "modern sophistic tricks", which had never occurred to the ancient thinkers even in their wildest dreams. Occasionally, he appears to forget his stated intention to counter the opinion of Porphyry as representative of the "young" philosophers, and not the ancient concepts that he was supposed to have refuted previously. His principal method was to avoid confronting the content of the interpretation, and instead to undermine it by proving it unauthentic and irrelevant. Subsequently (*PE* 3,8), Eusebius selects several passages from Plutarch and argues that they clearly refute Porphyry's statements. The refutation based on Plutarch seems superficial, however, unless Eusebius is suggesting that precedent can refute new opinions. But even the perceived contradiction, regarding the interpretation of images of the gods, is limited only to the nature of the materials from which they were created, and does not deal with their significance.[97]

---

[95] *PE* 3,4.
[96] *PE* 3,5.
[97] A good summary of the fragments of *On Images* can be found in Buffière, *Les*

Eusebius includes, in the following chapter,[98] a further, lengthy quotation from *On Images*, in which Porphyry presents an Orphic hymn to Zeus, together with an interpretation. Eusebius does not attack Porphyry's interpretation of the Orphic hymn but proposes his own, as if the words of the hymn were the issue under scrutiny, and not Porphyry's interpretation. Another question is whether Porphyry's interpretation of the hymn in fact represents his own view, for Eusebius later adduces a further interpretation of the hymn proposed by Porphyry. Eusebius dismisses Porphyry's interpretation of the hymn in a single sentence, as demonstrating Porphyry's view that Zeus constituted the visible world of the senses, a view that accorded with the Stoics and with Porphyry's own theology. This, however, is virtually the interpretation of the hymn as proposed by Eusebius himself. But he also presents Porphyry's second interpretation of the Orphic hymn, which apparently expresses Porphyry's opinion. According to the second interpretation, the god of creation was the creative intellect deified by the poet. Eusebius cannot reject Porphyry's idealistic interpretation and must indirectly attack the basis of the interpretation, namely the hymn itself, by arguing that from the outset, an Orphic hymn could not include an ideal, immaterial concept of god. He subsequently claims to have proved that Porphyry employed deceptive sophistry in his commentary on the poem—a claim that was patently false.[99] He further asserts that Porphyry thought the creator of the world to be identical with the soul of the world. This may have been true, but there is no evidence to support the claim in the statements made by Porphyry just previously. By presenting Porphyry's interpretation in this way, Eusebius had ample opportunity to be critical. He duly proceeds to criticize the initial part of Porphyry's first interpretation, though his critique focuses on the hymn itself and not on Porphyry's brief interpretive statements. He then presents a critique of the second part of the interpretation and argues, ostensibly in reaction to Porphyry, that the

---

mythes d'Homère, pp. 536–539. For a brief discussion, see E. Bevan, *Holy Images: An Inquiry into Idolatry and Image-Worship in Ancient Paganism and Christianity* (London, 1940), pp. 74–75. Behind the symbolic grasp of Porphyry lies an ancient philosophical tradition of internal pagan criticism against images, which commenced with Xenophanes and Heraclitus and continued with the Cynics, Zeno, Posidonius, and Plutarch. See Bevan, ibid., pp. 64–65.

[98] *PE* 3,9.
[99] *PE* 3,10.

rational human soul preserved within it the image of God and was immaterial—which was precisely Porphyry's meaning! Thus either Eusebius misunderstood the seemingly straightforward quotations from Porphyry, or else he may have deliberately distorted them. According to Porphyry, the anthropomorphic form that the deity assumes in the hymn is merely a manifestation of its reason. Eusebius proceeds to summarize his critique of Porphyry, combining all the arguments against the various ideological, mythological, physical, and symbolic methods.[100] At the conclusion of the chapter, Eusebius again attaches a philosophical interpretation (in this case by Porphyry) to mythological motifs to create the effect of absurdity, while making the seemingly generous gesture of accepting a philosophical concept for the sake of argument.[101] Thus it emerges that, for Eusebius, the disparity between mythological tradition and its philosophical interpretation according to Porphyry, was acceptable as grounds for refutation.

The discussion regarding the Orphic hymn is lengthy. Eusebius toys with sections of Porphyry's *On Images*, with the effect of ridiculing them. After a long quotation describing the gods as forces active in the universe, Eusebius takes Porphyry's evocation of the divine force present in the earth and presents it as a distinct cult of the earth and its power. He attacks the alleged absurdity of Porphyry's description of the forces of the universe, by arguing that Porphyry assigned important gods to an unimportant part of the universe, while ascribing to a significant part those who were not even gods.[102] He is not content with attacking Porphyry's views. He impugns Porphyry's personal morals because of his symbolic use of satyrs and bacchants. Having established his rival's absurdity, Eusebius relies on the reader's understanding of his own fundamental principles to complete the picture. Henceforth, he simply adduces further lengthy quotations by Porphyry that give his interpretation of Greek mythology and Egyptian religion.[103]

Further on in the polemic against Porphyry's metaphysical-symbolic interpretation of paganism, Eusebius assumes a magnanimous stance and gives credit to this concept, only then to refute it as metaphysical

---

[100] *PE* 3,10.
[101] Ibid.
[102] *PE* 3,11.
[103] Ibid.

polytheism, by ignoring its philosophical monotheistic basis, or *henothe-ism*.[104] In fact, the subsequent passage shows that he is acquainted with this concept. He presumably finds in Porphyry's interpretation of Egyptian religion views that are contradictory and mutually exclusive. He perceives two different interpretations in Porphyry's statements and chooses to see one as correct and authentic, the other as artificial, introducing foreign theological and idealistic principles.[105] In other words, he endeavors to present Porphyry's interpretations as distortions. In fact, Porphyry does not give two interpretations. Eusebius' "first interpretation" is based on statements from Chaeremon, quoted by Porphyry; he derisively sustains mythological motifs together with the symbolic-allegorical concept. This was certainly not Porphyry's intention. Here, we can again ask whether Eusebius intentionally falsified the symbolic concept, or else could not or would not grasp that this philosophical approach either emptied paganism of its content or cast it in a new mold. Perhaps he understood this only too well and was wary of the affinity with Christian beliefs. Later in the chapter, as noted, Eusebius acknowledges the henotheistic concept of different forces working in the universe as manifestations of the powers of one God. He dismisses this view as yet another theoretical concept of the philosophers that had no practical application in religious life. He asks, rhetorically: Why then did those philosophers not categorically reject mythologies and external manifestations of pagan religion. Here Eusebius requires philosophers to live according to their principles, even if they did not become Christians.[106] He persists in his attack against the philosophers, who observed the pagan cult only for the sake of appearance. In so doing, they simply reinforced the misconceptions of the masses.[107]

In *PE* 3,14, Eusebius includes quotations from Porphyry's *Philosophy from the Oracles*, a work that is positive about the oracles, in order to demonstrate their absurdity. As opposed to his symbolic interpretation, gleaned from *On Images*, Eusebius selects statements from this earlier work in order to make Porphyry look ridiculous and self-contradictory. These extracts are made to represent the simple truth as understood by Porphyry, whose interpretation of the oracles is

---

[104] *PE* 3,13.
[105] Ibid.
[106] *PE* 3,13.
[107] *PE* 3,14. Of course, there is more than that here. Many displayed a strong desire and profound need to preserve the social and world order; perhaps they even identified with it and had an inner impulse to give new content to old patterns.

omitted. The gods themselves are then presented as rejecting the physical-symbolic interpretation, thereby heightening the absurd effect.

In his discussion on oracles and demons, Eusebius declares that he selected Porphyry from among the many Greek historians and philosophers, since Porphyry was the most knowledgeable on the subject. He seemed to be a friend and an advocate of demons and had studied them in depth in his work, *Philosophy from the Oracles*.[108] Thus in addition to the disparaging presentation of Porphyry as a friend of demons, Eusebius attests to his erudition and thoroughness. Eusebius declares that he judges Porphyry according to his works.[109] In Book IV of the *PE*, he presents the various statements on sacrifices from Porphyry's *On Abstinence* in order to point out differences from the views expressed in *Philosophy from the Oracles*. Other inconsistencies in Porphyry's works are highlighted. Chief among these is the contrast between his negative attitude to sacrifices in *On Abstinence*, and his favorable interpretation of individual sacrifices to the gods, in *Philosophy from the Oracles*. With ostensible generosity, Eusebius praises Porphyry for his negative view of sacrifices in *On Abstinence*, attributing this to "correct thinking".[110] In the same chapter, however, he underlines the absurdity of the oracle quoted by Porphyry, which asserted that Plato is simply a demon. Such statements regarding Porphyry serve only as an introduction; in subsequent chapters, Eusebius has to proceed to the stage of textual proof, namely, the quotations that substantiate his statements.[111] The next chapter (*PE* 4,15) endeavors to present decisive proof of the internal contradictions between *On Abstinence* and Porphyry's own interpretation of the oracle in *Philosophy from the Oracles*. Eusebius proves that all demons are evil, and not only some of them, as Porphyry had thought.[112] Eusebius finds an internal contradiction in *Philosophy from the Oracles*, where the appearance of the good demon actually causes sudden death, thus negating his goodness. Moreover, in his oracle, Apollo contradicts Porphyry.[113] Similarly, Eusebius contrasts sections from *A Letter to Anebo* and *Philosophy from the Oracles*. He sub-

---

[108] *PE* 4,6.

[109] *PE* 4,8.

[110] *PE* 4,10.

[111] Quotations from *On Abstinence* (*PE* 4,11–14) concerning the spiritual concept of sacrifices, are discussed in Chapter 4 of this study.

[112] I have noted the similarities between the demonology of Porphyry and Eusebius in Chapter 5.

[113] *PE* 5,5–6.

sequently concludes that in the course of their struggles against each other, the gods had revealed the art of theurgy to men.[114] After praising Porphyry effusively as a "noble philosopher", "wonderful theologian", and "wise man of mystery", Eusebius proceeds to disparage his theology, basing his argument on a passage from *Philosophy from the Oracles.* The gods occupied themselves with matters of no relevance to humans and eschewed deeds that could be helpful.[115] Moreover, according to Eusebius' interpretation of this passage, the gods were aware of their limitations.[116] Eusebius follows this with a polemical summary: The gods were simply demons and the Christians acted wisely in abandoning them.[117] Finally, at the beginning of Book VI of the *PE*, Eusebius addresses Porphyry personally and then praises Oenomaus for his negative stance on oracles and fatalism, favorably contrasting his wisdom and superiority with the oracular deities of Porphyry. He scolds Porphyry and encourages him to learn from Oenomaus.[118]

The direct and open critique of Porphyry in *PE-DE* is actually limited to Books III–VI of the *PE*. It is addressed to Porphyry as the modern interpreter of pagan religion, and as chief spokesman of the neo-Platonic school and the metaphysical-symbolic interpretation of ancient religious traditions. Eusebius chooses Porphyry as interpreter of the pagan religion not only because he was the great enemy of Christianity whose image and stature had to be undermined, but also as Plotinus' senior disciple, who studied and wrote extensively on philosophical and religious subjects with a comprehensive erudition, and acquired a reputation, authority, and primacy in intellectual circles. Direct and open criticism of Porphyry does not occur elsewhere in the double composition—either in response to the anti-Christian charges of *Against the Christians*, or in relation to other views expressed in Porphyry's other works. The critique itself is rhetorical rather than substantive. The emphasis is less on assailing Porphyry's views than on exposing contradictions within and between his works. Since Porphyry bore a certain resemblance to Eusebius in the spirit of his theological concepts and in his tendency to asceticism, it was difficult for the latter to oppose these aspects. Where Eusebius could

---

[114] *PE* 5,10.
[115] *PE* 5,14.
[116] *PE* 5,15.
[117] Ibid.
[118] *PE* 6,6,52.

not expose Porphyry as inconsistent, he attacked him on the basis of the tradition that Porphyry sought to interpret, and argued that such a tradition, a priori, could not sustain Porphyry's interpretation. We have seen how Eusebius attributes to Porphyry himself oracular pronouncements presented in Porpyry's work, and how he manipulates quotations to determine Porphyry's purported standpoint. The element of ridicule and derision previously noted is present here; on occasion, a personal note enters the ostensibly relevant critique, reminding the reader that Eusebius' opponent was not just another of the many authors quoted in his works. Eusebius displays a great tactical finesse in choosing Porphyry's early work, *Philosophy from the Oracles*. The fact that Christianity's dangerous enemy had once been captivated by oracles and sacrifices made him a perfect target for Eusebius' criticism.[119]

Porphyry's mentor, Plotinus, displayed a special proclivity for oracles.[120] This was continued and enhanced in Porphyry's *Philosophy from the Oracles*, which regarded oracles as sacred sources of pagan prophecy, and included descriptions of magical practices. In *Philosophy from the Oracles*, the detailed instructions regarding sacrifices do not concur with the Pythagorean concept, which viewed animal sacrifice as serving the appetites of evil demons, nor with Apollonius of Tyana's negative approach to sacrifices, later adopted by Porphyry in *On Abstinence*. Through his questions, doubts, and struggles on theological issues, Porphyry evinced an openness on the problem of forms of pagan ritual; his desire to reform pagan religion was expressed in *On Abstinence*, the *Letter to Anebo* and *On Images*. This approach was perceived by Eusebius as weakness, to be exploited in his polemic in order to reveal the contradictions and negations inherent in the various manifestations of pagan religion.[121]

As we have stated, in the *PE-DE* Eusebius does not attribute to Porphyry any major or minor arguments against Christianity. This, despite his frequent mention of Porphyry as the bitter opponent of Christianity and its greatest adversary. Nonetheless, we have seen that

---

[119] Augustine followed suit. See Bidez, *Vie de Porphyre*, p. 28; Geffcken, *Last Days*, p. 59.

[120] See Geffcken, ibid., p. 54.

[121] Porphyry's *On the Return of the Soul to God* met with a similar fate. Christians seized upon its refinement of prevalent pagan beliefs and its vacillating stance on the subject. Only Augustine has preserved fragments of this work. See Geffcken, ibid., p. 68.

the major pagan arguments on which his work is based, and some of the minor arguments as well, are similar or identical to those found in the extant fragments of Porphyry's work against the Christians. For the most part, such arguments are not linked to quotations from Prophyry or to the polemic against him. On certain crucial issues, however, the arguments are juxtaposed with a quotation from Porphyry and the polemic against his statements. These instances may have indirectly preserved part of the direct polemic with Porphyry, otherwise assimilated by Eusebius into this work.

Early in the *PE*, as we have noted, key criticisms raised by Porphyry are presented as the motivation and polemical framework for the entire composition.[122] The Christian religion lacked a rational basis; it depended on blind faith without reason, on acceptance without investigation. Christians required from converts unquestioning faith, since their own faith could not be proved. Christians were innovators, deviating from ancient pagan traditions and from the religion of the Hebrews. They were without fear of God, atheists who had abandoned the cult of the gods to turn to an alien, atheistic, and barbarous religion. Similarly, *PE* 4,1, introduces the prevalent argument against the Christians, namely, that they had committed a grave religious sin by not worshiping the beneficent divine powers. They broke the law and created problems with their love of "innovations". Pagan enemies of Christianity were therefore justified in wanting the death penalty for Christians. At this point, Eusebius does not point specifically to Porphyry, but he may have had him in mind.[123] We have seen the quotation from *Against the Christians* in *PE* 5,1,7–8, where Porphyry states that the Christians were responsible for the plague in the city. For with the advent of Jesus, Asclepius and other gods had departed. Eusebius does not respond to the pagan argument here, but rather uses it as proof for the power of Jesus. He briefly juxtaposes pagan claims that Jesus was a mortal and a charlatan, attributing them to pagans in general.[124] In *PE* 14,10, immediately following quotations from Porphyry adduced as evidence of speculation, discord, and inconclusive proof in Greek philosophy, Eusebius repeats the pagan charge that the Christians

---

[122] *PE* 1,1–2. Porphyry is not mentioned by name; however, the arguments are identical to the point that Wilamowitz and Harnack regarded them as part of Porphyry's introduction to *Against the Christians*.

[123] See Chapter 1, the section on *Against the Christians*.

[124] *PE* 5,1,7–8.

deserted the Greeks in favor of the Hebrews. Here too, Eusebius does not attribute the argument to Porphyry. *DE* 7,3, recalls the anti-Christian charge that there were contradictions between the different genealogies of Jesus in the Gospels. Despite the fact that Porphyry attacked these contradictions, Eusebius does not mention him in this regard, nor does he mention Porphyry in his reference to his work dealing with this issue.

In Chapter 6 of this study, I have analyzed at some length the arguments against Jesus and the apostles in Book III of the *DE*, noting Stevenson's unproved suggestion that Book III is based on Eusebius' lost work against Porphyry. Despite the fact that Porphyry proposed arguments similar to those refuted by Eusebius, the latter does not attribute them directly to Porphyry. Stevenson's assumption belongs to the realm of speculation until such time as the lost work, *Against Porphyry*, emerges from oblivion. Nonetheless, as we have seen in *DE* 3,7, Eusebius apparently did not want to identify his anonymous rival as Porphyry. It was his wish, it seems, to argue with an imaginary pagan figure who represented all pagan opposition to Christianity.

In conclusion, Porphyry's role falls into two categories: that of auxiliary witness, and that of self-contradictory author. Quotations relating to the first are scattered throughout the *PE*; those concerning the second are limited to Books III to VI of the *PE*. Thus the open and direct criticism and polemic against Porphyry is confined to the context of a philosophical interpretation of religion, while Porphyry's testimony against pagan religion and philosophy, and his testimony on the Hebrews and Christians appear throughout. In the wider perspective of the double composition, the polemic against his opinions is limited, whereas his testimony against the pagans has a cumulative significance. In his double composition, therefore, Eusebius uses Porphyry on several levels: (1) He presents key anti-Christian arguments expounded by Porphyry as building blocks for the polemical structure of his work. (2) The polemic is directed at Porphyry as the representative of pagan religion and modern philosophical interpretation, and of neo-Platonic philosophy, on the basis of his philosophical-religious writings. (3) Porphyry's words are presented as testimony against pagan religion and philosophy.

Although his polemic does not specifically target Porphyry's *Against the Christians*, and he does not directly confront Porphyry's arguments, the achievement of Eusebius is broad in scope. (1) The comprehensive work is a general reply to the main arguments propounded by Porphyry. (2) Contemporary pagan religion and philosophy as represented by Porphyry is discredited. The result, even if achieved by means that are more rhetorical than logical, tends to undermine the position of Porphyry as the leading authority on philosophy in his generation, and thus reduce his status as the great adversary of Christianity in his day. (3) Porphyry, the enemy of Christianity and the greatest pagan of his time, helps to erode the principles of pagan religion and philosophy, and provides convincing proof of their lack of truth—and also, indirectly, invalidates the great pagan onslaught against Christianity. The few quotations from *Against the Christians* are short and insignificant, compared to the long passages from Porphyry's other works; they are included not to present Porphyry's arguments, but because Eusebius can use them to reinforce his own claims. In contrast, anti-Christian arguments that also appear in Porphyry, are included without attribution. In Book III of the *DE*, Eusebius conducts a sharp polemic against pagan claims regarding Jesus and the apostles, which are familiar, in part, from *Against the Christians*. The polemic is aimed at an anonymous pagan rival whom Eusebius addresses in second person; he takes care, however, to distinguish clearly between the anonymous rival and Porphyry, from whom he draws decisive evidence against that rival. Key anti-Christian arguments, identical or similar to those found in Porphyry, are basic foundations of the two-part work. In addition, many of the secondary arguments that I have listed have parallels in the well-known arguments of Porphyry, but Eusebius never identifies these as taken from Porphyry or *Against the Christians*, even though they are occasionally juxtaposed with a quotation from Porphyry, or even with a polemic or critique directed at the latter. On occasion, a personal tone enters Eusebius' polemical statements against Porphyry. As we have noted, Wilamowitz and Harnack identified a major anonymous pagan argument in the *PE* as Porphyry's preface to *Against the Christians*. It seems that Eusebius did not envision this composition as a specific reponse to Porphyry's book, but rather as a comprehensive anti-pagan campaign in which Porphyry was perceived as leading the opposing camp.

The instances of a direct polemic against Porphyry did not target his arguments, but the man himself, as the representative and leading contemporary interpreter of philosophy and religion. The way in which Eusebius undermined Porphyry's position and authority, and used his writings in order to discredit paganism, made a decisive contribution to the refutation of Porphyry's attack on Christianity. Eusebius conceived his work as more than yet another reply to Porphyry's *Against the Christians*. In an earlier, more detailed book, he had apparently dealt with Porphyry's arguments systematically, one by one. Here he wished to formulate a general response to pagan religion and philosophy based on a comprehensive strategy. In fact, Porphyry's work was a primary motivation for this undertaking as well. However, it was not conceived as a personal answer to Porphyry. Thus his major arguments are presented anonymously and *Against the Christians* is not mentioned at all in Eusebius' discussion of pagan arguments. On the three single occasions when this work is briefly noted, it is in the context of adducing evidence on behalf of the Christians, and not in order to raise pagan arguments. This accords with Eusebius' determination to use Porphyry as negative testimony regarding the pagans and as positive testimony for the Christians. This testimony was crucial, as it came from the great enemy of Christianity. It was apparently for strategic purposes, therefore, that Eusebius tried to minimize the direct personal polemic against Porphyry. He was not interested in producing yet another written response to Porphyry's onslaught. On the other hand, it is possible that his early response, *Against Porphyry*, was not sufficiently effective and convincing—as Philostorgius maintained[125]—and that Eusebius preferred to avoid a direct confrontation with Porphyry's arguments in his *PE-DE*. He may also have wanted to avoid giving a publicity to Porphyry's attack. Perhaps, both considerations came into play.

Porphyry's openness on the problematic issue of pagan cult practices was perceived as weakness by Eusebius and other Christian writers, and duly exploited. Subsequent pagan writers took the same view, and the issue became an embarrassing one in the difficult period of the final great struggle of paganism for survival. As a result, the influence of Porphyry on later pagan writers was perhaps less than that of Iamblichus, and only *Against the Christians* was widely used by pagan polemicists. Not until the close of the fifth century did his other works recover their honored status.[126]

---

[125] See the end of Chapter 2 of this study.
[126] See Geffcken, *Last Days*, p. 73.

CHAPTER NINE

THE THEOPHANY:
THE FINAL APOLOGETIC STATEMENT

General Analysis

The Theophany is Eusebius' final apologetic work. Preserved in its entirety only in a Syriac translation, it was probably written during Eusebius' final years, apparently between 333 and 337.[1] S. Lee, who first published the Syriac version together with an English translation, maintained that *The Theophany* preceded the *PE* and the *DE*.[2] However, subsequent scholars have indicated a later date, between 333 and 337—they differ as to the exact year of composition— towards the end of Eusebius' life. The precise date was unclear because the first three books of *The Theophany* include almost the entire second part of his late work, *In Praise of Constantine*, and because the two were written in such close succession.[3] Lightfoot believes that *The Theophany* had not yet been published when Eusebius delivered his sermon on the Holy Sepulchre, which may have been based mainly on *The Theophany*, just as his *tricennalia* sermon may have included material from *The Life of Constantine* before its publication. He argues that *The Theophany* preceded *In Praise of Constantine* but had been subsequently edited, and that Eusebius might not have finished it.[4] Harnack, on the other hand, contends this argument is not con-

---

[1] S. Lee, *Eusebius, Bishop of Caesarea on the Theophania or Divine Manifestation of our Lord and Saviour Jesus Christ. A Syriac Version* (London, 1842).

[2] Lee thought that the more organized, abridged, and popular form of *The Theophany* antedates the larger, more learned and comprehensive work, *PE-DE*. See S. Lee, *Eusebius' Theophania Translated from the Syrian Version of the Original Now Lost Greek* (Cambridge, 1843), p. XXI. The question arose because *The Theophany* contains much material parallel or even identical, word for word, to *PE-DE*, a feature that will be discussed. Beyond Lee's opinion, which is based on erroneous considerations, as Lightfoot has demonstrated ("Eusebius", p. 333), he overlooks the fact that in *The Theophany* Eusebius wrote about the *DE* as a work from which he cites (*Theophany* 4,37; 5,1), and did not identify the Syriac title of the work in 5,1, as Gressmann has shown. See H. Gressmann, *Studien zu Eusebs Theophanie*, *TU* 23,3 (1903), p. 38.

[3] See Gressmann, ibid., Introduction, p. V.

[4] Lightfoot, "Eusebius", p. 333. The subject at the end of Book V based on the *DE* seems to be somewhat abbreviated and incomplete.

vincing and that *The Theophany* may have been edited before the sermons.[5] Gressmann conducts a detailed examination of this question and concludes that *The Theophany* was written c. 333.[6] Schwartz generally accepts Gressmann's conclusion, namely, that *The Theophany* had been written before the sermons, and does not propose an exact year.[7] Laurin also concurs with Gressmann.[8] By contrast, Wallace-Hadrill rejects Gressmann's reasons for dating *The Theophany* before *In Praise of Constantine*, and dates the former to 337, close to Eusebius' death.[9] Barnes, on the other hand, opts for an earlier date (c. 325–326), basing this on the reference to the survival of temple prostitution in Heliopolis in Phoenicia, despite its abolition by Constantine.[10] The question of the exact year of composition is not crucial for our discussion. The significant fact is that the work was written in the latter part of Eusebius' life, after Constantine had undertaken the great transformation of the imperial order. It is worth noting that Eusebius does not quote *The Theophany* in any of his works, a fact that could serve as further evidence for a late date, although in his later books, as we have seen, Eusebius is capable of entirely ignoring some of his earlier compositions.

Although *The Theophany* was preserved intact only in its Syriac translation, many sections of its Greek original can be reconstructed on the basis of quotations and parallels from Eusebius' other works, mainly *PE-DE*, but also *In Praise of Constantine* and the *HE*. Similarly, A. Mai has identified many Greek fragments in *catenae* ascribed to Eusebius' *Theophany*.[11] But in many places the fragments are similar rather than identical, leaving large lacunae. Furthermore, *The Theophany*, notably in Book IV, also contains material that does not appear in his other extant works. Gressmann devotes the bulk of his research to philological examination, comparing the Syriac translation with the Greek fragments. He concludes that, for the most part, despite all the minor errors in translation, the Syriac version is exact and faithful to the original. But he warns against a total reliance on the Syriac translation, especially where no Greek parallels exist.[12] The

---

[5] Harnack, *Chronologie*, II, p. 121.
[6] Gressmann, ibid., pp. 39–42. He repeats his conclusion in the introduction to the German translation of *The Theophany*, *GCS*, III, 2, pp. XIII–XX.
[7] Schwartz, "Eusebios", p. 1429.
[8] Laurin, *Orientations maîtresses des apologistes chrétiens*, p. 386.
[9] Wallace-Hadrill, *Eusebius*, pp. 52–53, 58.
[10] *The Theophany* 2,14; Barnes, *Constantine and Eusebius*, p. 187.
[11] See the introduction to Gressmann's study of *The Theophany* mentioned above.
[12] Gressmann, *Studien*, pp. 48–50.

Syriac translation is early—probably close in time to the original work—and the textual tradition is relatively faithful to the presumed original.[13]

The Theophany is a popular work directed at a wider public than the more erudite and lengthy *PE-DE*.[14] It includes the main apologetic traits of the latter, and covers all its major subjects. Eusebius' motive in writing *The Theophany* may have been to present the enormous undertaking of the dual composition in a more accessible form for the wider public. This impression is strengthened by the fact that at least seven-tenths of this work is repetition, paraphrase, or even an exact reproduction of statements in *PE-DE*. The first two books of *The Theophany* are constructed mainly in parallel to the *PE* but without the numerous quotations from pagan, Christian, and Jewish authors. Book II, in particular, contains quotations of authors derived mainly from the *PE*, and covers the same subjects with few innovations, in a lofty, oratorical style. Book III follows the plan of the *DE* and contains many parallels, especially from Book IV of the *DE*. Book V is almost a repetition of *DE* 3,3–7, with occasional changes in the order of the passages and their phrasing.[15] Book IV is exceptional in that most of the text is not parallel to the *DE* or other known works by Eusebius. More sober in tone than the first three books, Book IV is reminiscent of Eusebius' more learned works. It is mainly a collection of the prophecies of Jesus and their fulfillment throughout history. As we have stated, both Lightfoot and Gressmann proposed that Book IV was based on a particular work that Eusebius devoted to these prophecies, mentioned in the *PE*.[16] We shall discuss this book later. The second part of Book III also contains material that has no parallel in the *DE*, mainly concerning the

---

[13] Lightfoot, "Eusebius", p. 332; Gressmann, *Studien*, p. 52.

[14] This is the general consensus among scholars. See Gressmann, ibid., p. 36; Schwartz, "Eusebios", p. 1431; Barnes, *Constantine and Eusebius*, p. 187. Wallace-Hadrill also held that *The Theophany* was not actually written as a literary work, but was perhaps a compilation of several sermons, homilies, or conversations (*Eusebius*, p. 58). This view—influenced by his assertion that the work postdated the sermons—appears unfounded, particularly in light of Book IV, which constitutes an inventory of the prophecies of Jesus and thus falls outside the category of sermon, discussion, or homily.

[15] Gressmann recorded the parallels between *The Theophany*, *PE*, *DE*, *HE*, and *In Praise of Constantine* in useful columns, and also the parallels between the Greek fragments printed in *PG* 24, 609–680. See Gressmann, *Studien*, pp. 143–147.

[16] *PE* 1,3. See Lightfoot, "Eusebius", p. 331, and Gressmann, Introduction to the Translation, pp. XIII–XX. See also Chapter 4 of this study.

Resurrection of Jesus, and this, too, will be considered later. However, both Book IV and the second part of Book III, deal with subjects treated in the *DE*, but with attention to detail, development,
and emphasis not found in the *DE*. In addition, Eusebius takes a
somewhat different approach to one or two subjects in Book II of
The Theophany. The fact that *The Theophany* is based largely on parallels from *PE-DE*, and the *HE*, including many quotations, that are
not, however, noted as such, may indicate that the unidentified material was taken from Eusebius' lost works. Hence, Lightfoot and Gressmann's theory for Book IV seems valid, and one may also assume
that the discussion of resurrection in Book III is based on the second, lost part of the *DE*. Thus the impression is that *The Theophany*
is based entirely upon earlier material, mainly from Eusebius' known
works, which was superficially adapted. This virtual absence of originality probably explains why there is no scholarly study of the contents of *The Theophany*, with the exception of the textual research by
Mai, Lee, and Gressmann.

We shall now briefly survey the contents of *The Theophany*,[17] and
then discuss the subjects on which Eusebius' attitude seems to have
changed. I shall further explore the treatment of resurrection in Book
III, and the contents of Book IV. The title of the work, *The Theophany* (Θεοφάνεια)—the manifestation of God in the Incarnation of
the Logos—indicates the central subject around which are arranged
all the ideas and issues that Eusebius considered crucial. In Book I,
Eusebius postulates that the structure of the world required a creator. There had to be an intermediary between the supreme God
and man—namely, the Logos. Eusebius examines the nature of the
universe and of man. Nature possessed an essential duality, the visible and the invisible, the material and the spiritual. Created in the
image of God, man had potential superiority over the rest of Creation. He was able to achieve perfection through the power of his
reasoning. However, men were corrupt and they degenerated to the
depths of evil because of their material and physical desires. The
concept of the Logos and the epiphany is presented as the antithesis of atheism and polytheism, and the errors of the polytheists and
pantheists. In this book we encounter the well-known polemic against
the errors of paganism, polytheism, and fatalistic determinism, against

---

[17] A full descriptive survey of the contents of *The Theophany* can be found in
Gressmann, *Studien*, pp. 1–34.

rejection of the concept of Providence, and the pagan error of sub-stituting the created for the Creator. The concept of the Logos is presented as a corrective. Eusebius summarizes his concept of how religion developed, of monotheism as an ancient form of religion before man was misled by demons, and of the Hebrews as the only ones who persisted with their monotheism, and were therefore rewarded by the manifestation of the Logos, prophecy, and correct philosophy.

Book II describes the degenerate state of humanity, which made the Incarnation necessary. Humanity became corrupt when people engaged in polytheism and moral depravity. People worshiped nat-ural phenomena, qualities, objects, passions, humans, and animals. The philosophers could not save them, and even they themselves were victims of various errors. Eusebius launches another—brief—attack on the various schools of philosophy, on the plagiarism from other barbarian nations and from the Hebrews, and on philosophers who sustained pagan religion, paying lip service to the cult of demons and thus reinforcing a partnership with them. He scorned the con-tradictions between philosophers and their internal debates. Plato was the closest to the truth but even he was in the grip of a major misconception. Demons drove humanity mad and captured it in their net through a highly sophisticated conspiracy. Thus many strange cults emerged throughout the world. The cult of sacrifices, wars, and other calamities, were the fruits of a demon plot to dominate human-ity. Here Eusebius includes a discussion on human sacrifice and the oracles as part of the plot. However, the power of the demon-gods was limited; they were not capable of defending their temples or protecting them from decay and destruction. Occasionally, God man-ifested himself through prophecies and natural disasters, and pre-pared the ground for the Redemption of mankind. When the time was ripe and the imperial Pax Romana had effaced national barri-ers and promoted political unity, the Logos appeared to humanity, heralding the divine truth. In contrast to the litany of wars and dis-asters caused by the demons, Eusebius pens a hymn of praise to the Pax Romana, brought about by divine providence.

Book III deals mainly with evidence of the truth of Christianity and the divinity of Jesus. Eusebius includes these in order to attest to the Epiphany by enumerating the beneficial effects of the Incar-nation—world peace and the prosperity of the empire, the decline of paganism, the fall of Christianity's enemies and persecutors, the remarkable historical triumph of the Church despite the persecutions, and the moral improvement bestowed on mankind—and thus prove the necessity of the major events in the Redeemer's life: the Incarnation, and his death and the Resurrection. Eusebius embarks on a defense of the concept of the Incarnation. The Incarnation did not damage the purely spiritual concept of the divinity of the Logos, which was not limited to any one place even at the time of the Incarnation. There follows a defense of Jesus' death and Resurrection. The Resurrection gave the disciples proof of Jesus' power to overcome death, and further strengthened their belief that they would attain eternal life. For Jesus died to offer atonement for sinful humanity. His death as a sacrifice was also to pursue, entrap, and crush the demons.

The purpose of Book IV was to prove further the divine manifestation of the Logos through prophecies and their fulfillment. He directs his words at those who had not yet acknowledged the divine revelation of the Logos. Most of these prophecies, however, are not derived from the Old Testament, but those uttered by Jesus himself and fulfilled during his lifetime and in subsequent generations. Jesus' miracles are divided into those that he performed during his life on earth, and those he performed up to the time of Eusebius. The first group were mentioned by the prophets and in the testimony of Jesus' contemporaries. The ongoing miracles of the second category were witnessed even in the present by Eusebius' generation. The major prophet of these miracles was Jesus himself and his prophecies were to be found in his sayings and parables in the Gospels. Book IV relates to the second category only, or, more precisely, to the prophecies of Jesus and their fulfillment in history, such as the growth of the Church and the spread of the Gospel throughout the world, the rejection and punishment of the Jewish people, universal redemption, persecutions, heresies, and internal divisions within the Church, and the End of Days. The function of Book IV within the general framework of this work is to prove the divinity of Christ and the truth of the Gospel from the unprecedented greatness of the wonder they represented, through the prophecies of Jesus and their fulfillment. The prophecies of Jesus proved that he was not a mortal prophet, but one who was also the force for their fulfillment in history. All of the above attested, like a thousand witnesses, to the divinity of Jesus and to the divine truth of the Gospel.

As we have noted, Book V repeats *DE* 3,3–7, refuting pagan accusations that Jesus and the apostles were frauds, charlatans, and prac-
titioners of magic, as discussed in Chapter 6 of this study.

Thus the apologetic-polemical subjects that appear in *The Theophany* are not new. From the point of view of apologetics, Eusebius
singles out pagan philosophers for especially harsh criticism. He seeks
to discredit their lack of belief vis-à-vis the Logos, the Son of God
who was made flesh to redeem mankind, and he endeavors to respond
to specific polemical arguments. Eusebius assembled from his earlier
works issues and arguments that seemed important and relevant, and
arranged them around the central subject of theophany, the revelation
of the Logos. The work is relatively short, with fewer and briefer
quotations, and Eusebius' tone is confident and casual. On occasion,
however, Eusebius' view on a subject discussed in previous works,
mainly in *PE-DE*, undergoes a change, exceeding the usual paraphrase or additional detail.[18] Occasionally, this shift reflects the evo-
lution of the status of Christianity in the empire, and its newly-confident
and belligerent attitude vis-à-vis paganism. Elsewhere, when the material is for the most part unfamiliar to us, the views expressed may
not indicate change but instead represent attitudes from earlier, lost
works. Nevertheless, the length and emphasis of such statements in
The Theophany, as opposed to their absence or negligible weight in
the *DE*, may indeed reflect a change in Eusebius' stance on such
subjects. Perhaps, rather than representing a substantial change, such
material formed a significant part of the lost half of the *DE*. I shall
first deal briefly with two issues that might indicate a definite shift on
the part of Eusebius between the writing of *PE-DE* and *The Theophany*,
and subsequently relate to the unfamiliar material in the *The Theophany*.

The Attitude to Plato

Plato had a special role in the *PE*.[19] The author most frequently
quoted, he is hailed as the greatest Greek philosopher, and the closest to attaining the truths of Christianity. His philosophy derived

---

[18] Examples of minor additions of details can be found, for instance, in 1,63,
where Eusebius briefly notes the power of exorcism among the pagans and their
magical and theurgic forces. In 1,65, he speaks of man's gift of prophecy, inspired
by the holy spirit, and of dreams as a true means of prophecy. These words represent a minor and insignificant amplification of earlier statements in *PE-DE*.

[19] See Chapter 3 of this study.

from the Hebrews and was identical to it in many areas. Platonic philosophy was in harmony with Scripture. He knew of the Holy Trinity and even prophesied the Passion and Crucifixion of Jesus.[20] Eusebius devoted three entire books of the *PE* to demonstrating the harmony between Plato and Scripture, and Plato's acknowledgment of the Bible and all branches of Hebrew philosophy. Likewise, he introduced Plato as a critic of religion, mythology, and several philo-sophical schools.[21] At the end of his discussion of Plato, he was forced to devote several chapters to an explanation as to why, despite all the above, Christians preferred the barbaric Hebrew philosophy to Plato.[22] He also expressed his admiration of and affinity to the philoso-pher, and felt he had to apologize for the criticism leveled at him.[23] Eusebius admired and respected him, despite the fact that Plato occa-sionally erred and did not reach the practical conclusions suggested by his ideas.[24]

Plato also occupies a central position in *The Theophany*. The dis-cussion of his "Christian" concepts and errors occupies about one-third of Book II (Chapters 24–46). It seems, however, that the treatment of Plato—a major part of Eusebius' critique of the differ-ent philosophical schools—is guided by a somewhat different pur-pose, and not the particular desire to prove that all that is good and true in Greek philosophy can be found in and derived from Hebrew philosophy and Scripture. Here, too, Eusebius says that Plato was closer than all other Greeks to the true philosophy, and that he advocated the correct theology regarding the Father and the Son, Creation, and the soul. He was the only Greek who recognized the concept of the creating Logos (24–29). He taught the doctrine of punishment and reward, of Judgment Day and divine justice for souls. He stated that man's greatest good was to resemble God, and regarded the gods as demons who had once been mortals (30). Euse-bius adds that Plato was the philosopher who belonged to the celestial

---

[20] See Chapter 5 of this study.

[21] *PE* 11–13.

[22] *PE* 13,14–19.

[23] *PE* 13,18.

[24] See Des Places, "Eusèbe de Césarée juge de Platon", pp. 73–76, on Eusebius' attitude towards Plato in *PE*, on the harmony between Plato and Scripture, and on Plato's qualities and defects. His conclusion was that Eusebius' attraction to Plato and the positive descriptions in *PE* are dominant. Eusebius recognized the major role played by Plato in paving the way to Christianity, or, in other words, in the "preparation for the Gospel".

intellectual world of the ideas, and who spoke truths in a superhuman voice (32). Nonetheless, he was more deserving of condemnation than all other philosophers, for he had attained knowledge of the supreme God, but did not worship Him as a God. He hid the truth from mankind and spread lies. To those whom he loved, he spoke openly, as a philosopher, about the Father and Creator, but he did not at all behave like a philosopher towards the Athenians. He participated in the cult with Socrates, at the latter's request. He was not embarrassed or evasive, nor did he blush when he admitted that his teacher, the father of philosophy, had instructed him to please the gods by sacrificing a rooster, namely, the earthly matter and traces of blood that constitute a dead chicken. Despite Plato's acknowledgment that the gods were simply mortals who had become demons, he deemed it proper that men worship them as gods. Since he participated with the masses in their cult, he should rightly be considered a party to their plots because he concealed the truth with a veil of philosophy and lies (30). He sank into the abyss of error (32). He now honored the world of phenomena—which he himself had claimed was ephemeral and lacking any complete and true existence—in the form of many gods. He condemned the authors of mythologies and theogonies for never telling a single word of truth, but himself later agreed with their words (34). His advice to adhere to the misconceived pagan cult sprang from fear of the capital punishment decreed by law. Fear of the law and of man had displaced fear before the truth and the law of truth. Whither, therefore, did the pure, great, and wonderful words of Plato disappear (35)? Here Eusebius comes close to addressing Plato personally, through disappointment that he did not behave in accordance with lofty ideals he preached (40). Thus Plato sinned through words and deeds that directly contradicted his philosophical ideas. He who scornfully expelled poets from his republic, called Homer, Hesiod, and Orpheus, the sons of God. Eusebius was therefore justified, he claims, in regarding Plato as more deserving of condemnation than other philosophers. He says that at one time he was attracted to Plato because of the affinity of their ideas and because, of all of the Greeks, he clung to the gates of truth and his words showed a closeness to the Christians. He deserved condemnation, therefore, because despite the fact that he recognized the truth, he exchanged a true life for one of lies and living for the moment (41). Critical of Plato's belief in the immortality of the soul of irrational animals and in the transmigration of human and animal souls, Eusebius feels obliged to doubt the sincerity of Plato's belief in the immortality of the soul. He inserts a sharp condemnation of Plato, stating that he deserved universal scorn. In describing Plato, Eusebius paraphrases Paul: "He knew God, but honored Him not as God, but worshiped and served creation instead of the Creator."[25] He even referred to the heavenly elements as gods and worshiped them, despite his acknowledgment that they were created and finite. Thus Plato sinned in his stupidity (46).

The detailed criticism of Plato and his deviations from "Christian philosophy", which Eusebius lists in the short chapters[26] of *The Theophany* are not new, coming directly from *PE* 13,14–19. In fact, the criticism in these chapters of the *PE* is far more detailed and includes additional points. The most conspicuous difference between the discussion of Plato in the *PE* and in *The Theophany* is the significance of the criticism within the respective works; In *The Theophany* the condemnation of Plato is sharp and scathing and its conclusions against him, radical. As noted, Eusebius devoted three books of the *PE* to a discussion on Plato. Books XI–XII give detailed attention to the concurrence between Plato and Scripture. Book XIII continues this discussion and concludes with Plato's deviations from Hebrew philosophy, in the last six chapters (14–19). Here, the proportions are also completely different. In the *PE*, Books XI–XII and most of Book XIII are devoted to the affinity between Plato and Scripture; only Chapters 14–19 of Book XIII note Plato's deviation in order to explain why, despite this affinity, Christians preferred the barbaric Hebrew philosophy to Plato's ideas. Eusebius expresses his admiration for and special rapport with Plato, and even apologizes for his critique.[27] In contrast, in *The Theophany* the critique of Plato in Book II constitutes a major part of the criticism of the philosophical schools, and singles him out as the chief representative of Greek philosophy.[28] Here the discussion is not intended to highlight the way in which

---

[25] *Theophany* 2,44; quoting the Epistle to the Romans 1 with minor changes, combining the verses 21 and 25.

[26] Most chapters of *The Theophany* are simply short items, mainly of one or two paragraphs.

[27] *PE* 13,18.

[28] Porphyry is not mentioned by name in *The Theophany* and the few quotations by him are indirect, from *PE*. See the list by Gressmann, *Studien*, p. 151, and the parallel references in *PE* by Lee, in the notes to his translation.

Plato's thought converged with Scripture and the truths of Christianity, but rather to attack his misconceptions and lack of truth. Furthermore, Eusebius makes relatively few statements about harmony between Plato and the Bible. He speaks of harmony mainly in Chapters 24–30, while Chapters 30–46 deal with Plato's errors.[29] Thus he devotes twice as much space to his attack on Plato as he does to the harmony between Plato and Hebrew philosophy. Here, too, Eusebius seems to vent feelings of triumph and exaltation. There was no need now for a detailed apologetic discussion on the correspondence between all that was good in Greek philosophy and the work of its greatest spokesman, Plato, and the truths of Christianity. From this point, an attack could be launched, direct and not apologetic, on all the philosophical schools combined, demolishing them by the discrediting of their greatest representative; he had attained proximity to the truth, but then retreated from it, through fear and a devotion to worldly vanities and ephemeral pleasures.

Peace, the Empire, the Incarnation, and the Success of Christianity

In *PE-DE*, the synchronism of the Incarnation with the Pax Romana and the empire was presented as auxiliary evidence—one of a series of portents—of the fulfillment of ancient prophecies, the divinity of Christ, and the truth of the Gospel;[30] in *The Theophany* the *Pax Romana*, and the historical success of Christianity after the triumph of Constantine, became a major apologetic argument. Eusebius states this explicitly. The Pax Romana, he claims, was prime evidence of the truth of Christianity and the divinity of Jesus.[31] The first half of Book III deals with proof of the truth of Christianity and the divinity of Christ, and opens with the subject of the Pax Romana and the Gospel. Peterson has noted the shift that took place in Eusebius' concept of synchronism and parallels between key developments in Roman and Church history: the establishment of the empire, and the expansion of the Church and its victory in the wake of the political changes, and the correlation between the *Pax Romana* of Augustus

---

[29] With the exception of Chapters 42–43, where he attacks the concept of the soul among the Aristotelians and Stoics.

[30] As I have shown in Chapter 7 of this study, in contrast to Peterson and Sirinelli, who claim that it was already a major argument in *PE-DE*.

[31] *Theophany* 3,33.

and the peace of Constantine.[32] Peterson describes the consolidation of Eusebius' concept as reflected in the *Life of Constantine* and the *In Praise of Constantine*. However, he, and subsequently Sirinelli, did not notice the apparent indication of this change in *The Theophany*. It occurs within an apologetic framework, featuring both in the polemical significance of the argument and in the concept itself as a reaction to the dramatic changes in relations between the Church and the empire.[33] The motif is thus an important new development in the apologetic sequence of *The Theophany*, underlining the need to redefine the relationship between Church and empire, but also the special significance of that relationship in light of its manifest historical consummation with the miraculous, simultaneous Constantinian peace and the Church success, and the cooperation between Church and Empire. The plan of God and the common destiny of the Church and the empire were now clearly revealed in the present, and not in the remote historical past of Augustus' reign. If, in the past, this argument had been problematic and fragile, it had now become solid and self-evident. For only the divine power of Christianity, that of the divine Christ active in history, whose victories continued to mount, could support such colossal historical events. Thus this motif became a salient factor in proving the divinity of Jesus and the truth of Christianity.

Resurrection

In addition to many references to the Incarnation and to relevant prophecies in the *DE*, Books VI–IX are constructed around prophecies and questions concerning the Incarnation, such as its date and location, pertinent historical prophecies, several of which have been noted in this study, and events in the life of Jesus up to his Crucifixion and death. In *Theophany* III, two long chapters, 39–40, and a short one, 41, briefly present the main points raised in the *DE*, but without the prophecies and extensive commentaries. Book X of the *DE* deals with the passion of Jesus, the Crucifixion, the sacrificial death, and his descent to Hell, through commentaries on the prophecies

---

[32] See Chapter 7 of this book.
[33] For the textual parallels between *The Theophany* and *In Praise of Constantine*, see the list in Gressmann, *Studien*, p. 144.

relating to these subjects, and concludes with a prophecy regarding
the Resurrection and the subsequent acts of Jesus. This book has
parallels in *Theophany* III, 42–54, which are also extremely brief. If
we recall that *Theophany* III, 1–39, is essentially parallel to *DE*, I–II
and IV–V, it emerges that *Theophany* III, in its sequence and subject matter, mirrors at least the first half of the *DE*, namely, the first
ten books in our possession. *DE* III, however, with its notable anti-
pagan polemic, was extracted as an independent unit and designated
as *Theophany* V. In terms of proportions, the first half of *Theophany*
III essentially duplicates the first, extant part of the *DE*. It is therefore possible that the second half of Theophany III[34] is based on
the lost, second part of the *DE*, for it is in no way parallel to the
text in our possession, even if occasionally there are ideas that were
presented in the first part. However, such a proposal is, at best, just
a reasonable hypothesis.

We have noted that the Incarnation and the Resurrection were
highly problematic for both pagans and Christians of pagan origin,
and that these concepts played a major role in polemics. Likewise,
we have noted Eusebius' personal difficulty in believing in these concepts and in attempting to give them a rational explanation. His
belief in these tenets came only as the result of the great divine wonder of Jesus' active power in the world and in history, that taught
him about the Incarnation and the Resurrection, namely, the great
and formative miracles of the past, from which all subsequent miracles derived. The above attests to the importance that Eusebius
attributed to the Incarnation, death, and, apparently, to the Resurrection of Jesus in his composition of the *DE*, and subsequently in
The Theophany too. For the most part, the interpretations of prophecies in the *DE* do not emerge from a direct polemical context as
refutations of specific arguments, but rather from Eusebius' grappling with the problems of the Incarnation and the Resurrection,
and as part of a wider nexus of discussion and proof, based on
prophecies regarding the divine activity of the Logos prior to the
Incarnation, during Jesus' lifetime, and also, apparently, after his
Resurrection and Ascension, in the context of history of Christianity and mankind. The same holds true regarding *The Theophany*.
Although the words of Eusebius are not in a directly polemical con-

---

[34] Chapters 55–80. Together, these are slightly shorter than the first fifty-five
chapters, many of which are brief passages.

text, the spirit of the polemic and the necessity of solving the problems clearly emerge. Nowhere else in Eusebius' work does this subject feature in an apologetic context, and these chapters of *The Theophany* therefore merit closer study.

In dealing with the Resurrection, Eusebius does not attempt to respond to critics who ridiculed the concept on the ground of logical absurdity; instead he continues to maintain that it was a wondrous miracle that had to have taken place, from the standpoint of intrinsic logic. In other words, his line of arguing is to prove the inevitability of Jesus' Resurrection.

Without the Resurrection, Jesus could not have overcome his final struggle against death, which dominated everything. On completing its service for the Logos, the human vessel—the body—had to meet an end worthy of God, after death. Either Jesus could have allowed his body to be destroyed, and thus withdrawn in shame from the struggle, or he could prove that his body was superior to death, and through divine power transform the mortal body into an immortal one. The first possibility was incompatible with the nature of the Logos, for the Logos promised life for all and thus could not neglect itself and allow its image to be corrupted by death. It had to achieve immortality for its body openly and publicly. If it had done so secretly, it would not have helped mankind. However, as a public act, it bestowed on everyone the benefit of a great miracle. Hence the Resurrection of Jesus was revealed for all to witness. Jesus did not flee from death, which would have been an act of cowardice, demonstrating that death could overpower him. Here Eusebius apparently introduces a new response to the well-known criticism of Jesus' weakness and helplessness, and the accusation that he could not save himself as Apollonius had.[35] Thus in his struggle against death, he transformed the mortal man into an immortal. This struggle took place in order to bring salvation and a promise of eternal life for all.[36]

Jesus' death and Resurrection form another stage in his struggle against the demons, which had begun while Jesus was alive. The beginning of his struggle took place on the physical plane, when he

---

[35] *Theophany* 3,55. In 2,46, Eusebius relates explicitly to this argument. He states that had Jesus chosen to disappear suddenly from the cross and not allowed his body to die, he would be considered only a ghost. See the parallel in *In Praise of Constantine* 15,2.

[36] *Theophany* 3,55.

was in the desert for forty days and nights.[37] Here, the importance
of the Logos' struggle against the demons lay in the fact that it was
conducted by means of his body and not as an incorporeal, spiritual force. As humanity had been dominated by demons from ancient
times, Jesus had to suppress them by means of a human body. Thus
the body that had been conquered by demons had to triumph over
them and save humanity. This body was superior to the demons
and could overcome them by its cooperation with the Logos.[38] His
initial struggle against the demons marked the start of his activity
among men. His final struggle against them was the beginning of
his domination over death. The flight of the host of demons and
their leader from the first battle was a tactical retreat in order to re-
group for the decisive encounter, or a maneuver of retreat to ambush
Jesus the man—the body at the time of the Crucifixion. The assumption of the demons was that Jesus would depart the world like all
mortals and that his body would come into their possession. They
had no way of knowing that there existed a human nature superior
to death, or that the trap of death was not designed for all mortals.
They thought that it was the final evil from which no one could
escape.[39]

The death of the body for three days was an experiment of sorts,
designed to prove its superiority over death, just as a man could
prove that a vessel could withstand heat, by placing it in fire and
removing it intact. Thus did the Logos act with the body of Jesus,
to proclaim the fact that the human means used for man's redemption could overcome death. The Logos departed the body only briefly
and decreed death upon it. The reason for physical death was punishment for the intrinsically sinful nature of the body. Perhaps the
intention here was not that the body of Jesus himself was sinful, but
the matter is unclear.[40]

The three reasons for the Resurrection were as follows:

1. The Resurrection was proof that the divine power of Jesus was
stronger than death.[41]

2. The Resurrection took place in order to prove that divine power
resided in the body of Jesus, and that this was not just another

---

[37] Matthew 4:1–11; Mark 1:13; Luke 4:2–10; *Theophany* 3,55.
[38] *Theophany* 3,56.
[39] *Theophany* 3,57.
[40] Ibid.
[41] *Theophany* 3,57.

instance of a mortal being deified after death, as happened at the beginning of polytheism according to Eusebius' concept. In contrast, through the Resurrection, the Logos had demonstrated a nature more powerful than death.[42]

3. Redemption and sacrifice. The sacrifice liberated the souls of men from the clutches of the error of the demons, who, when robbed of strength, lost their dominion. Here, it is not clear whether Eusebius is referring to such a sacrifice as appeasement of the demons, or as atonement before God the Father for the sins of mankind. The sacrifice was only the mortal human body and not the Logos who dwelt within. Jesus and Christ were two epithets. The Hebrew word "Messiah" also denoted the High Priest. Jesus, therefore, received two epithets. "Jesus" was the expression of the sacrifice of the body, and "Christ", the expression of the Logos as high priest of God the Father of all humanity and creation.[43] This third reason for the Resurrection, namely, redemption, was the most important, because it was vital for the disciples to witness with their own eyes life after death, thereby strengthening their belief in rebirth into a new life.[44] Thus there is an educational-didactic aspect for his disciples designed to dispel any doubts regarding the belief in the Resurrection. Hence it seems that without the appearance of Jesus after the Resurrection, the disciples may have doubted the resurrection of the body.[45] Disciples and apostles who were about to spread the Gospel had to be totally convinced of the truths of the faith and—the strongest proof— to witness them with their own eyes, in order to withstand the harsh trials awaiting them.[46]

Through fear, death had dominated mankind from ancient times and cast its shadow upon men until the Advent of the Redeemer. Death frightened all peoples, rich and poor. No cure for it was to be found in human knowledge, ancient writings, prophecies, or the revelations of angels. Death was stronger than everything and dominated everything. It was the source of all sin. Since human beings did not believe in life after death, they lived in sin and licentiousness

---

[42] *Theophany* 3,58. See the parallel in *In Praise of Constantine* 15,10.

[43] *Theophany* 3,59.

[44] *Theophany* 3,60.

[45] We have noted Eusebius' statements in *DE*, that only after the Resurrection and appearance of Jesus before his disciples, did they finally believe in his divinity. See Chapter 6 of this study.

[46] *Theophany* 3,60.

deserving of capital punishment, because there was no fear of future punishment. Thus all of life became an ongoing dialogue with death—the sole dominant force—in order to lengthen and enhance a once-only lifetime, until men elevated death itself to a divinity. The passions and their stimulants were likewise deified. This explained the many myths regarding the corruption and licentiousness of the gods.[47] The deification of passions is a subject that features in the *PE* and *The Theophany*. Here, however, the emphasis is on the deification of death as the source of all passions, and its dominance, which Jesus opposes through his Resurrection. Hence the necessity of a body that enters the corporeal and material world, in order to overcome death through the instrument of its very nature,[48] and thus bring about the greatest miracle for all mankind—the triumph of eternal life, which the Redeemer set against death. For the miracle to be clear and beyond any doubt, Jesus had to die a physical death like all mortals, thus proving his humanity, so that the victory of the power of life over death would be manifest to all and unconditionally acknowledged.[49]

The divine power, the Logos, departed from the body at the time of the Crucifixion. The body that remained on the cross attested to its human, mortal nature.[50] This body was given to the dominion of death, treated, and buried according to human practice. Here Eusebius attests as an eye-witness that the grave was an individual one, standing alone above the entire area. The fact that he was buried in a single grave, and not in a burial cave with multiple niches, was a great wonder as well. For had Jesus been buried in a common burial ground, the greatness of the miracle of the Resurrection would have been diminished. After the opening of the grave had been sealed, death celebrated its victory. The period when the body was in the grave was necessary in order to validate his death. But it was not sufficient. The three days in the grave was the minimum time needed to indicate a true death, in case people did not believe that he had died. The time in the grave, therefore, proved

---

[47] *Theophany* 3,61.

[48] Here there may be a variation on a theme of later pagan demonology, namely, the distinction between spiritual deities and material demons. One had to offer spiritual sacrifices to spiritual gods, and a material-physical sacrifice of animals, to demons. See Porphyry, *On Abstinence* 2,36. Both evil and good demons ruled the material world and bodies, and one therefore had to offer them material sacrifices. See Iamblichus, *On the Mysteries* 5,14.

[49] *Theophany* 3,61.

[50] We have encountered a similar idea in *DE*. See Chapter 6 of this study.

that his Resurrection was true and that it followed a true death. Thus the Logos planted in the hearts of men the hope of their rebirth in their old bodies.[51]

Eye-witnesses, such as his disciples and apostles, attested to and wrote about the Resurrection and bequeathed their faith in eternal life to subsequent generations. Thus humanity was liberated from its bondage to the overriding fear of death. Jesus provided direct and substantial proof of life after death, unlike the indirect evidence of statements and arguments by sophists and philosophers. Hence many followed in his footsteps, despising death and aspiring to the afterlife.[52] The miracle of the Resurrection and the subsequent strengthening of belief in eternal life led people to strive for moral and holy lives, and brought about a great moral improvement among all nations. These now spit in the face of idols, trampled the wicked laws of the demons, and scoffed at the erroneous traditions of their ancestors. Everyone abandoned forever their mistaken ways and began to acknowledge the creator and worship Him.[53] The demons were eternally dispossessed of their domination, for men learned to exorcise them from their bodies and souls.[54] In the final chapters of Book III, Eusebius writes briefly about the martyrs,[55] the spread of Christianity throughout the world,[56] the establishment of communities and schools for the teaching of Christian doctrine, and Christian practice throughout the world.[57] The Christian ritual of prayer and hymns was set at fixed times and was standard for all communities;[58] Christians around the world prayed in a similar manner—albeit in different languages—and at the same time of day.[59]

In his conclusion to Book III, Eusebius declares that, through the teachings of Christ, Christians became wise, they learned to stand strong and steadfast in the face of death, to attach little value to the

---

[51] *Theophany* 3,61.

[52] *Theophany* 3,62. The context here may be polemical. Porphyry argued that the revival of Lazarus from the dead (John 11:44) did not constitute proof of resurrection from the dead, for his body had not yet begun to decompose. He also argued that the Resurrection of Jesus was not proof of resurrection, for he had not been born, as others were, from semen (Harnack, *Against the Christians*, f. 92).

[53] *Theophany* 3,63.

[54] *Theophany* 3,70.

[55] *Theophany* 3,74.

[56] *Theophany* 3,75.

[57] *Theophany* 3,76–77.

[58] *Theophany* 3,78.

[59] *Theophany* 3,79.

life of this world, and to place their hope and confidence in the promise of the Redeemer. They learned that they would achieve the eternal life of the soul in heaven and in the Kingdom of God. Behind this promise stood the Savior, who proved its reality in his struggle against death, and who proved to his disciples that terrible death was nothing. He revealed before their eyes the life he promised, and through Resurrection he made his body a source of hope for the indestructible life of the body, and the exaltation of the Christian faithful to the level of angels after the Resurrection.[60] In Book III, the acts of Jesus relating to his Epiphany and his activity in the world, were only selected examples of the evidence of his divine power.[61]

In effect, all Eusebius' statements on the Resurrection are intended solely to emphasize or explain the necessity of the Resurrection. The effect is distinctly apologetic. An explanation was needed as to why Christians required the "paradoxical" belief of the body's resurrection, an idea vociferously attacked by pagans, and one which many Christians found difficult to accept, let alone understand. Eusebius does not propose in *The Theophany*, either, a rational physiological explanation for the great miracle of the resurrection of the body. Perhaps he still held his basic view that this miracle could not be explained rationally, and that if Scripture and other miracles performed by Jesus throughout history had not attested to it, the Resurrection would have had to be viewed merely as an absurd mythological tale.[62] All that remained, therefore, was to attempt to understand and explain why the Logos had sought to perform the wondrous and inexplicable miracle of the Resurrection.

The Fulfillment of the Prophecies of Jesus as Argument and Proof

Theophany IV is distinct from the four other books, which constitute a partial, brief paraphrase of the *PE* and the *DE*, and, on occasion, duplicate the latter. Book IV is an anthology of the prophecies of Jesus and a demonstration of their fulfillment throughout history, with prophetic quotations from the Gospels. Each prophecy is treated

---

[60] Ibid.
[61] *Theophany* 3,80.
[62] See Chapter 6 of this study.

individually. The structure is somewhat reminiscent of Eusebius' earlier work, *Prophetic Extracts*, and—even more, perhaps—many chapters of the *DE*, which contain prophecies classified according to
different subjects, with Eusebius' interpretations. The fact that *The
Theophany* adapts earlier material strengthens the assumption that it
integrates either Eusebius' previous work on the prophecies of Jesus,
as proposed by Lightfoot and Gressmann, or perhaps, an adaptation of this work in the lost portion of the *DE*.

We have noted that Jesus' prophecies occupy a relatively small
part of the *DE*. The argument that the fulfillment of Jesus' prophecies was proof of the truth of Christianity and of his divinity, appears
only peripherally, as an addition to other accumulated evidence and
claims. In the *DE*, Eusebius does not rely to any great extent on
the prophecies of Jesus, and refers sparingly to the Gospels and the
Epistles, in keeping with his general methodological principle of min-
imizing testimonies and proof that derived from Christianity itself.
In fact, the marginal place of Jesus' prophecies in the *DE* does not
corroborate the opening statement of the *PE*, which asserts that the
actual fulfillment of Jesus' prophecies, particularly in Eusebius' generation, furnished proof that was stronger than any argument, powerful enough to close the mouths of the most aggressive enemies.
The fulfillment of his prophecies was testimony and proof of Christian beliefs regarding Jesus and his divinity. By this, Eusebius meant,
first and foremost, the prophecy regarding the spread of Christianity throughout the world and its strong stand in the face of enemies,
troubles, and death. Here he recalls the special work in which he
collected sayings and prophecies of Jesus and showed their fulfillment in history, thus proving beyond all doubt the truth of the Christian views of Jesus.[63] From the context of these statements, it seems
that the short passage on the importance of Jesus' prophecies and
their fulfillment as proof—a passage that gives an example of the
prophecy that Christianity would stand steadfast in the face of its
enemies and death[64]—is based on that same earlier work. Perhaps,
this explains why such statements occur at the beginning of the *PE*,
before its tactical, methodical approach had been finalized. Subsequently, in the major work dealing with prophecy, namely the *DE*,
proof based on the fulfillment of Jesus' prophecies was considered

---

[63] *PE* 1,3,12.
[64] Matt. 16:18.

less important. Alternatively, we could surmise that Eusebius saved
any major discussion of this type of proof for the second, lost half
of the *DE*, because of Jesus' many prophecies regarding the more
distant future. Furthermore, despite the importance of this proof,
Eusebius may have preferred to minimize it for the methodological
and tactical reasons mentioned earlier.

As noted, the figure of Jesus as a prophet was well known, and
early apologists refer to him as a prophet without particular emphasis. Both Justin[65] and, later, Clement of Alexandria[66] and Origen,[67]
argued that Jesus' prophecies had been fulfilled in their own day
and would be fulfilled in the future. According to Clement, the apostles were also prophets.[68] In the *DE*, Eusebius makes the general
statement that Jesus had predicted the history of the apostles and
the subsequent history of Christianity.[69] Clement holds that he also
foresaw the disagreements that would arise within the Church.[70]

Eusebius' lost work, devoted to the prophecies of Jesus, may have
resembled the *Prophetic Extracts*—a collection of prophecies arranged
in order of their appearance in the Gospels. In fact, the assumption
of Lightfoot and Gressmann that the work served as the basis for
Theophany IV seems plausible; Eusebius apparently followed the order
of the Gospels, albeit not consecutively but according to major subjects. This assumption, however, presents complications because other
adaptations and changes may also be presumed. On the other hand,
Book IV bears a closer resemblance to many chapters of the *DE*
than to the *Prophetic Extracts*.

In *Theophany* IV, the small rubric devoted to Jesus the Prophet in
the *DE* occupies one-fifth of the entire work. The reasons for and
significance of this great change poses several questions. For even if
all or part of the work on Jesus' prophecies had been incorporated
into the *DE*, this would not explain the disproportionate treatment
of the subject in *The Theophany* compared to that in the *DE*. In fact,
as we have noted, a mere half of *Theophany* III corresponds to the
first half of the entire *DE*.

Within the general framework of *The Theophany*, the role of Book

---

[65] *Dialogue* 8,35.
[66] *Stromateis* 7,15.
[67] *CC* 2,13.
[68] *Stromateis* 5,6.
[69] *DE* 3,5.
[70] Matt. 13:28; *Stromateis* 7,15.

IV is to present the prophecies of Jesus and describe their fulfillment in history as proof of his divinity and the truth of the Gospel.
This takes the form of a series of additional, more cogent arguments
proving the divinity of Jesus, intended for those who were not satisfied
with previous proof.[71] Here, Eusebius discusses the divine prophetic
power of Jesus. His statements, made in a direct polemical context,
are intended for those who were not prepared to acknowledge the
divine nature of Jesus' acts.[72] According to Eusebius, the miracles
and prophecies of Jesus could be divided schematically into two periods: New Testament and post-New Testament, including Eusebius'
own times.[73] The subject of Book IV covers mainly the second period.
The author proposes the familiar logic that miracles performed in
the past should be believed because of the power of miracles and
the fulfillment of prophecies in the present. Eusebius himself attests
to witnessing miracles.[74] The prophecies of Jesus in *Theophany* IV
relate to the future of Christianity in the generations after Jesus, such
as the acts of the apostles and disciples, persecutions, the fate of the
Jews, heresies and internal dissension among Christians, and the success of Christianity throughout the world. In Matthew 8:11, Jesus
predicts the spread of Christianity throughout the world and casts
the Jews into darkness after rejecting them (Matt. 8:12). This prophecy
was fulfilled by the fate of the Jews, living in slavery and exile, forbidden to view their holy place, even from a distance.[75] The centurion mentioned in the text symbolizes the spread of Christianity
amongst high officials in Eusebius' day. Eusebius attests to the popularity of Christianity in Persia, India, and Britain in his own times—
a fulfillment of the prophecy in Matthew 8:11 regarding the spread
of Christianity: "Many will come from east and west and sit at table
with Abraham, Isaac, and Jacob in the kingdom of heaven."

Several of Jesus' prophecies which refer directly to the apostles
and disciples, and to the worldwide acceptance of Christianity, reflect common polemical arguments. For example, Jesus selected simple,

---

[71] *Theophany* 3,80.
[72] *Theophany* 4,1.
[73] Ibid.
[74] *Theophany* 4,1. In fact, the Gospels show an awareness of the divinity of Jesus,
even on the part of a Gentile (4,2; Matt. 8:5). It is noteworthy that this Gentile,
the centurion, appears in *The Theophany* as a chiliarch, namely, captain of a thousand.
[75] *Theophany* 4,3.

ignorant folk as his apostles in order to demonstrate clearly his divine power.[76] This statement reflects the polemical argument against the lowly origins of the apostles, and its refutation by Eusebius, which we have noted previously. He emphasizes that Jesus was not only a vessel for prophecy, or a type of prophet, but also responsible for fulfillment, as manifest in the great miracles of Jesus' time which he had predicted. Eusebius refers to Jesus' prophecy to Peter and his brother Andrew: "Follow me and I will make you fishers of men" (Matt. 4:19), expanding this promise into a full-fledged sermon, an allegorical parable on the advantage of being a fisher of men over a catcher of fish. Through the power of Jesus, Simon, a poor Galilean, had caught in his wonderful net that which others could not attain, including great men such as Moses. The mighty churches of Caesarea, Antioch and Rome, which Simon founded, were full of "intelligent fish" and attested to his endeavor.[77] Peter is considered the founder of the churches of these great metropolises. Eusebius elevates Peter to a leading role in the spread of Christianity. Through his disciple Mark, he was responsible for disseminating the faith in Egypt and Alexandria, and indirectly, in Italy as well.[78] Jesus also predicted the crucifixion of Peter (John 13:36; 21:18–19). Eusebius interprets this prophecy as relating to Peter's crucifixion in Rome and as granted exclusively to him, not to all of the apostles and disciples. For only Peter was destined to end his life in a manner similar to Jesus.[79] Perhaps this emphasis on the special status of Peter was an expression of local patriotism on the part of Eusebius, a resident of Caesarea; perhaps there is also an echo of the polemic of Porphyry who, according to the fragments, attacked the leading apostles, Peter and Paul, more than the others.[80]

The historical success of Christianity throughout the world, achieved through the prophecy and power of Jesus, furnished proof beyond any doubt regarding the divinity of the Redeemer.[81] The words of Jesus in Matthew 5:14–16 were additional proof of the dissemina-

---

[76] *Theophany* 4,6.

[77] Ibid.

[78] *Theophany* 4,6.

[79] *Theophany* 4,26.

[80] On Peter in the writings of the pagan opponents of Christianity, especially Porphyry, see also A. Harnack, "Petrus in Urteil der Kirchenfeinde des Altertums", *Festgabe für Karl Müller* (Tübingen, 1922) pp. 1–6.

[81] *Theophany* 4,6.

tion of Christianity throughout the world by the disciples. In fact, Isaiah had made a prophecy regarding them and had even predicted their Galilean origins.[82] The prophecy of Jesus also spoke of the glory of Peter whose reputation spread throughout the entire world. According to Eusebius, in his time, the memory of Peter was more honored among the Romans than that of their own ancestors, and throngs of people from all over the empire would visit his venerated tomb as if it were the temple of God.[83] As in the case of Peter, the apostle John was exalted through his Gospel, which was translated into many languages and read daily by all peoples. From John's tomb in Ephesus his fame and the light of his Gospel spread throughout the world.[84] The writings of Paul also illuminated men's souls. His death as a martyr and his grave had been venerated in the city of Rome until the present.[85] In the context of Eusebius' statements about Peter, John, and Paul, his remarks on Paul seem to be a mere footnote that he felt obliged to add. His comments on Paul are considerably shorter even than his brief remarks on John. Eusebius evidently wished to grant Peter not only the position of head of the early Church in the first generation after Jesus, but also to credit him with primacy in converting the world to Christianity.[86]

The conduct of the disciples exemplified Jesus' words about the city that was set on a hill and could not be hidden (Matt. 5:14); in other words, in the way they lived, the disciples had nothing to hide.[87] For despite their poor and humble origins, they were not innocent fools or dupes, as the pagans often charged. Rather, they carefully examined the miracle of Jesus' appearance after the Resurrection, before believing it; only then did they set out to proclaim it to all humanity.[88] In these statements, Eusebius hints at doubting Thomas (John 20:25–29). The command of Jesus to his disciples:

---

[82] *Theophany* 4,7. These statements emerge from the correlation between the last part of Isaiah 9:1 and the verse that follows (Isaiah 9:2): ". . . Galilee of the nations. The people who walked in darkness have seen a great light."

[83] *Theophany* 4,7. Such passages suggest mass pilgrimages to the tomb of Peter in Eusebius' day.

[84] *Theophany* 4,7.

[85] Ibid.

[86] Lee sensed this tendency and had difficulty reconciling himself to it. He went to great effort searching Eusebius' statements for indications that the other apostles, notably Paul, were granted a status at least equal to that of Peter. See p. 222, n. 1 in his translation.

[87] *Theophany* 4,7.

[88] *Theophany* 4,8.

"Go therefore and make disciples of all nations, baptizing them in the name of the Father and of the Son and of the Holy Spirit, teaching them to observe all that I have commanded you; and lo, I am with you always, to the close of the age" (Matt. 28:19–20) combines a command, a promise, and a prophecy of future events.[89] The disciples and apostles were hesitant about the burden of their mission, particularly in light of their humble origins and lack of education. The task, however, was forced upon them because of the greatness of the miracles and acts which they had seen and experienced. The prophecy of Jesus that he would be with them "until the close of the age" related not only to them but to all who followed and accepted the teachings of Jesus. Thus Jesus was also present for all those who had become his disciples in Eusebius' day.[90] He was present among his disciples in every generation.

The words of Jesus in Luke 24:44–47 constituted a prophecy that was based on an Old Testament prediction of his suffering, death, and Resurrection on the third day, and on the repentance and forgiveness of sins, which would be proclaimed in his name among all peoples, beginning in Jerusalem. Prophecies fulfilled in the present were proof of the fulfillment of his prophecies in the past, too, such as that concerning the Resurrection.[91] Jesus' words concerning the woman who poured precious oil on his head: "Truly, I say to you wherever this gospel is preached in the whole world, what she has done will be told in memory of her", (Matt. 26:13) prophesied the way the Gospel would be proclaimed to peoples throughout the world. According to Eusebius, Jesus foretold that these words, and the story of the woman, would be written by his disciples and circulated throughout the world.[92] Here Eusebius bases his interpretation upon the change in the term, "Gospel." Alternatively, he may have thought that Jesus was referring, in a literal sense, to a book that would be called "Gospel." He interprets as a form of prophecy Jesus' words about the founding of the Church on Peter, the rock. Peter was the rock and foundation, because of his understanding that Jesus was the Christ. This understanding served as the basis of the Church—the belief in Jesus as the Redeemer. All this could be

---

[89] Ibid.
[90] *Theophany* 4,8.
[91] *Theophany* 4,9.
[92] *Theophany* 4,10.

found in Jesus' words: "... that you are Peter, and on this rock I will build my church, and the powers of death will not prevail against it" (Matt. 16:18). The second part of this prophecy, "and the powers of death will not prevail against it", were to be fulfilled during the many persecutions that did not vanquish the Church. It was surprising, said Eusebius, that Jesus mentioned the word *ecclesia* (church) in his prophecy, and not the word "synagogue", although he frequented the latter. Hence it was clear that through his spirit he foresaw the presence of Churches, namely the large Christian communities that would be established in his name long after his death.[93] Thus Jesus' prophecy distinguished between the Christian church and the Jewish synagogue in his day, at a time when there was no acknowledged differentiation.

Jesus predicted that Christianity would cause discord and quarrels within families (Matt. 10:36; Luke 12:51–54). Pagans also argued that Christianity brought about dissension, separation, and hatred amongst family members. Eusebius attests that this prophecy continued to be fulfilled in his own time. The phenomenon of families split by differences over the new faith did not take place before Jesus nor at the time of his prophecies. Moreover, no philosopher or prophet, Greek or barbarian, possessed the power to sow seeds of dissension in every home and family throughout the world. This feature was additional proof of the divine power of Jesus—the power to sow dissension. Eusebius quotes a statement by Jesus from an apocryphal Gospel, which he said existed in Hebrew among the Judeo-Christians. It is not clear whether Eusebius meant the *Gospel According to the Hebrews*, or another apocryphal work. According to this statement, Jesus selected the best from every family.[94]

Jesus not only prophesied in clear and direct pronouncements, but in parables as well. His parables included predictions of the future. The parable of the vineyard (Matt. 21:33–44) was a prophecy against the Jews. According to Eusebius, the parable of the vineyard in the book of Isaiah (Isa. 5:1–8) served as background for the parable of Jesus, which in fact completed it. Jesus supplied that which the prophet omitted. In the parable, the vintners were the leaders of the people who had murdered prophets in the past. The vineyard was the people; the tower, the Temple; the winepress, the altar. According

---

[93] *Theophany* 4,11.
[94] *Theophany* 4,12.

to the prophecy, all of the above were taken from the Jews. In the
parable, Jesus predicted the murder of the son of God by the Jews
and the destruction of Judaism. The verse, "The very stone which
the builders rejected has become the head of the corner" (Matt.
21:42; Ps. 118:14–15), actually prophesied the Resurrection of Jesus.
Further on, the vineyard became "the kingdom of God" given to
others according to the decision of the leaders of the Jews; Eusebius
asserts that, as was well known, this prophecy had been fulfilled.
The transfer of the vineyard to another people was God's act of
electing the Christians, who bore the fruits most acceptable to God
throughout the world.[95]

The parable of the invitation to the wedding banquet (Matt. 22:
1–10) predicted the events after the Resurrection of Jesus. The bride-
groom was the Logos; the bride, the rational soul; their union, the
Church; the banquet, divine food. In the parable, the servants dis-
patched to call people to the banquet were the apostles—first sent
to the Jews—the evangelists, and seventy disciples. The Jews, however, were too preoccupied with commerce (!) to take time out for
the Gospel. Furthermore, the Jews harassed the disciples and murdered three of them: Stephen, James, the brother of John, and James,
the brother of the Lord—the first martyrs of Jerusalem. Jesus had
predicted all these events in the parable. The murder of the disciples was a sequel to the murder of the prophets. The parable also
contained the prophecy of the punishment and destruction that would
be visited upon the Jews by the Roman army, evidence of which
still existed in Eusebius' time. He states that the remnants of Jerusalem's
torching by the Romans were still recognized by every visitor. Josephus had handed down detailed testimony.

Eusebius also deals with internal contradictions in Jesus' sayings
regarding the preaching of the Gospel by the apostles. On one occasion, his designated audience was the Jews; elsewhere, he insisted
that disciples work among the Gentiles. However, this apparent contradiction was easily explained: the statements of Jesus limiting the
Gospel to Israel, and those that called for the Gospel to be brought
to the Gentiles, were in fact two stages of the same process. The
first stage ended with the rejection of the Gospel by Israel, where-
upon the second began.[96]

---

[95] *Theophany* 4,13–14.
[96] *Theophany* 4,16.

Eusebius does not hide the dissension and weakness within the Church, which the pagans used in their argument against the truth of Christianity. But he repeats here his earlier assertion, that such dissension was part of Jesus' prophecy and, in this case, the parable of the wedding banquet. But Eusebius is referring to more recent internal divisions in the Church and to evil elements incorporated into the Church, along with the good. The parable already includes Jesus' condemnation of rebellious and contentious Christians.[97]

Theophany IV also contains a group of prophecies relating to the destruction of the land, the city, and the temple. Jesus' words in Matthew 23:34 are a prophecy of the persecution of the apostles and disciples, as described in Acts of the Apostles. According to this prediction, the destruction was also a punishment for shedding the blood of the righteous in the generations before Jesus.[98] Jesus' prediction of the destruction (Matt. 23:37–38; Luke 13:34–35) was fulfilled by the Romans. Eusebius elaborates upon the difference between the destruction of the First Temple, and Jesus' prophecy of the destruction of the Second Temple. Jesus foretold total and final devastation, whereas the destruction of the First Temple was temporary and served as punishment for great cruelty, idol worship, and shedding the blood of prophets. The destruction of the First Temple was temporary because the event was not stated explicitly, whereas Jesus had proclaimed in Matthew 23:38, regarding the Second Temple: "Behold your house is forsaken and desolate." In contrast, the prophet Haggai (2:9) spoke of the glory of the Second Temple about to be rebuilt. Eyewitnesses to the complete fulfillment of this prophecy included all visitors to the site. Furthermore, Jesus prophesied: "There will not be left here one stone upon another, that will not be thrown down" (Matt. 24:2). The fulfillment of that prophecy continued to the time of Eusebius, who attested that one could still see ruins of the marvelous decorations of the Temple. The ruins were preserved as fragments and not as parts of a building. The power of the prophecy continued throughout the course of history, since the ruins of buildings survived as evidence of the destruction on the Temple Mount until Eusebius' time. In many places on the Temple Mount, there were no longer ruins even of the buildings' foundations, and in the *DE*, Eusebius remarks that he had seen oxen plowing a field

---

[97] Ibid.
[98] *Theophany* 4,17.

on part of the Temple Mount. The gradual destruction of the Temple Mount, therefore, constituted the fulfillment of Jesus' prophecy, which became stronger as his power increased in the world. The growth of Jesus' might was clearly evident from the strengthening of the Church, to the point that soon, "there will not be left here one stone upon another." In fact, Eusebius admits that here and there ruins of structures remained on the Temple Mount, although Jesus' active prophetic power would, he declares, eradicate them as well.

Eusebius was aware of certain difficulties regarding the total fulfillment of the prophecy. He proposed an alternative explanation for the problem of the existence of ruins on the Temple Mount—namely, that Jesus' prophecy referred only to the buildings at which the disciples had marveled (Matt. 24:1)! He presents this solution as a Christian exegetical tradition that he had heard. Another matter that required explanation was Jesus' prediction of the conquest of the city (Luke 19:43–44). Here Eusebius thought it necessary to explain why Jesus had wept for the destruction of Jerusalem (Luke 19:41). Why should Jesus have wept over the destruction of the city's buildings and the devastation of the land? Eusebius states that he pitied the people and the destruction that awaited them, not the buildings. Here, too, it was Josephus who had described the fulfillment of the prophecy.[99]

Another prophecy relating to the destruction can be found in Luke 21:12–27. In this instance as well, Eusebius emphasized that in contrast to previous destructions, that which was prophesied by Jesus was final and absolute. Eusebius, however, was grappling with another problem. The Jerusalem of his day was a rebuilt city—the Christian Jerusalem whose fame had spread throughout the world. Therefore, Eusebius had to explain Jesus' prediction of destruction, since reality did not bear out its fulfillment. The prophecy did not mean that the city would be devoid of human habitation. Jesus' words about the destruction referred not to the city in general, but to the Jewish city. Even the words of Jesus that "Jerusalem will be trodden down by Gentiles" (Luke 21:24) meant that Gentiles would rule and dwell in Jerusalem.[100] This is Eusebius' explanation for the presence of Gentiles in Jerusalem from the time of Emperor Hadrian and, especially, in his own times.[101] Thus the prophecy meant the

---

[99] *Theophany* 4,19.
[100] See also *DE* 7,1.
[101] On the problem of interpreting the new reality of Christian Jerusalem in the

destruction of the Jewish city, the prohibition of Jewish residence in Jerusalem, and the end of religious practice in the city. The fulfillment of this prophecy was manifest in the dispersion of the Jews among the nations and the residence of Gentiles in Jerusalem. The fulfillment attested to the great wonder of the prophecy. Eusebius argues that Jews can be found among Ethiopians and Scythians, and in every corner of the earth. However, the fact that the prophecy related only to the destruction of the Jewish city and to the prohibition of Jewish residence in the new city lent it great significance. For had the city remained in ruins, one could assume that the Jews did not live there because of its desolation. Hence the particular importance of the city's reconstruction and population by Gentiles. The realization of each detail of the prophecy of destruction could be seen in the description by Josephus. Thus Jesus' prophecy not only anticipated destruction in general, but also the details described by Josephus. In his prophecy, he also advised his disciples to remove the Christian community from Jerusalem before or during the Great Revolt,[102] and envisioned in his statement, "until the times of the Gentiles are fulfilled" (Luke 21:24) the length of time that Jerusalem would be trodden by the Gentiles. According to Eusebius, Jesus meant the end of the world.[103]

In addition to detailed predictions of destruction, Jesus prophesied the end of the Jewish ritual and adherence to the laws of Moses. This prophecy (John 4:19–24), deals not only with the abandonment

---

fourth century, as opposed to official Pauline theology and the prophecy of Jesus regarding total destruction, see J. Prawer, "Christian Attitudes Towards Jerusalem in the Early Middle Ages", in J. Prawer & H. Ben-Shammai (eds.), *The History of Jerusalem: The Early Muslim Period 638–1099* (Jerusalem, 1996), pp. 311–348; A. Linder, "Jerusalem as a Focus of Confrontation between Judaism and Christianity: Anti-Jewish Views in the Jerusalem Church from the Fourth Century", in B.Z. Kedar & Z. Baras (eds.), *Jerusalem in the Middle Ages: Selected Papers* (Jerusalem, 1979), p. 12 (Hebrew); M. Poorthuis & Ch. Safrai (eds.), *The Centrality of Jerusalem* (Kampen, 1996). For Eusebius' attitude to Jerusalem and to holy places in general, see P.W.L. Walker, *Holy City, Holy Places?* Part One, and R.L. Wilken, *The Land Called Holy*, pp. 82–100. On the specific issue of Eusebius' attitude to Jerusalem as determined by internal rivalry between the Christian communities of Caesarea and Jerusalem, see Z. Rubin, "The Church of the Holy Sepulchre and the Conflict between the Sees of Caesarea and Jerusalem", *The Jerusalem Cathedra* 2 (1982), pp. 79–105.

[102] See also *HE* 3,5,3, which relates an oracular prophecy (χρησμός) given to the Jerusalem community prior to the Great Revolt, telling it to depart for Pella in the Transjordan, and does not mention a prophecy made by Jesus during his lifetime. *Theophany* IV, 21–22, includes lengthy quotations from *The Jewish War* as evidence of the fulfillment of Jesus' prophecies of destruction.

[103] *Theophany* 4,22.

of Mosaic Law and Jewish worship in the Temple of Jerusalem, but also the end of the Samaritan worship on Mt Gerizim and their observance of the Law. In contrast, Jesus proposes a form of worship befitting God, which would take place in the Church.[104] Eusebius' comments relating to this prophecy reflect certain problems not hitherto encountered in his works. For even if the Jewish religious center and religious practice in Jerusalem were destroyed, observance of the Law, nonetheless continued to exist in some form among the Samaritans on Mt Gerizim. Thus Jesus' prophecy regarding the end of sacrifices had to pertain to the Samaritans as well. Eusebius states that during the reigns of Vespasian and Hadrian, both religious centers, in Jerusalem and on Mt Gerizim, were devastated. His statements regarding Mt Gerizim and Shechem also refer to a pagan cult that existed there for a time. He refrains any mention of a Samaritan cult on Mt Gerizim in his day. Perhaps he was satisfied that Jesus' prophecy concerning the Samaritans had at least been fulfilled in the past.[105] This prophecy was also valid regarding the other aspect of the cessation of sacrifices. For the true worship was that of the "spirit" and the "truth", in contrast to the Jews and Samaritans; this fact also explained the Christians' divergence from the Jewish religion.[106]

Jesus predicted that his teachings would spread among the Gentiles and would bring about their redemption.[107] He prophesied that his death would bring redemption to many, namely, to the Gentiles (John 12:23–24). As we have noted regarding the centurion (*i.e.* chiliarch), Eusebius was interested in discovering the Gospel to the Gentiles in the words and deeds of Jesus, and their recognition of his divinity during Jesus' lifetime. Therefore he interprets John 12:20 ("Now among those who went up to worship at the feast were some Greeks") as referring to Gentile Greeks and not Hellenistic Jews on pilgrimage. He concludes that Jesus uttered this prophecy to the Greeks who approached him. Eusebius even proposes the unusual argument that Jesus spent a lot of time with Jews because they knew the prophecies concerning him.[108] Here there may be traces of the

---

[104] *Theophany* 4,23.
[105] Ibid.
[106] *Theophany* 4,23.
[107] *Theophany* 4,24; John 10:14–17.
[108] *Theophany* 4,25.

pagan criticism that Jesus appeared before the Jews—a remote, uncivilized people in an unfortunate corner of the world—rather than in a major center of culture before the leaders of the empire. In any case, we can definitely discern an apologetic need to tone down the conspicuous jewishness of Jesus in the Gospels.

Jesus predicted the many persecutions awaiting his disciples in later generations (Matt. 5:11–12; 10:17). Eusebius gives a brief explanation of the persecutions, similar to that in the *DE*.[109] The persecutions were neither a divine punishment nor a test of strength before final victory. They occurred for their own sake, in order to prove and bear witness to the Redeemer. It was a great and unique wonder that no other teacher throughout history had prophesied persecutions as testimony to his disciples. This marvelous prophecy, which was fulfilled, served as further proof of the divine power of Jesus.[110] He predicted that subsequent generations would accuse him and his disciples of tempting men with magic and associating with demons. Eusebius attests to the fact that this argument was prevalent in his own time. Jesus himself had stated that this claim would be refuted by the sound moral quality of his disciples' lives and beliefs.[111] Jesus had predicted not only the heroic deeds of Christians during the persecutions, but also every detail of those historical events. In Matthew 10:21, he predicted the vacillation on the part of many Christians, and their participation in the cult of demons, in order to save themselves during the persecutions.[112] Jesus foresaw the heresies that would arise in the Church in his name, mainly in the form of Gnostic and Manichean teachings.[113] The parable in Matthew 13:24–31 and 13:36–43 predicted future heresies, with Satan sowing in men's hearts the seeds of heresy together with the seeds of faith. Eusebius offers an interesting interpretation for the term "Son of Man" as applied to Jesus. Jesus called himself "Son of Man" because of the time he spent among men. In the parable in Matthew, Jesus predicted that heretics all over the world would possess false scriptures and gospels in which his statements would be mixed with antithetical pronouncements and falsehoods attributed to him, which

---

[109] See Chapter 7 of this study.
[110] *Theophany* 4,27. We have encountered this argument in the *DE*. See also Chapter 6 of this study.
[111] *Theophany* 4,31.
[112] *Theophany* 4,28.
[113] *Theophany* 4,30; Matt. 7:15–17.

reflected their ideas. Eusebius declares that such works were in circulation in his own time—some attributed to heretical figures, such as Mani, Marcion, and others.[114]

Jesus foresaw the social-religious situation at the time of Eusebius. Matthew 19:9–12 constitutes a prophecy of the ascetic ways of many Christian men and women, who would lead lives of holiness and virginity, as stated by Eusebius in the *DE*.[115] He is not referring to the nascent monastic movement, but rather linking the ideal of abstinence to preparations for the imminent Kingdom of Heaven. He attests that he knew many Christians who applied literally the words of Jesus: "There are eunuchs who have made themselves eunuchs for the sake of the kingdom of heaven" (Matt. 19:12); there were similar reports concerning Origen.[116] In this act, Eusebius saw the wonderful fulfillment of the prophecy of Jesus in all its detail, and proof of the truth of his divine pronouncements.[117] On the other hand, Jesus' prophecy showed his awareness that Christianity would become a new social reality as a religion of the masses in later generations, especially after its victory. He spoke of those who converted to Christianity out of impure motives, and of their eventual punishment (Matt. 13:47–50). Here Eusebius recognizes that the large Church would not be monolithic and would include adherents who were good and evil, strong and weak. He attests to the Church's internal dissent and weaknesses in the Church in his day, as prophesied by Jesus.[118] The parable of the sower in Matthew 13:3–9 predicted three types of people who would accept his teaching out of base motives, in contrast to three kinds of good people who would accept Christianity in good faith. Likewise, his parable predicted three main motives for corrupting the seed of faith. Eusebius attests to many different kinds of people who became Christian but could not maintain their faith because of weakness, temptation, and various difficulties. He does not give details regarding those who were strong or weak in their faith.[119]

---

[114] *Theophany* 4,34.

[115] See Chapter 4 of this study.

[116] *HE* 6,8,1–3.

[117] *Theophany* 4,32. In fact, in *HE* (ibid.), he wrote that voluntary castration was an adolescent and immature act, despite the fact that it was proof of faith and self-control. Origen interpreted the words of Jesus too literally and radically.

[118] *Theophany* 4,29.

[119] *Thophany* 4,33.

Jesus predicted false Messiahs who would come in his name in the future, like a second coming of Christ (Matt. 24:3–5; 24:23–27); one such impostor was Dositheus, a contemporary of the apostles, who persuaded the Samaritans that he was the one of whom Moses had spoken (Deut. 18:15–19). He had fooled some so successfully that they declared him to be the Christ. Some regarded Simon Magus as the Christ who had returned; others thought it was Montanus of Phrygia; some regarded yet other people as the Christ in various places and at different times, up to Eusebius' day. However, as Jesus had taught, to prevent any mistake, his triumphant return would not resemble his first advent—limited to a single place in one corner of the world, and as a human being—but as ". . . lightning which emerges from the East and sheds light to the West, thus will be the coming of the 'Son of Man'."[120] The Second Coming would take place simultaneously across the entire world, unlike his local manifestation in the Incarnation. These claims bring to mind the well-known pagan arguments against the appearance of Jesus in a remote corner of the world. According to Eusebius, Matthew 24:6–14 predicted that, as a necessary preliminary to the End of Days, the Gospel would be promulgated throughout the world. Then, when only a few people did not possess the Gospel, the End of Days would take place.[121] Here we may sense from the words of Eusebius that he felt the end of the world was imminent; the persecutions carried out in his day augured the end of days, which would be fulfilled in his time.[122]

The words of Jesus contained many prophecies that had not yet been fulfilled. Just as many prophecies had come true before Eusebius' time, many others would be fulfilled in the future.[123] We may recall that Eusebius had used this argument to strengthen the belief in the fulfillment of Jesus' prophecies during Jesus' lifetime, or in the generations between Jesus and himself. Thus the realization of certain prophecies in the present attested to the fulfillment of the others, in both the past and the future.

In the final chapter of Book IV, Eusebius summarizes the argument

---

[120] *Theophany* 4,35 (Matt. 24:28).
[121] *Theophany* 4,36.
[122] Ibid. A brief discussion on the eschatological aspect at the end of *The Theophany* can be found in Theilman, "Another Look at the Eschatology of Eusebius of Caesarea", pp. 232–233.
[123] *Theophany* 4,34.

based on the prophecies of Jesus. The fulfillment of the prophecies
was proof of his divine manifestation and of the divinity of his actions.
Whereas in the past, such prophecies were simply heard, at present,
their fulfillment was manifest, and everyone could see that Jesus'
deeds were in the realm of the supernatural. Thus the prophecies
of Jesus and their fulfillment in the present constituted clear proof
of the divinity of Christ. Eusebius knew that such proof would not
suffice to persuade the staunchest enemies of the truth; on the other
hand, their opposition could not jeopardize the power of the proof.
In fact, he adduces additional proof of the truths of the Gospel
and the divinity of the Redeemer, in order to convince those still
in doubt. Here Eusebius states explicitly that he intends to present
again those facts investigated previously for the benefit of opponents
not yet persuaded by earlier evidence.[124] Here, he clearly means *DE*
III, which was meant mainly for pagan opponents who had not yet
acknowledged Scripture as proof. Such is the framework for *Theophany* V, which is no more than a long extrapolation from *DE* III.
He repeats these statements almost verbatim in the introduction to
Theophany V—virtually the only part of *Theophany* V not copied directly
from *DE* III. Here he explicitly refers to the *DE* as his source.[125]

It seems that the special significance which *The Theophany* attributes to Jesus' prophecies and their fulfillment, as testimony to his
divinity and the truth of the Gospel—in contrast to their marginal
importance in the *DE*—derives from the historic change that the
Church had undergone between the writing of the two works. Eusebius wrote the *DE* in a period of uncertainty and instability, either
during or immediately after the persecutions, and tried to minimize
his use of evidence from the New Testament in his arguments on
the truth of Christianity. Even if *Theophany* IV was based mainly on
the compilation of Jesus' prophecies written before the *PE*, Eusebius
did not wish to use it extensively in the *DE*.[126] In contrast, the sense
of triumph and exaltation that accompanied the enormous victory of

---

[124] *Theophany* 4,37.

[125] From this point *The Theophany* recapitulates statements from *DE* 3,3–7, responding to the arguments against Jesus and the apostles, and the charge of magic and
charlatanism, and presenting moral argument as response, expounded in Chapter
6 of this study.

[126] Unless we opt for the assumption that the work, or part of it, was incorporated in the lost second part of the *DE*, by reason of its extensive treatment of
Jesus' prophecies relating to subsequent generations—a feature that may have corresponded to the putative plan of the ten lost books of the *DE*.

Christianity, brought about a change of concept and emphasis. The marvelous victory could only be understood as a divine wonder, a great miracle, and the complete fulfillment of the prophecies of Jesus. Hence the total confidence that this fulfillment was clear to any beholder, and worth the testimony of a thousand witnesses to the divinity of Christ and his divine activity throughout history. This feeling of elation caused Eusebius to see himself as poised on the final run of history, and his time as the last days before the return of the Redeemer. The conditions had been fulfilled and time was short. However, he does not give free rein to his expression and, in fact, restrains himself. We may now better understand the major role of the collection of Jesus' prophecies and their fulfillment in *The Theophany*. As we have noted, Eusebius makes a distinction between the prophecies of Jesus that had come true in his own day, and those that were realized in subsequent generations, up to Eusebius' own time. Others had yet to be fulfilled. Virtually all the prophecies recorded by Eusebius were those fulfilled between Jesus' time and his own. The reason for this selection may be found in Eusebius' conviction that Jesus' great prophecies were coming true before his very eyes. It was less important, therefore, to include prophecies that had been fulfilled in Jesus' time or shortly afterwards, for being in the distant past, these were difficult to prove directly and were easily subjected to doubt. By the same token, there was no real reason to deal with eschatological prophecies. The newly enhanced status and significance attributed to these prophecies in his final apologetic work perhaps reflects a sense of superiority and power over the pagans, as evinced by the shift in tone in this apologetic-polemical work, from the defensive to the moralizing.[127] Freed from the tactical limitations of polemics and apologetics dictated by a position of inferiority, the author was able to promulgate his theological positions more forcefully.

In fact, *The Theophany* may be considered a popular apologetic review, in which Eusebius integrated the main points of some forty years of apologetic-polemical writing, becoming confident and complacent in light of Christianity's dramatic elevation to a position of predominance in the ancient pagan world.

---

[127] There is no mention of any direct polemic against Porphyry in *The Theophany*. He is not referred to by name despite the fact that he is quoted three times. The quotations, however, are taken directly from the *PE*. See Gressmann, *Studien*, p. 151.

CONCLUSION

Eusebius began his apologetic-polemical writing early in his literary career. The new polemics against Christianity, written by pagan authors, especially Porphyry, demanded a fresh, up-to-date response to the new challenge. Literary polemics quickly became linked to the socio-religious attacks on Christianity by the authorities. From the moment he joined the campaign, Eusebius never forsook the struggle and his apologetic works became a major part of his literary activity. Many of his writings have a distinctly apologetic character. Even those works that are not particularly apologetic-polemical in content have apologetic motives and motifs. He had in mind a specific audience and well-defined goals for early apologetic works such as those refuting the polemics of Hierocles and Porphyry, the *General Basic Introduction*, and texts composed to resolve the difficulties and contradictions in the Gospels that had been targeted by pagan critics. Eusebius' early works outline the major concepts and motifs that would be fully expanded and refined in his great apologetic project, the *PE-DE*.

This two-part work was conceived as a comprehensive response to the attacks of all the enemies of Christianity. Its encyclopedic structure relates to several major pagan arguments raised by the pagan-Christian polemic, rather than refuting individually the many different charges leveled by pagan polemicists, although several of their secondary arguments can also be found in the text. The main part of the *PE* is a critique of the philosophy and forms of pagan religion, for which Eusebius adduces copious quotations from pagan, Jewish, and Christian scholars. However, Eusebius saw the main thrust of his work as the presentation and demonstration of the truths of Christianity; this was the affirmative aspect of his apologetic undertaking—first in the *PE*, but mainly in the *DE*. This section of his work is distinguished by the way in which Eusebius deals with the problems posed by polemics.

In the course of this endeavor, Eusebius formulated his principal concepts and arguments. Thus the central concept of Christian prehistory evolved as a reply to the two-fold pagan argument that Christians had abandoned the traditions of their ancestors and deserted the gods for a strange and alien religion, and that they had perversely betrayed Judaism in order to blaze a convoluted trail in the wilderness guided by ignorance and irrationality. The reply to the second part of the argument also includes the refutation of Jewish arguments against Christianity—arguments that were actually expounded in the Jewish-Christian debate, or else, perhaps, presented by Christian apologists as Jewish arguments within the framework of the pagan-Christian polemic. Eusebius' main arguments are based on prophecy and miracles, but these became problematic in light of pagan criticism. Thus Eusebius had to examine these arguments and reformulate the fundamental principles of his work, which he had derived from many earlier apologetic texts, notably Origen's *Against Celsus*. On the other hand, motifs that had appeared only briefly in these writings were revised and expanded in his large work. He pledges that he will be a fair opponent, presenting an objective account of his rivals' views, and he states that his polemic is honest and unprejudiced. Nevertheless, he frequently resorts to rhetoric to cover the weak points in his argument. Considering, however, the sarcastic and caustic style of pagan polemics, Eusebius manages to keep his promise.

We have noted the major influence of Porphyry in stimulating Eusebius' earlier polemical writing. The question of Porphyry's role in *PE-DE* is more problematic. Although Porphyry was a key figure behind the work, close scrutiny of the text shows that Eusebius did not want the work to be seen as just another refutation of Porphyry's *Against the Christians*. There is no direct polemic against arguments presented in the latter work, despite the fact that pagan arguments identical to Porphyry's appear anonymously as the fundamental points around which *PE-DE* is structured. Direct polemic against Porphyry relates to him only as the leading representative of pagan philosophy and chief commentator on religion of his day; also targeted are his statements in various works, but not the criticism expressed in *Against the Christians*. Thus even if it was Porphyry's polemic that motivated the writing of *PE-DE*, the purpose of Eusebius' work extends beyond any limited polemic against Porphyry. In this work, Eusebius embarked on a comprehensive campaign against pagan culture, along with a defense of Christian tenets. Porphyry plays a leading role in the campaign, in the course of which his status and authority are undermined, thus devaluing his critique of Christianity.

Moreover, Porphyry himself contributes many statements to the critique of pagan philosophy and religion, and even appears to attest to the truth of Christianity.

The Theophany, Eusebius' last apologetic work written near the end of his life, is an abridgment and simplification of his major ideas in *PE-DE*. But it also contains new emphases and perspectives with regard to several issues. In addition, *The Theophany* introduces new material, not found in his other compositions, and probably taken from earlier, lost works. Examples include the detailed discussion of the Resurrection of Jesus and the detailed treatment in Book IV of the prophecies of Jesus as a major argument and proof of the truths of Christianity. The additions and new viewpoints reflect the great change undergone by Eusebius in the period between the *DE* and *The Theophany*, when euphoria reigned in the wake of the dramatic events that changed the course of Christianity in his generation.

This study has traced the development of Eusebius' apologetic-polemical writing. I have dealt with the main factors that shaped his great apologetic project, in the *PE-DE*, by closely examining the polemical context which formed his views, and the emergence of ideas from his experience of contending with pagan criticism. His intensive apologetic enterprise testifies to the vitality of pagan-Christian polemics in his day, and the importance of such writing for Eusebius and his contemporaries.

I have limited the scope of this study to a discussion of Eusebius' works and earlier apologetic literature, and have not broached the subject of his influence on subsequent apologetics. Porphyry's legacy to pagan polemics against Christianity in subsequent generations has been partially investigated by other scholars. In contrast, the influence of Eusebius on Christian apologetic literature has received only scant attention. Further study of this subject could reveal that his impact was considerable.

BIBLIOGRAPHY

Adler, W., "The Jews as Falsifiers: Charges of Tendentious Emendations in Anti-Jewish Christian Polemics", in *Translations of Scripture: Proceedings of a Conference at the Annenberg Research Institute, May 15, 1989* (Philadelphia, 1990), 1–27.

———, "Eusebius' Chronicle and Its Legacy", in H.W. Attridge and G. Hata (eds.), *Eusebius, Chirstianity, and Judaism*, (Detroit, 1992), pp. 467–491.

Aland, K., "The Relation between Church and State in Early Times: A Reinterpretation", *Journal of Theological Studies*, 19 (1968), pp. 115–127.

Altheim. F. & Stiehl, R., "Neue Bruckstücke aus Porphyrios *Kata Christianon*", *Gedenkschrift G. Rohde, Aparchai, Untersuchungen zur klassischen Philologie und Geschichte des Altertums* 4 (1961), pp. 23–38.

Amand, D., *Fatalisme et liberté dans l'antiquité grecque*, (Amsterdan, 1973).

Amir, Y., "Moses as the Author of the Torah in Philo", *Proceedings of the Israel Academy of Science*, 20,6 (1980), pp. 83–103 (Hebrew).

Anastos, M.V., "Porphyry's Attack on the Bible", *The Classical Tradition: Literary and Historical Studies in Honor of Harry Caplan* (Ithaca, N.Y., 1966), pp. 421–450.

Andresen, C., *Logos und Nomos, Die Polemik des Kelsos wider das Christentum* (Berlin, 1955).

Attridge, H.W., "The Philosophical Critique of Religion under the Early Empire", *ANRW* 16,1 (1978), pp. 45–78.

Avi-Yonah, M., *The Jews under Roman and Byzantine Rule* (Jerusalem, 1984).

Bacher, W., *Die Agada der palästinensischen Amoräer*, Vol. 1–3 (Strassburg, 1892–1899).

Bardy, G., "Saint Jérome et ses maîtres hébreux", *Revue Bénédictine* 46 (1934), pp. 145–164.

———, "La Théologie d'Eusèbe de Césarée d'après l'Histoire ecclésiastique", *Revue d'histoire ecclésiastique* 50 (1955), pp. 5–20.

Barnard, L.W., *Athenagoras, a Study in Second Century Apologetics*, Paris 1972 (*Théologie historique* 18).

———, "Early Christian Art as Apologetic", *Journal of Religious History* 10 (1978), pp. 20–31.

Barnes, T.D., "Porphyry against the Christians: Date and Attribution of the fragments", *Journal of Theological Studies*, N.S. 24 (1973), pp. 424–442.

———, "Sossianus Hierocles and the Antecedents of the 'Great Persecution'", *Harvard Studies in Classical Philology* 80 (1976), pp. 239–252.

———, *Constantine and Eusebius* (Cambridge, Mass., 1981).

———, *The New Empire of Diocletian and Constantine* (Cambridge, Mass., 1982).

———, "Scholarship or Propaganda? Porphyry *Against the Christians* and its Historical Setting", *Bulletin of the Institute of Classical Studies* 39 (1994), pp. 53–65.

Barthelemy, D., "Eusèbe, la Septante, et 'les autres'", *La Bible et les Pères* (Paris, 1971), pp. 51–65.

Baskin, J.R., *Pharaoh's Counselors; Job, Jethro, and Balaam in Rabbinic and Patristic Tradition* (Chico, 1983).

Baynes, N.H., "Eusebius and the Christian Empire", *Mélanges Bidez* (Brussels, 1934), pp. 13–18.

Benko, S., "Pagan Criticism of Christianity During the First Two Centuries A.D.", *ANRW* 23, I, pp. 1055–1117.

Benoît, A., "La 'Contra Christianos' de Porphyre: où en est la collection des Fragments", *Paganisme, Judaisme, Christianisme, Mélanges offerts à Marcel Simon* (Paris, 1978), pp. 263–270.

Benz, E., "Christus und Sokrates in der alten Kirche: Ein Beitrag zum altkirchlichen

Verständnis des Martyrers und des Martyrium", *Zeitschrift für die neutestamentliche Wissenschaft*, 23 (1950–51), pp. 195–224.

Berkhof, H., *Die Theologie des Eusebius von Caesarea* (Amsterdam, 1939).

Bevan, E., *Holy Images: An Inquiry into Idolatry and Image-Worship in Ancient Paganism and Christianity* (London, 1940).

Bidez, J., *Vie de Porphyre* (Ghent, 1913).

Bidez, J., and F. Cumont, *Les Mages hellénisés* (Paris, 1938).

Binder, G., "Eine Polemik des Porphyrios gegen die allegorische Auslegung des Alten Testaments durch die Christen", *Zeitschrift für Papyrologie und Epigraphik* 3 (1968), pp. 81–95.

Boer, W. Den, "A Pagan Historian and His Enemies: Porphyry against the Christians", *Classical Philology* 69 (1974), pp. 198–208.

Bowersock, G. W., *Greek Sophists in the Roman Empire* (Oxford, 1969).

Bowie, E.L., "Apollonius of Tyana, Tradition and Reality", *ANRW* II,16,2 (1978), pp. 1652–1699.

Brown, P., *The Making of Late Antiquity*, (Cambridge, Mass., 1976).

Bruns, J.E., "The 'Agreement of Moses and Jesus' in the *Demonstratio Evangelica* of Eusebius", *Vigiliae Christianae* 31 (1977), pp. 117–125.

Buffière, F., *Les mythes d'Homère et la pensée grecque* (Paris, 1956).

Calderone, S., "Il penserio politico di Eusebio di Cesarea", in G. Bonamente & A. Nestori (eds.), *I Christiani e l'ipero nel IV secolo* (Macerata, 1988), pp. 45–54.

Cameron, A., "The Date of Porphyry's *Kata Christianon*", *Classical Quarterly* N.S. 17 (1967), pp. 382–384.

Cameron, Av., "Eusebius' *Vita Constantini* and the Construction of Constantine", in M. Eduards & S. Suain (eds.), *Portraits: Biographical Representations in the Greek and Latin Literature of the Roman Empire* (Oxford, 1997), pp. 145–173.

Carolo, E. dal, "La filosofia tripartita nella Praeparatio Evangelica di Eusebio di Cesarea", *Rivista di storia e letteratura religiosa*, 24 (1988), 515–523.

Chadwick, H., *Origen: Contra Celsum* (Cambridge, 1953).

——, *Early Christian Thought and the Classical Tradition* (Oxford, 1966).

Chesnut, G.F., "Fate, Fortune, Free Will and Nature in Eusebius of Caesarea", *Church History* 42 (1973), pp. 165–182.

——, *The First Christian Histories, Eusebius, Socrates, Sozomen, Theodoret and Evagrius*², (Macon, 1986).

Chuvin, P., *Chronique des derniers païens* (Paris, 1990).

Coman, J., "Utilisation des Stromates de Clément d'Alexandrie par Eusèbe de Césarée dans la Preparation Evangélique", *TU*, 125 (1981), pp. 115–134.

Courcelle, P., "Propos anti-chrétiens rapportés par Saint Augustin", *Recherches augustiniennes* 1 (1958), pp. 149–186.

——, "Critiques exégétiques et arguments anti-chrétiens rapportés par Ambrosiaster", *Vigiliae Christianae*, 13 (1959) pp. 133–169.

Crafer, T.W., "The Work of Porphyry against the Christians and Its Reconstruction", *Journal of Theological Studies* 15 (1914), pp. 360–395, 481–512.

Croke, B., "Porphyry's Anti-Christian Polemic", *Journal of Theological Studies* N.S. 34 (1983), pp. 168–185.

——, "The Era of Porphyry's Anti-Christian Polemic", *Journal of Religious History* 13 (1984/5), pp. 1–14.

Crouzel, H., "L'Ecole d'Origène a Césarée", *Bulletin de littérature ecclésiastique* 71 (1970), pp. 15–27.

——, "Les Critiques addressés par Méthode et ses contemporains à la doctrine origénienne du corps ressuscité", *Gregorianum* 53 (1972), pp. 679–716.

Cumont, F., *Astrology and Religion among the Greeks and Romans* (New York, 1912).

——, "Les anges du paganisme", *Revue de l'histoire des religions*, 72 (1915), pp. 159–182.

———, *Lux Perpetua* (Paris, 1949).

Curti, C., "L'esegesi di Eusebio di Cesarea: Caratteri e sviluppo", in *Eusebiana, I: Commentarii in Psalmos* (Catania, 1987), pp. 195–213.

Daniélou, J., "Les sources juives de la doctrine des anges des nations chez Origène", *Recherches de science religieuse*, 38 (1951), pp. 132–137.

De Lange, N.R.M., *Origen and the Jews* (Cambridge, 1976).

DeMarolle, J.M., "Un aspect de la polémique païenne à la fin du IIIᵉ siècle: le vocabulaire chrétien de Porphyre", *Vigiliae Christianae* 26 (1972), pp. 87–104.

Dillon, J., "Iamblichus of Chalcis", *ANRW* 2, 36:2 (1987), pp. 863–909.

Dodds, E.R., *The Greeks and the Irrational* (Berkley, 1951).

Doergens, H., "Apollonius von Tyana in Parallele zu Christus dem Herren", *Theologie und Glaube* 25 (1933), pp. 292–304.

Dorival, G., "Un astre se lèvera de Jacob. L'interprétation ancienne de Nombre 24,17", *Annali di storia dell'esegesi* 13 (1996), pp. 295–353.

Drake, H.A., *In Praise of Constantine: A Historical Study and New Translation of Eusebius' Tricennial Orations* (Berkeley, 1976).

Drogge, A.J., "The Apologetic Dimensions of the Ecclesiastical History", in Attridge & Hata (eds.), *Eusebius, Christianity, and Judaism*, pp. 492–509.

Ehrhardt, C.T.H.R., "Eusebius and Celsus", *Jahrbuch für Antike und Christentum* 22 (1979), pp. 40–49.

Faulhaber, M., *Die griechischen Apologeten der klassischen Väterzeit. I. Buch. Eusebius von Cäsarea* (Würzburg, 1895).

Fedou, M., *Christianisme et religion païenne dans le Contre Celse d'Origène* (Paris, 1988).

Festugière, A.J., "Sur une nouvelle édition du 'De Vita pythagorica' de Jamblique", *Revue des études grecques* 50 (1937), pp. 489–494.

Fisher, E.A., "Greek Translations of Latin Literature in the Fourth Century AD", *Yale Classical Studies* 27 (1982), pp. 173–215.

Flusser, D., "The Jewish Origins of Christianity", in idem., *Jewish Sources in Early Christianity* (Tel Aviv, 1979), pp. 418–447 (Hebrew).

Foakes-Jackson, F.J., *Eusebius Pamphili* (Cambridge, 1933).

Frend, W.H.C., *Martyrdom and Persecution in the Early Church* (Oxford, 1965).

———, "Prelude to the Great Persecution: The Propaganda War", *Journal of Ecclesiastical History* 38 (1987), pp. 1–18.

Gager, J.G., *Moses in Graeco-Roman Paganism* (Nashville-New York, 1972).

Gallagher, E.V., "Eusebius the Apologist: The Evidence of the *Preparation* and the *Proof*", *Studia Patristica* 26 (1993), pp. 251–260.

Geffcken, J., *Zwei griechische Apologeten* (Leipzeg-Berlin, 1907).

——— *The Last Days of Greco-Roman Paganism* (Amsterdam-New York-London, 1978), an English translation of the second German edition of 1929.

Goulet, R., *Makarios Magnes, Monogenes*. Introduction générale, Traduction et Commentaire, Thèse inédite (Paris, 1974).

———, "Porphyre et la datation de Moïse", *Revue de l'histoire des religions* 184 (1977), pp. 137–164.

———, "Porphyre et Macaire de Magnésie", *Studia Patristica* 15 = *TU* 128 (1984), pp. 448–452.

Grant, R.M., *Miracle and Natural Law in Graeco-Roman and Early Christian Thought* (Amsterdam, 1952).

———, "Early Alexandrian Christianity", *Church History* 40 (1971), pp. 133–144.

———, "Porphyry among the Early Christians", *Romanitas and Christianitas* (Amsterdam-London, 1973), pp. 181–187.

———, "The Religion of Maximin Daia", *Christianity Judaism and other Greco-Roman Cults, Studies for Morton Smith at Sixty*, ed. J. Neusner (Leiden, 1975), pp. 143–166.

———, "Eusebius and his Early Lives of Origen", in *Forma Futuri: Studi in honore del Cardinale Michele Pellegrino* (Turin, 1975), pp. 635–649.

————, "Eusebius, Josephus and the Fate of the Jews", *Society of Biblical Literature 1979 Seminar Papers*, V. 2, Missoula, Montana, pp. 69–86.

————, "Civilization as a Preparation for Christianity in the Thought of Eusebius", *Continuity and Discontinuity in Church History. Essays presented to George Huntson Williams*, ed. F. Forrester Church and T. George (Leiden, 1979), pp. 62–70.

————, *Eusebius as Church Historian* (Oxford, 1980).

————, *Greek Apologists of the Second Century* (Philadelphia, 1988).

————, "Eusebius and Imperial Propaganda", in: Attridge & Hata (eds.), *Eusebius, Christianity, and Judaism* (Detroit, 1992), pp. 658–680.

Gressmann, H., *Studien zu Eusebs Theophanie*, *TU* 23,3 (1903).

Gronewald, M., "Porphyrios Kritik an den Gleichnissen des Evangeliums", *ZPE* 3 (1968) p. 96.

Hagedorn, D. & Merkelbach, R., "Ein neues Fragment aus Porphyrios 'Gegen die Christen'", *Vigiliae Christianae* 20 (1966), pp. 86–90.

Hägg, T., "Hierocles the Lover of Truth and Eusebius the Sophist", *Symbolae Osloenses* 67 (1992), pp. 138–150.

Harl, M., "L'histoire de l'humanité racontée par un écrivain chrétien au début du IVe siècle", *Revue des Études Grecques* 75 (1962), pp. 522–529.

Harnack, A., "Die Altercatio Simonis Judaei et Theophili Christiani, nebst Untersuchungen über die antijüdische Polemik in der alten Kirche", *Texte und Untersuchungen zur Geschichte der altchristlichen Literatur* 1,3, 1883.

————, "Die Griechiesche Übersetzung des 'Apologeticus' Tertulians", *TU* 8.4 (1892) pp. 1–36.

————, *Geschichte der altchristliche Literatur bis Eusebius* (Leipzig, 1893) I.

————, *Die Chronologie der altchristlichen Literatur bis Eusebius* II (Leipzig, 1904).

————, *The Expansion of Christianity in the First Three Centuries* (New York, 1905).

————, "Kritik des Neuen Testament von einem griechischen Philosophen des 3 Jahrhunderts", *TU* 37, 4 (1911).

————, *Porphyrius "Gegen die Christen", 15 Bücher: Zeugnisse, Fragmente und Referate* (Berlin, 1916).

————, "Neue Fragmente des Werkes des Porphyrius gegen die Christen", *Sitzungsberichte der preußischen Akademie der Wissenschaften* (1921), pp. 266–284; 834–835.

————, "Petrus in Urteil der Kirchenfeinde des Altertums", *Festgabe für Karl Müller* (Tübingen, 1922) pp. 1–6.

Hawthorne, A.F., "Tatian and His Discourse to the Greeks", *Harvard Theological Review* 57 (1964), pp. 161–188.

Hirshman, M., *A Rivalry of Genius, Jewish and Christian Biblical Interpretation in Late Antiquity* (New York, 1996).

Hoffmann, R.J., *Porphyry's Against the Christians, the Literary Remains* (Amherst, N.Y., 1994).

Hollerich, M.J., "Religion and Politics in the writings of Eusebius: Reassessing the first 'Court Theologian'" *Church History* 59 (1990), pp. 309–325.

————, "Eusebius as a Polemical Interpreter of Scripture", in Attridge and Hatta (eds.), *Eusebius, Christianity, and Judaism* (Detroit, 1992), pp. 585–615.

————, *Eusebius of Caesarea's Commentary on Isaiah: Christian Exegesis in the Age of Constantine* (Oxford, 1999).

Hulen, A.B., "The Dialogues with the Jews as Sources for the Early Jewish Arguments against Christianity", *Journal of Biblical Literature* 51 (1932), pp. 58–70.

————, *Porphyry's Work against the Christians: An Interpretation* (New Haven, 1933).

Irshai, O., "R. Abbahu said: 'If a man should say to you "I am God"—he is a liar'", *Zion* 47 (1982), pp. 173–177 (Hebrew).

Junod, E., "Polémique crétienne contre Apollonius de Tyane", *Revue de théologie et de philosophie* 120 (1988), 475–482.

Kannengiesser, C., "Eusebius of Caesarea, Origenist", in H.W. Attridge and G. Hata (eds.), *Eusebius, Christianity and Judaism* (Detroit, 1992), 435–466.

Keller, E., *Eusèbe: historien de persécution* (Geneva, 1912).

Kertsch, M., "Traditionelle Rhetorik und Philosophie in Eusebius' Antirrhetikos gegen Hierokles", *Vigiliae Christianae* 34 (1980), pp. 145–171.

Knauber, A., "Das Anliegen der Schule des Origenes zu Caesarea", *Münchener Theologische Zeitschrift* 19 (1968), pp. 182–203.

Kofsky, A., "Eusebius of Caesarea and the Christian-Jewish Polemic", in O. Limor & G.G. Stroumsa (eds.), *Contra Iudaeos: Ancient and Medieval Polemics between Christian and Jews* (Tübingen, 1996), pp. 59–83.

———, "Prophecy in the Service of Polemics in Eusebius of Caesarea", *Christianesimo nella storia* 19 (1998), pp. 1–29.

Krauss, S., "The Jews in the Writings of the Church Fathers", *Jewish Quarterly Review* 6 (1894), pp. 82–99.

Krivouchine, I., "L'époque préchrétienne dans l'*Histoire Ecclésiastique* d'Eusèbe de Césarée", *Traditio* 51 (1996), pp. 287–294.

Labriolle, P. de, *La Réaction païenne* (Paris, 1934).

Lachs, S.T., "Rabbi Abbahu and the Minim", *Jewish Quarterly Review* n.s. 60 (1969), pp. 197–212.

Lamberton, R., *Homer the Theologian. Neoplatonist Allegorical Reading and the Growth of the Epic Tradition* (Berkeley, 1986).

Lampe, G.W.H., "Miracles and Early Christian Apologetic", *Miracles: Cambridge Studies in their Philosophy and History*, ed. C.F.D. Moule (London, 1965), pp. 205–218.

Laurin, J.R., *Orientations maîtresses des Apologistes chrétiens de 270 à 361* (Rome, 1954 = *Analecta Gregoriana* 61).

Levine, L.I., *Caesarea under Roman Rule* (Leiden, 1975).

Levison, J.R., "The Prophetic Spirit as an Angel According to Philo", *Harvard Theological Review*, 88 (1995), pp. 189–207.

Lieberman, S., "The Martyrs of Caesarea", *Annuaire de l'institut de philologie et d'histoire orientales et slaves* 7 (1939–1944), pp. 395–446.

Liezmann, H., "Apolinaris und seine Schule", *TU* 1 (1904).

Lightfoot, J.B., "Eusebius", *DCB* 2, pp. 308–355.

Linder, A., "Ecclesia and Synagoga in the Medieval Myth of Constantine the Great", *Revue belge de philologie et d'histoire* 54 (1976), pp. 1019–1060.

———, "Jerusalem as a Focus of Confrontation between Judaism and Christianity: Anti-Jewish Views in the Jerusalem Church from the Fourth Century", in B.Z. Kedar & Z. Baras (eds.), *Jerusalem in the Middle Ages: Selected Papers* (Jerusalem, 1979), pp. 5–26 (Hebrew).

Lyman, J.R., *Christology and Cosmology: Models of Divine Activity in Origen, Eusebius, and Athanasius* (Oxford, 1993).

MacMullen, R., *Paganism in the Roman Empire* (New Haven-London, 1982).

———, *Christianizing the Roman Empire (AD 100–400)* (New Haven-London, 1984).

Malingery, A. M., "Le personnage de Socrate chez quelques auteurs chrétiens du IVe siècle", *Forma Futuri*, pp. 159–178.

Mayer, P., "De Vita Constantini", *Eusebiana, Festschrift dem Gymnasium Adolphinum zu Moers* (Bonn, 1882), pp. 23–28.

Mendels, D., *The Media Revolution of Early Christianity: An Essay on Eusebius's Ecclesiastical History* (Grand Rapids-Cambridge, 1999).

Mendelson, A., "Eusebius and the Posthumous Career of Apollonius of Tyana", in Attridge & Hatta (eds.), *Eusebius, Christianity, and Judaism*, (Detroit, 1992) pp. 510–522.

Meredith, A., "Porphyry and Julian Against the Christians", *ANRW* 23.I 2 (1980), pp. 1119–1149.

Moffat, J., "Great Attacks on Christianity, II: Porphyry, 'Against the Christians', *Expository Times* 43, 1 (1931), pp. 72–78.

Mosshamer, A.A., *The Chronicle of Eusebius and the Greek Chronographic Tradition* (Lewisburg-London, 1979).

Nautin, P., "Trois autres fragments du livre de Porphyre 'Contre les Chrétiens'", *Revue Biblique* 57 (1950), pp. 409–416.

Norris, F.W., "Eusebius on Jesus as Deceiver and Sorcerer", in Attridge and Hata (eds.), *Eusebius, Christianity, and Judaism* (Detroit, 1992) pp. 523–540.

Oliver, H.H., "The Epistle of Eusebius to Carpianus: Textual Tradition and Translation", *Novum Testamentum* 3 (1959), pp. 138–145.

Opitz, H.G., "Euseb von Caesarea als Theologe: Ein Vortrag", *Zeitschrift für die neutestamentliche Wissenschaft* 34 (1935), pp. 1–19.

Parke, H.W. & D.E.W. Wormell, *The Delphic Oracle* (Oxford 1956).

Parkes, J., *The Conflict of the Church and the Synagogue: A Study in the Origins of Antisemitism* (London, 1934).

Patterson, L., "Methodius, Origen, and the Arian Dispute", *Studia Patristica* 17.2 (1982), pp. 912–923.

Peterson, E., "Der Monotheismus als politisches Problem", *Theologische Traktate* (Münster, 1951), pp. 83–94.

———, "Das Problem des Nationalismus im alten Christentum", in idem, *Frühkirche, Judentum und Gnosis* (Vienna, 1959), pp. 51–63.

Petzke, G.G., "Die Traditionen über Apollonius von Tyana und das N.T.", *Studia ad Corpus Hellenisticum Novi Testamenti* 1 (1970), pp. 19–36.

Pezella, S., "Il problema del *Kata Christianon* di Porphyrio", *EOS* 52 (1972), pp. 87–104.

Pines, S., "Judaeo-Christian Materials in an Arabic Jewish Treatise", in *The Collected Works of Shlomo Pines, Volume IV, Studies in the History of Religion* (Jerusalem, 1996), pp. 285–315.

Places, E. des, "Eusèbe de Césarée juge de Platon dans la Préparation Evangélique", *Mélanges de Philosophie Grecque offerts à Mgr Diès* (Paris, 1956), pp. 69–77.

———, *Eusèbe de Césarée commentateur: Platonisme et écriture sainte* (Paris, 1982).

Poorthuis, M. and Ch. Safrai (eds.), *The Centrality of Jerusalem, Historical Perspectives* (Kampen, 1996).

Posnansky, A., *Schiloh: Ein Beitrag zur Geschichte der Messiaslehre*, I (Leipzig, 1904).

Prawer, J., "Christian Attitudes Towards Jerusalem in the Early Middle Ages", in J. Prawer & H. Ben-Shammai (eds.), *The History of Jerusalem: The Early Muslim Period 638–1099* (Jerusalem, 1996), pp. 311–348.

Puech, A., *Les apologistes grecs du IIe siècle de notre ère* (Paris, 1912).

Ricken, F., "Die Logoslehre des Eusebios von Caesarea und der Mittelplatonismus", *Theologie und Philosophie* 42 (1967), pp. 341–358.

Rokeah, D., "Ben Stara is Ben Pantera", *Tarbiz* 39 (1970), pp. 9–18 (Hebrew).

———, "The Jewish People and Religion in Pagan-Christian Polemics in the Roman Empire", *Tarbiz* 40 (1971), pp. 462–471 (Hebrew).

———, *Pagans and Christians in Conflict* (Jerusalem-Leiden, 1982).

Rubin, Z., "The Church of the Holy Sepulchre and the Conflict between the Sees of Caesarea and Jerusalem", *The Jerusalem Cathedra* 2 (1982), pp. 79–105.

Sansterre, J.M., "Eusèbe de Césarée et la naissance de la théorie 'césaropapiste'", *Byzantion* 42 (1972), pp. 131–195 and 532–594.

Sant, C., *The Old Testament Interpretation of Eusebius of Caesarea* (Malta, 1967).

Schreckenberg, H., *Die christlichen Adversus-Judaeos-Texte und ihr literariches und historiches Umfeld (1–11 Jh.)* (Frakfurt a.m, 1982).

Schwartz, E., "Eusebios", *PRE* 11, pp. 1370–1439.

Sellew, P., "Achilles or Christ? Porphyry and Didymus in Debate over Allegorical Interpretation", *Harvard Theological Review* 82 (1989), pp. 79–100;

Shaeublin, C., "Diodor von Tarsos gegen Porphyrios?" *Museum Helveticum* 27 (1970), pp. 58–63.

Simon, M., "Christianisme antique et pensée païenne: rencontres et conflits", Bulletin de la faculté des lettres de Strasbourg 38 (1960).

———, *Verus Israel: A Study of the Relations between Christians and Jews in the Roman Empire (135–425)* (Oxford 1986—an English translation of the second French edition of 1964).

Simonetti, M., "Eusebio tra ebrei e giudei", Annali di storia dell'esegesi 14 (1997), pp. 121–134.

Sirinelli, J., *Les vues historiques d'Eusèbe de Césarée durant la période prénicéenne* (Paris, 1961).

———, "Quelques allusions à Melchisédech dans l'oeuvre d'Eusèbe de Césarée", *Studia Patristica* 6 (1962), pp. 233–247.

Smith, A., *Porphyry's Place in the Neoplatonic Tradition* (The Hague, 1974).

Speyer, W., "Zum Bild des Apollonios von Tyana bei Heiden und Christen", *Jahrbuch für Antike und Christentum* 17 (1974), pp. 47–63.

Stemplinger, E., *Das Plagiat in der griechischen Literatur* (Leipzig & Berlin, 1912).

Stevenson, J., *Studies in Eusebius* (Cambridge, 1929).

Stroumsa, G.G., "Religious Contacts in Byzantine Palestine", *Numen* 36 (1989), pp. 16–41.

Thielman, F.S., "Another Look at the Eschatology of Eusebius of Caesarea", *Vigiliae Christianae* 41 (1987) pp. 226–237.

Timothy, H.B., *The Early Christian Apologists and Greek Philosophy* (Assen, 1973).

Trombley, F.R., *Hellenic Religion and Christianization c. 370–529* (Leiden, 1993).

Ulrich, I., *Euseb von Caesarea und die Junden* (Berlin-New York, 1999).

Urbach, E.E., "Homilies of the Rabbis on the Prophets of the Nations and the Balaam Stories", *Tarbiz* 25 (1956) pp. 272–289 (Hebrew).

———, "The Homiletical Interpretation of the Sages and the Expositions of Origen on Canticles, and the Jewish-Christian Disputation", *Scripta Hierosolymitana* 22 (1971), pp. 241–270.

———, *The Sages, their Concepts and Beliefs* (Jerusalem, 1975).

Volker, M.W., "Von welchen Tendenzen liess sich Eusebius bei Abfassung seiner Kirchengeschichte leiten?" *Vigiliae Christianae* 4 (1950), pp. 157–180.

Walker, P.W.L., *Holy City, Holy Places? Christian Attitudes to Jerusalem and the Holy Land in the Fourth Century* (Oxford, 1990).

Wallace-Hadrill, D.S., *Eusebius of Caesarea* (London, 1960).

———, "Eusebius of Caesarea's Commentary on Luke: Its Origin and Early History", *Harvard Theological Review* 67 (1974), pp. 55–63.

Wilamowitz-Moellendorf, U. von, "Ein bruchstück aus der Schrift des Porphyrius gegen die Christen", *Zeitschrift für die neutestamentliche Wissenschaft* 1 (1900), pp. 101–105.

Wiles, M. F., "Miracles in the Early Church", *Miracles*, ed. C.F.D. Moule (London, 1965), pp. 221–233.

Wilken, R.L., *The Christians as the Romans Saw Them* (New Haven-London, 1984).

———, *The Land Called Holy* (New Haven & London, 1992).

Williams, L. A., *Adversus Judaeos, A Bird's Eye View of Christian Apologiae until the Renaissance* (Cambridge, 1935).

INDEX

INDEX OF SOURCES